# Fairfield

# Fairfield

the biography of a community

*1639-1989*

By

*Thomas J. Farnham*

*Published for the*

FAIRFIELD HISTORICAL SOCIETY

*by*

PHOENIX PUBLISHING
*West Kennebunk, Maine*

Farnham, Thomas J.
  Fairfield: the biography of a community, 1639-1989 / by
Thomas J. Farnham.
      p.     cm.
  Includes bibliographies and index.
  ISBN 0-914659-37-5 :   $27.50
  1. Fairfield  (Conn.)—History.  I. Fairfield  Historical
Society (Fairfield, Conn.)  II. Title.
F104.F2F37     1988                              88-28347
974.6'9—dc19                                        CIP

Printed in the United States of America

*For my mother,*
*Marjorie Javery Farnham*
*and*
*for my father,*
*Harold Frederick Farnham,*
*in memoriam.*

# Contents

# Foreword

THE FAIRFIELD Historical Society was chartered by the Secretary of State of the State of Connecticut on the ninth of February 1903. The articles of association clearly indicate the *raison d'etre* of the organization: To foster a spirit of local patriotism and a cordial interest in local history; to hold occasional meetings for the presentation of antiquarian researches; to publish and circulate documents, old and new, which concern the life of Fairfield; to collect and preserve the letters, journals, papers, books, furniture, garments, and heirlooms handed down from an honorable ancestry; and to encourage the marking of historic sites. Over these past eighty-five years, the Society has taken many significant steps toward addressing these original guidelines and today finds itself as a respected and professionally managed community resource.

The publication of *Fairfield: The Biography of a Community, 1639-1989* can perhaps be seen as the pinnacle of the Society's efforts to collect, interpret, and disseminate information about our community. Although there have been several historical publications relating to specific aspects of the town's history written over the years, this is the only comprehensive examination that has yet been produced.

The concept for this publication grew out of informal discussions held nearly three years ago between the Society's director, Corwin Sharp, librarian Irene Miller, and immediate past president Lee Thomas. The intent of these discussions was to focus the Society upon a significant and timely project to coincide with the 350th anniversary celebration of the founding of Fairfield in 1989 — in short, to find an appropriate way in which the Historical Society might honor this event. The idea for a publication relating to the 350 years of the life of Fairfield quickly gained support throughout the Society, and a Publication Committee under the guidance of Pat Daly was formed. Stanley Crane, librarian at the Pequot Library in Southport; Lawrence Hughes, a publishing house executive; Joan Huntington, a noted local antiques dealer; Carol Hutchinson, former librarian at the Fairfield Public Library; W. Bradley Morehouse, a local historian and attorney; and Dr. Paul Siff, history professor at Sacred Heart University, along with the Society's director, curator, and head librarian, joined Mrs. Daly in the monumental task of overseeing the entire project. The committee determined the focus of the publication, selected the author and publisher, reviewed and commented upon the drafts, galleys, and page proofs, and provided numerous other services throughout the course of the project.

The financial direction of the endeavor was most ably administered by the Society's Development Committee under the leadership of Stephen Galpin. This committee, comprised of vice-chairman Archibald Smith, DeLoss Blackburn, David Crawford, Dorothy Doolittle, W. Bradley Morehouse, Carolyn Pichard, and David B. Smith, spearheaded a highly successful fund-raising drive to have the cost of the publication of the book primarily underwritten by local businesses, corporations, and foundations. The marketing plan for the sale of the work has been provided by two talented and enthusiastic members of the Society, William Cargill and Robert Horning, who graciously offered the professional services by which they normally make their livings. The author's fees for the research and writing of the history have been generously underwritten by the Town of Fairfield. For this major source of support, the Society wishes to thank First Selectman Jacquelyn Durrell, Selectmen Eunice Postol and Carl Dickman, and all of the members of the Representative Town Meeting for their hearty and unanimous support of the entire project.

This has truly been a community project, by, for, and about the town in which we live. As with the town, it should stand the test of time, for it is a living thing. It is more than a history—it is the story of people, the biography of our community.

Arthur C. Williams
President
Fairfield Historical Society

Fairfield, Connecticut
August 15, 1988

# *Preface*

AIRFIELD is one of Connecticut's grand old towns, the fourth community created in the colony of Connecticut. It was founded by Roger Ludlow, the person who as much as any single individual probably deserves credit for establishing the colony itself. For almost two centuries, Fairfield was the dominant town in southwestern Connecticut, and for even longer it was the shire town of the county that bears its name. Although it was hardly a bustle of activity during much of the nineteenth century, during the twentieth it became a diverse community that included both industrial areas and some of the most desirable neighborhoods in the northeastern United States. It also became a town that included a variety of social, religious, political, cultural, and ethnic groups — groups that have adjusted sufficiently well to each other to live in harmony.

Despites its importance, Fairfield has never been the subject of a general history. About one hundred years ago, Elizabeth Hubbell Schenck wrote a two-volume history of the town from its settlement to the American Revolution. More a chronology than a history, the work is a treasurehouse of information but beyond a year-by-year listing of events is almost entirely without organization. In the century that has elapsed since the publication of Schenck's book, several talented professional historians have examined specific aspects of Fairfield during the colonial and revolutionary years. Their studies have greatly expanded what is known about the town. But except for one gifted sociologist who has studied some of the implications for the town of suburbanization, scholars have ignored nineteenth- and twentieth-century Fairfield.

Writing a history that encompasses 350 years is an ambitious task. It required the author to be as much an authority on the Native Americans of the early seventeenth century as on the suburbanites of the late twentieth. From my perspective, the task would have been an impossible one had I not constantly attempted to focus my attention on the community of Fairfield. What I have attempted to do is to write a biography of that community, a study of the development of a living and changing entity. I have concentrated on those persons, events, institutions, and neighborhoods that have altered the development of that entity. I have made no attempt to mention individuals or organizations merely to include them in the history. I have had to ask myself one question over and over again: How did he, or she, or it bring change to Fairfield? Those persons or events that did bring change were important to me.

I have also attempted to be conscious of my audience; an audience of general readers, not of professional historians. I have kept footnotes and other scholarly apparatus to a minimum. While hoping the notes do contain enough bibliographical information to be useful to future students of Fairfield history, I want their presence not to discourage readers who hope to find only a few pleasurable hours in this book. For those who would dig deeper, all of my working notes for this study are available at the Fairfield Historical Society. Again aware of my audience, I have simplified all dates for the years before 1752, the year the English-speaking world adopted the Gregorian calendar. January, 22, 1662/3, for example, will appear as January 22, 1663.

My task would have been totally impossible had I been without the help of a whole army of able and energetic individuals. Consequently my debts are great and my sense of gratitude deep. Irene K. Miller first gave me the idea of writing a history of Fairfield. Pat Daly and the other members of the Publications Committee of the Fairfield Historical Society—Stanley Crane, Lawrence Hughes, Joan Huntington, Carol Hutchinson, W. Bradley Morehouse, and Paul Siff—then not only provided the opportunity to write this history but also generously placed their collective talents at my disposal. They have my thanks. Without the logistical support, the encouragement, and the good humor of L. Corwin Sharp and Mildred C. Glotzer of the Fairfield Historical Society, my work would have been substantially more difficult and less enjoyable.

Many librarians and archivists gave unstintingly of their time. I am indebted to the staffs of the Bridgeport Public Library, the Connecticut Historical Society, the Connecticut State Library, the Fairfield Historical Society, the Fairfield Memorial Library, the Pequot Library, and the Buley Library of Southern Connecticut State University. In particular I want to thank Linda M. Mulford, Arley L. MacDonald, and Roderick B. MacKenzie of the Fairfield Historical Society, Stanley Crane and Tom Kemp of the Pequot Library, and Claire Bennett at Buley Library. Martha Rockwell and Laura MacKenzie, volunteers at the Fairfield Historical Society, graciously answered my myriad of questions.

John J. Sullivan, former first selectman of Fairfield, Attorney John T. Fitzpatrick, Joseph Wakeman, W. Eben Burr, and Benjamin Plotkin all found time to talk with me about Fairfield and its history. Evelyn Hiller, Fairfield's town clerk, provided me with full access to the important records in her care.

I owe a special debt of gratitude to Christopher Collier, Christopher Bickford, Paul Siff, and Christopher B. Nevins. Their deep and profound knowledge of Connecticut and Fairfield history has saved me from innumerable faux pas and added greatly to this work. Matthew S. Magda, a gifted historian, shared his skills with me and also contributed mightily to this volume. John Menta and William Alpern shared their knowledge of Connecticut Indians with me.

Finally I wish to thank my editor, Anne D. Lunt, for her precision and her forebearance and Southern Connecticut State University for its encouragement of this project. And my wife, Gwen, who, as always, was like a cloak from the cold, has my deep and humble thanks.

Thomas J. Farnham

North Haven, Connecticut
September 6, 1988

# Fairfield

# PART I

From 1639 until 1800, Fairfield grew from a small, Puritan, corporate community into a significant urban center in Yankee Connecticut. Founded by Roger Ludlow, an aggressive colonizer who refused to allow native Americans, Massachusetts Bay, New Haven, or the Dutch to forestall his plans for a plantation he would control, Fairfield was a community marked by its independence throughout the seventeenth and eighteenth centuries. It, like Ludlow, remained willing to pursue its own interests diligently, able to find a formula for prosperity, and in many ways unique among Connecticut towns throughout these years.

# The Ludlow Years

FAIRFIELD was the offspring of Roger Ludlow, and as surely as if the town had been a real son or daughter, the child bore an amazing resemblance to the parent. Although Ludlow fathered other communities — Dorchester in Massachusetts and Windsor, one of Connecticut's original towns — Fairfield was the one upon which he left his mark. For the first century and a half of its existence, Fairfield tended to do things as Ludlow had, tended for better or worse to bear his personality; and for this reason, Fairfield was as conspicuous among Connecticut's towns as Ludlow was outstanding among Connecticut's early leaders.[1]

Some aspects of Ludlow's character were less than appealing. He was a stubborn and arrogant man, one who rarely doubted the wisdom of a decision he had made. He believed the world, especially the world of seventeenth-century New England, to be a hostile place, a place where rivals constantly sought advantage at the expense of those who failed in diligence. He believed it was impossible to maintain the status quo: one must move forward or fall behind. Ambitious to a fault, Ludlow refused to fall behind, even if to avoid doing so required harshness or brutality.

Ludlow also had admirable qualities. He was forthright. Only one of his enemies ever suggested he was anything less than honest. John Lee called him a "false hearted knave, a hard hearted knave, a heavy friend, &c." The General Court of Massachusetts Bay, unconvinced by the characterization, however, ordered Lee whipped for his remarks.[2] One who loved adventure and demanded to be independent, Ludlow was both physically and intellectually courageous. The idea of marching off to unknown lands where violent death might lurk intimidated him no more than did the thought of scolding John Winthrop, the most formidable of the Massachusetts Bay elders, and pointing out to him precisely how and why he was wrong. By character and temperament, Ludlow was ideally suited to be a colonizer. For twenty-four years, he was vitally important to the development of the colonies in New England; and for fifteen years, with the pride and protection only a parent could offer, he oversaw the infancy of Fairfield.

3

Ludlow was born in Dinton, Wiltshire, in 1590, the son of Thomas and Jane Pyle Ludlow, who presented him for baptism on March 7, 1590. He spent his youth in Dinton, living there until his father's death in 1607, when he and his mother moved to one of the other Ludlow estates, at Baycliff, where he remained until he was twenty.

He enrolled in Balliol College, Oxford, on June 16, 1610. How long he remained at Oxford is uncertain. Whether he graduated or not is also unclear. On January 28, 1612, he gained admission to the Inner Temple, where he began the study of law. He was still studying law a year later and probably did complete the prescribed curriculum. His older brother, Thomas, and his uncle, Sir Edmund Ludlow, were, as his father had been, prominent men in Wiltshire. To take advantage of their influence in furthering his career, young Roger moved to Warminster, Wiltshire, once he had completed his studies. Sir Edmund's willingness to act as Roger's "proponent" probably ruled out any other choice.

Ludlow also welcomed the thought of returning to Wiltshire, and especially to Warminster, because the area was the site of increasing Nonconformist activity in the early seventeenth century. While technically a member of the Church of England, he and his family had embraced Nonconformity in seeking to eliminate all vestiges of Catholicism from the Anglican church. For those of Ludlow's persuasion—history refers to them as Puritans—the English Reformation had been inadequate, had failed to create sufficient distance between the Church of Rome and that of England. But this was an error they believed could yet be corrected.

About 1620 Ludlow married Mary Cogan of Chard, Somersetshire. Mary died while she was still a young woman, but the circumstances and even the date of her death remain a mystery. Ludlow's second wife was Mary Endicott. Little is known about her except that she was the sister of John Endicott, a man who assumed a large role in the life of Ludlow and in the establishment of New England. Endicott became interested in New England in 1623, when a group of English businessmen formed themselves into the Dorchester Adventurers, a company whose purpose was to open what eventually became the northeastern part of Massachusetts for trade. The company established a post at Cape Ann, where Roger Conant served as plantation manager. Two years later, its resources exhausted, the endeavor was about to collapse, but some of those who had actually gone to Cape Ann decided to remain, hoping that Conant could eventually make the post profitable. Back in England, Reverend John White, Rector of Old Trinity Parish, Dorchester, Dorset, encouraged Conant to stay by promising to find additional support for the struggling settlement. White hoped to secure a patent from the Council for New England that could give the Cape Ann plantation additional legitimacy. He won the support of Sir Henry Rosewell, a man of considerable influence with the council. On March 19, 1628, the council granted a patent to Sir Henry and five other associates, one of whom was John Endicott. The six men formed The New England Company, with the center of its operations in New England in Conant's Salem. Endicott became the first governor of the company and on June 20, 1628, left England for Salem.

To provide a more substantial basis for the colony, The New England Company secured from the Council for New England a grant of land that included everything from three miles north of the Merrimack River to three miles south of the Charles and from the Atlantic Ocean to the Pacific. On March 4, 1629, Charles I ratified this grant in a charter to the company and designated it The Governor and Company of the

Massachusetts Bay in New England. Thus the Massachusetts Bay Company came into being. Roger Ludlow, interested in the affairs of his brother-in-law, bought stock in the venture.

The leaders of the Massachusetts Bay Company met on February 10, 1630 at the home of Thomas Goffe in London. Samuel Sharpe, one of the persons nominated to be an assistant or magistrate of the company, was unable to attend the meeting or take his oath of office. In his place, the leaders chose Roger Ludlow. Thomas Prince, who had supported Ludlow, described his candidate as a "pious gentleman of good family" and a man generally in sympathy with the religious ideas of the Puritan gentlemen who controlled the company. Never again would the Massachusetts Bay Company meet in London. Both it and Ludlow, then forty years of age, were about to leave England for the New World.

Now one of the leaders of the company, Ludlow, on the *Mary and John*, a ship that he owned, sailed from Plymouth on March 20, 1630. He traveled with the Reverend John Warham and his congregation. Ludlow and Warham apparently agreed on many matters of religious doctrine, including the idea that church membership ought to be available to all who tried to live decent and godly lives and not merely to those who could actually demonstrate their grace by describing a conversional experience. Ludlow's apparent theological liberalism failed to make him politically liberal as well, however. A thoroughgoing aristocrat, he thought the colony should be directed by men like himself. As one who had been born to status and wealth, he believed such considerations should weigh heavily, very heavily, in selecting leaders. A man of independence in both his religious and his political opinions, Ludlow, as important as he was to the founding of Massachusetts Bay, would often find himself out of favor with the other leaders of the Bay.

About May 30, 1630, Thomas Squibb, master of the *Mary and John,* discharged his passengers on barren Nantasket Point. From there the party struggled up the Charles River in small boats until the stream became narrow and shallow. There Ludlow oversaw the construction of a temporary home for himself and his family, located sites for other dwellings, and named the settlement Watertown.

Despite the name Ludlow had given his new home, he and the other settlers were unable to find adequate pure water, and so decided to move to a neck of land that the Indians called Mattapan. Here existed an abundance of fresh springs, and here the Englishmen built new shelters. Ludlow renamed the neck Dorchester after the place in England that so many of his new neighbors had called home. By the end of July, skilled craftsmen were constructing the most substantial home in Dorchester for Ludlow. He had come to the New World because he saw opportunity there, opportunity to create a community that would be pleasing to God and one in which he could seek his own political and economic fortunes. Certainly he had not come with the idea of resigning himself to the life of a frontiersman.

The first meeting of the General Court of Assistants of the Massachusetts Bay Company assembled on August 23, 1630, on the *Arbella*, the flagship of the fleet that had delivered John Winthrop to Boston. Present were Governor Winthrop, Deputy Governor Thomas Dudley, Sir Richard Saltonstall, and Roger Ludlow. Ludlow served as an assistant from the time of his original election in London in 1630 until the spring of 1634, when he became deputy governor of the colony.

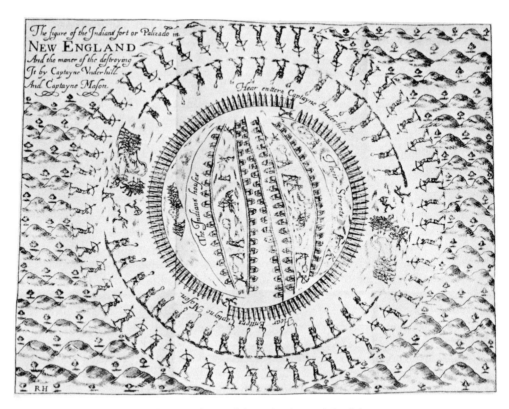

*Engraving depicting the annihilation by the English of the Pequot's*
*fortified village near present-day Mystic, Connecticut.*

At the meetings of the governor and assistants, Ludlow spoke his mind openly, so openly, in fact, that on several occasions he incurred the animosity of Governor Winthrop. In his journal Winthrop mentioned a meeting in Boston in 1632 when "Mr. Ludlow grew into a passion" because the people of the colony wanted a larger voice in the selection of officers. Ludlow argued that if that should happen "we should have no government, but there would be an interim, wherein every man might do what he pleased, etc." Such a point of view was totally in line with Ludlow's aristocratic perspective. Winthrop noted that "this was answered and cleared in the judgment of the rest of the assistants, but he [Ludlow] continued stiff in his opinion." Incidents like this gradually wore down any kindred feeling that might have existed between the two men.[3]

In October 1634, while he was deputy governor, Ludlow received a delegation of Pequot Indians from Long Island Sound at his Dorchester home. The Pequots had sought a meeting because of difficulties between themselves and the Dutch traders who maintained a post—they called it Redfoort—at the present location of Hartford. The Pequots feared that the Dutch were about to make an alliance with the Narragansett Indians, the traditional enemies of the Pequots. The two tribes lived in close proximity, the Pequots in what is today eastern Connecticut and the Narragansetts in modern-day Rhode Island. In this situation, proximity tended to breed animosity. To avoid being caught between the Dutch and the Narragansetts, the Pequots came to Ludlow to seek an alliance. Sassacus, the Pequot sachem, sent a gift for Ludlow with his delegation. Ludlow accepted the gift and sent one of equal value—a moose coat—to Sassacus but then announced that he was unwilling to negotiate with the members of the delegation because they were of insufficient stature to parley with Englishmen. Ludlow used the time it took to dispatch new Pequot envoys to seek advice from the other leaders of the Bay.[4]

Two weeks later a new commission, this one including two leaders or sagamores, called upon Ludlow. They were empowered, he learned, to urge the English to come into their domain—which included much of what is now Connecticut—and to acquire whatever land they wished. In return the Pequots asked for a trade agreement and the good offices of Massachusetts in attempting to establish peace between themselves and the Narragansetts. Ludlow liked the Pequot proposals and brought the Indians to Boston to see Governor Dudley. On November 4, 1634, the Pequots and Massachusetts Bay signed an agreement that provided for, among other things, the English settlement of Connecticut. As Winthrop explained it, "They [the Pequots] offered us also all their right at Connecticut, and to further us what they could, if we would settle a plantation there."

Ludlow was determined to take advantage of the special situation the treaty had created, providing the opportunity for a tranquil English advance and Pequot contraction in Connecticut. He wanted to move ahead as quickly as possible, but other Massachusetts leaders were less eager. Winthrop viewed English expansion into Connecticut as a dissipation of the Commonwealth's already limited resources. He argued that the project was less than urgent and that delay would be an appropriate response. Ludlow reminded his colleague that a smallpox epidemic had recently decimated the Indian population in Connecticut. That, and the treaty, made action imperative.

Although he was unable to convince his fellow leaders, Ludlow refused to abandon the plan. Sometime during the winter of 1634-35, he decided he would go to Connecticut himself. The decision meant forsaking a bright future in Massachusetts for a questionable future in yet another wilderness. A letter that Israel Stoughton, one of Ludlow's neighbors in Dorchester, wrote from Massachusetts Bay to his brother in England in May 1635 describes what Ludlow was giving up: "So allso our Mr. Ludlow is now no Magistrate: tho within 6 days before it was most probable & almost past question that he would be chosen governor.... Now he is neither governor nor assistant, so did divine providence dispose it." Uncharacteristically, John Winthrop refused to assign Ludlow's political misfortune to divine providence; he blamed the man's arrogance. In fact, even before the election, Ludlow had announced that he was going to pursue the opportunity the Pequot treaty provided. In his mind, the favorable circumstances in Connecticut were even more promising than prospects in Massachusetts. Typically, Ludlow made his decision without regrets.[5]

By June 16, 1635, he was already on the banks of the Connecticut River. There he found a trading post manned by persons from the Plymouth Plantation. He traveled upriver as far as what is today South Hadley Falls, Massachusetts, looking for a site as advantageous as the one held by the Plymouth men. Finding nothing that pleased him, he returned to the location of the Plymouth trading post in July 1635 and made plans to take control of that area. There he encountered an agent of Sir Richard Saltonstall, Francis Styles, who was in Connecticut to establish a plantation under a patent granted by the Earl of Warwick to Sir Richard, Lord Say & Sele, Lord Brook, and others. Typically unintimidated, Ludlow informed Styles that the area was controlled by Massachusetts Bay, that he had arrived in Connecticut before Styles, and that he intended to take possession of that part of the Connecticut River Valley. Styles left to take up the matter with Saltonstall in Boston, and Ludlow began to lay out a plantation. Saltonstall later complained to Winthrop: "There hath been done some abuse & injury done me by Mr. Ludlow & others of Dorchester who would not suffer Francis Styles & his men to empayle grounds wheare I appointed them at Connecticute."[6]

Ludlow also managed to offend the Plymouth traders. Governor William Bradford of Plymouth denounced his "usurpation" and accused him of "casting a partial if not covetous eye upon that, which is your neighbors, and not yours." Not to be outdone, the Dutch informed the leaders of Massachusetts Bay that Ludlow's behavior was reprehensible in their eyes as well.[7]

Ludlow continued to press forward. Lands had to be surveyed, shelters constructed, and Indians convinced of the wisdom of selling their lands to the English. Initially Ludlow called the plantation Dorchester, after the place where he and his associates had resided in Massachusetts. Later he decided that Windsor would be a more appropriate name (a choice perhaps dictated by his fondness for his maternal grandmother, Edith Windsor). Gradually the Dutch and the Plymouth Plantation abandoned their claims to lands along the Connecticut. The only important setback Ludlow encountered came in the form of cold weather. During the winter of 1635-36, unusually frigid temperatures forced him and his colleagues back to Dorchester.

That winter saw interest in migration to Connecticut grow in Massachusetts as the Reverend Thomas Hooker prepared to lead his followers southward as soon as spring arrived. John Winthrop and other Massachusetts leaders were determined that Connecticut should remain under the control of the Bay. The area was clearly outside the boundaries of Massachusetts as established by its charter, but Winthrop in particular was convinced that Connecticut had to remain subordinate to Massachusetts and prevented from developing an existence of its own.

On March 3, 1636, the General Court of Massachusetts Bay granted a commission to Roger Ludlow and seven other gentlemen to govern the people "at Connecticut in a judicial way" for a year, "to hold a Court," and "to levy taxes & fines." In accepting this commission, Ludlow and the others agreed to remain subordinate to both Massachusetts and to the Saybrook Company, a group of adventurers who had received a charter to establish a settlement at the mouth of the Connecticut River. John Winthrop, Jr., then in London, was the governor of the Saybrook Company, "appoynted by certain noble personages and men of quallitie interested in the said ryver, which are yet in England." The Winthrops, father and son, intended that Ludlow and the others should govern Connecticut only until Massachusetts could find some means of exerting direct control over it.[8]

The most important limitation placed upon Connecticut was that it had to restrict its belligerent activity to "defensive war." The Winthrops and Massachusetts wanted to be as certain as possible that Connecticut was prevented from laying claim to territory on the basis of conquest. When the time was right, Massachusetts would carry on the wars of conquest and so add to its own domain.

Ludlow was quick to return to Connecticut. By April 26, 1636, he was not only

*John Winthrop, first governor of
the Massachusetts Bay Colony.*

back home, but had summoned and was presiding over the first "Corte" there. To avoid confrontation, Ludlow had agreed to accept the commission presented by Massachusetts, but once back in his new home, in his usual fashion, he felt that the commission restricted him and his colleagues in no serious way. He had refused to be intimidated by Winthrop in Massachusetts; why should he be now that he was in Connecticut?

This thought must have occurred to John Winthrop and the other "elders of the Bay," because before the summer of 1636 had passed they began to take steps to bring Connecticut under their control. On August 25, a punitive expedition left Boston under the command of John Endicott, Ludlow's brother-in-law. The expedition was first to attack the Narragansett Indians on Block Island and then the Pequots on the coast of Long Island Sound. Its objective was purportedly to avenge the murders of Captain John Oldham, a Massachusetts trader who had been killed on Block Island, and Captain John Stone, an itinerant West Indian trader who had met his death two years earlier on the Connecticut River. The Narragansetts had indeed killed Oldham, but Stone's murderers were the western Niantics. In neither instance were the Pequots involved. The Pequots became an object of the Massachusetts attack because Massachusetts wanted their lands, in particular the harbor at what eventually became New London. Were the Connecticut River towns of Hartford, Wethersfield, and Windsor to conquer the Pequots, these settlements would have a legitimate claim to the Pequot domain along the shore of Long Island Sound. Massachusetts was determined to prevent this by striking first.

The Endicott expedition did little actual damage, but it did invoke the wrath of the Pequots. Regarding themselves as innocent victims of aggression, especially in the

*The Ludlow Years*

wake of their invitation to the English to come to Connecticut, the Pequots began a series of attacks on Saybrook. Designed by Lion Gardiner, a military engineer, Saybrook was invulnerable to the Indian raids. On April 23, 1637, the Pequots selected an easier target; they attacked Wethersfield, killing six men and three women and taking two girls captive.

On May 1, Roger Ludlow presided over a special session of the Connecticut General Court that declared an "offensive warr" on the Pequots, thus specifically defying the Bay Colony's sanctions. A force of ninety men, under the command of Captain John Mason, was authorized to attack the Indians. The measure was a desperate one. In the spring of 1637 Connecticut consisted of only the three river towns; Saybrook was a completely independent entity. To send ninety men against the Pequots was to leave the three towns, all barely a year old, without any defense. Ludlow understood the danger. Once the expedition had departed, he wrote to William Pynchon in Springfield of his predicament: "Our plantations are so gleaned by that small fleet we sent out that those that remain, are not able to supply our watches, which are day and night; that our people are scarce able to stand upon their legs." But, in Ludlow's mind, the danger was necessary if Connecticut was to establish rights of conquest, and to build a legal case for a separate charter.[9]

Captain Mason and his men, supported by a contingent of Mohegans led by their chief, Uncas, descended the Connecticut River. Despite the efforts of a small delegation of Massachusetts troops sent by Winthrop to talk Mason into delaying until additional Massachusetts reinforcements arrived, Mason and his men attacked a Pequot village on the Mystic River on the night of May 26, 1637. By killing as many of its inhabitants as possible, Mason hoped to dishearten the Pequot warriors, who were awaiting attack in another fortified position about five miles from the village and who never imagined that the English would make war on women and children. To a large degree the plan worked. Mason ignited the village, and when the holocaust drove the inhabitants into the open, he and his men killed them. They slaughtered between three and seven hundred Indians, almost all of them women, children, and elderly persons. When Sassacus, the Pequot sachem, and his warriors arrived at the scene, they found only death and a smoldering ruin. The Pequots' anger gave way to grief, astonishment, and fear. Sassacus and what was left of his tribe fled their tormentors and fled a scene too horrible for them to bear.

Ludlow had remained in Windsor. When news reached the river town of Mason's success and of the subsequent arrival weeks later of a new Massachusetts expedition under Israel Stoughton, the Connecticut General Court appointed him and John Haynes to go to Saybrook "to treate & Conclude with their friends of the Bay about prosecuting the war against the Pequots, — & to parley with the Bay about setlinge downe in the Pequoitt Country." Connecticut was winning the war; Ludlow and Haynes were to prevent Massachusetts Bay from claiming the victory and so the lands in question.[10]

Ludlow, Haynes, and Stoughton agreed to pursue the fleeing Pequots along the coast of Connecticut. On July 14, a force of Connecticut, Massachusetts, and Mohegan men — that included Roger Ludlow — cornered a sizable contingent of Pequots in a great swamp in the territory of the Sasqua Indians. There, in what the twentieth century knows as that part of Fairfield called Southport, the English tried to exterminate as many Pequots as they could, one more in a series of atrocities against these Indians.

*Monument in Southport marks the site of the battle*
*that ended the Pequot War on July 13, 1637.*

Some Pequots survived. Some managed to hide themselves among the Mohegans, whose leader, Uncas, was Mason's ally but who was willing to accept the Pequots in order to strengthen his own tribe. Sassacus and forty of his warriors successfully reached New York, where they hoped to find allies among the Mohawks. Instead the Mohawks, eager to curry favor with the English, murdered Sassacus and his followers, took their scalps, and sent their gruesome trophies to Ludlow in Windsor. On August 5, John Winthrop noted in his journal: "Mr. Ludlow, Mr. Pinchon and about twelve more, came [from *Connecticut*] the ordinary way by land, and brought with them a part of the skin and lock of hair of Sasacus [*sic*] and his brother, and five other Pequod [*sic*] sachems." Ludlow had made his point. Connecticut was now in a position to assert its own claim to charter rights; Massachusetts domination was over.[11]

Legend has it that Roger Ludlow was so impressed by the beauty of Uncoway, the general vicinity where the Pequots were surrounded and the area that eventually became Fairfield, that he decided to make it his home. Without question, the comely, the fair fields of Uncoway must have caught Ludlow's eye. But if beauty is in the eye of the beholder, it meant something quite different to Ludlow than it might to a man with a more highly refined sense of aesthetics. The beauty that he saw was beauty that a man like himself, the quintessential colonizer, could best appreciate. His considerations were practical ones.

What attracted his attention in Uncoway initially was its open fields. The first task that usually faced a pioneer farmer in New England—as difficult as any task he undertook—was to clear land for cultivation, cutting the trees and brush and burning the debris. A strong man working at a steady pace might hope to clear three acres in a month if he left the stumps in place. Any lands that had been cleared by the Indians, therefore, immediately attracted the attention of settlers. Along the coast and beside the principal rivers in Uncoway were several hundred acres that the Indians had cleared and cultivated. Such fields as these were indeed fair in the eyes of Ludlow.[12]

He found other attractions in Uncoway. Early New England farmers were almost as impressed by an abundance of feed for their cattle as they were by cleared lands. Besides Uncoway's open fields, the area contained a wealth of natural hay marshes, salt and fresh. Even if crops should fail, as they did with great regularity in the seventeenth century, these marshes would enable the livestock, and therefore the settlers, to survive.

Access to a location on the water was essential. It was no accident that Hartford, Wethersfield, Windsor, and Saybrook — the only communities then in existence in what became Connecticut — were located on navigable bodies of water. Uncoway was similarly situated. Whether Ludlow saw all the advantages Uncoway offered in this respect is unclear. He may have had an idea of the fine harbor facilities the area possessed. Eventually Black Rock Harbor would come to be recognized as an excellent natural facility, and Mill River, later known as Southport, would also become an important port, at least for the coasting trade. Ludlow's vision may have been sufficient to recognize at least some of the benefits of these two ports.

Without question, he realized that the forests of Uncoway were an important asset. These were hardwood forests, primarily oak and chestnut. The advantages of both of these woods, strength and resistance to insects and moisture, were well understood in 1637. The forests would provide a third crop, timber, in addition to those offered by the cultivated fields and the pastures. Many a pioneer farmer helped to sustain his family by taking advantage of what the forest offered, lumber or shingles or clapboards or staves.

The Native Americans in the area may have provided some general information about the climate of the region, but Ludlow probably failed to understand how good the climate actually was. Today we know that in parts of Fairfield the first frost of autumn waits to arrive until nearly the end of October, and the last frost of winter rarely comes after the middle of March. This means that in the warmest sections of Fairfield, farmers could enjoy a growing season of close to 190 days. Had Ludlow known this fact, he would have given it serious consideration.

Had he possessed the means to evaluate it, he also would have given earnest attention to the quality of Fairfield's soil, which is nearly as good as any in Connecticut. Only Stamford, Norwalk, Stratford, Wallingford, and Wethersfield have soil that is generally better. About 20 percent of Fairfield's soil was favorably suited for the production of vegetables, grain, and orchard products, and about 50 percent was ideal for the cultivation of grain and hay. Even the poorest lands were adequate for pasture.

These physical features were to be important to Ludlow. There was also a human factor to be considered. The Native American population of the area presented little threat to any potential settlement. The population was not large, perhaps numbering a few hundred persons from the Pequonnock River to the Saugatuck. These Indians were members of the Pequonnock band, which was part of the Paugussett nation. The English referred to several subdivisions of the Pequonnocks according to their place of residence: the Uncoways, who lived between Black Rock Harbor and the Mill River, as these landmarks eventually came to be known; the Sasquas, whose home stood between Mill River and Sasqua Creek; and the Maxumux, who lived between Sasqua Creek and the Saugatuck River, especially around Componaug or Compo, and at Aspetuck, located in what is now Weston.[13]

These Native Americans were farmers, and probably good farmers. They enjoyed all the advantages that Fairfield would one day bestow on Ludlow and his neighbors, and they also benefited from an agricultural culture that had been many centuries in the making. Before the European invasion, they had known a fairly high standard of living. Corn and beans and squash provided the essential items in their diet, supplemented in various ways, most importantly from the waters that were so prominent around Fairfield. Gathering and hunting were also important to them, but one would be mistaken to think of these first inhabitants of Fairfield as hunters and gatherers. They had a technology that the English settlers were eager to learn.

Ludlow appreciated the placid temperament of these people. Generally peaceful and ignorant of the ultimate motive of the English — complete domination of the land — the Pequonnocks would welcome the outsiders, share their technology with them, and surrender their vast domains for a pittance.

When Ludlow assessed all these factors, he concluded that Uncoway was an attractive area, probably more attractive than Windsor, his current home. But he demonstrated no great impatience about returning to southwestern Connecticut. He had been there in July 1637 in pursuit of the Pequots; he did not return, as far as is known, for more than two years. Impressed as he was by Uncoway, he was content to continue his life in Windsor.

The years between his first and second visits to Uncoway were particularly productive for Ludlow. During 1638, he began work on a document that would eventually become the Fundamental Orders of Connecticut, the basic law of the colony until the Charter of 1662. Ludlow worked with others in drafting the Fundamental Orders; John Haynes, former governor of Massachusetts Bay, Edward Hopkins, who would one day be Connecticut's governor, and Thomas Hooker all provided assistance. But Ludlow was a principal author. If one reads the preamble to the Fundamental Orders in conjunction with Ludlow's letter of May 29, 1638, to John Winthrop and in conjunction with the preamble to the Code of 1650, which Ludlow is acknowledged to have written, one cannot avoid being impressed by the similarities in all three in terms of both thought and literary expression.

The river towns adopted the Fundamental Orders on January 14, 1639, and the first elections under them took place on April 11. Roger Ludlow became deputy governor of Connecticut. While Uncoway may have been on Ludlow's mind between the summer of 1637 and the autumn of 1639, he was hardly preoccupied with the subject.

A series of events reawakened his interest in Uncoway. Trouble had cropped up in Wethersfield. A group of men, finding themselves at odds with the Wethersfield minister, had decided to leave Connecticut and move to the New Haven Jurisdiction, which consisted of a group of towns — New Haven, Branford, Guilford, Milford — that before 1662 functioned independently from the Connecticut plantations. Ludlow had heard rumors that New Haven's leaders were encouraging these men to establish a new settlement on the coast, south and west of Milford. The idea dismayed Ludlow. Having fought the Pequots to justify a claim to lands in southeastern Connecticut, he was unwilling to watch the New Haven upstarts establish themselves in the southwest.

During the summer or early autumn of 1639, Ludlow obtained a commission from the Connecticut General Court granting him authority to establish a plantation at Pequonnock, the area that would shortly become easternmost Fairfield and westernmost Stratford and would subsequently become the city of Bridgeport. He then set out with several men and a herd of cattle, supposedly to sell some cattle in New Haven and then to proceed to Pequonnock to winter the rest of his animals there. But "att his coming downe to Quinnipiocke [New Haven] the hand of the Lord was upon him in taking away some of his Cattle, wch prevented him in some of his purposes there for selling some of them." Whether Ludlow actually intended to sell cattle in New Haven is unclear. What is certain was his determination to learn more about the plans that New Haveners were making for a new settlement. Apparently what he uncovered confirmed his suspicions.

He then proceeded to Pequonnock, but what he found at that location caused him "to alter his former thoughts of wintering his Cattle there." In Pequonnock he learned, either from squatters or the Indians, "that some others intended to take up the sayd place [Uncoway], who had not acquainted this Court with their purposes therein, wch might [be] preuidiciall to this Comon wealth." Having heard this disturbing news, "he adventured to drive his Cattle thither, make provition for them there, and to sett out [for] himself and some others house lotts." In other words, Ludlow learned, perhaps in New Haven but more likely in Pequonnock, that others—probably the disgruntled men of Wethersfield—were interested in establishing a settlement either at Uncoway or close by. To prevent what he regarded as a disaster for Connecticut, Ludlow acted to keep the Wethersfield men and the New Haven Jurisdiction out.[14]

In doing so he violated the letter of his commission. He asked the court to decide if he had violated the spirit of it as well. At its October 10, 1639 session the General Court decided that "his proceedings could not be warranted by the Comission, nor can he be excused of neglect of his duty, that he had not given notice to these plantacons of what he did." But the court agreed to establish a committee "to repaire thither and take a view of the aforesayd occasions, and if in their judgments both persons & things settled by him be . . . [as] confirmed, they may remayne as they are." While the court fined him £50 for exceeding his authority and five shillings for missing the September General Court, it also promised to consider making the settlement at Uncoway permanent and to take the matter up at the next General Court, in January 1640.[15]

The committee that was dispatched to Uncoway consisted of Governor John Haynes and Thomas Wells. What Haynes and Wells found was hardly a typical New England settlement. Ludlow had been accompanied by only four other settlers: Thomas Staples, Thomas Newton, Edward Jessop, and Edmund Strickland. Normally one would expect to find a much larger initial contingent making the trek into the wilderness. While others, most of them from Watertown, Massachusetts, would follow shortly, Fairfield originally consisted of but eight or ten families. These families lived along five roads that Ludlow and the others had established, two running northeast/southwest and three running northwest/southeast. The roads created four squares, each comprising twenty-five or thirty acres.

Ludlow purchased the land from the Pequonnocks. He acquired all the land west of the Pequonnock River to the Sasqua or Mill River and then along the coast to the bounds of the Maxumux Indian lands. From Long Island Sound, the purchase extended seven or eight miles into the interior. The Indians also agreed to pay an annual tribute of furs, wampum, and corn to Ludlow and the others, and to reside on certain reservations within the tract, principally Golden Hill, located near what would become the Fairfield-Stratford boundary.

Haynes and Wells had to have been impressed with the land that Ludlow purchased and must have been pleased with Ludlow's efforts generally. On January 16, 1640, they announced their decision to confirm the settlement at Uncoway. While on the coast, they had taken time to give the settlers "the oath of fidelity, make such free as they see fitt, order them to send one or two deputyes to the two Generall Courts in September and April, and for deciding of differences & controversies under 40 s. among them, . . . give them power to choose 7 men from among themselves, with liberty of appeale to the Court here." The settlement also enjoyed the power to dispose of its undivided lands as it saw fit, a power granted to Connecticut towns by the Fundamental Orders. Thus the General Court confirmed the existence of Connecticut's fourth town.[16]

During the spring of 1640, a problem arose that would occupy Uncoway's attention for years to come. This was the problem of the town's boundaries. Obviously little land along the coast had been surveyed by this time, and almost none in the interior. Thus no one was sure where Uncoway ended and its neighbor to the east—what came to be called Stratford, Connecticut's fifth town—began. The vagueness of geographical information, combined with the acquisitive nature of the Uncoway settlers in general and Ludlow in particular, created a problem that seemed beyond solution. The list of Connecticut notables who worked on this dilemma includes almost every political leader from the colony's early years.

Ludlow's acquisitive instincts prompted him to purchase additional land along the coast. He wanted room for Uncoway to expand and so negotiated for the land from the Saugatuck River to the Norwalk River and back a day's walk into the country. At almost the same time, he bought a large tract of land in what is today Salem, Westchester County, New York. Ludlow displayed a particular interest in land speculation, and the land in Salem was certainly intended for this purpose. His purchase of the land between the Saugatuck and the Norwalk was part of his plan to add as much territory to the town of Uncoway as the General Court would allow.

He was being overoptimistic in hoping that his town would ever extend as far west as the Norwalk River. In fact, it was not until 1650 that the General Court finally recognized that Uncoway reached as far as the Saugatuck River. In May the court granted the town the land to the Saugatuck provided the river was not more than two miles west of the existing boundary of Uncoway. This became the basis of another extended boundary dispute.

By that time, Ludlow and his neighbors had largely abandoned the name "Uncoway." They now called their plantation Fairfield. Perhaps they selected the name because of the advantages that the town offered: cleared land, an abundance of hay, huge stands of timber. Perhaps Fairfield was a variation of "far field." The Indian word *uncoway* meant "place beyond," and possibly the settlers merely intended to anglicize the original name of their home. They may well have been adopting the name of an English hamlet. There were two Fairfields in England at the time. One was in Kent, its Old English name having been Faierfeld, meaning "beautiful field." The origins of the name of the other in Worcestershire, were considerably less picturesque—it had been called Forfeld, Old English for pig field. Since Worcestershire was much closer than Kent to the former homes of Ludlow and the other early Fairfield residents, let us hope that Fairfield was a translation of the word *uncoway*.

During the first decade of its existence, Fairfield had to provide for its own defense.

The river towns of Connecticut were too far away to offer any assistance, and nearby Stratford, the name that much of Pequonnock and all of Cupheag came to assume about the time Uncoway became Fairfield, was even smaller and weaker than Fairfield. During the fall of 1639, the General Court had created a trainband or militia at Uncoway and appointed John Nichols "to train the men in military discipline." Even though the local Indians were friendly, Fairfield was too exposed to neglect its defenses.[17]

In August 1642, an Indian who lived only a short distance from Ludlow approached the deputy governor while he was overseeing the haying of his fields and asked if he could speak in private with him and one of his Indian servants, Adam. Ludlow agreed that he and Adam would met the mysterious native in the woods by the side of the field. There the Indian explained that Miantonimo, a Narragansett sachem, had traveled to Long Island to seek allies for a war against the English in Connecticut. Miantonimo had the support of all the Indians "on the Island & upon the main from the Dutch to the Bay," he warned. The Indians believed that they had lost all of their best lands and must now fight to win them back.[18]

Ludlow took the warning seriously. He traveled to New Haven to relay the message to the settlers there. In New Haven, he learned that Governor Theophilus Eaton had also heard the story of Miantonimo's conspiracy. So Ludlow hurried to Hartford, only to discover that that community knew of the threat as well.

The General Court sent word of the danger to Massachusetts Bay and then ordered each of the Connecticut towns to establish a regular watch and to provide weapons, "twenty half pikes of ten foot in length, at least in the wood." The court also outlawed the sale of iron or steel items to the Indians and forbade them entry within the central parts of towns. In Fairfield, one man from each family went to Sabbath services fully armed. Ludlow assumed responsibility for training the soldiers "upon the sea coast," Fairfield and Stratford. His men trained six days a year, once during each of the first weeks of March, April, May, September, October, and November.[19]

Tensions were exacerbated in the spring of 1643 when a Massachusetts man was murdered by an Indian near Stratford. Ludlow demanded that the culprit be surrendered to the English. The Indians agreed, asking that ten Englishmen be sent to arrest the murderer. As the ten men approached, the Indians released their prisoner, who made good his escape. Ludlow refused to brook such defiance; he immediately seized eight Indians and announced that they would be held until the murderer was turned over to him. He then sent an urgent request for assistance to New Haven, which supplied twenty armed men for the defense of Stratford and Fairfield.

Tensions eased slightly during the autumn of 1643 when Miantonimo, who had been captured by Uncas and his Mohegan warriors, became a prisoner in Hartford. They were further reduced when the English arranged the murder of the Narragansett sachem, thus demonstrating to his allies the folly of such schemes as his. By the early months of 1645, the Indian threat had faded to a point where the General Court could reduce the number of training days a year from six to three.

Ludlow's years in Fairfield were years during which he continued to serve the colony of Connecticut. From 1639 until 1654, he held the office of either deputy governor or magistrate. In 1649, the General Court requested him "to take some paynes in drawing forthe a body of laws for the government of this Comon welth." The result was the famous Code of 1650, the first complete statement of law in Connecticut. The Code and the Fundamental Orders, the two great political documents to arise from early Connecticut, were both Ludlow products.[20]

At the same time, he did not neglect his own affairs. He acquired a great deal of property in Fairfield, including his home, located at the corner of what is now South Benson and Old Post roads, and his fields, which were scattered about the part of the town that had already been surveyed. Ludlow used the land to grow crops, to support his livestock, and to provide firewood and other necessities. Because of the extent of his holdings, he produced more than he and his family needed. This surplus he traded, his most important customers probably being persons who had recently arrived in town and who had yet to gather harvests of their own. He also traded with the Indians for furs and sent these pelts to Boston, perhaps with some agricultural goods.

Fairfield's population had been growing steadily, although very slowly. In 1644, the first important influx of population since 1639 appeared. Led by the Reverend John Jones, about twenty families, or one-seventh of the population of Concord, Massachusetts, moved to Fairfield. Several factors had encouraged them to leave Concord, including that area's poor soil, the perception among Concord inhabitants of overcrowding, and burdensome taxes caused by the town's insistence upon supporting two ministers. On the other hand, the Connecticut General Court had recently passed legislation that required the towns to grant one hundred acres of plowing ground and twenty acres of meadow to those who would improve twenty of these acres the first year, eighty the second, and the remainder the third. After years of struggling to survive, the offer was difficult for the Concord people to resist. They came to Fairfield, settling both in the central village but also in that part of Pequonnock that was within Fairfield, the area that would later become Black Rock. Thomas Wheeler, Sr. may well have come from Concord as early as 1640 to settle in Pequonnock, but he surely was there by 1644. So were about a dozen other families.

The year 1644 brought other newcomers to Fairfield besides the Concord group. Most important among these were Jehu and John Burr. They were brothers who had come to the Connecticut River Valley at the same time Ludlow had arrived in Windsor. They had made their home at Agawam, later called Springfield, Massachusetts. The Burrs would eventually become as important to Fairfield as any single family.

Probably no real church existed in Fairfield until the arrival of Jones and his followers. That the town went without a church for five years, while unusual in Puritan New England, should hardly be taken as evidence of heresy in Ludlow and his neighbors. Until 1644, Fairfield was so small it may have been unable to attract a minister. The arrival of the Concord group nearly doubled the town's population. The town's deliberate behavior might indicate how much importance Fairfield people attached to the question of finding a minister. Even during the eighteenth century, the town was willing to endure long periods between ministers rather than to rush into the selection of one who might prove unsatisfactory.

Jones, an ordained Anglican clergyman whose zeal to purify that church had led to his dissent, became Fairfield's first minister. In 1645, the Reverend Thomas Hooker, surveying the churches of Connecticut, found the Fairfield church to be in good standing. Whether Jones had already been selected as a permanent minister or whether he was serving on a provisional basis at that time is unclear. It is certain that Fairfield, as of 1645, was without a meetinghouse. A building designed to serve as both a town house and a schoolhouse may have existed then and may have also served as a meetinghouse. But in January 1645, William Frost gave the town "tenn pounds, in good pay, towards the building of a Meeteing howse, to be paid when it is halfe built."[21]

The lack of a meetinghouse was only one of Jones's problems. On March 5, 1647, he wrote John Winthrop indicating his wish to leave Fairfield: "I, despairing of a convenient passage unto you before the spring, did engage myself to keep a lecture here untill the season of the yeare would permit me to remove, so that my engagements here being ended with the winter, it is my desire and full resolution (if God permit) to take the first opportunity of coming to you, either by land or water." Jones may well have found himself at odds with Ludlow over certain theological issues. Ludlow's views were far from orthodox, especially on the question of church membership, and one can be assured that he was in no way reluctant about expressing them. Whatever the cause of Jones's malaise, it must have passed, because he remained at his post in Fairfield for twenty years, until his death in 1664.[22]

That the earliest settlers in Fairfield lacked a meetinghouse would surprise few who understood their circumstances. Many of the first to arrive in Uncoway lived in the crudest of homes. These were called cellars, square pits dug six or eight feet deep in a location that was, the residents hoped, dry during most of the year. The sides might be lined with rushes or some other vegetation, and a roof, certainly not impervious to water, was improvised. The cellars provided protection of a sort for many Fairfield families until they could find the time and capital for more adequate dwellings. A man of Ludlow's position, while he may have had to endure crude accommodations for a time, would quickly arrange for the construction of a large residence, with many rooms. He had had such a home both in Dorchester and in Windsor before his move to Fairfield.

For most, clothing was as simple and as crude as their homes. With survival at issue, any items that were not absolutely essential became superfluous. Crockery, glassware, and pewter were luxuries that few people could afford. Even among the families of gentlemen, furniture was also scarce, trestleboards of different sizes serving as tables and as seats.

The first residents of Fairfield did not lack for work, however. The first crop to be planted was Indian corn. It could be planted without plowing, it ripened quickly, and it yielded more per acre than any other crop. With the corn, the early farmers were likely to plant squash and beans. Probably most families during their first years in Fairfield had, besides some beef, pork, and fish, little more to eat than the corn, beans, and squash from their gardens.

Hogs were easier to raise than cattle, as they could be relied upon to fend for themselves. Hay was abundant, but harvesting it meant the expenditure of valuable labor. Underestimating the severity of the climate, many farmers lost cattle because they neglected to provide shelter for them. Generally herds were small, and the settlers produced only enough animals for themselves. As breeders of livestock as well as cultivators of crops, these early farmers were inefficient and wasteful. Yet they managed to put enough food on their tables to keep the population growing.

Life in Fairfield during its earliest years must have been, at least from a modern perspective, intensely intermeshed. The entire range of human activity had to take place within a few hundred square yards between the forests on one side and Long Island Sound on the other. From the home of a man like Ludlow, one could see virtually every other dwelling in Fairfield, except those in Pequonnock. Sixty or seventy families, three or four hundred souls, made up the community in 1650. Each resident knew all other townspeople well, saw them on a regular basis, dealt with them within numerous different contexts—economic, social, political, and religious.

Such intensity inevitably bred strain. Most of the tensions have been forgotten, but one can still catch an occasional glimpse of the controversies that plagued Fairfield. One such instance involved Roger Ludlow and two of the men who accompanied him to Fairfield in 1639, Thomas Newton and Thomas Staples. All three men were prominent in Fairfield; all three were prosperous. Staples came to own vast amounts of land. Newton, a carpenter by training, owned a ship in addition to large tracts of land; he traded with the towns on the Connecticut River and made an occasional voyage to Manhattan, when he was able to accumulate enough agricultural produce to make such a trip worthwhile.

Newton had a tendency to get into trouble. He was frequently the defendant in law suits. He was slow about paying his debts. He chose to move out of the central part of town to a desolate spot he bought from the Maxumux Indians. He even, in 1649, fathered an illegitimate child by Elizabeth Johnson, the wife of Peter Johnson. For this last offense, Connecticut officials arrested Newton in December 1649, and held him in prison in Hartford.[23]

Bad blood had existed between Newton and Ludlow for several years. An independent man himself, Ludlow failed to appreciate the quality in others. He regarded Newton as an insolent troublemaker. By contrast, Newton and Staples were fast friends, one of the ingredients of their friendship being their mutual dislike for Ludlow. They shared their antipathy for Ludlow with several other important men in town. Henry Gray and John Green, neighbors of Newton, resented Ludlow's arrogant nature. They attempted to provide bail for Newton after his arrest for adultery, but because he was charged with a capital offense, the court rejected their effort. After a jury found Newton guilty on May 20, 1650 and ordered his execution, John Banks, Edward Adams, Phillip Pinkney, John Hoyt, and George Goodwin conspired with Staples to facilitate Newton's escape to the Dutch in Manhattan.

Even with Newton out of Fairfield, the division among Fairfield's leaders continued to widen. In July 1650, for reasons that have been lost, Ludlow sued Staples for defamation of character, and in March 1651, the court ordered Staples to pay the plaintiff ten shillings in damages as well as costs.

The tensions among Fairfield's leaders may well have been exacerbated by fears of possible attack by the Dutch and by concerns over Indian violence. In 1648, Indians in Stamford had killed John Whitmore of that town; and during that same year, Governor Peter Stuyvesant, of the New Netherlands, had stated that Connecticut rightfully belonged to the Dutch and that he might seize at least part of that territory by force. These events were sufficient to cause the General Court to dispatch Ludlow to Stamford to apprehend the murderers and to designate him to see that the soldiers of Fairfield and Stratford were prepared for war with either the Dutch or the Indians.

The danger passed without further violence, but in 1652, England and Holland actually went to war. What the war would mean for the colonies was unclear. John Cable, a Fairfield man who reacted to the crisis much as Ludlow did, was ready for a fight. In April he and some followers seized a Dutch vessel and its cargo and brought them to Fairfield as a prize. In May the General Court ordered both vessel and cargo returned. Heads were apparently cooler in Hartford than in Fairfield.

During the spring of 1653, rumors began to spread about Stuyvesant's efforts to incite the Indians against southwestern Connecticut. The alarm was so great that Fairfield farmers neglected their plowing in order to maintain watch day and night. Stamford and Norwalk, both in existence by this time, were more exposed than Fairfield, but this thought failed to ease the concerns of Fairfield families.

Connecticut had allies who should have been willing to help. In 1643 Connecticut, Massachusetts Bay, Plymouth, and New Haven had agreed to form a confederation, "a firm and perpetuall league of friendship and amity, for offense and defense, mutuall advice and succour." Roger Ludlow and John Cullick were the Connecticut delegates to the United Colonies, as the four collectively were called. The delegates met in April 1653, agreeing to settle the number of men each colony should provide in the event of war, to distribute arms and munitions that had recently arrived from England, and to send agents to Manhattan to evaluate the disposition of the Dutch.

Gathering again in May, the delegates studied the report of the men who had gone to Manhattan. Seven of the eight agents concluded that the colonies should declare war on the Dutch. William Bradstreet was the only delegate opposed. But he was an influential man—and he represented the colony, Massachusetts Bay, that was to provide 333 of the 500 men the United Colonies had decided would be an appropriate number to send against the Dutch. Without the full agreement of Massachusetts, declaring war would be an empty act. The delegates sought out the "elders of the Bay," but they advised against war, asserting that "it would be safest for the colonies to forbear the use of the sword." Connecticut, whose contribution toward the Army would have been sixty-five men—eight of them from Fairfield, was left frustrated.

At its June 1653 session, the Connecticut General Court ordered that "their shall forth[with] bee presented to the Bay, the present stresses, fears & dangers that the English bordering uppon the Dutch . . . are in." The Court also sent Ludlow and John Haynes to New Haven to plan joint defensive strategies.

When the delegates to the United Colonies reassembled in September, Massachusetts Bay remained adamant in its opposition to war. The Connecticut, New Haven, and Plymouth delegates came away feeling that they had been betrayed. No one felt this more acutely than Ludlow. Aggressive as ever, he believed that war was a necessity and would result in great benefits for Connecticut.

Rhode Island, because of long-standing differences between Roger Williams and the leaders of the Bay Colony, was not a member of the United Colonies. Free to follow its own course, it recognized a state of war with the Dutch and proceeded to issue commissions to Rhode Island seamen to capture Dutch vessels. Captain Thomas Baxter, a holder of one of these commissions, seized a Dutch ship at the west end of Long Island Sound and brought it as a prize to Black Rock Harbor in Fairfield during the winter of 1653-54. The Dutch retaliated by sending two warships with one hundred marines to the Fairfield harbor, where they threatened to attack any departing vessel.

Fairfield's townsmen (the elected officials who would later take the name selectmen) voted, not surprisingly, to protect Fairfield but then went a step further and declared war against the Dutch. Ludlow, who must have supported the townsmen's vote, agreed to take command of Fairfield's army and sent a letter to Governor Eaton of New Haven describing what had happened. Eaton urged Ludlow to take no action until the General Court of Connecticut learned of recent events. The General Court was not scheduled to meet for another three months, that is, until March 1654; but because no actual fighting had erupted at Fairfield and because the seventeenth century tended to think of warfare as a warm-weather activity, no effort was made to convene a special session of the legislature.

When the General Court did assemble in March it largely ignored the danger of war with the Dutch but did issue a warrant for the arrest of Captain Baxter, still in Fairfield. The General Court of the New Haven Jurisdiction also ordered his arrest for various breaches that had occurred in Stamford, which was at the time under the control of New Haven.

Baxter was arrested in Fairfield and delivered to the New Haven authorities. On March 10, they charged him with seizing a vessel without proper authority as well as "with many miscarriages of a high nature at Fairfield." Baxter argued in his defense that he believed his Rhode Island commission was all that was required to conduct war against the enemies of England. During the course of the hearing, John Odell of Pequonnock testified about events in Fairfield after the arrest: "As Baxter's men went up & down the streets of Fairfield, with the swords drawn in their hands, he heard William Ellitt sweare with a great oath (but knowes not the words) that with them hands of his, he would be avenged upon the blood of some of them, which had taken his Captain, & he supposed their was about a dozzen of them, which so runn with their swords drawn." Edward Parker and Daniel Hopper also gave their versions of the events that had transpired in Fairfield. They told of a riot in Fairfield when a group of Baxter's men assaulted the guards in charge of him. In the course of the melée, one of Baxter's men was killed and one of the guards wounded. Fairfield in 1653 was a frontier town; the type of violence associated with frontier communities had obviously created near chaos there during the Baxter incident.[24]

Baxter's treatment at the hands of the Connecticut General Court, to whom New Haven shifted responsibility for passing judgment on him, was hardly severe. The court fined him £70, required him to provide bond of £200 for his good behavior for a year, and ordered him to pay £150 to the owner of the Dutch ship he had captured. While the fine and damages, totaling £220, represented a vast amount of money, Baxter could have been charged with insurrection and faced the death penalty.

Ludlow's role in all of this is unclear. He did, while Baxter was still in Fairfield, put the Rhode Island man under bonds. But this was an action required by the courts and gives no indication of his position on Baxter's activities. Ludlow's willingness to take up arms against the Dutch in what looked like an effort to protect Baxter's prize must have associated him in the minds of many with the erratic Rhode Islander. Ludlow had argued long and vigorously for war with the Dutch, had seen his arguments rejected by Massachusetts Bay which controlled the United Colonies, and then appeared to have acted on his own initiative in offering protection for the captured Dutch ship.

The prosecution of Baxter failed to relieve the tensions that plagued the town. Baxter's activities, conflicting perceptions of Ludlow's role, and fears of a Dutch attack exaggerated the divisions among Fairfield's leadership even further. The feud between Ludlow and Staples entered a new, more sinister phase.

At the time that Ludlow was arguing for war before the United Colonies, Goodwife Bassett, the wife of Thomas Bassett, was on trial in Stratford for witchcraft. Found guilty, she was awaiting execution when she informed several persons in Stratford that she knew of another witch, one, she claimed, who lived in Fairfield and who held her head high. She refused to reveal the witch's name. A short time later, Fairfield brought charges of witchcraft against Goody Knapp. Knapp, however, failed to fit Bassett's description of a woman who held her head high. Goody Knapp was the wife of Roger Knapp, a poor man who had lived in New Haven and on Delaware Bay before moving to Fairfield with his wife and two sons. She did fit the stereotype historians have discerned for women accused of witchcraft in seventeenth-century New England. She was middle-aged, married but with only two children, frequently involved in disputes, abrasive, and without status.[25]

The timing of the accusations, however, is surprising. For the most part, witchcraft proceedings occurred in New England after periods of great turmoil. Generally communities were so occupied with whatever conflict was happening that they had little time to hunt witches. In the case of Goody Knapp, Fairfield acted during a period of major strife rather than after such an interval.

The peculiarity of the situation failed to help poor Goody Knapp. She asserted her innocence throughout the trial, but was found guilty as charged. The conviction was based upon the discovery of witchmarks on her body. Many seventeenth-century people believed that imps or familiars accompanied witches to assist in their evil work. These imps generally took animal or human form but required nourishment directly from the witch. To provide this nourishment, witches had "some big or little teat upon their body and in some secret place where he [the imp] sucketh." A committee of Fairfield women claimed to have found witchmarks on Knapp.

While awaiting execution in the custody of Richard Lyon, Knapp was visited by Lucy Pell, whose husband, Thomas Pell, was a physician in Fairfield; Lucy's daughters by a previous marriage, Elizabeth and Mary Brewster; Susan Lockwood, wife of Robert; and Mary Purdy, wife of Francis. These women came to urge Knapp to confess and to try to extract from her the name of the witch in Fairfield who "held her head high." They repeatedly told Knapp that Mary Staples, wife of Thomas Staples — Ludlow's old archenemy — had been the last to testify against her and had been largely responsible for her conviction.

Knapp refused either to confess or to implicate anyone else. But the following day she sent for Lucy Pell, who returned to Knapp's cell, accompanied again by her daughters and also by Hester Ward, wife of Andrew. Now Goody Knapp began to hint that Mary Staples was Fairfield's other witch. Encouraged by her audience, she described how Mary had once told her about an Indian who had come to her from the forest and presented her with two talismans that glowed more brightly than the day. Mary Staples, Knapp continued, said she had refused the magic items.

At this point Susan Lockwood and Mary Sherwood arrived. Lucy Pell and her daughters continued urging Knapp to reveal the name of the other witch, suggesting again that Mary Staples might well be the individual in question. Knapp refused. She would reveal the secret to either Roger Ludlow or the Reverend Jones at the time of her execution, she declared. Elizabeth Brewster warned her that the devil might take her in the meantime, to protect the identity of his other agent. Aware of the women's motive and as abrasive as ever, Knapp retorted: "Take heed the devil have not

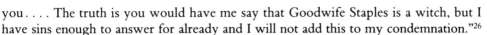

you. . . . The truth is you would have me say that Goodwife Staples is a witch, but I have sins enough to answer for already and I will not add this to my condemnation."[26]

Unaware of the pressure that Lucy, her daughters, and Hester Ward had placed on Goody Knapp, Mary Sherwood came to the defense of Mary Staples, pointing out that her testimony had been no more significant than that of several other witnesses. Knapp replied that she had heard differently within the past half-hour. Mary Sherwood departed shortly after this; she returned later in the day to find Joan Baldwin, wife of Nathaniel, with the condemned woman urging her to implicate Mary Staples. Mary Sherwood left again, this time returning with Martha Gold, the wife of one of Fairfield's most notable residents, Nathan Gold. Martha Gold warned Goody Knapp against sowing seeds of dissension, then listened as Knapp related how she had been tempted by others to do precisely that. She stated that she was unaware of any witch in Fairfield.

This whole bizarre episode came to an even more bizarre climax at Goody Knapp's execution. Mary Staples, having learned of the events that had taken place in Knapp's cell, attended the execution. On the way to the gallows, Ludlow and the Reverend Jones pressed Knapp to tell all she knew about the activities of witches in Fairfield. Distraught, Mary Staples implored the two men to stop harassing the poor woman. After the hanging, Staples rushed forward and demanded to see Knapp's witchmarks. Finding herself ignored, she seized the corpse of Goody Knapp, ripped the clothing from the dead body, and began examining it for unusual marks. "Will you say these are witch's teats?" she demanded of her neighbors. "Here are no more teats that I myself have or any woman."[27]

Why Lucy Pell and her daughters, Hester Ward, and others had tried so hard to convince Goody Knapp to testify against Mary Staples is unclear from the perspective of more than three hundred years. But their close ties to Roger Ludlow, Ludlow's precarious situation because of his earlier support of Baxter against the Dutch, and the intense hostility that existed between Ludlow and Thomas Staples suggest that Knapp's tormenters saw her as a means of attacking Staples and of relieving some of the pressure then on Ludlow.

Not only did their plan fail, it resulted in even further damage to Ludlow's reputation. Thomas Staples was as relentlessly stubborn as Ludlow. When his wife came under attack, his strategy was to counterattack rather than to retreat to a defensive position. Ludlow had mentioned certain suspicions he had about Mary Staples to the Reverend John Davenport, one of the founders of New Haven. Because Ludlow had opposed several schemes for New Haven expansion, he was not a favorite of Davenport's, who informed Staples of his remarks. Staples, on behalf of his wife, sued Ludlow for slander. The New Haven Court heard the suit on May 29, 1654, John Banks of Fairfield representing Staples and Alexander Bryant of Milford defending Ludlow. The court found for the plaintiff and awarded Staples £10 in damages, as well as costs. Ludlow and Staples, men who had together risked their futures by coming to Uncoway in 1639, had become the bitterest of enemies.

By the end of May, Roger Ludlow had abandoned Fairfield. He had made his decision several months earlier, well before the Staples suit. In January 1654, he had begun to sell his lands. In February he cleared the title to about three hundred acres so that they could be sold. He disposed of the land he had purchased between the Saugatuck and Norwalk rivers to the planters of Norwalk on April 13. Six days later, he was in

New Haven trying to untangle some confusion over a ship he had hired to transport his family and his property from Connecticut. He sold his remaining lands in Fairfield on May 10 to Alexander Bryan, his lawyer. In May 1654, for the first time since it came into being, the Colony of Connecticut failed to list Roger Ludlow as one of its magistrates or as its deputy governor. To the end, Ludlow wished the colony well. When he sold the lands west of the Saugatuck to the Norwalk settlers, he added a condition "that they will set upon the planting. . . with all convenient speed" and "not receive in any that they be obnoxious to the publique good of the Commonwealth of Connecticut."[28]

Ludlow may have gone from Fairfield to Virginia to visit his brother, George, but his ultimate destination was the British Isles. He was sixty-four when he left. The Civil War in England had resulted in the establishment of the Commonwealth in 1649, with a government dominated by Puritans. He believed England and the British Isles had a bright future, probably brighter than that which Fairfield could anticipate. Many New Englanders , sharing his opinion, were returning to the Old World. William Pyncheon, the founder of Springfield, went back home. So also did Edward Hopkins, six times governor of Connecticut, and Henry Whitfield, who had brought the first settlers to Guilford. Both founders of New Haven, Theophilus Eaton and John Davenport, almost returned in 1654. Ludlow's departure was hardly surprising; the idea of a new adventure was one that he usually relished.

On November 3, 1654, the lord deputy and council for Ireland appointed him to the post of commissioner for the "receiving, hearing and determining of all claims in or to forfeited lands in Ireland." A month later, the lord deputy ordered that "Roger Ludlow, Esq., be appointed Commr. for the administration of justice at Dublin." He was still alive in February 1660 and probably died five or six years later in Dublin.[29]

The Fairfield that Ludlow had known was characterized by factionalism, exemplified by the Ludlow-Staples feud; by conflict, with neighboring plantations over boundaries and with the Indians and the Dutch over more vital issues; and by a high turnover in population — of the original settlers, only Thomas Staples died in the town he had helped to establish.

By 1654, Fairfield was the fourth most populous of nine Connecticut towns. It counted ninety-four households within its borders. Life in town was to become less frantic. The English and the Dutch settled their differences during the summer of 1654. The old leaders now largely gone, Fairfield would discover a new and more stable group of men to direct its affairs. Factionalism refused to disappear entirely, but became of little importance. Differences with Norwalk and Stratford gradually vanished, and fears about Indian attacks subsided. Fairfield men and women learned to find new ways to improve their standard of living, began to open new lands to settlement, and decided, in most cases, that the town offered as good a life as they could hope to find. Unlike the first settlers, they were there to stay. But Fairfield could not forget Roger Ludlow. His imprint was too enduring.

1. No adequate biography of Roger Ludlow exists. The best studies are R.V. Coleman, *Roger Ludlow Goes for Old England* (Westport, Conn., 1935); Herbert F. Seversmith, "Roger Ludlow (1590-1665/6)," *National Genealogical Society Quarterly* 51 (Sept. and Dec. 1963) 154-64, 224-34; John M. Taylor, *Roger Ludlow, The Colonial Lawmaker* (New York, 1900).

2. Nathaniel B. Shurtleff, ed., *Records of the Governor and Company of Massachusetts Bay,* 5 vols. (Boston, 1853-54) I, 114.

3. John Winthrop, *Winthrop's Journal,* ed. J. K. Hosmer, 2 vols. (New York, 1908), I, 78.

4. Relations between the Pequots and the English are examined in Francis Jennings, *The Invasion of America: Indians, Colonialism, and the Cant of Conquest* (Chapel Hill, N.C., 1975) and Neal Salisbury, *Manitou and Providence: Indians, Europeans and the Making of New England, 1500-1643* (New York, 1982).

5. Quoted in Seversmith, "Ludlow," 158.

6. Ibid., 159.

7. Ibid.

8. *Records of the Court of Assistants of the Colony of the Massachusetts Bay,* 3 vols. (Boston, 1901-8, I, 170.

9. Quoted in Elizabeth Hubbell Schenck, *The History of Fairfield,* 2 vols. (New York, 1889-1905), I, 313.

10. *The Public Records of the Colony of Connecticut,* ed. J. Hammond Trumbull and Charles J. Hoadly, 15 vols. (Hartford, Conn., 1850-90), I, 10. Hereinafter cited as *Connecticut Colonial Records.*

11. *Winthrop's Journal,* I, 229.

12. The importance of the lands being cleared by the Indians is discussed by Howard S. Russell, *A Long, Deep Furrow: Three Centuries of Farming in New England* (Hanover, N.H. 1976) and Bruce C. Daniels, "Economic Development in Colonial and Revolutionary Connecticut: An Overview," *William and Mary Quarterly,* 37 (July 1980), 429-50.

13. The best study of Fairfield area Indians is Franz L. Wojciechowski, *The Pauqussett Tribes: An Ethnohistorical Study of the Tribal Interrelationships of the Indians of the Lower Housatonic River* (Nijmegen, The Netherlands, 1985).

14. Ludlow's expedition is described in *Connecticut Colonial Records,* I, 35-36.

15. Ibid.

16. Ibid.

17. Ibid., I, 36.

18. Quoted in Schenck, *Fairfield,* I, 27.

19. Ibid., I, 28, 37.

20. *Connecticut Colonial Records,* I, 138.

21. Ibid., I, 465-66.

22. Frank Samuel Child, *An Old New England Church* (Fairfield, Conn., 1910), 38.

23. William K. Holdsworth, "Adultery or Witchcraft? A New Note on an Old Case in Connecticut," *New England Quarterly* 48 (Sept. 1975) 394-409.

24. Schenck, *Fairfield,* I, 79-83.

25. The best studies of witchcraft in colonial New England are John Putnam Demos, *Entertaining Satan: Witchcraft and the Culture of Early New England* (New York, 1982) and Richard Weisman, *Witchcraft, Magic, and Religion in 17th-Century Massachusetts* (Amherst, Mass., 1984). R. G. Tomlinson, *Witchcraft Trials of Connecticut* (Hartford, Conn., 1978), should also be consulted.

26. Quoted in Tomlinson, *Witchcraft Trials,* 6-8.

27. Ibid.

28. Edwin Hall, *The Ancient Historical Records of Norwalk* (New York, 1847), 32-33.

29. Coleman, *Ludlow Goes for Old England,* 29.

# The Town Takes Shape

LUDLOW'S DECISION to leave Fairfield for what he believed to be better opportunities in Ireland should not be taken as evidence that the plantation was faltering. In fact, its best years lay ahead. The people who lived there as of the summer of 1654 were men and women determined to create a Christian community in which all residents would live in loving harmony. Whether they could accomplish this depended upon their ability to blend themselves into a single whole, a corporate community with a solitary mission. "We must knit together as one man . . . and . . . must delight in each other, make other's condition our own, rejoice together, mourn together, labor and suffer together, always having before our eyes our commmission and community in the work," John Winthrop had told the early settlers of Massachusetts Bay; the people of Fairfield understood that they must work for the same end.[1]

Fairfield's inhabitants indeed became a single body, each a part of the whole. They lived huddled together, worked and worshiped together, and shared both good experiences and bad. Farmers depended upon each other to offset deficiencies in their own production; one man whose corn crop was small but whose orchards yielded an abundance would hope to find a neighbor with the opposite and complementary predicament. Interdependence was essential for survival. The tradition of mutual help, the core of community life in many English villages, encouraged the growth of a corporate identity. The Puritan sense of mission, the desire to create a community that would be pleasing in the eyes of God, made that identity even stronger.

But while the community was one body, the people who made up the parts of the body refused absolutely to regard themselves as equals. Fairfield people classified themselves by rank, persons of the same rank tending to live close by each other, to occupy the same positions in the town, to socialize, and to intermarry. The modern reader might expect tension to have existed between the idea of the town as a commonwealth and the idea of society as a hierarchy, but the inhabitants of mid-seventeenth-century

26

Fairfield saw no conflict. From their perspective, this was all part of God's plan, the way life should be.

The town meeting was the most important political institution. The meeting gathered regularly, handled important matters, and included practically all male inhabitants. It addressed matters of religion, defense, economics, and morality. Because the town and the parish were conterminous in the early years of Fairfield, the town meeting handled all secular and monetary concerns pertaining to the church. The membership of the church gathered separately to discuss doctrine, discipline, provisions of the covenant, and potential new members, but strictly parish affairs fell within the domain of the town meeting.

Because the meetings were so important, residents who failed to attend were fined. Residents were summoned by a drummer, the same one who also gathered them on the Sabbath and on election days, to a building that certainly existed by the time of Ludlow's departure, the meetinghouse, the site of all important town assemblies. The drummer also was responsible "to cause the meting house to be swept and the dogs kept out." Those who indulged "in disorderly speaking" or in "speaking w[ithou]t leave" risked fines as surely as those who failed to attend.[2]

On February 26, 1658, the Connecticut General Assembly defined those eligible to participate in the town meetings — called "admitted inhabitants" — as "householders that are one & twenty years of age, or have bore office, or have £30 estate." Two years later the court added another criterion: "None shall be received as Inhabitant into any Towne in the Colony but such as are known to be of honest conversation, and accepted by a major part of the Towne." Typically Fairfield followed its own course, refusing, within this context, to make any distinction between inhabitants generally and admitted inhabitants.[3]

Fairfield's most important elected officials were the townsmen or, as they came to be called after 1703, the selectmen. They acted as an original court in controversies involving less than 40 shillings, warned of town meetings "as ocation shall require," appointed "anny persons to anny bisines about highways fences and about Common feilds," and acted on the "prudentials of the town in all particulars" for the town's well-being, except the granting of lands.[4]

Besides the townsmen, Fairfield elected a whole array of town officers. The function of the constables was what one would anticipate, to keep the peace. The sheepmasters hired shepherds for the town flock and looked after the welfare of the sheep generally. The recorder was early Fairfield's version of the town clerk. One man was chosen "to seal wayts and measurers," four to see that farmers' fences were properly maintained, and two to watch over the condition of the roads. From time to time, the town would choose persons to perform other specific tasks, perhaps "to sweep the meting house and keep out the hoggs" or to serve as "Clark of the market for wheat & other grains" or, when the town had become sufficiently affluent to afford a bell for the meetinghouse, "to ring the bell at nin of Clock every night."[5]

Ad hoc committees were an essential part of Fairfield during the seventeenth century. Whenever the town was unable to resolve a disagreement or to find someone to accomplish an especially burdensome job, it would appoint an ad hoc committee to handle the matter. Such committees divided newly surveyed lands, collected taxes to pay the minister, oversaw the plastering of the meetinghouse, settled disputes between neighbors, and, in particular, handled grievances that developed between inhabitants and the town. Fairfield was eager to avoid alienating any of its inhabitants, eager to maintain a loving harmony in town. These committees worked to keep conflict to a minimum.

Political power during the second half of the seventeenth century was widely distributed in Fairfield. Nathan Gold, Jehu Burr, and his brother John Burr were the most important men in town. All three had come to Fairfield as well-to-do men and remained in town until their deaths, all in the 1690s. Gold was certainly the wealthiest and most respected man in Fairfield and the Burrs were second only to him. Most men who served as townsmen served one, two, or three terms, and a large majority of the men of town held public office at least once during their lifetime, the one exception being the poorest inhabitants, who were generally excluded from office. Gold and John Burr each served fourteen terms as townsmen and Jehu Burr thirteen.

Most of the matters before the town represented the concerns of any small agricultural community: fences, livestock, land, and roads. But the town was in many respects a stern father, determined to control the lives of its residents in a variety of ways. The town might decree that every proprietor of a dwelling must possess a ladder long enough to reach the ridge of his house and that each must see that his chimneys were cleaned fortnightly in the winter and monthly in the summer. It might decide that firearms were to be discharged only away from the center of town. It could order inhabitants to refrain from exporting clapboards, shingles, pipe staves, hogshead staves, or barrel staves cut on the town's common lands, or from sowing peas "for the spac of three years."[6] Town orders could be entirely personal; one prevented Peter Clapham from selling any of his woodlands to Edward Lacy.

The town kept a constant watch for breaches of morality, no matter how small. Boys were a particular problem, especially in the gallery on Sabbath days, but adults also required supervision. In 1686 Fairfield ordered its constables "uppon saboth days in time of exersies to take note who they are are lying or sleeping or playing and Inform those with whom they are conserned that they may reform such evell practises." Fairfield watched its female population as closely as it did its males. In 1685 Mary Shervington, the wife of Thomas, "was Complayned agst for being drunke and selling rum to the Indians." The town fined her and ordered her to "sitt in the Stockes not Exceeding Three hours" for her disorderly behavior, plus another two hours for her contempt of court.[7]

Six young men, all sons of prominent Fairfield families, appeared before the Fairfield court on January 3, 1686, for assembling at an "Unseasonable time of night from their usual places of abode without leave from said Masters." The court fined each ten shillings and ordered that two shillings and six pence from each fine be paid to the person who had informed against them. The use of informers was a common and accepted method of social control and of maintaining "the peace of the neighborhood."[8]

The town's greatest power was the power to determine who could live in Fairfield. Newcomers found themselves undergoing close scrutiny before they would be allowed to take up residence within town. Fairfield rejected anyone likely to become a burden on the town, a public charge; and the town assumed the worst about strangers until there was good reason to believe otherwise. For the most part, unless he was from a prominent family in a nearby community or came by marriage to a Fairfield daughter or widow, any outsider could assume that the town meeting would reject him.

Even among those who were admitted for good reasons, there were instances when the town changed its mind. Edward Howard gained admission to town in 1685 when he married Abigail Dimon, the widow of Moses Dimon and the daughter of Andrew Ward. When evidence revealed that Howard was embezzling Dimon's estate, the Fairfield court fined him 40 shillings for "his contemptuous cariage and Language;" and the town forced him to find a home elsewhere. William Tomson arrived in town in 1684 and received permission to remain "during the Towne's pleasure." But two years later the town ordered that "no person shall build a hous or dig a seler upon anny of the towns land without thar leave and it being Complained that william tomson hath settled him a sellar . . . [he was required] to remove himself and family out of the Towne."[9]

The problem Fairfield faced in maintaining its exclusiveness seldom came from those who applied to the town meeting for admission; it came from sojourners," people who were illegally "entertained" by town residents and who moved into the community "without town leave." The General Court in 1637 had decreed that "noe Mr of a Family shall give habitacon or interteinment to any yonge man to soiourne in his family, but by the allowance of the inhabitants of the saide Towne where he dwelles under the like penalty of 20 s. pr weeke." Again in 1682, it warned of "sundry persons of an ungoverned conversation [who] thrust themselves into our townships and by some underhanded ways . . . become inhabitants . . . such persons often proveing vicious and burthensome and chargeable"[10]

Fairfield was diligent in its efforts to keep these illegal residents out. Once it discovered them, it was quick to send them away. In August 1673, it ordered Enocke Boulton to "depart the Town within this fortnight" and warned all town residents against entertaining him after that time. Women found in town illegally faced the same fate as men. The town granted Aaron Fountain temporary permission to remain in Fairfield in 1685 until the winter on the condition that he remove "his mayd he formarly brogt to the town and free the Town of anny Charge about her." Five years later, the town learned that Daniel Frost was sheltering a strange woman at his home. It ordered "sd danill frost to Convay her to her Unkell bushey at New Haven and if shee bee sent back again thn to bee sent westward from whear shee Cam to claer the town of her."[11]

Fairfield frequently reminded its inhabitants of the fines that could be imposed for entertaining persons without proper authorization. On December 12, 1678, it ordered that anyone who "shall give entertaynment for future to any person That the Towne or Townsmen shall give warning to not to Inhabit any longer in the Towne but to depart the Towne . . . shall forfeit a fine of the Towne Treasury of nineteen shillings for such entertaynment and five shillings for every hour he shall soe continue to entertayne." On several occasions, the marshal or some other prominent citizen, upon orders from the town, made "diligent enquiry who entertains sojourners without the towns consent."[12]

Year in and year out, the most important matter before the town was the distribution of land. The General Court had given Connecticut towns the power to dispose of the lands within their borders. During Fairfield's earliest years this was an easy task. The town provided each newcomer with a home or building lot, the amount of land a person received depending upon his contribution to the cost of purchasing Indian lands and the size of his family. The lots were located around the four squares that originally comprised the town. Outlying lots—planting fields, meadows, and pastures—were established around the central village. Ludlow and the other original settlers were too

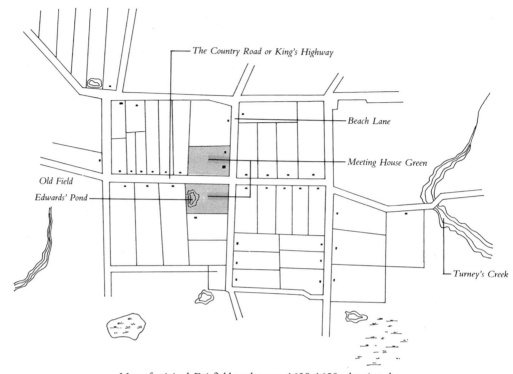

The Country Road or King's Highway

Beach Lane

Meeting House Green

Old Field

Edwards' Pond

Turney's Creek

*Map of original Fairfield settlement, 1639-1650, showing the "four squares" with home lots clustered around the town green.*

individualistic — and too self-seeking — to organize their planting according to the open-field system, that is, one where the fields were worked in common, a practice widely followed in England. But following another English tradition, their fields were small parcels scattered about among those of neighbors, guaranteeing that no one monopolize all the best land and that no one be burdened with exclusively inferior land.

In 1641 the General Court of Connecticut ordered that new settlers be granted "one hundred acres of plowing ground & twenty acres of meadow, provided twenty acres were improved the first, & eighty the second year." Anyone Fairfield admitted could assume that he would receive land, the amount beyond the stipulated 120 acres and the location being determined by an ad hoc committee. During these early decades, the town refused to distinguish between inhabitants and proprietors, proprietors being those individuals, including widows, who were taxpayers and therefore entitled to receive a share in each dividend. [13]

This unhurried system of land distribution continued for about twenty years, while England, preoccupied with civil war, the overthrow of the monarchy, and the establishment of the Commonwealth, paid little attention to New England. Connecticut, which would not receive a charter until 1662 and which therefore had no legal basis in the eyes of the mother country, was unconcerned about interference from abroad while England was so busy at home. But in 1660, England restored the Stuart family to the throne and turned an attentive eye once more toward the New World. Throughout

*Fairfield: the biography of a community*

Connecticut settlers began to worry about what the new king, Charles II, might do with those lands that remained undivided. Fairfield decided to distribute these lands as quickly as possible so that title could be transferred from the town to individual owners and thereby be made more secure. In some cases, the town was so eager to put its lands into the hands of its residents that it made the divisions even before the property had been fully surveyed.

The first major division came in January 1662. The town ordered that about 320 acres located in both southeastern and southwestern Fairfield should be divided among the town's taxpayers, with no more than six acres going to a single family. Sixty-nine families participated in the division, which the town originally intended should be only a grant of use for ten years but which it eventually made a permanent dividend. The formula for determining how much land each family received was based upon the grant of a half-acre to each "master of family" a quarter-acre for his wife and for each child, and two acres for each £100 of taxable property. A typical family received 4.6 acres in this first division.

By the beginning of 1669, the town was ready to make another division, this one located west of the Mill River and known as the Sasqua dividend. It involved 415 acres to be distributed among sixty-eight families, with the average family receiving 6.1 acres.

The Sasqua grant was only the beginning of an ambitious plan to transfer title to an amazing quantity of land in a short period of time. At the time the Sasqua grant was being made, the town ordered Nathan Gold, Jehu Burr, John Banks, James Beers, and William Hill to buy any lands within the town, except reservations, that were still in Indian hands. In September 1670, Fairfield bought "the last six miles of the Indians: of the Towne Commons: and they having agreed that the Towne shall give them 36 pounds for it." Fairfield paid the purchase price in "trucking cloth" valued at 10 shillings a yard. The following month, John Banks, Seriant Seely, and James Beers went with the Indians to "bound the land to the end of the Towne bounds that we are buying of the Indians."[14]

This purchase was a prelude to the dividend of 1671. The town had to attend to other preliminaries. At the time of the 1662 division, Fairfield had made a distinction between inhabitants and proprietors. Sixty-nine persons had participated in the 1662 dividend and sixty-eight in the Sasqua division. The town meeting voted that essentially the same group should take part in the forthcoming division, the town's object being to exclude newcomers from participation. But John Burr and William Ward argued that this also permanently excluded the adult sons of proprietors who, because they still lived at home, were not taxpayers. The best such a young man could hope for would be one day, after the death of his father, to share with his brothers his father's single right to participate. This point remained unresolved until January 26, 1671, when the town decided to include some children and some absentee owners or their tenants among the proprietors. The number participating increased from 68 or 69 to about 100. Those who failed to be included in this group were, with one or two exceptions, permanently excluded.

The amount of land a proprietor could expect to receive in 1671 was determined "by persons and the present list of estate: the persons to be vallued as followeth: a master of a family thirty pounds a wife Ten pounds and a child at Ten pounds: which vallu shall be added to the list of estates: & according to the Totall sum pertayning to each

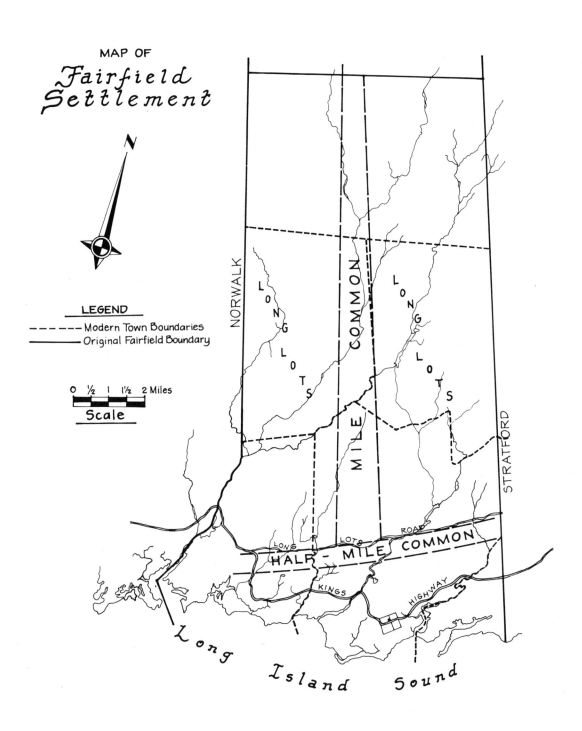

MAP OF
*Fairfield Settlement*

N

LEGEND
- - - - - Modern Town Boundaries
——————— Original Fairfield Boundary

0   ½   1   1½   2 Miles
Scale

NORWALK

LONG LOTS

MILE COMMON

LONG LOTS

STRATFORD

LONG LOTS ROAD

HALF - MILE COMMON

KINGS HIGHWAY

Long Island Sound

*Fairfield: the biography of a community*

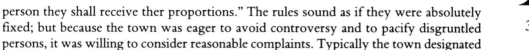

person they shall receive ther proportions." The rules sound as if they were absolutely fixed; but because the town was eager to avoid controversy and to pacify disgruntled persons, it was willing to consider reasonable complaints. Typically the town designated an ad hoc committee to act as arbitrators in these cases.[15]

The plan for the 1671 division was a simple one. A Half Mile of Common was established all the way across Fairfield, from the Stratford line to Compo. Just below the Half Mile of Common, the town created tiers of building and pasture lots. Above the Half Mile of Common and intersecting it at approximately its midway point was a Mile of Common, which ran back to Fairfield's rear boundary. On either side of the Mile of Common, the town created Long Lots that paralleled the common and began at the Norwalk line on one side and the Stratford line on the other.

While the building and pasture lots averaged only twelve and eleven acres respectively, the Long Lots were vastly larger. In the first place, they were about 13.5 miles long, although town residents were unaware of this at the time, surveyors having only established a base line in the area of the Half Mile of Common; decades would pass before they would complete their work in this huge area. The width of the lots depended upon the size of one's total dividend. Phebe and Deborah Barlow, the orphans of John Barlow, received a lot that was only about 3 rods, or 50 feet, wide. Nathan Gold, on the other hand, found that his was more than 53 rods wide, or about 875 feet. The average Long Lot contained over 490 acres.

Fairfield granted more than 52,000 acres or approximately 81 square miles in the dividend of 1671. The average grant—including Long Lot, building lot, and pasture lot—was 513 acres. The Barlow girls received a smaller amount than anyone else in town, 97 acres. Nathan Gold, the wealthiest man in Fairfield, received the largest grant, 1500 acres, to add to his already vast holdings. Thomas Staples, the only original settler of Fairfield still in town, added 1128 acres to his estate.

The following year, 1672, Fairfield divided another 800 acres. This land was located in Compo and included everything between Sherwood Island and the Saugatuck River and south of the Long Lots. One hundred and one proprietors participated in this division, one that included, according to the Town Records, 300 acres of good land and 500 acres of "worss land."[16]

In 1664 Charles II had granted all the land between the Delaware River and the Connecticut River to his brother, the duke of York. Beginning in the middle 1670s, Sir Edmund Andros, as governor of New York, began to assert the duke's claim to western Connecticut. Aware that Andros might push this matter to the point of challenging Fairfield's title to its lands, the town decided to establish a general Indian deed to cover all previous purchases. On October 6, 1680, all the Indian sachems from whom Fairfield had purchased lands, or their descendants, were assembled to sign a new deed. By the terms of this deed, the Indians acknowledged that they had sold and had been duly compensated for lands mentioned in the deeds of March 20, 1657, which had confirmed the Ludlow purchases; of March 21, 1661, the Sasqua purchase; and of January 19, 1671, when Fairfield bought the last six miles of land at the rear of its boundary. The Indians continued to reserve for their use lands at Sasqua, Pequonnock, Uncoway, Old Indian Field, Wolves Pit Plain, and Aspetuck, all within Fairfield. Still concerned about Andros, Fairfield's leaders decided to purchase the Old Indian Field, which they did May 18, 1681. The next year, they divided its sixty-three acres among ninety proprietors.

*The Town Takes Shape*

Before the town could make any other substantial grants, it was forced to watch Massachusetts fall victim to the designs of first Charles II and then James II and their agents in America. In 1684, Charles II, after years of effort, finally managed to revoke the charter of the Massachusetts Bay colony. His successor, James II, then proceeded to create the Dominion of New England, which brought Massachusetts, New Hampshire, and Maine under one government headed by the notorious Sir Edmund Andros. In July 1685, Edward Randolph, collector of customs for New England, began *quo warranto* proceedings against the charters of Connecticut and Rhode Island. Clearly those colonies were destined to be included in the Dominion.

To prevent the loss of the undivided lands in Connecticut, the General Court in 1685 changed the legal form of ownership of these lands. Whereas before 1685 the towns had held these lands in common, now title was vested in the specific persons named as proprietors. At the same time the General Court conferred upon each town a patent by which it "do give, grant, ratify & confirm" the town's ownership of all lands purchased from the Indians.

Fairfield responded to the General Assembly's actions by voting on November 1, 1687, that "those of the Town that did divide pasture, building & the Long Lots, Shall be, and be deemed to be with their heirs & lawfull Successors . . . the proprietors of all the Comons of Fairfield; that is of the two half miles of Comon, and the mile of comon, & all other Lands lying in the Comon." Thus the former town-owned lands became the property of the proprietors. Both town and colony wanted to be as prepared as possible for the onslaught.[17]

Unbeknownst to Fairfield, it had actually come on October 31, 1687, when Andros, without waiting for the outcome of the *quo warranto* proceedings, took control of Connecticut. He failed, however, to gain possession of the charter, which, according to legend was hidden in an oak tree. Actually Andros's incorporation of Connecticut into the Dominion of New England had little impact upon Fairfield. Life proceeded much as it had before. And the Dominion had but a short existence. On April 18, 1689, the people of Massachusetts Bay, encouraged by the Glorious Revolution that toppled James II, revolted, overcame the Dominion, and threw Andros into jail.

The impact of the Dominion was so slight in Fairfield that the last two substantial land divisions took place while the town was technically under Andros's control. In 1688, the town divided 21 acres on Paul's Neck among 103 proprietors and 83 acres at Wolf Swamp among 104 proprietors. Even after these last important dividends, the proprietors continued to meet and to oversee the distribution of the common and undivided lands. Their meetings were separate from the town meeting, and they continued well into the eighteenth century.

The land system that developed in early Fairfield had a profound and indelible impact upon the town. Without great difficulty the modern resident can still discern the location of the four squares, the original central village. The regularity of the streets in that part of town are reminders of Ludlow's original plan. The old Half Mile of Common, with its northern limits at what the twentieth century knows as Hulls Farm Road, also betrays its former identity in its roads, many of which even today follow the land contours as once they did as swine and cow paths. Above Hulls Farm Road the parallel highways reveal the direction the Long Lots originally took three hundred years ago.

Anything involving the town lands Fairfield regarded seriously. When an Indian who called himself both John Wampus and John White claimed to be the owner of a large section of Fairfield, the town immediately took notice. Wampus was the husband of Anne Praske and the son-in-law of Romanock, once the sachem of both the Sasqua and Aspetuck Indians. Romanock, on September 11, 1661, had given his daughter some of his land, in particular, a parcel located in that part of Fairfield once controlled by the Aspetucks. Wampus, who had never lived in Fairfield, claimed the land as Anne's husband, married women being unable to own real estate under existing Connecticut law. He came to Fairfield and asked the town clerk, William Hill, to examine the deeds relating to the property in question. Hill refused, telling Wampus that he must obtain the permission of townsman Nathan Gold before he could see them. Gold, a man as committed as any to maintaining Fairfield's control of all of its lands, denied his permission. Undeterred, Wampus pressed his demand onto the other townsmen. They supported Gold, and when Wampus refused to accept their verdict, they ordered him imprisoned and then out of Fairfield.

Wampus carried his case to England. There the Lords of Council not only heard his petition but ordered the governor and magistrates of Connecticut to "proceed in such manner as his Majesty's subjects may not be forced to undertake so long & dangerous Voyages for obtayning Justice, which his Majesty expects shalbe speedily & impartially administered upon them in place." Wampus was unable to take advantage of the Lords' decision because he died just before it was rendered.[18]

Attorney Richard Thayer of Milford, whom Wampus had hired to pursue his case, continued to push the Indian's claim. On July 25, 1681, he asked Governor William Leete to intercede on his behalf in attempting to gain access to Fairfield land records. Leete and the magistrates replied that they would normally be willing to intervene but refused to in this case because "to suffer strangers to draw lines within townships without order or consent of the town, we think not safe to encourage."

Thayer then went to court. He sued Peter Clapham and Isaac Frost, two individuals who had received grants from Fairfield that included lands claimed by Wampus. The town meeting voted that if the two "will take direction from the Townsmen in the defence of the case, then the necessary Charge arising in the defence of the said case shall be defrayed out of the Towne Treasurie." Indians living in Fairfield undermined Thayer's case. They testified that the English had purchased all the land in question and that the Sasqua and Aspetuck Indians had fought with the Pequots against the English, had been defeated, and so had lost their claim to most of their land. Thayer's case totally collapsed when the jury learned that neither Wampus nor his wife had enjoyed possession of the land for more than twenty years; by Connecticut law, the land was considered abandoned and became the property of the town to do with as it saw fit.[19]

Wampus's case was important because it demonstrated the degree to which Fairfield residents would go to preserve what they believed belonged to the town. They were uncompromising in attempting to amass enough land within the town to provide for the needs of their children and grandchildren. The case also marked the last time that Fairfield's purchase of its lands from Native Americans would be brought into question.

A less vexatious issue was the question of the Maxumux or Bankside farmers. In the late 1640s, a group of men—men like Thomas Newton, Henry Gray, and John Green, men who placed a great premium upon independence—bought about a mile of land just west of Fairfield's original boundary on Long Island Sound. The area came to be called Maxumux or Bankside. The relationship between the Bankside farmers and the town was first defined in an agreement of November 1648. Fairfield maintained its right to graze cattle along the shore and to drive them back and forth across the Bankside lands. The farmers agreed to provide adequate fences for their planting fields and to pay all town taxes from which they might reasonably expect to benefit.[20]

Eventually, on March 21, 1661, Fairfield bought the land beyond Bankside from the Indians, thereby encompassing the farmers' lands within the town boundaries. But the farmers maintained their ambiguous independence until January 1665, when the Fairfield town meeting insisted upon determining the precise "relation they stand in to us." As a consequence, on June 29, 1666, a second agreement was made between the farmers and the town. By its terms, Bankside was completely united with Fairfield, and the farmers became full inhabitants, enjoying equal privileges and subject to equal taxes and to all the orders of the town.[21]

Establishing firm boundaries for Fairfield was a problem of greater magnitude than those created by either John Wampus or the Bankside farmers. Fairfield was without recognized boundaries when it was established. In typical fashion, Ludlow extended the town's boundaries until they ran into conflict with a neighboring town. Those who followed him as leaders pursued a similar policy.[22]

By 1641 the boundary between Fairfield and Stratford had become an issue. Several attempts to establish the boundary failed, largely because the issue was complicated by the presence of the Pequonnock Indians, through whose lands the boundary passed. In 1659, the governor and magistrates of Connecticut ordered Fairfield and Stratford to be sure that the Indians had sufficient land to sustain themselves. Fairfield could assemble little enthusiasm for providing for the Pequonnocks. The town replied to the governor's directive by complaining that Fairfield had hardly enough land for its own people and that Stratford should be responsible for them.

Faced with what the governor called Fairfield's "peremptory persisting," the General Court took it upon itself to resolve the issue that same year. It ordered Fairfield to compensate Stratford for its grant of Golden Hill to the Indians and to assume responsibility for them as if they resided within Fairfield. Fairfield residents resented the decision and, in May 1661, asked the General Court to review it. The court, which had been plagued with this problem for twenty years, wasted few words in denying the petition: "This Court declare their unwillingness to admit a further hearing of the case twixt Fairfield & Stratford." To resolve the problem definitively, the court then appointed a committee, including one representative each from Fairfield, Stratford, and Norwalk, to run the boundary between Fairfield and its neighbor to the east.[23]

The Norwalk-Fairfield boundary was an even more complicated problem. In 1650 the General Court granted Fairfield the right to extend its western boundary to the Saugatuck River, provided the river was within two miles of Fairfield's existing western boundary. This began the controversy. Various efforts to resolve it were futile, and for years the boundary remained uncertain. At its October 1666 session, the General Court reestablished Fairfield's western boundary as a line seven miles south and west of its Stratford boundary, the same western boundary that had existed before 1650. This still left open the question of ownership of the lands between this line and the Saugatuck

River. Once again years of indecision and procrastination followed.

Fears of Sir Edmund Andros and the Dominion of New England eventually prompted some action by the General Court, and it created a committee to try to reach a full settlement of the issue. A final disposition proved to be as elusive as ever, however; ten more years passed before the boundary was settled. A December 14, 1697, agreement established the line at the Saugatuck River, finally ending nearly a half-century of conflict, much of it created by Fairfield's single-minded determination to add as much land as it possibly could to the town's domain. In 1697 Fairfield was as large as it ever would be, encompassing nearly 140 square miles.

In the minds of its early inhabitants, the town could never be too large; they understood that each additional generation meant more population and more pressure on the land. Fathers anticipated both the day when they would divide their land among perhaps several sons and the day when those sons would repeat the process. Such a geometric progression meant smaller estates and shrinking standards of living for a progeny yet unborn, a situation they could postpone only by being determinedly acquisitive.

## NOTES

1. John Winthrop, "A Modell of Christian Charity," *Winthrop Papers*, 2 vols. (Boston, 1931), II, 294-95. Particularly useful in the preparation of this chapter have been Joan R. Ballen's "Fairfield, Connecticut, 1661-1691: A Demographic Study of the Economic, Political, and Social Life of a New England Community," M.A. thesis, University of Bridgeport, 1970; Thomas W. Jodziewicz, "Dual Localism in Seventeenth-Century Connecticut: Relations between the General Courts and the Towns, 1635-1671," Ph.D. dissertation, College of William and Mary, 1974; Bruce C. Daniels, *The Connecticut Town: Growth and Development, 1635-1790* (Middletown, Conn., 1979); Christopher Collier, "Saybrook and Lyme: Secular Settlements in a Puritan Commonwealth," in George J. Willauer, Jr., *A Lyme Miscellany* (Middletown, 1977); and Kenneth Lockridge, *A New England Town, The First Hundred Years: Dedham, Massachusetts, 1636-1736* (New York, 1970).

2. Fairfield Town Records, vol. B, part II, 1661-1741, Connecticut State Library, Feb. 23, 1664, Jan. 14, 1677. All citations of the town minute records from the years 1661-1741, with the exception of citations to meetings held between June 24, 1664 and Feb. 15, 1669, are to this original volume of the minutes. Other copies of these minutes, including vol. B, part I, 1661-1826, at the State Library and typescripts available at both the Fairfield Historical Society (hereinafter cited as FHS) and the Fairfield Town Hall, contain serious inaccuracies. In many instances, vol. B, part I had to be used because it remains the only source of information about town meetings held between June 24, 1664 and Feb. 15, 1669 and between 1741 and 1826. The original town meeting records for the years since 1826 are located in the Office of the Town Clerk, Fairfield Town Hall. The minutes will hereinafter be cited as FTR, B, II,

in instances where the reference is to vol. B, part II; as FTR, B, I, where the reference is to vol. B, part I; and as FTR where the reference is to the originals in the office of the Town Clerk.

3. *Connecticut Colonial Records*, I, 293, 351.

4. FTR, II, May 21, 1688; Feb. 15, 1670; FTR, B, I, Feb. 15, April 29, 1665.

5. FTR B, II, Feb. 16, 1679, May 7, 1691.

6. Ibid., Feb. 12, 1692.

7. Ibid., Aug. 17, 1686; *Connecticut Colonial Records*, III, 181.

8. *Connecticut Colonial Records*, III, 214; quoted in Ballen, "Fairfield," p. 182.

9. *Connecticut Colonial Records*, III, 190-92; FTR, B, II, Oct. 3, 1684, Aug. 10, 1685, Dec. 22, 1686.

10. *Connecticut Colonial Records*, I, 87; III, 111-12.

11. FTR, B, II, Oct. 14, 22, 1673, Jan. 21, 1690, Apr. 10, 1685, Jan. 21, 1691.

12. Ibid., Dec. 12, 1678; FTR, B, I, Jan. 15, 1665.

13. Schenck, *Fairfield*, I, 22.

14. FTR, B, II, Sept. 10, Oct. 21, 1670.

15. Ibid., Jan. 14, 1671.

16. Ibid., Feb. 22, 1672.

17. Ibid., Nov. 1, 1687.

18. The best source of information about the Wampus case is in the "Trumbull Papers," *Collections of the Massachusetts Historical Society*, 5th Series, IX, 93-138.

19. FTR, B, II, June 12, 14, 1684.

20. Schenck, *Fairfield*, I, 56-57.

21. Ibid., 133.

22. Jodziewicz's "Dual Localism" skillfully untangles the seemingly incomprehensible process of establishing Fairfield's boundaries.

23. Connecticut Archives, 1st Series, Towns and Lands, I, i, 55; *Connecticut Colonial Records*, I, 336.

# To the End
## of the Seventeenth Century

E ARLY FAIRFIELD was a land of farmers. All other economic activities were incidental to agriculture. Fairfield's most important crop was corn, the same crop that had been the staple of the Indians of the area. It was easy to raise, could be planted in hills, thus avoiding the necessity of plowing entire fields, and was simple to harvest. Farmers needed only to pick the ears; hogs and cattle then enthusiastically devoured what was left of the plants, the stalks. The ears of corn could either be roasted and eaten fresh or dried and then turned, by industrious farm wives, into a variety of dishes, Indian pudding being popular, or, most likely, cornmeal. Beans and peas, frequently planted with corn, would most often be cooked in pork or beef pot liquor, a concoction that could be eaten hot or allowed to jell to provide a cold meal.[1]

The other essential crop besides corn for seventeenth-century farmers was apples. Apples did well in Fairfield, and the harvest proved useful in a variety of ways. The apples might end up in pies, might be dried and eaten during the winter, or might, especially if they were inferior, be used to feed hogs. But most of them would be crushed and turned into cider. Finding Fairfield generally unsuited for the cultivation of the ingredients needed for beer, which was, of course, what they had been accustomed to drink in England, Fairfield men and women turned to cider. It was as close a substitute as they could find.

Toward the end of the seventeenth century, Fairfield farmers began to pay more and more attention to the production of grains other than corn. Winter wheat could be grown in town, although it required soil of the highest quality Fairfield could provide. Rye was also possible and when combined with corn made delicious bread. Farmers used oats exclusively as fodder.

Fairfield never had to endure a "starving time," as did Jamestown, Virginia, for example. This disaster was avoided by the town's early interest in animal husbandry. Hogs were an ideal source of meat. They found their own food, surviving on acorns, roots, shellfish, and what farmers threw away. They provided hams, bacon, salt pork, and lard. For at least two centuries, salt pork was the basic meat of Fairfield farmers. Cattle were less independent. Farmers had to provide them with hay, but Ludlow had been attracted to Fairfield in part because of its abundant hay, both salt and fresh. Fairfield's herds produced milk, at least in the summer, butter, cheese, and, of course, meat. Sheep failed to become popular with Fairfield farmers until they had eliminated the problem of predators.

The farms of early Fairfield were hardly examples of up-to-date agricultural efficiency, even by seventeenth-century standards. The problem was not that Fairfield farmers were bad farmers; the problem was that they had too much to do to keep abreast of the latest developments in agriculture. They and their wives lived lives of continuous labor, trying to provide shelter, food, fuel, and clothing. The tools available to them were simple, the hoe, scythe, maddox, ax, spinning wheel. That their crops were initially small and their animals scrawny is less surprising than the fact that they survived at all.

Besides their livestock and their crops, Fairfield farmers had a third crop, wood products from their forests. From the forest they extracted the materials with which they built their houses and outbuildings, fenced their livestock, heated their homes, cooked their food, and created barrels for their salt pork, their cider, their cornmeal, and whatever else they had to package.

If new ways of doing things around the farm seemed to make sense, Fairfielders would try them. To improve the quality of their soil, they dug peat from local swamps and spread it on their fields. They were eager to attempt new crops once they were confident they could provide enough of the basic foods for their families. Many Fairfield families were growing turnips and onions well before the end of the century.

The town always stood ready to assist farmers in whatever ways it could. Besides distributing land and building roads, the town provided other services. In 1664, it paid John Hoitt to drive the town's dry cattle to pasture along the Saugatuck River. A mysterious "poyson weed" was costing Fairfield farmers cattle in 1665; the town ordered its residents to destroy the weed on their lands immediately or face a fine. Because native hay, despite its abundance in Fairfield, was inferior to English hay, the town in 1666 appointed Cornelius Hull to collect money with which to purchase hayseed from England for the common meadows.

The town expended a vast amount of energy trying to keep unruly animals under control, especially voracious hogs and amorous rams. The pound seemed to require constant attention, always "defective," always in need of "repaire." The town imposed fines on those whose animals were impounded, auctioned off any swine that had done damage to the town fields, and gave specific directions for the pound keepers. The owners of "several swine in the Towne of Fairfield [that] are Ravenus and kils the young lams" were in serious trouble with the town fathers in 1680.[2]

Fairfield was convinced that it was easier to prevent damage by contumacious livestock than it was to cure the damage once it had occurred. Both the economic well-being and the harmony of the town depended on good fences and good gates; Fairfield knew this well.[3] The town issued countless orders concerning fences. In February 1664, it decreed that "all possessors of all the home lots in the Towne shall make and mayntayn

*To the End of the Seventeenth Century*

*The Capt. John Osborne House, late seventeenth century farmhouse on King's Highway West, Southport.*

ther deviding fence . . . as also ther share of common fence . . . with a sufficient fence." If the fence viewers found any "defactive," they were to notify the owner, who then had two days to make the necessary repairs. In April 1671, Fairfield instructed John Green to build and maintain a gate "to be well hung with necessary ketches to it" for the common field.

Fairfield residents wanted to keep sheep but were afraid to as long as the area forests were home to so many predators. Bounties were paid on wolves from the earliest times. Once Fairfield did have sheep, the sheepmaster, who had the general responsibility for the welfare of the flock, often paid a bounty to hunters above that paid by the town, the money coming from the sheep treasury, to which all who placed their sheep under the care of the sheepmaster contributed.

Two other predators were regularly a problem, bears and dogs. The town established bounties on bears like those on wolves. Wandering dogs were killed, although no bounty was paid. In 1671, the town ordered that because "the dogs of sum of the Inhabatants of the Towne have worried and killed severall sheep: and sum of the owners of the dogs refuseth to kill their dogs: for the prevention of dammage: the Towne orders that if any dogs of any of the Inhabetants of the Towne have killed or worried sheep . . . the owner having notice thereof shall kill such dogg or dogs." In 1707 the town required "the severall Inhabitants that have dogs . . . [to] Restraine them either by tyeing them up or killing them." Fairfield had little more patience with unruly dogs than it did with wolves or bears.[4]

The list of town services provided for farmers went far beyond bounties on predators and maintenance of the pound. The town also supervised the branding of horses and cattle and the earmarking of hogs. This business was handled by "the keeper of the brand book." The town kept several bulls, at times as many as six or eight, for servicing farmers' cattle, many herds being too small to justify farmers owning a bull in their own right. The sheepmaster performed several services. He hired shepherds to watch the town flock, sold the dung it produced, decided where the sheep were to be pastured, ordered rams that were "preiedeciall to the flocks by ther badness of breed" to be killed or gelded, bought rams that were well suited for breeding, and saw to it that shepherds did not do "the flock great damage by hurrying Inoderably the sheep." On at least one occasion, the sheepmaster went to Boston to buy twenty bells "to hang on the flock of sheep." His work paid off. By 1699 they were so many sheep in Fairfield that a town meeting had to be postponed because "moste of the Inhabitants of the Towne [were] busy aboute sheareing of sheep," and in 1704 Sarah Kemble Knight, a visitor in town, remarked that Fairfielders "have aboundance of sheep, whose very dung brings them great gain, with part of which they pay their parsons sallery, and they grudg that, prefering their dung before their minister."[5]

Fairfield farmers required the services of a variety of tradesmen and artisans, the vast majority of whom were also farmers, at least part of the time. The miller was the most essential of all. Fairfield could never have developed without a gristmill and a sawmill. Thomas Sherwood built the first mill in Fairfield, located on the Sasqua River at what came to be known as Mill Plain. Shortly thereafter John Green built another farther upstream. This concentration of mills led the residents to change the name of the Sasqua River to the Mill River. To service the other end of Fairfield, Henry Jackson in 1649 erected another mill, this one located on Uncoway Creek (now Turney Creek) close to the spot where the creek emptied into Uncoway River, or, as it is currently known, Ash Creek.[6]

Because millers were so important, Fairfield closely regulated their activities, granting them certain privileges, such as authority to dam streams, in return for their acceding to certain price and quality controls. In 1662, Nathan Gold, John Burr, and John Banks formed a committee to bring a miller to Fairfield to replace a man who had recently departed. They had the power to offer a likely prospect ten acres of upland and six acres of meadow. Until a substitute was found, Thomas Sherwood, who was operating a sawmill at this time, agreed to grind all grists brought to him "upon munday and Thursday in every weake" at the stipulated rate, one-sixteenth of the flour or meal he produced. In time Gold, Burr, and Banks found a miller, Richard Ogden of Long Island, and used the inducement of "a new damm & trench to be made for the mill" to convince him to come. He bought the mill and agreed to grind grain at the rate the town had prescribed.[7]

A miller could live a comfortable life. When Richard Ogden died in 1687, he left an estate of almost £425, a considerable sum when one considers that his mill was worth only about £45. But the miller could expect to hear from the town if his services were inadequate. Richard Ogden, Jr. was accused of "faylyer in grinding for the Inhabitanc." The Fairfield town meeting created an ad hoc committee to investigate and to "reform" the younger Ogden if that should be required.[8]

Besides several grist- and sawmills, before the end of the century, Fairfield also had a fulling mill, a mill that cleansed and thickened cloth to make it more dense—

*To the End of the Seventeenth Century*

fuller—and consequently warmer. In the middle 1660s, in fact, the town had actively sought a fuller; whether it found one then is unclear from the town records, but by the 1680s, John Jackson, who already operated a gristmill in Fairfield, had opened a fulling mill. Ten years later, John Edwards opened another, an indication of the growing importance of wool to Fairfield's economy.

Next in importance to the miller among town artisans was the smith, and finding a smith was a chore for Fairfield. In 1672 the town offered an acre of land "by way of encorigment to a smith that is an honest man & able workman" and who would settle in town. Richard Burgiss of Boston came "to take the benefit of what is granted" but died within a few months. The town then negotiated with a series of men, some of whom rejected the town's inducements outright and some of whom came for short periods of time. Not until the next century did Fairfield find a reliable smith who was willing to settle permanently in town.[9]

Tanners were also a problem. The town granted Ezekiel Sanford ten acres on the conditions that he "erect a tan yard upon the said Land . . . to tan such hides for the Town as shall be brought to him," and that he maintain the highway near his tanyard. He may have met these conditions, but only after the town had reminded him that he could lose his land for failing to do so. Other tanners came and went, but not with the regularity with which the smiths moved in and out of town.[10]

Other tradesmen were also slow about settling in town. In 1644 the Connecticut General Assembly ordered that each town should include a tavern or "an Ordinary, for provision & lodgeing, in some comfortable manner, that such passengers and strayngers may know where to resorte." Twenty years passed before Fairfield established an ordinary. But the business must have been profitable, because prominent persons, such as John Banks, sought to be appointed ordinary keepers.[11]

At the end of the seventeenth century, Fairfield had begun to blossom economically, and a whole group of new trades suddenly came to be represented. Peter Twiss arrived in town "to make and burn a kill of Brick" in 1681; twenty years later bricks were still being made in Fairfield. The year 1683 saw Henry Rowland open "a hop yard"; Fairfield men and women could now afford beer. Benjamin Dunen arrived in 1686 to follow his trade as a shoemaker. At the same time, a Mr. Glaswell came to make "carsy and sarges"; he took advantage of Fairfield's bountiful wool crop to make cloth.[12]

The town still took its role as economic regulator seriously. When Glaswell arrived the town agreed to allow no other clothmaker to settle in town provided Glaswell did his work well and charged a fair price. His successor was accused of overcharging customers, and the town was quick to examine his prices, "about which sume declar themselves dissatisfyed." Even as late as the end of the seventeenth century, the town of Fairfield continued in many respects to play the role, as it had in Ludlow's time, of a stern father.[13]

No one can say when Fairfield farmers first began to produce more than they and their neighbors consumed. But as early as 1648, Thomas Newton, a Bankside farmer with a propensity for trouble, owned a ship, the *Virginia*. Within a few years, John Cable, a Pequonnock man, also owned a ship. In addition Henry Gray, one of Newton's Bankside neighbors, was involved in business dealings with Ludlow before the founder's departure for Ireland; these involved activities other than the buying and selling of land, activities that probably included collecting produce and livestock from local farmers and selling these goods, possibly to the new settlements that were appearing on both the Connecticut and the Long Island coasts. As early as 1661, some agricultural goods from Fairfield had made their way to Manhattan. No regular trade between these two settlements existed at that time, however. But blessed with two ports, Fairfield not surprisingly took readily to the sea.

Throughout the seventeenth century, the Wheeler family dominated Black Rock Harbor (or Ship Harbor, as the first members of that family would have known it). Thomas Wheeler came to Fairfield between 1640 and 1644 and settled at the head of the harbor. According to local tradition, he built a stone house with a flat roof upon which he installed two cannon, one directed at Long Island Sound from which Dutch raiders might appear and one aimed inland, the origin of possible Indian attacks. Much of Thomas Wheeler's land became the property of John Wheeler, his grandson. This John Wheeler won the right in 1677 to erect a wharf at Black Rock, a wharf that extended from the high-water mark to the channel and one that was tall enough to be above all ordinary tides. In granting this authority, Fairfield reserved the right for those inhabitants who "have such goods of thers that are proper goods that are exported & Imported. . . [to] give only sixpence p Tun for wharfage." Obviously enough trade existed by 1677 to justify the construction of the wharf. By the end of the century, an occasional ship left Black Rock bound for the West Indies, probably carrying corn, salt beef, and salt pork south and returning with sugar, molasses, and Caribbean rum.[14]

Probably most of Fairfield's maritime activity took place at Black Rock, but ships also used the port at Uncoway River (soon to be called Ash Creek), and especially the port on Mill River. Thomas Hill of Fairfield owned a half-interest in a vessel called *The Two Brothers*. He might have kept her in any one of these locations, as she was a ship of only 32 tons burden. When the ship known as the *Experiment* was in Fairfield, as she often was, she must have been at Black Rock because of her size, 106 tons.

Fairfield was, by the standards of the time, an important maritime center. Governor William Leete in 1680 reported that Connecticut's most important towns were Hartford, New London, New Haven, and Fairfield, "in which towns is managed the principall trade of the colony." He noted that ships as large as three hundred tons could be accommodated in Fairfield (obviously at Black Rock). He also put Connecticut's trade into perspective: "We have neither had leasure or ability to lanch out in any considerable trade at sea, haveing onely a fewe small vessells." Fairfield was important, but important only by the modest standards of Connecticut.[15]

The independence of Fairfield's residents, their willingness to break out of the mold of subsistence agriculture, explains in part the town's economic growth. In other ways, this same independence was a nuisance. The matter of taxes is a case in point. Although the burden that seventeenth-century Fairfield residents bore was light by modern standards, the people did have to pay several different taxes: a minister's rate, a tax to support the pastor; at times a purchase rate, a tax to pay off the debt created by purchasing lands from the Indians; a town rate, the general local tax; and a colony rate, to support the government of Connecticut.

Fairfield people did not accept these rates graciously. At times the town had to order that the tax be collected in a week or ten days or the collection would be turned over to the marshal. At other times the town was forced to order the townsmen to seize the property of delinquent taxpayers. Individuals attempted to hide taxable property.

*To the End of the Seventeenth Century*

In 1664 Cornelius Hull took action against Obediah Gilbert for not putting "his horse flesh into the town list." That taxes were normally paid "in merchantable provisions at current prices" failed to make the taxpayers any more enthusiastic about meeting their obligations.[16]

If the inhabitants were slow about paying the town tax, the town was also slow about collecting the colonial tax. Until 1650 Fairfield, like the other seaside towns, paid a greatly reduced colonial rate. The Code of 1650, established in May of that year, created a more uniform system. Fairfield was in trouble almost immediately. In November, the General Court fined Fairfield for not submitting a proper list of estates, that is, taxable property. The 1655 and the 1660 lists were also improper and brought admonitions from the General Court.

Perhaps Fairfield's attitude toward colonial taxes can best be seen in its reaction to the so-called patent rate. Governor John Winthrop, Jr. had served the colony well when he went to England in 1662 and managed to secure a royal charter for Connecticut. During the course of his efforts, Winthrop had incurred various expenses. Connecticut planned to pay these debts by collecting a special tax, the patent rate, sending the proceeds—in this case corn—to New London, where it would be sold, and then dispatching the necessary funds from New London to England. At the town meeting on April 7, 1663, Fairfield protested against certain features of the tax, in particular the General Court order that required the towns to pay the cost of transporting their corn to New London. If Fairfield men and women thought they could avoid a tax, or an expense associated with a tax, they would try.

Few projects within Fairfield actually required the expenditure of tax funds. Certainly the signpost that assumed a prominent position on the green in 1682 was an expense. The same was true of the bell "Hung in the Turret of the meting house" the following year.[17] But many elected officials were unpaid, donating their time out of a sense of duty. The money spent on roads and bridges was insignificant, town residents being obliged to contribute a certain number of days each year to the construction and maintenance of highways. In many instances, property owners were responsible for the roads that crossed or bordered their lands. Fairfield could afford to neglect its roads because of the abundance of water transportation that was available. Even bridges were often privately built. In August 1666, the town authorized Thomas Oliver to build a bridge across Uncoway River and to finish it at his own cost. He hoped to recover his costs by charging a toll.

One of the biggest expenses the town had to bear was the cost of keeping a prison. Fairfield ordered in February 1676 "that the prisson shall be forthwith repaired fit to answer the end of a prisson: & for the use of a watch house alsoe ther shall be a Stone Chimney built to it." Apparently the repairs needed to make the prison functional proved impossible, because just four years later, the town granted a small piece of land on the green "to build a prisson with a dwelling house thereon alsoe a garden plot & yard plot."[18]

The care of the poor also entailed expense. About a quarter of Fairfield's householders owned very little property. In some cases, these were single men who required only a small income to provide for themselves. In other cases, they were young men who had had little opportunity to accumulate land. But in some instances, these were families that were perpetually poor. Joseph Patchin came to Fairfield about 1645; he was poor all his life. He had three sons, two of whom lived their lives in poverty as well. Thomas Bassett, whose wife had been executed as a witch in Stratford, moved to Fairfield in 1653. He seems to have enjoyed a few prosperous years before falling on bad times and finding himself, by 1668, a charge on the town.[19]

Precisely what the town would provide to a pauper depended upon individual circumstances. In the case of Bassett, the town empowered the constables "to take care of him for his necessary supply: upon the Town charge." Patchin had participated in the land divisions and so owned real estate. When he became unable to care for himself, he asked the town for help selling his property. Jehu Burr and John Wheeler, appointed by the town, helped him improve his land in order to realize as much as possible from it. Patchin used the proceeds to support himself for a time, but in 1682 the town paid Thomas Bennett £13 "provided he mayntayn old patchin with meat drink clothing washing and Lodging for the Term of a Twelve month & render him in clothing at the years end as he is at this present."[20]

The town might help in other ways. In 1692, it gave Widow Wakeman the hay from two acres of common lands. It forgave Widow Gruman's taxes in 1697 and 1698. It made allowances for handicapped persons and for persons suddenly left without support. The town paid Robert Turney for caring for his blind brother. It gave John Bennett £10 for "building a hous and what else may be for ther releef in ther afflicted condesion." Richard Burgiss, who came to Fairfield as a smith in 1676, died eight months later, leaving a widow and a daughter and no estate. The Fairfield Court appointed Thomas Wilson to care for the Burgiss girl "for her education and bringing up." When Robert Risden died in 1666, leaving five children with neither a father nor a mother, the town ordered Nathan Gold and George Squire, both prosperous men, to provide for the children's needs without cost to the town.[21]

As exclusive as Fairfield was about admitting strangers to the town, it would assume responsibility for all its inhabitants, even those who were in town only temporarily. Aaron Fountain, unable to obtain permission to reside in Fairfield permanently, lived from town meeting to town meeting in Compo. Yet the town paid Mary Weir "on the acount of her tending Aran fountains wif at Compo when sick." Reluctant though it was to surrender its taxes, Fairfield seemed to accept the idea of attending the needs of its poor willingly, even graciously.[22]

Fairfield's concern for education was less consistent. It had direct control over education within its jurisdiction, but the General Court established the general perimeters within which the town was to operate. The Code of 1650 required parents or masters to attend to the fundamental education of their charges and required towns of fifty or more families to hire a schoolmaster to teach reading and writing. The law, however, contained no attendance requirements and no stipulation that the towns had to pay, either in part or whole, the salary of the teacher, but left the ultimate responsibility for education squarely on parents or their proxies.

As early as 1661, Fairfield was contributing toward the schoolmaster's salary, the remainder being supplied by the students' families. In February 1663, the town appointed Sergeant Thomas Squire and Robert Turney to canvass the town's population and "make Tryall what scollers are to be payable scollers to the schoolmaster & bring in a list of ther names to the secretary that ther may be a rate made to pay the schoolmaster." Fairfield's commitment to education was reaffirmed three years later, in May 1666, when it voted that town lands should be used to produce income to help pay a schoolmaster "who shall attend the Calling for the educating of Children of the Town." In 1668 Henry Jackson gave his dividend in the new field at Sasco to help support a school.[23]

But this initial enthusiasm for education began to disappear in the 1670s. When Fairfield hired a new teacher, one Mr. Shute, in December 1670, he was "to Take the benefit of his Scollers for his mayntenance." Apparently Shute and the town were unable to decide upon mutually satisfactory terms, because in January 1672 Fairfield agreed that Samuel Robinson was to be the schoolmaster, "he to be payd by the parents or masters of the scollers." At the time, Fairfield had no school building. Instead it rented a room on an annual basis and required the families of the students to pay the rent. In addition, the scholars had to provide the firewood used to heat the school.[24]

Connecticut's General Court in 1672 reenacted those provisions concerned with education from the Code of 1650 and added another stipulation requiring all towns with one hundred or more families to establish a grammar school, a secondary school that would provide training in Latin and Greek as well as additional instruction in reading, writing, and arithmetic. Having more than one hundred families, Fairfield was to be the seat of one of these schools. To ease the burden of creating such a school, the legislature granted six hundred acres apiece to Fairfield, Hartford, New London, and New Haven. Fairfield's grant was meaningless, however, because it took the colony until 1711 to make the land available.

Fairfield's interest in education seemed to be reawakened by the process of creating the grammar school. In 1674 it hired Josiah Harvey to be master of the grammar school and by 1677 was paying him. The contract he signed with the town was typical of those that would be signed by other teachers. He agreed to teach all those students sent to him "in the rules of grammar both Lattin & greeke & to read write & cast acctt. as any parents or guardians of such youth shall desire." The school year was to begin on September 29 at a location that had yet to be determined when the contract was signed. Harvey was, during the three winter months, to hold school for an hour and a half each evening; this was to provide for the older boys, whose families were unable to afford the loss of their labor during the day. The town agreed to pay Harvey £40 a year "to bee paid by a rate to bee levied upon all the Inhabitants of the sd Towne according to their list of estate." Harvey could expect to receive his salary in wheat, peas, pork, and Indian corn. The scholars were responsible for providing firewood.[25]

Fairfield still had no schoolhouse, but in 1678 another "petty," or elementary, school was created. The community at Pequonnock had grown to the point where the creation of a separate school there made sense. Forty-seven children from the area were attending school in Fairfield when their parents were able or saw fit to send them. The walk was a long one, long enough, thought the General Court, to justify their having their own school. The Pequonnock residents would support their school but were released from their obligation to pay the Fairfield school rate.

As late as 1690 Fairfield was still without a school building. Jehu Burr, one of Fairfield's representatives in the General Court, introduced legislation to provide subsidies for the grammar schools in Fairfield and New London like those granted to the schools in Hartford and New Haven. Burr's bill indicated more about Fairfield's desire to participate in the colony's largess than it did about the town's concern for education. Even the colony's commitment to education, in fact, was inevitably weighed against other considerations. In the same year that the General Court rejected the Burr legislation, it allowed the town schools to be kept for only six months a year instead of nine. In both Fairfield and the colony, the value of education had to be carefully balanced with the overwhelming burden of work that faced each family; frequently the immediate demands of chores to be done outweighed the long-range advantages of education.

But Fairfield managed as best it could. By 1695 it finally had a school building, a twenty-three-by-sixteen-foot structure built specifically for the purpose. The town sold sheep manure from its flock to pay the schoolmaster, and it eventually convinced the General Court to include Fairfield among the towns that received a subsidy for their grammar schools. The same body, after 1699 called the General Assembly, also agreed in 1700 to provide aid to both the petty and grammar schools throughout the colony. Neither the town nor the colony was able to eliminate illiteracy in Fairfield by 1700. In fact perhaps as much as one-seventh of the adult, male population of Fairfield was illiterate, but given the time and the circumstances, this figure was hardly shocking, on a par with the rest of New England and comparing favorably with the literacy rate in England.

The extent to which Fairfield did value education probably resulted more from the population's religious beliefs than from their economic circumstances. A land of subsistence farmers could tolerate an illiterate element among its population; a community of Puritans was less willing to suffer the unschooled within their midst. And the level of respect that Fairfield showed for its church indicates that it was indeed a community of Puritans.

As mentioned earlier, the Reverend John Jones found his early years in Fairfield difficult ones. His congregation was composed of the first generation of Fairfield settlers, a group that tended to be restless, mobile, and probably less concerned with religion than successive generations. By the time of Ludlow's departure, the uncertainty that had characterized Fairfield's earliest years had disappeared. Growing stability made Jones's work easier. By the time of his death in 1664, he and his congregation were gathering in a new meetinghouse, one that certainly must have been a great pride to the town not merely because it meant the congregation could move out of the town house but also because the new structure was an impressive one; perhaps not all that the town might have hoped for, but still impressive.

Jones's successor was the Reverend Samuel Wakeman, ordained in 1665. The most disruptive issue he had to face was the question of the Half-Way Covenant. To become a church member in colonial Connecticut was no easy task. Accepting the idea of original sin, the Puritans believed that most of humanity was condemned to an eternity in Hell: God chose only a few for salvation. As much as possible, the settlers intended to include as church members only the chosen ones, "the visible saints" who gave evidence of having been saved. Those who were unable to describe a profound conversion experience had to support and attend the church but could never aspire to the benefits of membership: the right to receive communion, to have their children baptized, to participate in church business, and to own the covenant—that is, declare their acceptance of Christ, their intention to live Christian lives, and their willingness to attend public worship and to heed the discipline of the church.

By 1660 church membership throughout the colony had declined to the point where it was causing problems in many communities. Massachusetts Bay had faced a similar dilemma and had found its answer in the Half-Way Covenant, adopted there in 1662. By the terms of the Half-Way Covenant, a person who did not profess conversion could still own the covenant, be enrolled in the church register, take part in church business, and present children for baptism. The creation of this form of partial membership caused immediate controversy. Some Connecticut citizens liked the concept; others wanted to continue with the old, exclusive system; still others advocated any number of variations on both the old plan and the new one.

On May 16, 1668, the General Court asked the Reverend James Fitch of Norwich, the Reverend Gershom Bulkley of Wethersfield, the Reverend Joseph Eliot of Guilford, and the Reverend Wakeman to meet at Saybrook or Norwich to "consider of some expedient for our peace . . . in matters of discipline respecting membership and baptism." For Wakeman, a young man just out of Harvard, to have been selected for such an important committee was a great honor. He and his colleagues endorsed the Half-Way Covenant and paved the way for its acceptance in Connecticut. That Wakeman avoided as much dissension as he did in Fairfield also attests to his talents. His willingness to allow doctrinal variation within his congregation certainly contributed to his maintaining "a loving harmony" within his church.[26]

When Wakeman died on March 8, 1692, after twenty-seven years of serving the Fairfield Ecclesiastical Society, the congregation was careful in its selection of a successor. It interviewed several men and brought three to town to preach on a trial basis. One of the three was Joseph Webb, a graduate of Harvard, class of 1688. On August 9, 1692, the town decided that Webb was the man for the position. He and his family moved to Fairfield permanently on October 13, 1692, the beginning of forty years with the church. Within a year Webb had convinced the town of the necessity of building a new meetinghouse, and by 1698 the new building was finished, ready for use.

The fact that both Sherwood and Webb were Harvard graduates indicates the dominant role Harvard played as the only college Connecticut's young men could attend during the seventeenth century. In 1701 the General Assembly created a Collegiate School, appointing ten ministers as undertakers or trustees; among the ten was Joseph Webb. For thirty years he would continue to serve that institution, which after 1718 came to be called Yale College, with the same enthusiasm he provided to his congregation in Fairfield. In both circumstances, he perceived his mission to be the preservation of orthodoxy, a mission he undertook with a zeal born of real commitment.

Whatever Fairfield was able to accomplish, whether in terms of caring for its poor or educating its people or establishing its church on firm ground, it accomplished in a world that was frequently unfriendly, a world where hostility often lurked nearby. Town defense was the subject of regular concern. In July 8, 1667, the townsmen ordered that the town should have "Thirty half Pikes and twenty large pikes to pertain to the town magazien to be disposed of as shall be thought necessary by the Military Officers of the Town." Procuring these pikes was a great expense, but one that Fairfield thought essential. The panic that occurred in 1667, like the one that would follow in 1673, came as a result of rumors of war between England and Holland. But even when the town faced no particular crisis, defenses had to be maintained, pikes had to be available for the "tryned band" and powder and lead available in the "magazeen."[27]

The year 1675 brought more anxiety to Fairfield than any since 1653, when the two Dutch men-of-war had positioned themselves off the coast. In June 1675, Philip, the son of Massasoit and the chief of the Wampanoags, together with his various allies, began a desperate attempt to recover from the English the planting grounds that had supported their ancestors for generations. Philip and his followers had decided to end the abuse they had been suffering from their unscrupulous neighbors. The result was King Philip's War. On October 18 the town voted "that the metinghouse shall be fortifyied by the publicke." This was an initial measure. On November 30, fortifications were expanded to include "a considerable part of the Towne," to be "erected by all the Inhabetants of the Towne with all ther Teems all male persons from Ten years old to seventee the maior [Nathan Gold] and the minister [Samuel Wakeman] excepted." Families that were unable to use their homes and lands because they were outside the fortified area were to "have free liberty of the use of the houses & lands contayned within the said fortification," and those that suffered losses from attack could anticipate reparation from the town.[28]

Fortunately King Philip never brought his warriors as far south as Fairfield. But Fairfield men took part in the war in various ways. Nathan Gold oversaw the gathering of foodstuffs in Fairfield and the shipping of this produce from Black Rock to Massachusetts. William Ward and Josiah Harvey, both surgeons, attended wounded Connecticut soldiers. Nathaniel Seely commanded many of these troops. Both Seely and Ward lost their lives during the campaign. Even the Reverend Wakeman participated in the war. He met in New Haven with a group of clergymen who attempted to discover "those evils amongst us, which have stirred up the Lord's anger against us," the colony typically insisting that the disaster of war must be an indication of God's displeasure and denying any legitimacy in the Indians' grievances.[29]

King Philip's challenge to New England passed just as that of Edward Randolph and Sir Edmund Andros was beginning. Randolph first demanded that Massachusetts answer charges brought against the colony in England. Then, in 1679, he endorsed New Hampshire's becoming a royal colony. By 1681 Randolph and Andros were urging royal officials to begin proceedings to revoke the charter of Massachusetts. Fearing the worst, the Fairfield town meeting in April 1681 voted to build "a stone wall Twenty or twenty four or five rods square four foot Thicke at the bottom and Twelfe foot high on the meting house green for a fort with sufficient fflankers and gates for that end." The town abandoned the plan after eleven prominent men protested against this use of the meetinghouse green, but the fact that it was ever endorsed demonstrates the level of fear that Randolph and Andros created, a level that lasted until Andros was at last overthrown.[30]

In April 1690, Connecticut acknowledged that a state of war existed between England and France. Fairfield went on the alert, building new fortifications in the center of town and, for the first time, at Grover's Hill, from which Black Rock could be protected; and Fairfield men, including Captain John Burr, Captain Matthew Sherwood, and Ensign Nathan Gold, Jr., marched off to defend Connecticut by stopping the French and their Indian allies at Albany, New York.

If King Philip's War had convinced Connecticut of God's displeasure, the combined impact of that war, the threats created by Randolph and Andros, a measles and smallpox epidemic in 1679, and finally the war between England and France was enough to create a sense of extreme anxiety throughout the colony. Connecticut men and women were convinced that they had wandered far from the path that God had set for them,

*To the End of the Seventeenth Century*

and they yearned to understand where they had gone wrong, how they had sinned. During this period of profound soul-searching, they looked at themselves to see how they had transgressed as individuals, but they also examined their community to see how it might have gone amiss.

What Fairfield residents concluded from all this introspection was that they needed to reaffirm their own sense of community. Many of the ideals that they had brought to Fairfield in the beginning, ideals such as neighborliness and corporateness, had been under attack. The abundance of land in Fairfield had stirred acquisitive feelings at the expense of the tradition of commonwealth. The incentive to grow and to change that being in this new place fostered produced individual, not community, values. To many Fairfield citizens, the time had come to correct an imbalance that had developed in their town, to reassert the ideal of community and to tame individualistic instincts.

Fairfield's householders tried to reassert their own commitment to the town's original way by showing how others had strayed from it, had become deviants. The process, one that was much like that which was occurring in Salem, Massachusetts, at the same time, began when people in Fairfield first took seriously the rantings of Catherine Branch, a servant girl employed in the home of Daniel Westcott. Branch, who was subject to fits and to wild hallucinations, accused Elizabeth Clawson and Mercy Desborough of having bewitched her. Significantly, both Clawson and Desborough had quarreled with Westcott in years past.

On May 27, 1692 Westcott made a formal complaint against the women. The court ordered a committee of females to search the accused for witchmarks. The searches were inconclusive, but the two women found themselves imprisoned to await trial. On June 2, a special court heard the case during which the alleged witches underwent the water test. Because both floated despite efforts to submerge them, the trial proceeded. A variety of witnesses testified about the malefic workings of Mercy, about her ability to cause cattle to die and children to fall ill.

By the middle of June, Catherine Branch was expanding her list of Fairfield witches. She named one Goody Miller, who fled to New York to avoid prosecution, as well as Mary Staples, who had already been accused by Goody Knapp in 1653, and Mary's daughter, Mary Harvey, and granddaughter, Hannah Harvey.

When the General Court in Hartford learned of these events, on June 22 it authorized the convening of a Court of Oyer and Terminer in Fairfield. The governor himself, Robert Treat, as well as the deputy governor and seven assistants, sat on the court, which met in September 1692. The charges against Mary Staples and her relatives were quickly dropped; the social position of Mary and her daughter, who was the stepdaughter-in-law of Nathan Gold, totally contradicted the popular understanding of a malefic witch. Clawson and Desborough, both of whom fit the folk image of a witch, went on trial, a trial that had to be delayed because of the jury's inability to reach a decision but which resumed again on October 28. The case against the women ultimately came down to the question of witch marks. Another examination was conducted, the committee of searchers reporting about Elizabeth Clawson that they "found on her secret parts, just within the lips of the same, growing . . . something an inch and a half long in the shape of a dog's ear which we apprehend to be unusual to women." As for Mercy Desborough, the committee discovered "on her secret parts growing within the lip of same a lose piece of skin and when pulled it is near an inch long. Somewhat in the form of the finger of a glove flatted. That lose skin we judge more than common to women."[31]

The jury declared Clawson innocent, and she went free. It found Mercy Desborough guilty of familiarity with Satan. Although the court expressed dissatisfaction with the jury's decision, the governor ultimately decided to accept it and sentenced her to die. Fortunately the court later reconsidered the matter and granted Desborough a full pardon.

Thus the witchcraft delusion of 1692 came to an end. That it happened when it did and in the way that it did was certainly no accident. After fifteen years of crisis and turmoil, Fairfield was left wondering if it, as a community, had wandered too far from its original goals. By identifying Elizabeth Clawson and Mercy Desborough as witches, the ultimate outsiders, the town hoped to define its own oneness, its corporateness; and in the wake of this cathartic experience, it in fact did briefly uncover a new sense of mission.

By the end of the seventeenth century, Fairfield, although still a small agricultural plantation, was no longer a frontier outpost. Its population had grown from eight or so households in 1639 to more than 150 by 1700. Longevity failed to account for the population growth; even if a boy lived to reach adulthood, he would probably die before his sixty-third birthday. Neither were large families responsible for the increase in numbers; a typical family had five children who would reach maturity, despite a much larger number of pregnancies. The increase came because the sons and daughters of Fairfield settlers made the decision to stay in town. Nearly 80 percent of them remained.

These young people stayed because it was to their economic and political advantage to do so. A typical young man would marry at about twenty-five years of age, his bride being a little younger and almost certainly a native of town. Finding a place to live constituted no great problem; a single room would do, makeshift, to be sure, but easily constructed. The bride's dowry would include household goods while the husband would bring his tools, some livestock, and a small amount of land, perhaps as little as forty or fifty acres, of which half would be improved. The couple could more than survive, saving £1 or £2 a year to be invested in land. Barring disaster, the couple could count on enjoying a comfortable, albeit modest, existence by their middle years, an existence probably based on agriculture, although almost a third of the householders were artisans either full or part time. At the same time that he left his parent's home, a young man would begin a political apprenticeship that might eventually lead to his holding a responsible position in the town.

Not all Fairfield families were so fortunate, but the availability of land almost precluded a class of permanently poor people. Most of the town's propertyless laborers were young, single men still living with their parents or married men just getting a start in life. Most of these would eventually own their own farms.

An important exception to all this would be the black slaves who lived in Fairfield. The town's slave population, while not large, was as substantial as that of any Connecticut town, perhaps accounting for about 4 percent of the total population. These were persons without hope for the future, persons relegated to a permanent inferiority, living anonymous lives of service.

But almost 90 percent of Fairfield's seventeenth-century population lived above the subsistence level, and perhaps 50 percent enjoyed some comforts. Fairfield's wealthy

*To the End of the Seventeenth Century*

population, those men — and there were never many of them — like Ludlow and Thomas Pell had deserted New England for a brighter future elsewhere. But for the others, dwellings were adequate, often small and crowded, but still adequate. Food was abundant in quantity if not variety, and herds were becoming larger and healthier.

Beyond the material comforts, the inhabitants could take satisfaction in knowing that they were carrying on the plans of the town's founders. With all the change that had come, Fairfield remained a Puritan village, its people still under the care and watch of the church, its society still a hierarchy where everyone knew his place, and its sense of community harmonious.

## NOTES

1. Russell, *A Long, Deep Furrow*, and Daniels, "Economic Development," carefully describe the agriculture of this period.

2. FTR, B, II, April 12, 1680.

3. Ibid., Feb. 23, 1664, April 18, 1671.

4. Ibid., Feb. 15, 1671, Dec. 26, 1707.

5. Ibid., April 1, 1672, Aug. 8, 1679, April 24, 1693, May 31, 1699; Sarah Kemble Knight, *The Journal of Madam Knight* (Boston, 1972), 34.

6. Daniels, "Economic Development," is useful in understanding all aspects of Connecticut's colonial economy.

7. FTR, B, II, March 25, June 19, Oct. 21, 1662.

8. Ibid., Jan. 2, 1692.

9. Ibid., Jan. 28, 1672, April 1, 1673, Feb. 12, 1677.

10. FTR, B, I, Oct. 3, 1665.

11. Schenck, *Fairfield*, I, 41; FTR, B, I, Feb. 28, 1665.

12. FTR, B, II, July 18, 1681, Dec. 7, 1683, Nov. 15, 1686.

13. Ibid., May 7, 1691.

14. Ibid., Feb. 16, 1677.

15. *Connecticut Colonial Records*, III, 297, 308.

16. FTR, B, II, April 9, 1664, Jan. 28, 1672.

17. Ibid., March 18, 1683.

18. Ibid., Feb. 21, 1676, Feb. 16, 1680.

19. A careful reading of Jackson T. Main, *Society and Economy in Colonial Connecticut* (Princeton, N.J., 1985), is essential to understanding colonial society in general and the place of the poor within that society in particular.

20. FTR, B, II, Nov. 13, 1669, April 27, 1681, Nov. 30, 1682.

21. Ibid., Sept. 29, 1685; *Connecticut Colonial Records*, III, 154-55, 221.

22. FTR, B, II, Feb. 15, 1688.

23. Ibid., Feb. 10, 1663; FTR, B, I, May 24, 1666.

24. FTR, B, II, Dec. 17, 1670, Jan. 31, 1672.

25. Ibid., Sept. 11, 1677.

26. Child, *An Old New England Church*, 41-42.

27. FTR, B, I, July 8, 1667; FTR, B, II, Dec. 15, 1673, Feb. 24, 1675.

28. FTR, B, II, Oct. 18, Nov. 30, 1675.

29. Schenck, *Fairfield*, I, 185.

30. FTR, B, II, April 4, 1681.

31. Quoted in Tomlinson, *Witchcraft Trials*, 60.

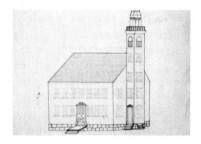

# Undermining
# the Puritan Village

DURING the first six or seven decades of the eighteenth century, Fairfield underwent a gradual metamorphasis from a Puritan village to a Yankee town. More easily noticed by history than by those living at the time, the transition started when Fairfield men and women began shifting part of what they had invested in the community and its interests to their own personal concerns. Puritans regarded the pursuit of self-interest at the expense of the commonweal as a violation of both the tradition of neighborliness and God's law; but by the end of the eighteenth century, Fairfielders, in part forsaking the concept of a corporate community, had learned to tolerate self-interest to a degree that would have horrified their forefathers. Many of the forces creating this change had been at work during the seventeenth century. When townspeople detected trends in this direction during the early 1690s, just before the trials of Goody Clawson and Goody Desborough, they sought to reassert the importance of the community, hoping in this way to solve the problem. For a time the treatment seemed to be working, but during the eighteenth century, other influences came into play that made change inevitable.[1]

Few of these forces were more powerful than the growing tendency of Fairfielders to leave the central village. This process had begun when part of Fairfield's population moved to Pequonnock, to take advantage of its harbor and salt marshes, and when others withdrew to Bankside, which offered abundant grazing lands and the isolation increasingly desired by a uniquely independent group of families. Others left the village because of disputes. Richard Hubbell, one of Fairfield's deputies to the General Assembly, departed the central village for Pequonnock because of a dispute with John Burr, who presided over a trial in which Hubbell's wife was convicted of selling strong drink without a license. After the conviction, Hubbell, in a rage, accused Burr's wife of the same crime, but the magistrate had the last word, ordering the irate husband out of court. Unable

53

to tolerate the idea of living near Burr, Hubbell took his family to Pequonnock.

Most of the families that left the village (they are called *outlivers*) moved in order to consolidate their lands. When the town granted lands it was absolutely unconcerned about the location of a person's grant relative to his existing holdings. A farmer might find that he owned a few acres in Sasqua, several more near Pequonnock, a great many north of the Half Mile of Common, and some at Compo, all in addition to his home lot in the central village. For the sake of efficiency, he naturally hoped to consolidate these separate parcels. Prosperous farmers were able to create contiguous tracts close to the village. Those who were less affluent were more likely to concentrate their lands in outlying areas where land values were lower.

Once a man's lands were unified, he might continue to reside in the central village, that being understood to be the appropriate place for him and his family to live, close to the meetinghouse, the town house, friends and relatives, and the schoolhouse. The farmer's commute, on foot, to his fields might add hours to the enormous load of work he was already carrying. But he would tolerate it, at least for a time. Eventually he and his sons might spend part of each week during the summer living on the land they worked. Having had his fill of masculine company, he could decide, after a summer or two, that he wanted his wife and daughters to join him for part of the season. To accommodate them, he would build a slightly more elaborate shelter than that which had served him and the boys. The expense of maintaining two homes, one of them perhaps as primitive as any that would have been found in early Fairfield, would finally convince him to move his family to the remote location of his lands permanently. The decision to become an outliver was anything but easy. It meant giving up all the conveniences of village living, friends and schools and the watch and ward of the church. It also meant long walks to church and to town meetings. But economically the move made sense.

This process was repeated again and again. Soon small settlements appeared in various parts of town. They reflected the growth of Fairfield, and they also reflected changing values. The town had originally been organized around the central village because such a pattern of settlement was ideally suited to existing notions of neighborliness and the necessity of maintaining the population under the watch and ward of the church. By moving away from the village, the outlivers were stating that they valued their land, their independence, and their hopes for worldly success more than they did community life. This was, although not understood as such at the time, a revolutionary statement.

Once several families had gathered in one of these outlying settlements, they would begin to consider establishing some public conveniences for themselves. Pequonnock, which straddled the Fairfield-Stratford line, began to think in these terms at an early date. It had come into existence perhaps as early as 1640 and grown slowly, and by 1678 was ready to petition the Connecticut General Court for the freedom to establish a school of its own and to be "freed from paying to the town in reference to *their* school." Being four miles from the center of Fairfield and having already hired a teacher, Matthew Bellamy, the Pequonnock residents believed their request was reasonable. So too did the Reverend Wakeman; he endorsed the petition "as an unfeighned wellwiller to the (as I thinke) honest scope of your said petitioners." The General Court readily granted authority for the school but wanted to avoid antagonizing Fairfield over the question of tax monies. It therefore created a convoluted scheme whereby Pequonnock continued to pay the school rate to Fairfield while at the same time the Fairfield County Court donated an equal sum to Pequonnock for its school. On January 25, 1679, Fairfield accepted the plan.[2]

Pequonnock residents waited eleven years before submitting their next request for a major privilege. In May 1690, forty-six petitioners, thirty-three from Fairfield and thirteen from Stratford, requested the General Court to allow them to maintain their own minister and to free them from the Fairfield minister's rate. The court refused to make a decision on so important a matter and recommended "to the towne of Fayrfield and the people of Paquanaug to meet and loveingly discourse to agree about this matter." Fairfield rejected the idea outright thereby creating the colony's first contested attempt to create a new congregation. The ensuing struggle became a prototype.[3]

At its next session, October 1690, the General Court appointed a committee— Governor Robert Treat of Milford, Magistrate William Jones and the Reverend James Pierpont of New Haven, and the Reverend Samuel Andrew of Milford—to work on the dispute. The committee met with delegates from Fairfield and Pequonnock on April 14, 1691. Both sides presented their cases. Believing that this petition was a precursor to a request from Pequonnock to be established as a separate town, Nathan Gold, the principal Fairfield spokesman, was adamant in his opposition. He argued that the General Court lacked the power to forfeit the town's patent. The court could not, he contended, "interpose or meddle in anny of the prudentiall concerns of our Towne, with out apparent violating & brekeing our just and legal libertyes in an arbitrary manner." As tenacious as Ludlow had ever been, Gold continued by explaining that the people of Fairfield "expose our humillaty in that we condescende to intreate for what you cannot take from us." To make his position as clear as possible, Gold provided the General Court with a list of twenty-four questions relating to the subject. Question #6 summarized Gold's position: "Whither itt be according to rule or Equity, that this one of your first borne a lovely butyfule child should be disinherrited & lose itts berthright to an inferiour bratt."[4]

Undeterred by Gold's vehemence, Pequonnock pushed its request before the next General Court in May 1691. The court finally granted Pequonnock's petition, giving the settlers there permission to establish their own minister provided they continued to pay the ecclesiastical rate to Fairfield until either Fairfield or the General Court freed them from this tax. In October, after Fairfield had declared itself totally opposed to the idea of releasing Pequonnock from this obligation, the General Court did so on the condition that the area inhabitants "maintain an orthardox memestar in poquonet."[5]

The man Pequonnock selected as its minister was the same man who had instigated the Pequonnock petition, Charles Chauncey. Born in Stratford in 1668 and graduated from Harvard in 1686, Chauncey had come to Pequonnock about 1687 to work as a teacher, but then decided the ministry was his true calling. Six months after he became Pequonnock's first pastor, he married Sarah Burr, the daughter of John Burr and the granddaughter of Jehu Burr. Both men had vigorously denounced Pequonnock's request for parish privileges, but neither seem to have opposed the marriage.

Chauncey was a minister without a church, because the General Court had authorized him to preach but had yet to establish an ecclesiastical society in Pequonnock. Made up of a parish, which was concerned with temporal matters such as the minister's salary and the maintenance of the meetinghouse, and a church, which addressed matters of doctrine and the church covenant and membership, the ecclesiastical society was the essential religious institution of colonial Connecticut. Finally, in May 1694, the General Court created the Fairfield Village Ecclesiastical Society, which would serve Pequonnock. Seven years later, the court renamed the body the Stratfield Ecclestiastical Society, a more appropriate name because the parish included both Fairfield and Stratford territory.

Stratfield, as Pequonnock came to be known, grew more autonomous. It developed its own trainband, John Beardsley serving as lieutenant and Isaac Wheeler as ensign. It enjoyed other aspects of independence. It had its own constable, its own collector of the ecclesiastical rate, its own officers who could summon meetings to consider the minister's salary and "what concerns may be needfull about their meeting house," and its own recorder or parish clerk.

The creation of the Stratfield Society was one step in a process that would eventually confuse the loyalties of Fairfield persons. Did Stratfield residents owe their primary loyalty to their society, Stratfield, or to their town, Fairfield? Concerned about its own society, its own trainband, its own school, Stratfield had less and less time and inclination to worry about Fairfield. Although Nathan Gold had been mistaken in believing that Stratfield wanted complete independence from Fairfield, the creation of the new society began the breakdown of the old homogeniety associated with the central village. The effects of outliving were beginning to tell.

Stratfield was only the first of many separate societies that sprouted up in Fairfield. The Bankside or Maxumux farmers had departed the central village shortly after people first settled in Pequonnock, and the Bankside section of Fairfield developed much as Pequonnock had. In 1703 Bankside farmers received authority to establish their own school, hired a schoolmaster, and built a schoolhouse on their green. Five years later, in January 1708, they petitioned the General Assembly seeking a separate ecclesiastical society and relief from the Fairfield minister's rate. Predictably, Fairfield opposed this, realizing that the loss of the Bankside revenues would place a larger burden on those who remained within the original society. The General Assembly referred the request to "the reverent elders in the county of Fairfield" but, because of Fairfield's opposition, took no additional action on the petition.[6]

When Bankside renewed its petition in October 1710, the legislature decided that the request should be granted if Fairfield would give its consent. Fairfield was again ready to stand opposed, but enough individual householders endorsed the Bankside request to convince the assembly of its worthiness. In May 1711 the General Assembly established another society within Fairfield and released Bankside families from the Fairfield minister's rate. It designated the new society the West Parish and included within it Compo, Bankside, and the area west of Sasco Creek. Two hundred and seventy persons lived within the new parish, now the third in town.

The families of the West Parish were so confident of the ultimate success of their petition that they had already erected a meetinghouse and hired a minister, Daniel Chapman. A graduate of Yale's class of 1707, Chapman was formally ordained in October 1715. The long delay between the establishment of the society and the ordination of its first minister was entirely in keeping with the society's lackadaisical approach to matters generally; it took the parish several years to build a house it had promised the minister when he accepted his post and until 1720 to complete the meetinghouse that was standing

*Fairfield: the biography of a community*

in 1711. Chapman remained the minister at the West Parish until 1741, when the society had to dismiss him for having been on several occasions "overtaken with too much drink." Daniel Buckingham, who had in common with Chapman his Yale background but not, fortunately, his propensity for strong drink, took over the post in 1742.[7]

As in Pequonnock, the creation of the separate society led to the development of other automomous institutions within the parish. By 1717, in addition to its own train-band and parish officials and constable, the West Parish selected its own sheepmaster, who oversaw a sheep treasury distinct from that of Fairfield itself, and appointed a separate tavern keeper, Abigail Couch.

The name "West Parish," while not inappropriate, was hardly one with which the local population could identify. They had known part of the area as Maxumux or Bankside and the remainder as Compo. About 1730 they began referring to the West Parish as Green's Farms, a name derived from the holdings of John Green, one of the original (1648) Bankside farmers and one of the largest landowners in that part of Fairfield. The West Parish of Fairfield remained the legal name of the society until the American Revolution, when it officially became Green's Farms.

On December 11, 1724, the Fairfield town meeting heard from "Sundry of the livers in the North West part of the Town distinct moving to this meeting that they might have liberty to hire some meet person to preach the gospel among them . . . for the Winter months ahead and that at their own Cost & Charge." The memorialists specifically stated that they were not seeking "to be abated any thing of their part of the Revd. Mr. Webb's rate." The meeting failed to find any fault with this request and granted the northwest section a winter ministry, as it was called.[8]

The following May, the same persons asked the General Assembly to organize them into a new parish. Thomas Hill and sixty-nine other men made the request on behalf of fifty-five families, all of them living two and a half to six miles from the Fairfield meetinghouse, which "utterly incapacitates many persons, old & young, to go to the house of God" and all of them combined owning £4000 worth of taxable property, certainly a sufficient base for a separate society. The fifty-five families came meekly before the legislature: "Hoping and humbly begging and praying that the honorable gentlemen of the Assembly will pity us, and be nursing fathers to us, and deal with us as they would be dealt with."[9]

The Fairfield Society was again reluctant to see so substantial a segment of its tax base lost, but Hill convinced the assembly to examine his and his neighbors' circumstances. On October 14, 1725, after the committee reported on its tour of inspection, the legislature decided to establish a new society, calling it the Northwest Parish of Fairfield, a name the legislature would change two years later to the Greenfield Parish or Society.

The first minister at Greenfield was only nineteen years old when he assumed his duties. Born in 1706 in Stratford, John Goodsell had been a member of the Yale class of 1724. His first sermon was delivered in a crude, diminutive building that had been built as a school. It remained the meetinghouse until 1730, when a new one, still unfinished, replaced it. The society, which was preoccupied paying Goodsell's £100 a year salary, finally accumulated enough money to complete its interior in 1743.

The origin of what would become Fairfield's fifth parish was unique. Located along Fairfield's northern boundary was a stretch of unoccupied land, surrounded by Fairfield, Danbury, Newtown, and Ridgefield, but itself part of no town. Called the "oblong" or the "Peculiar," this parcel was claimed by several Indians, members either of the Potatucks of Newtown or the Paugusetts of Stratford. The General Court had made grants of land within the Peculiar in 1687 and 1700 and 1706, but in 1712 decided that the remainder should be sold at public auction. Various factors delayed the sale until August 1722, when two Fairfield men, Samuel Couch and Nathan Gold, Jr., bought the ungranted lands on speculation. By May 1723, enough people lived in the area to justify their asking the General Assembly for permission to establish their own ecclesiastical society. Rejected again and again, they petitioned once more in May 1729, requesting on that occasion also that enough land be transferred from Fairfield to make the proposed parish more or less square.

Initially Fairfield denounced the idea; but eventually the town came to see some advantages in the plan, especially if the proposed parish were made part of Fairfield. On December 31, 1729, Fairfield granted two miles of land located at the rear of the Long Lots to the parish if the General Assembly would agree to its formation. The legislature decided that establishing the new parish was justified "and that said parish may be annexed to Fairfield, and that it be named Redding." Redding's development, in terms of schools and trainband, paralleled that of Stratfield, Green's Farm, and Greenfield.[10]

Once five societies existed in town, the question of the parsonage lands became an issue. These were lands that the town had granted to the original society — often now called the Prime or Ancient Society — when it was the only one in town. By the time Redding came into existence, the Prime Society owned a considerable amount of real estate, the income from which went to the pastor of that congregation. As the General Assembly created additional societies, it refused to entertain the idea that the parsonage lands should be divided. Greenfield residents in particular believed that allowing these lands to remain in the hands of one society, even if it were the original one, was unfair to the others. On March 15, 1733, after lengthy and frequently heated negotiations, the Prime Society, Stratfield, Green's Farms, Greenfield, and Redding agreed that the parsonage lands should be sold, one-half of the revenue derived to go to the Prime Society and the other half to be divided among the four newer societies. Each society would then lend the money "to best advantage and the interest therof to be improved for the maintenance and support of the present ministers" and the schools.[11]

The process of hiving off new parishes from old ones continued. In October 1756, the inhabitants of the northern part of Green's Farms and the northwestern part of Greenfield petitioned the General Assembly for their own ecclesiastical society, claiming that they lived at a great distance from the meetinghouses at Green's Farms and at Greenfield and asserting their ability to support their own minister. In May 1757, the General Assembly granted their request and created the Norfield Society. Four years later, inhabitants of northern Stratfield, northern Greenfield, and western North Stratford also requested parish privileges, which the General Assembly granted in 1762, creating the North Fairfield Society. Thus by the autum of 1762, Fairfield, which had originally been conceived as a community built around a single church, contained seven ecclesiastical societies, each of which claimed at least a share of the loyalty that had once belonged exclusively to the single community and church.

The town was undergoing other changes, changes that the founders of Fairfield would have regarded even more frightening than the appearance of additional societies.

*Fairfield: the biography of a community*

Whereas English Puritans had generally remained within the Church of England, those who came to New England had followed a different road, in the process becoming what later generations would know as Congregationalists. All seven of the societies that existed by 1761 were Congregational societies, and Congregationalism had been the New England way since the mid-seventeenth century. The idea that there was room in New England for other denominations was one that the early eighteenth century regarded as subversive, a concept that would inevitably destroy the basis of community as different religious groups struggled with one another for domination.

But shortly after the beginning of the eighteenth century, another religious force began to appear in New England, including Fairfield. On April 4, 1707, the Reverend James Muirson of the Church of England reported to his superiors at the Society for the Propagation of the Gospel in Foreign Parts that he "was lately invited to preach & baptize some children in a town called Fairfield." He asked town officials for permission to use the meetinghouse, but they refused. Muirson then assembled his followers in a private home, "but so cruelly was the Independent party [Congregationalists] set against us, that they railed & scoffed at the Church, making her as idolatrous as Rome, & denied us the liberty of ringing the bell, or beating a drum to give the people notice." Still Muirson "found a considerable number of people in a ready disposition to be received into the Church."[12]

Muirson's untimely death in 1708 hindered the cause of Anglicanism in southwestern Connecticut. Years passed before his replacement appeared. During part of this interim, James Laborie, a physician who was inclined to the Church of England, labored to keep Anglicanism alive in Fairfield. When the Society for the Propagation of the Gospel in Foreign Parts dispatched George Pigot to Stratford in 1722 with instructions to conduct services in both Stratford and Fairfield, Laborie and the other Anglicans were delighted.

But even with Pigot on the scene, Anglicans continued to encounter abundant hostility. Laborie wrote the SPGFP in March 1723 describing "the persecutions & threatening we are exposed to having in this town of Fairfield, the Lieut. Governor [Nathan Gold, Jr.] against us, & the pretended minister of the Independency [Joseph Webb] continually declaiming against the Church, terming her services Popery, the way to hell, & themselves Bishops as regular as the Bishop of London, with many other extravagant expressions." Gold, who was as adamant against Anglicanism as his father had been against the creation of the Stratfield Society, went so far as to introduce legislation in the General Assembly that would have prevented Pigot from exercising "his ministerial function" outside the town of Stratford, but Laborie prevented the bill from becoming law by threatening to take his case to England.[13]

Reverend Webb, like Nathan Gold, found the Anglican onslaught alarming. He wrote to Cotton Mather to report about "the revolt of several persons of figure among us unto the Church of England." He continued: "I apprehend the axe is hereby laid to the root of our civil and sacred enjoyments, and a doleful gap opened for trouble and confusion in our churches. It is a very dark day with us." Town leaders felt justified in doing all they could to keep the evil influence of Anglicanism out of Fairfield.[14]

Samuel Johnson, replacing Pigot in 1723, found "no abatement of persecution." Fairfield officials insisted that all inhabitants, regardless of religious connections, either pay taxes to support one of the town's Congregational societies or go to prison. In

February 1727, the Reverend Johnson reported to the SPGFP that he had "just come from Fairfield, where I have been to visit a considerable number of my people, in prison for their rates to the dissenting [Congregational] minister." He noted that others could expect the same treatment despite his efforts "to gain the compassion and favor of the government. . .; and both I and my people grow weary of our lives under our poverty and oppression."[15]

Unable to obtain relief from their town, the Anglicans turned to the General Assembly and in May 1727 asked to be excused from the payment of taxes to support the Congregational ministry. The assembly responded by asserting that all persons were responsible to pay taxes to support "the churches established by the laws of this government," but added that "if it so happen that there be a society of the Church of England. . . so near to any person that hath declared himself of the Church of England that he can conveniently & doth attend the public worship there, then the collectors, having first indifferently levied the tax above said, shall deliver the taxes. . . unto the minister of the Church of England."[16]

Heartened by this victory in the General Assembly, Fairfield Anglicans set to work completing a small church they had begun at Mill Plain in 1725. It was the second Anglican or Episcopal church in the colony and came to be served by Henry Caner, Jr., a graduate of Yale, class of 1724, and the son of a devout Anglican from Stratford. Because Fairfield's Anglican population was so small, it could afford to pay Caner only £10 a year, the SPGFP adding another £60. Besides Fairfield proper, Caner also served Stratfield, Green's Farms, and Greenfield on a regular basis and occasionally traveled to Norwalk, Stamford, Greenwich, and Redding to preach. He found Fairfield leaders relentless in their hostility. "Notwithstanding this discouragement," Caner reported to the SPGFP, "the Church grows & increases very much, four families being added since my coming."[17]

Apparently some of the tension between the Anglicans and the town had subsided by 1738, because in that year the town granted permission to the members of the Church of England to erect "a house for public worship on the highway [Old Post Road] near the old field gate" between what modern Fairfielders know as Rowland and Penfield roads. Trinity Church was completed in "a very decent manner with a handsome steeple and spire of one hundred feet, and a good bell of five hundred weight." The local church members could never have afforded such a magnificent structure. Most of the construction costs were borne by the Society for the Propagation for the Gospel in Foreign Parts and by Anglicans in New York, where the Church of England was the established church.[18]

The fortunes of the Anglican church continued to prosper in Fairfield. In October 1732, John Beach, a missionary of the SPGFP, began officiating at a small church, Christ Church, in the Redding parish, and in 1748, the Episcopalians in Stratfield, under the guidance of Joseph Lamson, Caner's successor at Fairfield, erected St. John's Church, which included among its supporters Colonel John Burr and Timothy Wheeler, two of Stratfield's most important men. During the summer of 1763, Lamson also directed the building of an Episcopal church in North Fairfield. Four Anglican churches, served by only two clergymen, existed in Fairfield by the end of 1763. Also, by that date, the General Assembly had conferred upon Trinity Church the power to establish and collect its own taxes. In this respect, it stood on an even footing with Fairfield's Prime Society.

The Prime Society had woes in abundance during the first half of the eighteenth century. In addition to the loss of revenue and membership to the new societies and the uneasiness created by the presence of Anglicanism within Fairfield, the society encountered problems with its minister. By the 1720s, the Reverend Webb's health had begun to decline. He was unable to attend public worship regularly. The town decided in 1724 to hire a man to assist Webb, a practice that had to be repeated year after year until Webb's death in the year 1733.

Noah Hobart, who succeeded him, had to contend with both the problems created by a decade of neglect and with what he referred to as "the Episcopal Separation." Hobart believed the Anglicans were as dangerous as Webb had thought them to be. But the younger man insisted on confronting the Anglican challenge and devoting as much of his energy as required to fend off the dangerous intruder. He argued that it was "a necessary part of a Minister's Duty, to write upon Controversy and even to contend earnestly for the Faith." He denounced the tendency toward Anglicanism in *A Serious Address to the Members of the Episcopal Separation in New England*, a pamphlet that explained the dangers of allowing a diversity of religious points of view within society. *A Second Address to the Members of the Episcopal Separation in New England* carried the battle even further, demonstrating Hobart's conviction that the Church of England represented for his generation a force almost as evil as the Church of Rome had been at an earlier time.[19]

While he was in the midst of this struggle another intrusion demanded his attention. This was the Great Awakening. By the 1730s, many Connecticut citizens had become dissatisfied with the type of Congregationalism being practised. Some, seeking more latitudinarianism in their religion, had already turned to the Church of England. The success of Anglicanism in Fairfield reflected in part the malaise within Congregationalism. But other men and women would attach more importance to what they called piety, spiritual awareness that must surpass the intellect if one were truly to understand his dependence upon God and the necessity of conforming to His will. These persons believed that the Congregational societies, in their efforts to avoid controversy within the church and with their emphasis upon the intellect as the most appropriate means to come to know God, had wandered too far from the original teachings of the founders of New England. The societies had abandoned too much of their autonomy to the Saybrook Platform, which created the county consociations, a modest form of church government; had tolerated too much civil interference, the General Assembly regularly making decisions affecting the churches; and had substituted too much rationalism for the emotionalism that had been so important to the older religion.

Just as those who sought more toleration found it in the Anglican Church, those who sought more piety found it in the revival meetings that spread across Connecticut in the late 1730s and the early 1740s. At these meetings, itinerant ministers, appealing to their congregations' emotions, insisted that all persons recognize their dependence upon God and the dreadful consequence of refusing to do so. The ministers would terrify their listeners to a point where some would moan in anguish while others, unable to bear the desperation of their plight, would swoon. On October 28, 1740, George Whitefield, probably the most powerful of these revivalists, preached to a large and responsive Fairfield audience during an unanticipated early snowstorm. Turmoil followed his visit. Many now rejected the calm and reasoned services that were the order of the day in the Reverend Hobart's meetinghouse. To the Anglican challenge was added that of men like Whitefield and his followers, the New Lights, who emphasized piety and emotion as essential to genuine religious awakening.

Hobart responded to the New Lights by warning his congregation of the chaos they caused. During the spring of 1742, news began to spread that the Reverend James Davenport was coming to Fairfield. A Yale graduate and a zealous revivalist who on at least one occasion preached for twenty-four hours straight, Davenport frightened Hobart. On May 9, the Fairfield minister addressed a letter to his congregation. "Mr. Davenports manner of Preaching and acting appear to me extreamly different from the Example of Christ & his Apostles, and to have a Tendency rather to destroy than to promote Religion," he began. Hobart acknowledged that he had heard Davenport preach in New Haven. On the basis of Davenport's performance there and on the basis of "the unhappy Effects of his Preaching in many Places," he advised his congregation "not to attend upon him if he comes. I would particularly caution you against attending unseasonable night meetings to the preventing the worship of God in your Families & in your Closets." He concluded by praying "that God will appear either to hinder his coming hither, or to prevent such Consiquences attending it among us as have in many other places."[20]

Hobart also kept the New Light ideas at bay by being aware of and responsive to new trends in society. He was aware, for example, of a new materialism in Fairfield, a new belief among Fairfield people that seeking wealth was not necessarily reprehensible. The Puritan founders of New England had made a subtle distinction between the vigorous pursuit of one's earthly calling, which was entirely admirable, and the chasing after wealth, which they denounced as covetousness. The distinction was one of motive. Was one following his calling and as a consequence incidentally becoming prosperous, or was one's goal the acquisition of the treasures of the world? In the one instance the motive was legitimate; in the other, an offense against God. Slow to condemn wealth, Hobart was usually willing to assume that prosperity came as a result of one's honest labors, and so sought to avoid creating a vast reservoir of guilt in his congregation; guilt that had caused many Connecticut congregations to turn in desperation to the teachings of men like Davenport. While it would be hard to prove that Hobart's relaxed attitude about changing social values was a conscious effort to thwart the New Lights, clearly his congregation's fidelity was due at least in part to his refusal to denounce covetousness whenever he saw affluence, to his acceptance of the town's new materialism.

Hobart lost ground to the Anglican church, which was even more forgiving than he of wordly pursuits, but he managed to keep the New Lights at bay, to maintain Fairfield as the most solidly Old Light—that is, antirevivalist—town in Connecticut, and to enjoy a prominent position among the colony's Old Light leaders. In 1751 the Prime Society completed a new meetinghouse, a building sixty feet long and forty-four feet wide adorned with a steeple that extended 120 feet above the Fairfield green, a symbol of the society's stability in a time of change.

While the Prime Society stood firm, the Great Awakening was pommeling the Stratfield Society. The Reverend Samuel Cooke, "a man of great dignity of character, highly respected by his people, although it has been said that they stood somewhat in fear of him," served the society from 1715 until his death in 1747. His fondness for New Light ideas and his "fervid and pungent" style of preaching alienated several of

*The Stratfield Baptist Church at the corner of Stratfield
and Churchill Roads was built in 1814.*

his most prominent parishioners, among them Colonel John Burr, John Holburton, and
Timothy Wheeler, These men, in 1744, withdrew from the society to become founders
of St. John's Episcopal Church in Stratfield.[21]

After Cooke's death, the society selected Lyman Hall, a Wallingford man who had
graduated from Yale in 1747 and was ordained two years later, to replace him. The choice
was a bad one. Hall, who supported the Old Lights with the same fervor that Cooke
had endorsed the New Lights, was unable to control the enmity that existed in his congregation. By the time his pastorate ended on June 18, 1751, the society was in a shambles.
His replacement, Robert Ross, a Princeton graduate who was nearly as conservative as
Hall, was a warm and generous man who managed eventually to bank the fires of antagonism that burned in his congregation.

Shortly after Hall's departure and before Ross had taken his place, a group of Stratfield men gathered at the home of Captain John Sherwood. Formerly a prominent
member of the Stratfield Society, having served that society on its Committee of Prudentials, as its clerk and as a frequent representative to the consociation, Sherwood led a
group of New Lights who, dissatisfied with Hall's conservative preaching, withdrew
from his congregation. At Sherwood's home, the dissidents listened to the preaching
of Joshua Morse, a Baptist clergyman who had been converted by Whitefield, and
witnessed Morse's baptism of ten of their number. This was the beginning of the Stratfield Baptist Church, the first in Fairfield County, though at that time it had neither
a minister nor a church building.

In December 1757, elders from the Baptist churches in Groton and New London
met with the Stratfield congregation and ordained John Sherwood, "a man of large stature,
of superior strength, & possessing no small degree of energy & Firmness in carrying

out the convictions of duty & right," as the minister of the Stratfield church. Still without a building of their own, the Baptists ordained their new minister in Stratfield's Anglican church, another congregation formed by disgruntled members of the Stratfield Society.[22]

By 1763 one Baptist, seven Congregational, and four Episcopal churches existed in Fairfield. Seven parishes controlled a variety of matters, such as the collection of the ministers' rates, the administration of schools, and the direction of trainbands. The idea of one community organized around a single church was dead. In its place Fairfield men and women found a variety of institutions competing for their loyalties, the upshot of which was to encourage increased preoccupation with personal, as opposed to community, matter. The community remained the object of much affection and much attention, to be sure, but priorities were changing. Fairfield men and women, once Puritans, were becoming Yankees.

## NOTES

1. Richard L. Bushman, *From Puritan to Yankee: Character and Social Order in Connecticut, 1690-1765* (Cambridge, Mass., 1967), is the standard study of the transformation of Puritans into Yankees.

2. *Connecticut Colonial Records*, III, 8.

3. Ibid., IV, 29-30.

4. Connecticut Archives, Ecclesiastical Affairs, I, 125-26.

5. *Connecticut Colonial Records*, IV, 47, 61.

6. Ibid., V, 42.

7. B. J. Relyea, *The Historial Discourse* (New York, 1865), 28-9.

8. FTR, B, II, Dec. 15, 1724.

9. *Connecticut Colonial Records*, VI, 522.

10. Ibid., VII, 231-32.

11. George H. Merwin, *Ye Church and Parish of Greenfield* (New Haven, 1913), 21.

12. Schenck, *Fairfield*, II, 14.

13. Ibid., II, 72-73.

14. E. Edward Beardsley, *The History of the Episcopal Church in Connecticut*, 2 vol. (New York, 1865), I, 39.

15. Ibid., I, 57, 59.

16. *Connecticut Colonial Records*, VII, 107.

17. Schenck, *Fairfield*, II, 89-90.

18. FTR, B, II, July 27, 1738; Beardsley, *Episcopal Church*, I, 101-2.

19. Child, *An Old New England Church*, 57.

20. Noah Hobart to the Church and Congregation in Fairfield, May 9, 1742, in the Hobart Family Papers, FHS.

21. *The Bi-Centennial Celebration of the First Congregational Church and Society of Bridgeport* (New Haven, 1895), 28-29.

22. Schenck, *Fairfield*, II, 214.

# Becoming Yankees

THE TOWN MEETING reflected the changes that came to Fairfield during the first two-thirds of the eighteenth century. During the early 1700s, the meeting considered business much like that which had been important in the seventeenth century. Timber remained a subject of interest. On April 29, 1718, the meeting ordered that town residents refrain from taking "any timber or Trees brought up or that shall be brought up by sd. sea on the Beach." Having a competent smith in town continued to be important. In 1706 the town authorized John Winto to erect a smith's shop where William Malery had "wrought." An even greater interest was providing the town with adequate milling facilities. Grist, saw, and fulling mills remained an item of vital interest to the town meeting.[1]

Before the century was twenty years old, certain types of business began disappearing from the town meeting agenda. The town had for years been responsible for the appointment of tavern keepers. This task, along with many others, fell to the parishes early in the eighteenth century. Stratfield, Green's Farms, Greenfield, and later the others appointed their own keepers of ordinaries and public houses, and chose their own sheepmasters, highway surveyors, fence viewers, constables, pound keepers, sealers of weights and measures, and horse branders.

At the beginning of the century, the town oversaw the schools of Fairfield. It hired schoolmasters and maintained the schoolhouses, both for the petty or elementary schools and the grammar school. When in 1711 Fairfield finally received the six hundred acres the legislature had promised in 1672 to subsidize the cost of the grammar school, the town appointed a committee to rent the land and to use the revenue derived for the benefit of that school in particular.

This situation changed in 1712. In that year, the General Assembly placed responsibility for the elementary schools with the parishes. The parishes regulated all school affairs except those relating to the grammar school, which continued to be under the town's control. The parishes hired and paid the schoolmasters, collected the school rates, and provided quarters for the school. The location of schools within the parishes could be a troublesome issue. While the parishes were still sparsely populated, the school committees might decide to rotate the school to different parts of the parish, spending a few months here and a few months there. Eventually one or more schools would be permanently located in the parish, according to the needs of the population. Greenfield, for example, on November 11, 1725 ordered a school to be kept six months of the year in the building that was then being used as a meetinghouse, located in the center of the parish. Five years later, this plan was altered to allow a school to be kept twelve months of the year, four months in the center, four months at Hull's Farm, and four months at Banks's Farm. When the parish created a fourth school, this one at Lyon's Farm, the school committee decided that each of these schools should meet for three months a year.

After 1712 the parishes became the recipients of colonial subsidies for education. Connecticut in the 1730s sold the land in the seven northwestern townships and used the revenue to establish a fund to assist the parishes with the cost of education. In addition Stratfield, Green's Farms, Greenfield, and the Prime Society received income from the old parsonage lands, which had been divided in 1733.

Though under the control of the parishes, these schools were not religious institutions. The education provided was, by the standards of that intensely religious age, secular. Reading, writing, and some arithmetic were as much the order of the day before 1795, when the parishes supervised the schools, as they were after that date when newly created school districts took control.

At the town grammar school one could prepare for college by studying ancient languages and perhaps a bit more arithmetic than had been available in the petty school. Much of the support for the school came from the six hundred acre grant. In May 1722 the General Assembly authorized Captain Joseph Wakeman, Captain Moses Dimon, and Lietenant Jonathan Sturges to sell the land, lend the money from the sale at interest, and use the income to help finance the school. Other costs were shared by the town and by the parents of the students, the concept of free public education still being part of a new world that had yet to arrive in Connecticut.

Additional educational opportunities in town meant that some young men were able to attend college. Daniel Sherwood, a precocious lad who would later serve Fairfield in a variety of capacities, grew up on the substantial farm of his father, also Daniel, in Greenfield. He went off to Yale in 1752. The privilege of attending college was one that only a miniscule part of the population enjoyed in eighteenth-century Connecticut, and Sherwood understood his special situation. "I shall endeavor to improve all the advantages which I am favoured with here for the better to fit & qualify myself so that I may be useful to mankind in my day & generation," he wrote his father on January 28, 1754. Even for a family as prosperous as the Sherwoods, having a boy in college meant a heavy financial burden, which they attempted to ease by providing as much for him as possible from the family farm. His father wrote on March 23, 1754, informing Daniel that he had "put your chest on board Capt. Sturges sloop and in the same I have put some apples and butter. I would have you git a good lock and put upon it."[2]

Without such items from home, young Daniel frequently had to go without. He told his father that "he missed it very much in not bringing over my butter for there is none to be had here." He also asked his father for some quills and warned him that "I shall want a wig at commencement very much." More than any of these specific items, however, Sherwood generally needed money. "I don't think that less than £12-00-00 old tenor will clear me of all the debts I owe in New Haven," he informed his father in February 1756. While genuinely grateful for anything his parents did for him, he still had to admit that if he "had a little more it would doe me no hurt for the present. I have bought me a new hebrew grammar which cost 45d. I must buy my wood & candles which are dear."[3]

William Wheeler was another eighteenth-century Fairfield boy whose family managed to finance four years in New Haven, although he had reached nineteen before his parents found the means to send him. Most of his classmates were closer to fourteen than nineteen. Daniel Sherwood had arrived at college when he was only sixteen. Wheeler was the son of Captain Ichabod and Deborah Burr Wheeler. His family, who resided near Black Rock Harbor, was involved in both farming and maritime enterprises, shipbuilding in particular. Like Daniel Sherwood's father, Ichabod Wheeler impressed upon his son the unusual opportunity the boy was enjoying and the great hardship that the cost of his education was imposing on the family. Ichabod also warned William that in New Haven he might encounter temptations the likes of which were unheard of around Black Rock. And the father's admonitions stood the youth in good stead. "And as every place furnished some temptation." he later recalled, "there is always some female of easy virtue in Town that the Scholars are acquainted with. At the period of my residence there was two — Mima Wedger & Sal Umberfield." William found these young women fascinating. He described Mima as being "about 15, well looking, small & a good figure — I have often heard her from her window as I passed on to the College from the long wharf." Sal was no less intriguing to him: "Sal was a tall brunette — the Scholars called her 'Copper Bottom.'" Fortunately for the sake of William's virtue, he remembered his father's warnings. "My father when I was young took great pains to instill into me a hatred of such characters and a proper respect for virtuous females & in this he succeeded fully." William was, certainly in his own eyes at least, a paragon of virtue: "Perhaps no person had a greater antipathy then myself to immodest females of this sort. A young lady whom I tenderly loved lost all command of herself but the temptation did not succeed." That all unchaperoned Fairfield lads of the time were as well behaved as Wheeler would be hard to prove and even harder to believe.[4]

If the sexual behavior of Fairfield's adolescents in the eighteenth century remains a mystery, the political behavior of Fairfield adults at the same time is anything but a riddle. Unlike the previous century, when political life had been characterized by widespread officeholding and the regular rotation of officials, eighteenth-century Fairfield saw a high concentration of political power in the hands of a few, generally affluent, men. Nathan Gold, the son of Nathan Gold, Sr., and Peter Burr, the son of Jehu Burr, dominated Fairfield political life during the first twenty years of the century. Both men were rich; their wealth deriving from their vast landholdings, and both eventually served as assistants of the colony, the most prestigious office in Connecticut besides that of governor.

The importance of the Burr family in Fairfield grew enormously during the next four or five decades. John, Andrew, Samuel, Thaddeus, John II, and Nathaniel Jr. all enjoyed political prestige comparable to that which Peter Burr had possessed earlier. All were also wealthy men. John Burr, Sr.'s estate in 1750 of £15,000 was probably the largest Fairfield knew during the entire colonial period. The family's wealth was certainly one of the factors in their political success; it allowed them the leisure to devote to politics. But other factors contributed to their prominence. Jehu, the progenitor of the family, who arrived in Fairfield in the seventeenth century, had four sons, Jehu, Jr., John, Daniel, and Nathaniel. Each was a man of some importance, and each had several sons, some of whom would become significant to Fairfield's history. By size alone the Burr family was an important ingredient in the town's political life.

Education was important to the Burrs. Several sons benefited from attending Harvard or Yale. The seventeenth and eighteenth centuries understood a college education as preparation for leadership, and the graduates of such institutions acccepted the idea that their attendance in college carried with it a special responsibility for service. The Burrs did not limit their activities to politics and business. Peter, John, and Andrew, all lawyers, regarded the law as more than a means of providing for themselves and their families; they became leaders within the legal profession, helping to create a legal community within Connecticut. Like Burrs before and after them, John and Andrew were also active members of the militia; active to the point of dominating the local militia units.

During the late 1760s and the early 1770s, the influence of the Burr family, though still impressive, did diminish. This decline represented no weakening of the family's talents, but indicated how the growth of Fairfield meant more competition for political power. The power that the Burrs had unintentionally surrendered had been seized by men of affluence like them. The ascendance of men like Ebenezer Silliman, Nathan Bulkley, Samuel Wakeman, David Rowland, and Jonathan Sturges hardly represented a democratic trend in Fairfield politics. Right through the end of Connecticut's life as a British colony, political life continued to be dominated by a small élite, an élite that now happened to include persons with a variety of surnames besides Burr.

If Fairfield's political life changed during the eighteenth century, its economic life changed even more. The seventeenth century had for the most part been an era of barely more than subsistence agriculture in Fairfield. The problems of survival had demanded so much time and energy that little of either was left over to refine the economy. But by the beginning of the eighteenth century, several new trends—encouraged by an increase in trade between Connecticut and the West Indies and by the realization by Connecticut farmers that certain soils and areas were better suited to particular crops than others—forced the economy into new directions.

The agriculture of Fairfield became more specialized and more commercial. As it had since its beginning, Fairfield continued to produce grain, but now its farms regularly yielded more than the local population could consume, enough to provide surplus trading goods. Much of the soil in town was ideally suited to the cultivation of flax, which became an even more important item of trade for Fairfield. An annual plant, flax was useful for its fiber, which could be spun into thread and woven into linen, and for its seed, which could either be sold as seed or pressed to produce linseed oil. Aware of the potential value of a successful flax crop, Connecticut had encouraged its production from the colony's earliest years. In 1640, the colonial government ordered that each family was to sow at least a rod of flax or hemp. Fairfield had also supported the cultivation of flax by pegging its value at an artificially high level and then accepting it as payment for taxes. By the middle of the eighteenth century, Fairfield farmers had come to realize that the flaxseed was more valuable than the fiber. Ireland, the center of the linen industry but a location where flaxseed rarely matured satisfactorily, could consume all the seed that they could ever produce. In 1750, £80,000 worth of flaxseed went from Connecticut by way of New York to Ireland, at least a fifth of it from Fairfield.

Sheep, hogs, and cattle continued to be important on Fairfield farms. The markets for meat and dairy products remained strong in Boston and especially New York. Grocers in both cities made a point of mentioning the Connecticut origin of their meat, an indication of the colony's reputation for quality. The early eighteenth century also found more and more horses in Fairfield. The mild climate, abundant feed, and level terrain of coastal Fairfield were ideally suited for horse breeding, and Fairfield horses commanded high prices, both on the mainland and in the West Indies.

As trade become more important to Fairfield, larger and larger quantities of agricultural goods were consumed on board ship; these products were required to feed crews and the livestock they frequently transported. Each horse shipped from Black Rock to the West Indies consumed between four and five hundred pounds of hay during the voyage plus ten or fifteen bushels of oats. Multiplying these figures by the hundreds of horses and other animals that made the journey during the eighteenth century provides some idea of the quantity of agricultural goods needed to keep just this aspect of the trade thriving. Although the seamen were doubtless less voracious than their equine passengers, feeding Fairfield's sailors provided further income for local farmers.

Along with other areas of Connecticut's western coast, Fairfield, with its good land, mild climate, access to New York, Boston, and the West Indies, and sheltered ports, began to blossom economically. During the frequent warfare between England and France, the British army's demands for goods more than filled any shortfall that might otherwise exist. King William's War (1690-97), followed by Queen Anne's War (1702-13), King George's War (1744-48), and then the French and Indian War (1754-63), meant boom times for Fairfield. As early as the 1720s, the town's land values exceeded those of interior Connecticut by 50 percent. Reclaiming wetlands by "Daming, Deaching and Draining" became a popular pastime in Fairfield, already the third wealthiest town in the colony, exceeded only by Hartford and New Haven.

Recognition of Fairfield's growing economic importance came in 1702, when royal officials designated it one of the eight lawful ports of the colony of Connecticut and appointed a naval officer in charge of entering and clearing ships. Just two years later John Edwards, who for many years served as the Fairfield naval officer, and John Sturges began, with the town's approval, to construct a wharf on Ash House Creek, Black Rock Harbor then being entirely under the control of the Wheeler family. Ash Creek remained an important shipping area until the mid–eighteenth century. On December 26, 1733, the town granted authority to Peter Thorp and Ebenezer Dimon to build a warehouse along the creek.

But Black Rock Harbor (or Ship Harbor, as it was initially called) soon dominated maritime activity in Fairfield. Because the harbor was accessible to large ships at both low and high tide, it became the port for Fairfield vessels engaged in the West Indian trade. About 1740, Ichabod Wheeler built the first shipyard at Black Rock, just north of the wharves that his family had built earlier in the century.

In March 1750, Samuel Squires, Jr. and Ebenezer Wakeman convinced the town to allow them to build a wharf "on the ship harbour near the Parsonage meadow and a Ware house on or near the same."[5] The project languished for more than a decade, principally because the central village and the harbor were so far apart and travel between the two points was so difficult. Peter Penfield's decision to build a tide mill at the lower end of Ash Creek in 1750 encouraged plans for a new road between the center of Fairfield and Ash Creek. By the time this road reached Ash Creek, Samuel Squire was back before the town seeking a renewal of his authorization to build a wharf. This came on December 10, 1760, but Squire continued to procrastinate until 1765, when at last a bridge across Ash Creek and a road from the creek to the harbor convinced him to act. The Squire Wharf, also called the Lower Wharf, became in modern times the location of the Black Rock Yacht Club.

The growing interest in the harbor encouraged David Wheeler III, Ichabod's cousin, to deed land to the town on January 21, 1767, for a street to run from the harbor to the main highway to Fairfield's center. Wheeler then began dividing the land along his new road into home lots and offering them for sale. Captain Joseph Silliman and Captain Thomas Holburton were the first to buy in Wheeler's development, which eventually became the home of many seafaring families.

On December 17, 1760, the town granted Ichabod Wheeler permission to build a new wharf near the location where his family had owned a pier for decades and where he operated his shipyard. Deciding that he was more interested in building ships than in developing docking facilities, Wheeler sold five-sixths of his interest in the project in March 1770. His partners, James Smedley, Samuel Bradley, Jr., Ebenezer Bartram, Jr., Robert Wilson, and Nathaniel Wilson, completed the wharf, which became known as Upper Wharf.

Black Rock Harbor eventually accommodated three wharves along its western shore. On December 23, 1766, the town agreed to allow Job Bartram and several partners "to build a Wharf at Black Rock Harbor adjoining to Capt. Ichabod Wheeler's Wharf to begin at the Southerly Side of Wheeler's Wharf and Extend one Hundred feet along the shore." These men built their dock several hundred feet from the original site, however, on land they bought from David Wheeler III at the end of his new road. This became the Middle Wharf.[6]

By 1770 Black Rock Harbor was a considerable maritime center. It included the Wheeler shipyard and the three wharves, around each of which stood warehouses or stores, sheds that served a variety of needs, chandleries, and the tackle required to load and unload ships. It was as busy as any location in Fairfield, ships arriving and departing, or in various stages of repair and construction, livestock and other cargo waiting to be loaded. Seventy years earlier, such activity could only have been conjured up in a fantasy.

At the opposite end of town, the economic revolution was also having its effects. During the 1740s, the General Assembly authorized Nathan Disbrow to operate a ferry from Fairfield to Norwalk across the Saugatuck River. Traffic between the two towns had increased to such a point by 1761 that Fairfield voted to join Norwalk in building "a good Cart bridge over Saugatuck River at the Banks," each town to bear half the expense of the construction.[7]

By December 1758, David Osborn's wharf and a shipyard, operated for a time by Charles Lewis, already stood along the Mill River, and enough commerce existed on the river to justify Samuel Whiting's building a storehouse on its banks. Eight years later, in December 1766, the town authorized two important projects along the river.

It voted to allow Hezekiah Sturges and Moses Bulkley to build a second wharf, eighty feet in length, and agreed that Talcott Bulkley could construct a third.

With three wharves of its own, Mill River (later called Southport) was nearly as busy as Black Rock. The two ports competed but also complemented each other. Few vessels bound for the West Indies called at Mill River. The West Indian trade developed at Black Rock. Ships engaged in the coastal trade operated from both ports, in which case Mill River suffered under no great disadvantage, its waters being sufficiently deep for coastal vessels, its location being convenient to the rich agricultural parishes of Greenfield, Green's Farms and Norfield, and its position on the coast being closer to New York than Black Rock's. Captain Stephen Thorp of Mill River was typical of the men trading out of that location. His trade was almost exclusively with "York" where he delivered flour, wheat, rum, and "Seader Shingles" and took on a variety of manufactured goods that had been imported from England.[8] Black Rock sent mariners off to more distant ports, neither England nor Europe but Barbados, St. Kitt's, and St. Thomas, where Connecticut livestock, salted meat, and flour could be traded for West Indian sugar, molasses, rum, and salt.

With few exceptions, Fairfield merchants and farmers bought and sold goods and services by means of an elaborate system of debits and credits. They kept detailed account books in which they recorded myriad transactions: goods for goods, services for goods, services for services. At various times, not necessarily annually, they made reckonings with customers and neighbors, possibly exchanging cash or merchandise but more likely merely reconciling credits and debits to allow the transfer of the account to a new and uncluttered page. The system worked well for a population that, despite its prosperity, possessed little money. The 1768 account of John Thorp, a Greenfield merchant and farmer, with Seth Perry, a blacksmith, indicates that Perry acquired a variety of goods from Thorp and provided various smithing services to him. During the course of the entire year, the two exchanged no money. At the time of reckoning, Perry agreed to settle by acknowledging a credit to his account in Thorp's journal. Thorp's 1770 account with Samuel Squire, a cooper, involved several transactions, Squire settling matters by paying Thorp a small amount of cash. Thorp and Increase Bradley, a farmer, managed to end the year without exchanging any cash; Thorp paid Bradley with a load of walnut wood and accepted five bushels of clams as change.

All this economic activity meant both new population and wealth for Fairfield. In 1756, the year of one of Connecticut's irregular enumerations, Fairfield included 4455 persons — 4195 whites and 260 blacks — making it the fourth largest town in Connecticut, behind Middletown, Norwich, and New Haven. In terms of taxable property it ranked second in the colony, only Norwich enjoying a larger list of estates.

Connecticut conducted another census in 1774. Unfortunately, comparisons between it and the 1756 census are difficult, because the General Assembly in 1767 made what had been the Fairfield parish of Redding into an independent town, thus depriving Fairfield of a significant amount of population and taxable property. With a population of 4863, Fairfield was the eleventh largest town in Connecticut in 1774. (Had Redding still been part of Fairfield, the town would have maintained its position as the third largest town in the colony, with a population of 6097.) The 4863 persons included 4544 whites and 319 blacks, giving Fairfield the highest percentage of black population in the colony. The Fairfield list of estates, that is, the town's grand list, was the fifth largest in

Connecticut, the same relative position the town held in terms of the size of its average per capita estate.

By 1774 Fairfield's trade was bringing affluence to Fairfield merchants like David Judson or Moses Bulkley, not men of great wealth as could have been found in Boston or Philadelphia, but still prosperous men who enjoyed a standard of living as high as any in Connecticut. This trade also meant affluence for some of the town's farmers, especially those who, like Thaddeus Burr, belonged to one of the leading families that owned so much of the town's real estate. Furthermore, the town was home to many lawyers, who found Fairfield attractive both because of the amount of legal business generated by the trade and because it was the location of the Fairfield County Court. Fairfield had been the court's home since 1666, the beginning of counties in Connecticut. The first courthouse was built in 1718, but precisely where it stood remains a mystery. In 1768, after Isaac Frasier, a convicted thief, set fire to the jail and courthouse in a futile effort to escape, Fairfield County built a new courthouse and jail on the meetinghouse green in Fairfield, "a little northwesterly of the New School House."[9] Frasier had the distinction of being the first criminal to go to the gallows at the new facility. Twice a year the Superior Court of Connecticut met there as well; it was that court's practice to hold two sessions annually in each county.

Skilled craftsmen found a place in Fairfield now that the town could afford to support a more specialized labor force. The days had passed when a man had to be a jack-of-all-trades. The growth of maritime affairs had forced more men to work as laborers than ever before. Ships had to be loaded and unloaded, repaired and maintained, and, of course, sailed. Men whose fathers had been farmers now made their living at Black Rock and Mill River or on the ships that journeyed forth from those ports.

Fairfield's growing trade encouraged the growth of its black population. Approximately three out of every four blacks in Fairfield in the 1770s were slaves. Most of them were men who worked as laborers or household servants; a smaller number of women were household servants; and an even smaller number were children. Most slaves were denied the pleasure of residing, with or without the benefit of marriage, with a member of the opposite sex. Captain David Judson owned a married couple and their child, but more typical was Hezekiah Gold, who owned four men, a "wench," a young man, and two boys. Slavery was a luxury that Fairfield came to afford as it became affluent. Most free blacks in Fairfield worked as laborers, either on the docks or on board ship.

Other, more palatable, evidence existed of Fairfield's growing affluence. On February 14, 1760, the Greenfield Society voted to build a new meetinghouse. The old one had been in use only thirty-three years but was plain and had neither a steeple nor a place for a bell. The congregation, conscious of its recent abundance, demanded a meetinghouse that reflected its improved situation. By 1762 the new edifice, far more imposing than any of the other seventeen meetinghouses that could be seen from its steeple, was ready to receive worshipers. Only two years elapsed between the date the congregation decided to build and the time the building was ready for use. Earlier Fairfield congregations had taken decades to complete similar, although less elaborate, projects, the parishioners requiring years to raise the necessary funds; funds that would have seemed a pittance compared to the more than £1000 that Greenfield spent on its 1762 meetinghouse.

*Fairfield: the biography of a community*

*Ogden House, built circa 1750 by David Ogden as it appeared in 1928 prior to restoration by Annie B. Jennings. It is now owned by the Fairfield Historical Society.*

The Stratfield Society, impressed by what had taken place in Greenfield and eager to demonstrate its own prosperity, voted on September 19, 1770, to add a steeple to its meetinghouse. When the steeple was in place, the society agreed to add a bell and "to have the bell ringed at the usual time on Sabbath days, and other days at 12 of the clock in the day and at 9 o'clock at night." Such luxuries were becoming commonplace.

But a glance at an eighteenth-century estate inventory helps to put that century's idea of affluence into perspective. David Ogden, who was forty-eight when he died in Fairfield in 1775, was, while not wealthy, a prosperous man; his estate, valued at £1515, clearly placed him among the most affluent 20 percent of the town's population. His houses, milk house, barn, and the twenty-eight acres upon which these structures stood were worth £455. He owned an additional seventy-two acres, worth £529. Ogden, his wife, and their five children lived in a substantial, six-room center chimney house. Their furniture at the time of David's death consisted of four bedsteads, three looking glasses, a desk, a case of drawers, two round and two square tables, a chest of drawers, a trunk, an old chest, a cradle, a great chair, twelve black chairs, six crookbacked chairs, and five "old chairs." These items — total value, about £14 — would hardly begin to satisfy the needs of the most humble twentieth-century family of seven. The Ogdens did not own a single piece of upholstered furniture; upholstered items were reserved for those wealthy enough to import them from Boston or New York.

David Ogden's entire wardrobe would barely fill a modern traveler's suitcase. He operated a hundred-acre farm with fewer tools than modern suburbanites need to maintain an acre lawn, and his wife, Jane Sturges Ogden, had no more dishes and utensils

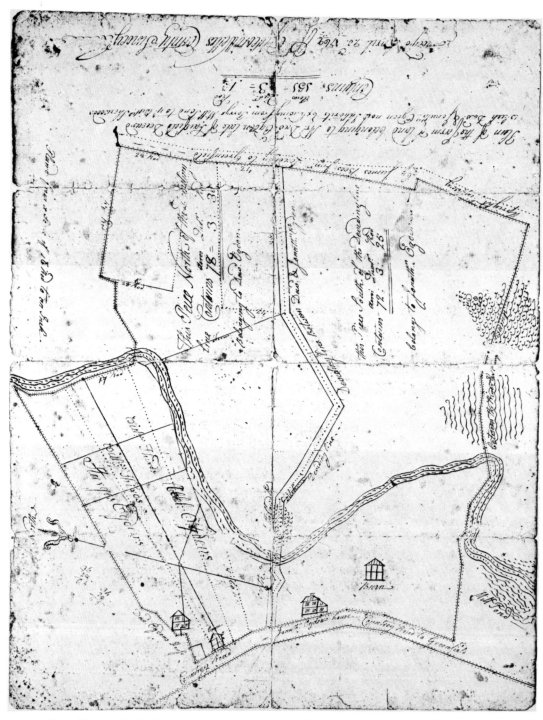

*Plan of the farmland of David Ogden showing division of property for his heirs. The Country Road to Greenfield is now Bronson Road and the river is Mill River.*

in her kitchen than a modern homemaker could fit in the family dishwasher. Relative to the scarcity that Fairfield had known in the seventeenth century, Ogden and his neighbors, the beneficiaries of the new prosperity, did enjoy many luxuries; but relative to modern times their homes were austere, their lives practically devoid of material goods beyond what was essential for a modicum of comfort.

Many Fairfield residents shared barely at all in the new prosperity. The fortunes of the town's slaves failed to improve with their masters'. Fortune also refused to smile on the "lesser sort," those who owned no productive property and who lacked any permanent place in the community. Most who started life destitute managed to escape poverty by the time they reached their forties. The "lesser sort," however, never achieved economic independence and often became, from time to time at least, wards of the town or of relatives. The town assumed responsibility for such persons when necessary, the practice being "to vendue the Poor," which meant that the town would receive bids from residents for the care of specific individuals and would then expect "that those who bid them off shall support them at the price bid at."[10] The number of persons who found themselves in this embarassing predicament was fortunately small, no more than 5 percent of the population.

Well over two-thirds of Fairfield families enjoyed a decent standard of living by the 1770s. Except for the slave population, the town provided its residents with a solid chance to make a good life for themselves and their families. The town's growing economic diversification meant new opportunities, and its social values encouraged an open society, in which a person could improve his lot in life. The town offered no incentives for great wealth beyond what it granted for simple success, had no tradition of lavish hospitality such as existed in Virginia, and placed no particular value on great mansions or rich furnishings, as were found in Philadelphia or Boston. When a man died his estate was divided among his sons, thus reducing the level of inequality that did exist. So Fairfield's prosperity managed to exist without inflicting crushing poverty on many and without creating an élite whose dominance was assured.

The new prosperity did not eliminate uncertainty from the lives of Fairfielders, however. Occasional threats to the town's physical security still existed. Indians were no longer a military problem; in fact, Nathan Birdsey told Ezra Stiles in 1761 that there were no longer any Native Americans living in the area, "only here & there a scattering Squaw and scarcely a Poppoose." Even as early as 1728, the Reverend Henry Caner had written that "the Indians in numbers were very small about Fairfield, by reason of the vicious lives they led, with their excessive drinking, which destroys them apace." Significantly, Caner blamed their proclivity toward drunkeness as well as their "inveterate prejudice against Christianity . . . on the shamefully wicked lives of us its professors."[11]

If the local Indians were no longer a menace, the French in Canada were. In each of the colonial wars—King William's, Queen Anne's, King George's, and the French and Indian War—men left Fairfield, traveled for days to some remote location in northern New England or New York or in Canada, and fought to keep the French menace from their homes on Long Island Sound. In 1745, during King George's war, five hundred Connecticut men, including a company from Fairfield County led by Jabez Banks of Fairfield, participated in the successful siege of Louisbourg on Cape Breton Island.

The French and Indian War placed much greater demands on Connecticut and on Fairfield. Two thousand Connecticut men fought at the Battle of Lake George in

September 1755, including Colonel John Burr, Colonel Andrew Burr, Colonel John Read, Captain James Smedley, and Private James March, "an Indian mulatto fellow,"[12] all from Fairfield. Town men also participated in the conquest of Ticonderoga and Crown Point during the summer of 1759 and then fought at Quebec, which fell on September 18, 1759. Back home Ebenezer Silliman and David Rowland were busy convincing Fairfield residents that additional taxes were essential, that donations of food were required to keep Connecticut men at the front healthy, and that more men needed to enlist to keep the French at bay.

In 1758 Fairfield underwent a new experience when regular British army troops, part of His Majesty's 48th Regiment of Foot and the men of Colonel James Frasier's Highland Battalion, were quartered in town. The presence of the troops created problems, as indicated by the fact that Captain James Cockburn and Captain William Edmondston, of the 48th Regiment, appeared before the Fairfield County Court to answer charges that they had refused to deliver to civil authorities certain soldiers accused of misdemeanors in town. The court found them reprehensible for their indifference to the civil authorities of the colony of Connecticut, but imposed no specific penalties.

One of the most positive results of the French and Indian War was the arrival of Francis Forgue, a highly respected physician captured during the war and brought to Fairfield as a prisoner. He grew so fond of the place that when the war was over he sought naturalization and married Sarah Thompson Dennie, widow of James Dennie and daughter of David Thompson. He practiced medicine in Fairfield until his death, in 1783, at the age of fifty-four. Trained in Europe, Forgue brought a degree of sophistication to the medical profession in Fairfield far beyond anything it had known earlier.

On the eve of the American Revolution, Fairfield was vastly different from the town of eighty or so years earlier. The central village, which had provided an ideal setting for the encouragement of New England's brand of Christianity, fell victim of the tendency of Fairfielders to want to consolidate their lands and to live close to the lands they farmed, had become one of several hamlets that existed in Fairfield—hamlets that served practical and economic needs more than they did ecclesiastical considerations. The single church that had been at the heart of Fairfield's existence now competed with several others, some of them also Congregational, others Anglican and Baptist. Much of the power that had once belonged exclusively to the town Fairfield now had to share with its various parishes. Except in the case of vagrants or other persons it might identify as clearly undesirable, the town no longer warned people out of its limits. The corporate community was a thing of the past; and loyalties were confused.

Coming on top of this was a prosperity that exceeded any of the expectations of earlier generations. Fairfield men and women, at least many of them, were becoming accustomed to luxuries and had begun to attach more and more value to material goods. By the 1770s, the pursuit of gain, which the earlier generations had seen as cupidity, became largely acceptable. In an attempt to preserve something of the old morality, Fairfield in 1761 granted additional powers to its tithingmen, elected officials who were to protect the town from moral turpitude. Their position itself was an anachronism. Diligently as they might try, the tithingmen could never hope to stem the flow of cultural change.

The change was everywhere. During Fairfield's early years, for example, the pews in meetinghouses were assigned "by dignity, age and estate," that is, according to a system of status that rewarded individuals' contributions to the town, their longevity, and their material success. When Greenfield built its new meetinghouse in 1762, it voted "to sell the spots or pews then voted to be laid out in our new meeting-house;" the most desirable pews simply went to the highest bidders.[13] Norfield used the same system when it built its meetinghouse in 1760. Green's Farms followed the pattern in the meetinghouse that it voted to build in 1783. Wealth alone was becoming the basis of status in Fairfield.

On May 23, 1700, the Reverend Joseph Webb noted that "a prodigious tempest of wind, thunder, rain and hail" struck Fairfield. He was, as anyone of his generation would have been, convinced that the storm was a sign that God was less than happy with developments in Fairfield. In July 1771, lightning struck the Stratfield meetinghouse and, according to William Wheeler, "killed uncle John Burr & ripped open the Shoes of his brother Ozias that stood near him & killed likewise David Sherman."[14] What grist this would have been for Webb's mill! But for Wheeler and his contemporaries, it was no more than an unfortunate accident.

The town, public morality, even religion had all changed by the 1770s. Founded and nurtured by Puritans, Fairfield was now a Yankee town, a town of men and women who probably put their own interests ahead of those of the community, who probably valued freedom more than they did order, who might unashamedly covet their neighbor's fine home or broad fields, and who might be a bit uncertain about how they or their community fit into God's plan; a plan about which they may have been less than clear.

## NOTES

1. FTR, B, II, April 29, 1718; Dec. 26, 1706. This chapter, like the one before it, has benefited from my reading of Bushman, *From Puritan to Yankee.* Bruce C. Daniels has written extensively and well on eighteenth-century Connecticut political institutions. Especially helpful was his "Large Town Power Structures in Eighteenth-Century Connecticut: An Analysis of Political Leadership in Hartford, Norwich and Fairfield," Ph.D. dissertation, University of Connecticut, 1970. Other essential reading for this period includes Main, *Society and Economy,* and Gaspare John Saladino, "The Economic Revolution in Late Eighteenth-Century Connecticut," Ph.D. dissertation, University of Wisconsin, 1964.

2. Daniel Sherwood, Jr., to Daniel Sherwood, Sr., Jan. 28, March 23, 1754, in the Sherwood Family Papers, FHS.

3. Same to same, July 31, Nov. 6, 1755; Feb. 11, 1756, all in ibid.

4. William Wheeler's Journal, in Cornelia Penfield Lathrop, *Black Rock, Seaport of Old Fairfield, 1644-1870* (New Haven, 1930), 38.

5. FTR, B, I, March 27, 1750.

6. Ibid., Dec. 23, 1766.

7. Ibid., Dec. 31, 1761.

8. Account Book of Stephen Thorp, Thorp Family Papers, FHS.

9. Schenck, *Fairfield* II, 267.

10. FTR, B, I, Dec. 28, 1785.

11. Ezra Stiles, *The Itineraries and other Miscellanies of Ezra Stiles, 1754-1794* (New Haven, 1916), 437-38; Schenck, *Fairfield,* II, 91.

12. Indenture of James Marsh, March 4, 1747, in Bradley Family Papers, FHS.

13. *Bi-centennial of . . . of the First Church . . . of Bridgeport,* 28-29; Merwin, *Ye Church and Parish,* 17-18.

14. William Wheeler's Journal, in Lathrop, *Black Rock,* 26.

# Revolution

THE FRENCH AND INDIAN WAR left Great Britain deeply in debt and determined to force her North American colonies to begin to pay at least a part of what it cost each year to administer and protect them. Fairfield men and women believed that their contribution to the recent war had been monumental. British attempts to impose taxes upon them were motivated by a broader scheme to limit their freedoms, they thought, and they determined to resist any British efforts to change their way of life. Fairfield's population was hardly a radical one—most of the town's residents had remained loyal to the conservative, Old Light position during the Great Awakening, and the deferential political system that still flourished in town was probably as antiquated as any in the colony. But life was good in Fairfield, and by standing up to Great Britain, the town sought to keep what it had, to resist the changes it saw being inflicted upon it.[1]

The Stamp Act, passed by Parliament in March 1765, taxed a variety of items, including newspapers, pamphlets, legal papers, mortgages, college diplomas, almanacs, tavern licenses, and advertisements. The governor of Connecticut, Thomas Fitch, argued that the law was unconstitutional, a violation of Connecticut's charter, which guaranteed that the people of Connecticut would be taxed only with their consent. He sent Jared Ingersoll, a New Haven attorney, to England to work for the measure's defeat. But once the bill became law, Fitch reluctantly decided that it must be enforced in Connecticut, and on October 31, 1765, took an oath to that effect. Jared Ingersoll also abandoned his opposition and, believing himself better suited that some royal official who could barely find Connecticut on a map, agreed to become the stamp distributor for the colony.

The people of Connecticut were furious with both Ingersoll and Fitch. The recently organized Sons of Liberty intimidated Ingersoll into quitting his post, and in the spring of 1766, the electorate summarily turned Fitch out of office. Also denied office in the 1766 elections were the four assistants, or members of the upper house of the General

Assembly, who had administered the Stamp Act oath to Fitch. One of the four was Ebenezer Silliman of Fairfield.

Born in 1707, Silliman was the grandson of Daniel Sillimandi, an Italian Protestant who had grown up in Geneva, where his family had fled to escape religious persecution. Daniel had arrived in Fairfield in the middle of the seventeenth century, and by the third quarter of the eighteenth his grandson Ebenezer was probably the most influential man in town. At various times he served as a justice of the peace, probate judge for Fairfield County, delegate to the General Assembly, major in the militia, and, after 1739, an assistant. In 1743 he became one of the five assistants who acted as the justices of the Superior Court of Connecticut, a position he held until 1766.

Fairfield condemned the Stamp Act as adamantly as almost any town in Connecticut, and the Sons of Liberty prospered in town. Jonathan Sturges served as secretary of the entire Connecticut organization. On November 12, 1765, the Sons of Liberty placed an effigy of Jared Ingersoll on a cart which a man in hangman's garb drove through the streets of Fairfield to cries of "Liberty and Property!" Erecting a makeshift gallows, the crowd hanged and burned the dummy, into which a charge had been implanted. The resulting explosion tore it "Limb from Limb."[2]

As vehement as Fairfield was in opposing the Stamp Act and as much as Silliman was defiled in other parts of Connecticut, in October 1766 the town, true to both its independent nature and its general conservatism, elected Silliman a deputy to the General Assembly, a position he would continue to hold, save for two terms, until May 1774. He became Speaker of the House in 1773 and, by virtue of his position as Speaker, one of the nine-member Connecticut Committee of Correspondence, established in May 1773 by the General Assembly to encourage communication between Connecticut and the other colonies. When Silliman attempted to regain his position as an assistant, he foolishly attached his fate to that of Fitch by supporting the former governor's election to the same body. Both men were defeated. Silliman lost his position on the Committee of Correspondence and Fairfield refused to send him back to the General Assembly.

Silliman's politics would best be described as moderate. He found it difficult to look with favor on the activities of Fairfield's most zealous advocates of colonial rights, the so-called Whigs. On November 30, 1765, for example, he wrote to Noah Hobart, still pastor of Fairfield's Prime Society, to complain about "the Late publick conduct of Job Bartram one of the communicants in the Church." Bartram played a prominent role in the Fairfield Sons of Liberty. Silliman took offense at Bartram's "calling upon God to damn all that had any hand in makeing the bill of Parliament called the Stamp Act: and in Libelling in the most Ignominious manner some in the most Elevated Stations in Civil authority." Old-fashioned and conservative, Silliman found such behavior reprehensible.[3]

At no point between the Stamp Act and the outbreak of fighting in April 1775 at Lexington and Concord, Massachusetts did Fairfield shrink from the Whig position. When Boston, in the wake of the Tea Party, became the particular object of British reprisals, Fairfield answered that city's call for assistance. The town meeting on September 20, 1774, voted "that a Committee be appointed to take in Subscriptions for the Relief of the Poor in the Town of Boston." Abraham Gold, Joseph Strong, and Moss Kent, members of the committee to collect the subscriptions, sent 634 bushels of rye and 116 bushels of wheat to Boston. Henry Hill expressed the Bostonians' gratitude: "The testimony which the patriotic inhabitants of the town of Fairfield have given of their attachment to the common & glorious cause of Liberty by their liberal donations of seven hundred & fifty bushels of grain by Capt. [Stephen] Thorp, had afforded much comfort as well as seasonable relief to their friends in Boston, who are now suffering under the cruel rod of tyranny & oppression."[4]

When the First Continental Congress approved the Association, a "non-importation, non-consumption, and non-exportation agreement directed against Great Britain," on October 20, 1774, Fairfield inhabitants, choosing "rather to die freemen than live in a state of servile subjection to any man or body of people on the face of the earth," voted "that any person or persons who shall directly or indirectly, with intent to dissuade, disunite or otherwise prevent us from strictly complying & conforming to said agreement & association" would have to face the community's wrath. At the same meeting, the residents appointed Gold Selleck Silliman, Jonathan Sturges, Andrew Rowland, Job Bartram, and Thaddeus Burr to consult with other towns in Fairfield County to determine the best means of enforcing the Association.[5]

The selection of Andrew Eliot, Jr. to take the place of Noah Hobart, who had died in 1773, as minister of the Prime Society also indicated Fairfield's support for the Whig or patriot cause. The son of the pastor of North Church in Boston, Eliot graduated from Harvard College in 1762, became a tutor at the college in 1768, and a fellow in 1773. The enthusiasm with which he supported the patriot cause created some apprehension among a few parishioners. During the debate over Eliot's appointment, Israel Bibbins, speaking for Eliot, described a dream in which he was carried off to "Satan's dominion." Bibbins found Satan in the middle of a conference in which he and his advisors were discussing the most expeditious means of keeping Eliot from the pulpit in Fairfield. Satan considered sending some of his imps to do his work, but then changed his mind. "You needn't go," he ordered. "I recollect that Mr. — — [the leader of Eliot's opposition] is on hand. He can do more to get them fighting than a dozen like you." Tradition says that the object of Bibbins's attack stormed out of the meeting, which then proceeded to elect Eliot unanimously.[6]

On Saturday morning, April 22, 1775, Fairfield learned that fighting between British troops and American militiamen had erupted in Massachusetts earlier in the week. Without hesitation forty-two Fairfield men, under the command of Captain David Dimon, Lieutenant Peter Henrick, and Lieutenant Edward Burroughs, left Fairfield for Boston to join the colonial defenders beginning to assemble there. Other members of Dimon's company, fearing that New York was a likely target for British attack, marched to that city to partcipate in its defense.

The troops had hardly departed when Stephen Thorp, Increase Bradley, and Peter Whitney, owners of sloops that operated out of Fairfield, sailed to Massachusetts with corn, rye, and rye flour for the American soldiers there. It had been many years since Fairfield had seen such a flurry of activity. General George Washington, on his way to assume command of the colonial soldiers at Boston, passed through Fairfield, conferring immortality on the home of Thaddeus Burr, where he spent the night. To Ellen Lothrop, there seemed no end to "the mighty armament & the vast preparations making to defend our country from the arm of tyranny."[7]

Fairfield contributed many sons to both the Continental Navy, which was never

*Portrait of Mary Fish Silliman (1736-1818), wife of Gold Selleck Silliman, painted by Reuben Moulthrop in 1794.*

large, and the Connecticut Navy, which sent fourteen vessels against the enemy during the course of the war. Two of these ships, the schooner *Mifflin* and the brig *America*, patrolled the waters off Fairfield County from Black Rock Harbor.[8]

    Captain Samuel Smedley's exploits on the high seas earned him a reputation as a great naval commander. Born in Fairfield on March 5, 1753, the son of James and Mary Burr Smedley, young Samuel grew up around Black Rock Harbor, where his father owned a one-sixth interest in Ichabod Wheeler's Upper Wharf. It was around the harbor that the boy met and came to idolize Captain Ebenezer Bartram, a West Indian trader who operated out of Black Rock. Upon learning of the war between the colonies and the mother country, Bartram joined the crew of the *Defense*, a 230-ton vessel that carried sixteen six-pound cannon and several swivel guns, required a crew of 130 men, and was commanded by Captain Seth Harding of Norwich. Smedley enlisted with Bartram, and before the year 1776 was out, the young man—barely twenty-three—had become captain of the *Defense*, a post he would hold until 1779, when the ship went down off New London. He later commanded two other vessels, the *Recovery* and the *Hibernia*. During the course of his service, Smedley captured eight large vessels and several smaller ones, was captured by the enemy twice, escaped the Old Mill Prison in England and found his way to Holland, and survived it all to return to Fairfield and the West Indian trade.

Fairfield's most important military leader was Gold Selleck Silliman. The son of Ebenezer, Gold Selleck Silliman had graduated from Yale in the class of 1752. He studied law and in 1768 became the king's attorney for Fairfield County and in 1772, a justice of the peace, a position he would hold for the rest of his life. In May 1774, as tensions between the colonies and England became acute, Governor Jonathan Trumbull appointed Silliman a major in the 4th Regiment of Militia. The following October his rank became lieutenant colonel and in May 1775 full colonel.

The burden on him and his family was heavy. His wife, Mary Fish Silliman, wrote her parents in Stonington in March to tell them "with a heart most tenderly affected that this morning an express comes in with orders from the Governor for my dearest Beloved to march forthwith to New York with a part of his regiment, there to wait the arrival of General Washington." The British had evacuated Boston and were about to turn their attention to New York, or so Washington believed. Silliman and his son William left Fairfield on March 27 for New York. Mary prayed that "the great happiness we have enjoyed may not end here . . . how happy we have been — such a husband, such a father few can lose." When she learned that the British were indeed headed for New York, Mary, as she had been taught by her father, the Reverend Joseph Fish, could only "commit my dearest Husband and dear Son to the care of that God that directs the lightning under the whole heaven, and can preserve you safe, tho instruments of death fly thick around you."[9]

Gold Silliman and his son survived the fighting in New York, but only to come home to Fairfield to more responsibility. In December 1776, the General Assembly restructured the militia, organizing it into six brigades and making Brigadier General Silliman commander of the 4th Brigade.

Some Fairfield men and women saw the conflict between the colonies and England in a totally different light from Smedley and Silliman. They were loyalists. The percentage of the town's population that remained loyal to George III was small. In 1774, 969 men between the ages of twenty and seventy lived in Fairfield; of this number, fewer than sixty — about 6 percent — were loyalists. This small minority quickly learned to keep its opinions to itself. During the fall of 1774, Whig mobs attacked loyalists to frighten them into silence. One Whig ruffian who joined others to terrorize the king's friends in Fairfield described a doleful scene when loyalists were discovered hiding in a loft: "Some [loyalists] were taking an everlasting leave of their families, whilst others were crying ready to kill themselves, for they all expected to be hung immediately on coming down."[10]

By 1776 official action was being directed against those loyal to England. In May of that year, Benjamin Huntington informed his wife that thirty-nine loyalists were currently imprisoned in the Fairfield jail. Their stay in prison would have been short unless Connecticut officials believed them to be dangerous. Joseph and Benjamin Hoyt remained in jail only a matter of weeks before they were released after paying the costs of their stay. Connecticut needed money to finance the war more than it needed full jails, so fines and special taxes were more suitable punishments than incarceration. In 1781 Fairfield imposed special taxes on David Adams, Thomas Turney, Hezekiah Jennings, and Increase Burr because they all had sons who went "over to the enemy of the United States."[11]

Loyalists from other parts of the United States, especially New York, did inflict real damage in Fairfield from time to time, but the local ones were too few, and too discreet, to menace the town.[12] They were more of a nuisance than a threat. In 1780, the people of Greenfield set up a liberty pole in their parish and "drank confusion to King George & hurra for Liberty." That night several loyalists, perhaps from Redding, slipped into Greenfield and cut the pole down. The Whigs set it in place again and plated it with iron as high as a man could reach. Several nights later their adversaries returned, this time armed with a saw and a ladder, and again leveled the pole.

Fairfield Whigs watched the adherents of the Anglican Church with particular care to see that they did nothing to damage the colonial cause. During the Stamp Act crisis, the Reverend James Lamson, Fairfield's Anglican pastor, complained to his superiors in England "that anarchy & disloyalty prevailed throughout the country in general; & that the missionaries were urging their parishioners to be loyal to the mother country by submission & quiet deportment." This position, he explained, has led to Anglicans being "threatened with having our houses pulled down over our heads."[13]

Lamson died in 1773, and the Reverend John Sayre, formerly of Newburgh, New York, took his place in 1774. An outspoken loyalist, Sayre brought the wrath of the community down upon himself. On January 28, 1777, the Fairfield County Court declared him to be "a person inimical and dangerous to the interests of the United States" and sent him to Farmington, where Colonel Isaac Lee was to supervise his activities. The court allowed him to return to Fairfield in the summer of 1777 only after Peter Bulkley, Jonathan Sturges, and Thaddeus Burr had interceded in his behalf. Upon his return, Sayre decided that the situation demanded prudence and so abandoned open advocacy of the king's cause, even holding his tongue when Whigs subjected the North Fairfield church, which was under his care, to "the most beastly defilements."[14]

Fairfield men and women had more important things to do during the war than harass local loyalists. Providing the town's share of soldiers for the Continental Army was an onerous task that involved, in addition to finding recruits, furnishing suitable clothing for them and caring for the families they left behind. Accomplishing this required the town to lay special taxes on several different occasions.

Special taxes were also necessary to provide bounties to men who enlisted in the Continental Army, a practice that became necessary toward the end of the war as the pool of men who had yet to serve became smaller, as weariness with the war became overwhelming, and as direct danger to the town increased. Beginning in June 1780, the town paid £10 to each man who enlisted. When even the incentive of the bounty proved insufficient to attract recruits, Fairfield empowered the selectmen "to hire for the deficient Classes such Recruits as are wanting to make out the Quota of soldiers in the Continental Army agreeable to an Act of Assembly made in October Last." This also failed to solve the problem; in 1782 the General Assembly issued "*Dooms* against the Town for neglecting to raise men for the service of the Last year." By this time the fighting was practically over, although technically a state of war existed with Great Britain until the autumn of 1783.[15]

Fairfield supplied provisions as well as men to the revolutionary effort. The war created huge demands for agricultural goods, of course, and supplying the needs of Connecticut, Continental, and French troops brought prosperity to many Fairfield farmers. In 1779 a Continental officer boasted that he could "procure anything" in Fairfield. Grain, especially wheat, remained important, and thousands of head of cattle came from Fairfield to provide meat for the armies. At the peak of demand, forty thousand head of cattle were grazing in the pastures of Fairfield County, the area of Connecticut that Governor Jonathan Trumbull asserted raised the "greatest surplus of provisions."[16] In addition, farmers such as Joseph Wakeman of North Fairfield exported thousands of pounds of pork and mutton. Fairfield horses, which already enjoyed a reputation for quality, did everything from carrying cavalry to pulling caissons to moving earth for fortifications.

Flax, long one of Fairfield's most lucrative crops, was also in demand. Connecticut commissioned Thaddeus Burr in February 1777 to obtain ten tons of well-dressed flax, Gold Selleck Silliman a month later to purchase thirty tons, and both Burr and Silliman in June to provide five tons. Just what Connecticut was doing with so much flax is unclear, but certainly, without the means to convert such quantities of flax into linen cloth, it was trading the crop for war materials. Burr and Silliman were ideally situated to obtain the flax, Fairfield still being the largest producer in Connecticut.

Some Fairfield farmers and merchants discovered that the British in New York City, where they were ensconced from 1776 until 1783, paid even higher prices for agricultural products than the Americans did. Trade with New York City was illegal but easily accomplished. Boats loaded with produce might legitimately depart for Stamford but mysteriously arrive in New York. Cattle or horses that were to be driven to Danbury might find their way to Westchester County and from there to the British in New York. Those suspected of engaging in this trade vehemently denied it; but the trade nevertheless existed, and Fairfield families, most of whom supported the American cause in all other respects, prospered because of it. On August 30, 1782, Fairfield appointed a committee "to inspect the behavior of Persons respecting the carrying on an illicit Trade with the enemies of the United States of America; and to assist the informing officers in their Duty in carrying into execution the Law of this state against illicit Trade." Unfortunately, the trade was too lucrative to be eliminated so easily.[17]

Fairfield's good times came to an end in 1778. By then raiding parties attacked and plundered the coast with such regularity that only in the interior were farmers immune to loss. But the raids had begun before 1779. As the Reverend Eliot explained, "Upon the removal of the seat of War from Boston [in 1776], the town became a place of danger. We were frequently in anxiety & doubtful Expectation, as it hindered many in the prosecution of their Schemes & plans of business." The pastor's brother, John Eliot, described Fairfield as "the center of danger" in 1777, and Mary Fish Silliman told her parents that her husband and his troops "have not gone so much as to the house of God for this great while without their *Arms*, daily expecting an attack."[18] During June 1777, Long Island loyalists raided and burned the home of William Palmer of Mill River. They took Palmer's daughter, Mary, when they departed, but Captain Amos Perry, Palmer's neighbor, overtook the raiders before they reached New York, rescued Mary, and captured their vessel.

In 1781 Andrew Eliot described the town's plight: "Plundering is carried on from both sides & we are in frequent alarm as well as constant uneasiness on account of the refugees [loyalists] who are embodied & are continually on the water & near or upon our shore." The particular object of their attention, he said, was Black Rock Harbor which "a kind Providence" had seen fit to preserve. Generally he believed "our situation however is very precarious."[19]

Fairfield had paid careful attention to its defenses. In February 1776, Thaddeus

*Silhouette of Rev. Andrew Eliot, minister of*
*First Church during the Revolutionary War.*

Burr and Gold Selleck Silliman called the General Assembly's attention to Fairfield's exposed position and to the vulnerability of Black Rock Harbor. The Connecticut Council of Safety ordered that twenty-five men be raised in Fairfield to improve the defenses at the harbor. Lieutenant Jonathan Mills oversaw the refurbishing of Black Rock Fort, located on Grover's Hill. In August 1776, he directed the installation of cannon, double-fortified twelve-pounders, these guns to be manned by twenty Connecticut soldiers, supplemented at night by twenty-six members of the Fairfield coast guard. Each night thirty other members of the guard—men from the militias of the Prime, Green's Farms, Greenfield, and Stratfield parishes—patrolled the shore from the Sasco River to Stratfield.

As the danger grew, Fairfield increased the size of its guard. In addition to the men at the fort, in 1779 the town stationed six men to patrol the coast near Stratfield; six at McKenzie's Point; six at Frost Point; and six at Compo. In the event of attack, their job was to spread the alarm. At the same time, Fairfield provided a modicum of comfort for the men at Black Rock Fort by building a barracks for them.

Governor Trumbull was particularly worried about the plight of Fairfield County's coastal communities. Because they had produced such large surpluses of provisions, he believed the British were intentionally maintaining pressure on them to "divert farmers . . . from their . . . husbandry." In January 1778, at his urging, the General Assembly ordered fifty matrosses to be stationed in Fairfield, and the Council of Safety authorized additional defenses to be built at Black Rock Fort.[20]

Neither the town's efforts nor the state's made Fairfield secure. The pace of the

*Revolution*

raids quickened after 1778. Andrew Eliot explained that "we are very much troubled on this Connecticut shore by marauding parties who pay us almost a weekly visit — somewhere or other — we live — we sleep in constant fear."[21] Albert Chapman of Green's Farms was at his home when he was kidnapped in 1779. On July 16, 1780, Captain Nehemiah Whitney was asleep in the cabin of his ship at Mill River. Hearing a noise on deck, he roused himself to investigate. Before he could determine what had awakened him, he was hit on the head and killed. Mill River, which had no fort to protect it, was the scene of another incursion on November 28, 1780. Twenty invaders landed, stole some animals, and killed some others. On December 9, sixty men attacked Compo. Raiders struck Mill River again on February 18, March 1, March 4, and March 22, 1781. On March 1, the raiders burned two houses and a barn and on March 4, two tide mills. They plundered two houses and kidnapped two persons on March 22. On April 18 and May 16, 1781, Black Rock Harbor was the object of attacks. Two hundred men landed at Compo on May 31, 1781, and stole cattle, sheep, and hogs and burned the guard-house before being driven off by Fairfield defenders, one of whom was killed and two others seriously wounded.

Prominence in the community made one more likely to be a target. About one o'clock on the morning of May 2, 1779, Mary and Gold Selleck Silliman were jarred from sleep by a noise at their door. Immediately aware of what the disturbance meant, Silliman reached for his gun and demanded to know who was there. "God damn you, let us in or your're a dead man," came the intruder's reply. Silliman saw eight or ten strange men in his front yard. He tried to fire his gun to frighten them away, but fortunately for his family's safety, the gun misfired. Before he realized it, the raiders had broken through a window, were in his home, and had taken him captive. They accompanied him to his bedroom so that he could dress, and withdrew only when they saw his pregnant wife trying to comfort their eighteen-month-old son, Gold Selleck Silliman, Jr. Silliman put on his clothes, embraced his wife and baby, and reluctantly went with his captors.[22]

Listening as they left, Mary Silliman realized that the raiders had seized their elder son, William, as well as her husband. She sent servants to spread the alarm and ran to the top of the house to see the direction the party was taking. She watched helplessly as the men crossed the two miles from Holland Hill, the site of the Silliman residence, to the head of Black Rock Harbor. For a few minutes she hoped that the gathering defenders could catch the invaders before they got away, but her husband's captors reached the harbor well before their pursuers, got into their whaleboats, and headed for Long Island. Mary heard nothing from or about her husband and son for three weeks.

Turned over to British officials in New York, the Sillimans had no more idea of what awaited them than Mary had. William was so ill at the time of his capture that the British, realizing he was of no value to them either sick or dead, paroled him almost immediately. His father, however, a rebel general, was to be held until the British could exchange him for a British prisoner of equivalent rank. The chances of an English officer or official of comparable position falling into the hands of the Americans were slight. General Silliman resigned himself to a long imprisonment.

By the autumn of 1779, with Silliman still in British hands, two of the general's friends, Captain David Hawley of Stratford and Captain Samuel Lockwood of Norwalk, decided to attempt to win his release themselves. Their plan was to kidnap loyalist Thomas

Jones, chief justice of the Superior Court on Long Island, who had himself been a prisoner in 1776 in Connecticut before being released pending an exchange that had yet to take place. Hawley and Lockwood assembled a crew of twenty-five men and on November 4, 1779, embarked in a whaleboat for Long Island. They reached Jones's home two days later, seized him, and began the hazardous march back to their boat. Six of their number fell behind and were captured by Long Islanders loyal to England. The others, with Jones, returned safely to Fairfield.

On the morning following his arrival in Connecticut, Mary Silliman received Jones as her guest for breakfast. She entertained him for two or three days, the judge generally proving to be "very unsociable."[23] Connecticut leaders, believing a rescue attempt was possible so long as Jones was held in coastal Fairfield, ordered his removal to Middletown, where he would be absolutely safe. While the judge himself was less than gracious while at the Silliman home, Mrs. Jones wrote to Mary Silliman to thank her for the hospitality she had shown her husband and sent her a pound of green tea as a token of her gratitude.

The taking of Jones failed to win Silliman's immediate release. Months of frustration ensued. On April 27, 1780, officials brought Jones back to Fairfield and at Black Rock put him aboard a boat that Mary Silliman had hired. If all went according to plan, the boat would take Jones to New York and immediately return with Mary's husband. On the morning of the twenty-seventh, the boat sailed out of Fairfield; Mary resigned herself to a long day of waiting and anxiety, at best; or perhaps disappointment once again.

By one o'clock that afternoon, Mary, watching from Holland Hill, saw the boat returning—hardly a good sign as it had not had enough time to make the round trip to New York. She described what happened next: "When our vessel came within call of our fort and battery on Grover's Hill near Black Rock, one called to know if they had Genl. Silliman on board. He then leapt on deck and waved his hat, when there was so loud a shout that we heard them plainly at our house (at the distance of two miles), and then all the cannon were fired off." Back on Holland Hill, the general, gone for almost a year, discovered that Gold Selleck Silliman, Jr., now two and a half years old, did not recognize him and that he had a new eight-month-old son whom he had never seen, Benjamin.[24]

Not all of the sights that greeted Silliman upon his return were welcome ones. While he had been held captive, the British army had visited Fairfield; the results were devastating. This was the second time that regular British troops had been in Fairfield during the war. On April 25, 1777, General William Tryon, former royal governor of New York, led a sizable army ashore at Compo. Danbury, where large quantities of American stores and provisions had been gathered, was Tryon's destination. He was eager to pass through Fairfield as quickly as possible, making his way to North Fairfield, what is called the town of Easton today, and Redding and then to Danbury. Fairfield escaped this incident generally unscathed. Tryon's second visit, which came during the summer of 1779 while Silliman remained in British hands, was a totally different matter.

The 1779 attack on Fairfield was one of three successive raids the British carried out in Connecticut during July. They struck New Haven, then Fairfield, then Norwalk. Sir Henry Clinton, who ordered the attacks, hoped to accomplish several objectives. First, he hoped that General Washington, who was then safely ensconced with his men in an almost invulnerable position at West Point on the Hudson River, would be drawn out of his bastion to come to the rescue of Connecticut; at which point Clinton, with

*Revolution*

fresh reinforcements, would force a decisive battle on the Americans, a battle that the forty-nine-year-old British commander was convinced he would win. Clinton also believed that the raids would destroy the rebel privateers that had been preying on British and loyalist shipping on Long Island Sound. Sir George Collier, who was temporarily in command of British naval forces in North America, stated that the privateers had "almost totally destroyed the trade of His Majesty's faithful subjects passing through the Sound." Even if Washington refused to be drawn into battle, the raids would eliminate the privateers.[25]

William Tryon, a vain and ambitious man but one with no particular appetite for cruelty, became the overall commander of the operation. Sir George Collier, a distinguished naval officer, was in charge of the British fleet that would convey the troops to Connecticut, and General George Garth, who heartily disliked the idea of fighting civilians, was third in command. Tryon and his men, 2600 soldiers, left New York on July 2. His force included the 54th Regiment, which had fought so valiantly at New York in 1776; the Regiment Landgraf, a Hessian unit; the King's American Regiment, made up of loyalists; the 7th Royal Fusileers; the famous 23rd Royal Welsh Fusileers, who had won the respect of the Americans at Bunker Hill; a regiment of Jaegers, which was a German light infantry force; and the flank companies of the Guards, the most élite companies within the most élite regiments in the British army. This was clearly no makeshift army; it was an army that meant business.

If any Americans had doubted this, their doubts were swept away by what happened in New Haven. Arriving on the morning of July 5 and departing on the evening of July 6, the British troops demonstrated that they were well-disciplined, effective soldiers. All had not gone according to plan in New Haven, but this was more a compliment to the bravery of American defenders than a criticism of the British soldiers.

The Fairfield coast guard first sighted the British fleet just before four o'clock on the morning of July 7. Isaac Jarvis, who commanded Black Rock Fort, ordered a gun fired to warn the town's residents. But even at this point, the British force's intention remained unclear. As Jarvis and the rapidly assembling defenders watched, the fleet disappeared in a heavy fog that began to roll in from the Sound.

Fairfielders assumed the worst. Ichabod Wheeler and his son, William, drove their livestock to Toilsome Hill, where they thought the animals would be safe. Mary Fish Silliman, who was in charge of the family while her husband was a prisoner, believed that Holland Hill was too close to the shore to be safe; pregnant though she was, she organized her family and fled to North Stratford, now Trumbull. There she would give birth to her son Benjamin, who would eventually become one of America's great scientists. Isaac Burr, a goldsmith, also fled, but only after climbing down his well to hide his inventory. Prudent Phillips was a washerwoman; fearing that her laundry might attract the attention of British plunderers, she took the time to conceal it in a thicket before she left town.

Priscilla Burr, the wife of Gershom Burr, had anticipated the worst when the British attacked New Haven. She had asked a friend in Norfield to bring his team to town and to help her remove her family and possessions in the event the British visited Fairfield. As soon as she heard the alarm she began to pack. Leaving her servants to hide what she was unable to take, she fled to the home of the Reverend Samuel Sherwood in Norfield, where she found his house filled with refugees from Greenfield and Green's Farms.

While the residents of Fairfield frantically prepared for the onslaught, the British fleet remained off the coast. At about ten in the morning, the fog began to clear, revealing the ships lying lazily off McKenzie's Point. Some Fairfielders hoped the fleet would move on, perhaps to some other part of the coast, perhaps, some optimists suggested, back to New York.

Hope turned to despair about three o'clock as the fleet came to life. Seamen began lowering small boats, and soldiers, equipped for combat, assembled on deck. The flank companies of the Guards were the first into the boats, followed by the Landgraf Regiment and the King's American Regiment. Within half an hour the boats, filled with soldiers, headed for the beach, and by four o'clock the troops, unopposed, began coming ashore near the foot of today's South Pine Creek Road. With the loyalist George Hoyt serving as guide, Tryon marched his men along the beach and then up what came to be known as Beach Road.

Tryon and his men had proceeded only a short way on the road when they came under heavy fire. Isaac Jarvis, from his position at Black Rock Fort, waited until the British were clearly within range and then ordered his men to begin firing their twelve-pounders, loaded with both grape and ball. At the same time, the men of the Fairfield militia, who had hidden between the center of town and the shore, opened fire with small arms.

The British halted and returned the fire. Tryon ordered the Guards forward, and Collier, aboard the *Camilla*, his flagship, directed his gunboats to commence firing on Black Rock Fort. Jarvis had to turn his attention to the navy, and the militia, unaccustomed to facing the likes of the Guards, fell back, allowing the British to proceed into the central part of Fairfield.

Tryon assembled his men on the meetinghouse green, commandeered the home of Benjamin Bulkley to serve as his headquarters, and waited for General Garth and his men to arrive. Garth's force had had to wait for the return of the small boats that had delivered Tryon's men to Fairfield before it could begin to come ashore. Garth's men eventually landed near Mill River and began the march over Sasco Hill to join Tryon.

In the meantime, the Fairfield defenders had fallen back to Round Hill, where Colonel Samuel Whiting was organizing his men to prevent Tryon's further penetration into town and to launch a small counterattack. Captain Thomas Nash and thirty men moved within range of the green and fired a volley or two at the British before being driven back to the safety of Round Hill.

While most of his men improvised fortifications on Round Hill, Whiting dispatched a smaller group to the Upper Bridge on the Boston Post Road, which provided the only possible route for large numbers of men to cross Ash Creek. They were to tear up the bridge's floor—an easy task for a farmer with a heavy chain and a yoke of oxen—and to set up defenses on the far side of the river. In this way, Whiting hoped to prevent the British from attacking Black Rock Fort from the rear.

While Tryon waited for Garth, he sent out parties to test the American defenses on Round Hill and to seize the Upper Bridge. Whiting had done his work well. The defenders at Round Hill refused to surrender any of their territory to the British, and the men at the Bridge, having dismantled its floor, managed to keep the attackers on the west side of the river. Tryon was furious when he learned that he would be unable to cross Ash Creek. He had planned to lead both his own and Garth's force into Stratfield,

*Thaddeus Burr, wealthy landowner and builder of the Burr homestead which still stands on Old Post Road.*

*Fairfield: the biography of a community*

*John Singleton Copley's matching portrait of Eunice Dennie Burr, painted between 1758 and 1760.*

*Revolution*

strike Black Rock Fort from the rear, destroy the shipping at the harbor, and reembark from that location. Now he had to revise his plans, and as he did, more and more defenders were arriving in Fairfield. Units that two days earlier had answered the New Haven alarm began trudging into Fairfield, exhausted but determined.

By this time, few civilians remained in town. A few women, confident that British soldiers were invariably gentlemen, had foolishly stayed behind. Eunice Burr, whose husband, Thaddeus, was a dominant political figure in town, thought she was safe within her home. Some soldiers broke in, found her in her bedroom, tore down her curtains and destroyed her furniture, then stole her silver shoe buckles and silver buttons. The invaders were less gentle with Lucretia Radfield. They demolished her furniture and, as she later testified, "attempted, with threats and promises, to prevail upon me to yeild to their unchaste and unlawful desires." Because she "obstinately denied them my body, these men then and there dragged me to bed and attempted violence, but thanks to God there appeared that instant to come two persons who rescued me." Her rescuers must have been invaders; no Americans were in a position to save anyone in the area controlled by General Tryon and his troops.[26]

While Tryon and Garth remained in town, their troops behaved themselves amazingly well. A Mrs. Beardsley went into labor while the British controlled the town. Ruana Robertson, after spending the night trying to make Mrs. Beardsley as comfortable as possible, later testified that "all the officers appeared disposed to treat her, and her assistance with decency." Eunice Burr reported after the raid that General Tryon, upon learning that she had been roughly treated by some of his men, "was kind enough to order two centrys at the house, which caused me a more quiet night than I feared."[27]

Tryon's consideration extended only to Fairfield residents, not their property. Unable to force his way to the rear of Black Rock Fort, he tried to intimidate the Fairfield defenders by burning some houses. Just before sunset he ordered his men to set fire to the house of Isaac Jennings. Elijah Abel's home was the second to burn. After only a few houses had been destroyed, Tryon sent the Reverend Sayre to Colonel Whiting with a message informing the defenders that peaceful Americans who remained at home would be spared any harm, either to their person or to their property. Whiting's reply came back with Sayre: "Connecticut having nobly dared to take up arms against the cruel despotism of Britain and as the flames, have now preceded the answer to your flag, they will persist to oppose to their utmost, that power exerted against injured innocence."[28] While less than a master of syntax, Whiting made his point clear.

Tryon ordered more houses burned. As the flames spread, a thunderstorm struck Fairfield. It was enough to make one believe, said Timothy Dwight, "that the final day had arrived, and that, amid this funereal darkness, the morning would speedily dawn to which no night would ever succeed, the graves yeild up their inhabitants, and the trial commence at which was to be finally settled the destiny of men." The flames were clearly visible to the defenders on Grover's Hill.[29]

The Reverend Sayre went to Tryon to ask him to stop the burning. Tryon refused but did agree to grant protections to some homes, including Sayre's and the Reverend Eliot's and the two houses of worship in the center of town. Garth, apparently appalled by Tryon's tactic, "treated the inhabitants with as much humanity as his errand would admit," said Eliot. By morning, much of the central section of Fairfield remained untouched by the flames.[30]

*Fairfield: the biography of a community*

The most serious fighting of the raid broke out just before sunrise, when Tryon sent word to Collier and the navy to destroy Black Rock Fort. The navy began its bombardment about four o'clock on the morning of July 8. The *Hussar*, a galley, fired seventy-five balls at the fort. Jarvis and his men held their ground, answered the British cannonade with one of their own, and added insults shouted through a speaking trumpet. When the fleet withdrew, after about three hours, the Americans remained in the fort. Aware that returning by the Beach Road would mean coming within the range of Black Rock Fort, Tryon ordered his men to march to Mill River and to board the small boats there. The British withdrawal began about eight A.M., the militia harassing them, Whiting reported, "very much at their embarkation, till afternoon when they all got on board."[31]

Tryon ordered the Jaegers to cover the withdrawal. Concerned only with their own safety, the Jaegers left havoc in their wake. They bayoneted three men to death: the elderly black servant of Jonathan Lewis; Solomon Sturges, the father of David Ogden's widow; and a man who worked for Samuel Penfield and who had just recently arrived in Connecticut from Ireland. Joseph Gold was shot and killed when he ignored a soldier's order to halt. The Jaegers pulled one woman "about by the hair of her head, tore her cloaths of [sic] and swore they would kill her." Andrew Eliot later reported: "The rear guard, consisting of a banditti the vilest that was ever let loose among men, set fire to everything which General Tryon left." They burned the houses of Eliot, Sayre, and Thaddeus Burr and even the two churches in town and then fled "persued through the burning houses by the enraged inhabitants." To get them off the shore, Collier had to order gunboats to drive the defenders back from the beach.[32]

With the departing raiders went the Reverend Sayre, who believed he could no longer safely remain in Fairfield, and his wife and eight children; he died in Burton, New Brunswick, in 1784. George Hoyt, who had served as Tryon's guide, also left. In addition, the British took several prisoners, including Joshua Beers and Jonathan Bulkley, Hoyt's brother-in-law. David Beers had also been captured by the British but he avoided being taken to New York by explaining to Tryon "that he had a large family of small children and wife, that he supposed his house and property was destroyed, [and] the genl. at the place of embarkation released him."[33]

By two o'clock the British fleet was sailing away from Fairfield. Its next stop— after a brief visit to Green's Farms, where a raiding party burned fourteen houses, twelve barns, and a meetinghouse—was Norwalk, where it left even more destruction.

With the British gone, Whiting was eager to calculate the extent of his losses, but an urgent call for assistance prevented him from doing so. Mrs. Jonathan Bulkley, whose brother, George Hoyt, had served as Tryon's guide and whose husband had departed— many mistakenly believed voluntarily—with the British, had sent the plea for help when she discovered that Captain Jonathan Sturges and his militiamen had brought a cannon to her home and had promised to blow it and its inhabitants to pieces in retaliation for the misery that her brother, and supposedly her husband, had brought upon the town. Sturges was supported by 150 men, but Whiting was no more intimidated by them than he had been by Tryon. He promised to arrest any who refused to disburse immediately. The irate and exhausted militiamen went home.

According to Whiting, nine or ten Americans died defending Fairfield. He was unable to determine the number wounded or missing. Nine of the British soldiers lost their lives, thirty were wounded, and five missing. Town officials estimated that the

British did £34,359:5:6 worth of damage in Fairfield including Green's Farms, a figure that the General Assembly considered exaggerated and reduced to £23,893:12:8. Among the property destroyed were ninety-seven houses, sixty-seven barns, twenty-eight shops and stores, twenty storehouses and outbuildings, two schools, three churches, the jail, and the courthouse.

Despite repeated entreaties, Fairfield men and women who suffered losses during the raid received no indemnification from the General Assembly until 1792. In that year, after the legislature had again investigated the damage done by the British in all the Connecticut towns raided, it granted "to the sufferers, named on the state record, or to their legal representatives if deceased, and to their heirs and assigns forever, 500,000 acres of land, owned by Connecticut, situated west of Pennsylvania." The 500,000 acres, part of the Western Reserve, was known as the Firelands. Fairfield's share was 47,500 acres. Few of the Fairfield people who lost property during the raid were either alive in 1792 or willing to abandon Connecticut for the wilderness of northeastern Ohio. For the most part, the "sufferers" or their heirs sold the land for much less than it was worth to speculators, who in turn sold it for all that it was worth.[34]

Rebuilding Fairfield was a task of gigantic proportions. The agricultural surplus that had been the key to Fairfield's prosperity for so many years was now consumed purchasing materials to rebuild houses. Tryon had barely left when Captain Stephen Thorp loaded his ship with twenty barrels of pork, thirty barrels of flour, four thousand pounds of flax, and six hundred bushels of Indian corn to take to Boston to trade for lumber. Individual citizens were left to their own resources to rebuild.

The Prime Society and the Green's Farm Society shared £1,000 that the state granted to them to rebuild, the money derived from the sale of confiscated loyalist properties in Fairfield County. The Reverend Eliot, an accomplished fundraiser, convinced friends and relatives in Boston that rebuilding the Fairfield meetinghouse was a worthy cause. Long accustomed to frugality, the parishioners shifted through the ashes of their old meetinghouse to salvage nails and iron that could be sold. Even with the best efforts of Eliot and his congregation, it took seven years to assemble the funds needed for the new structure, which finally received worshipers on March 26, 1786.

The plight of Fairfield Anglicans was even more severe. Since Sayre had fled with Tryon, the church had to rely on the services of a lay reader, Philo Shelton, for several years. Shelton read in the homes of John Sherwood in Greenfield or Abraham Bulkley near the meetinghouse green or Hezekiah Sturges at Mill Plain on some Sundays and in the churches at Stratfield and North Fairfield the rest of the time. Shelton, a native of North Stratford and a member of Yale's class of 1775, was ordained in the Episcopal Church in 1785, took charge of the Fairfield congregation, and became the impetus for the new church. After receiving permission to build on the military parade green at Mill Plain, the Episcopalians began work on a church, which was finally opened on September 5, 1790.

Public buildings had to be replaced more rapidly. The courthouse, which had only been built in 1768, was too expensive a structure to rebuild immediately, so the town voted to construct a temporary building that would serve until Fairfield County could find the means to build a suitable replacement. In May 1791, the General Assembly authorized the county to establish a lottery to raise £1300 to erect a courthouse in Fairfield and a jail in Danbury. The new courthouse, which served as both the county courthouse and Fairfield's town house and which still stands as the central part of the town hall, was completed in 1794. The Fairfield jail, never as elaborate as the Danbury prison, was reconstructed at its former location. The Prime Society, which controlled both the schools that had been lost, lacked the means to rebuild them and was reduced to holding classes in the makeshift town house. Only after 1795, when the General Assembly removed control of the schools from the parishes and placed it in the hands of newly created school districts, were they rebuilt.

Tryon's raid cost Fairfield more than buildings; it put an end to the prosperity the town had enjoyed during the early years of the war. That prosperity had been slowly withering before 1779 as the town's maritime commerce shrank under British restrictions. Fairfield's shipbuilders had already forsaken Mill River for the upper areas of Black Rock Harbor, which was better hidden from the prying eyes of British sailors cruising on Long Island Sound and was protected by the fort on Grover's Hill. But the raid crippled the shipping industry. Fairfield's maritime population, which was considerable, had to find new ways of making a living.

Privateering impressed many as a solution. Since 1776 Judge Gold Selleck Silliman, who was a justice of the peace as well as a general in the militia, and Judge Thaddeus Burr had had the power to warrant ship captains to attack and capture British vessels, and since that same year, Judge Abraham Davenport, a Stamford man, had served as judge of the Fairfield County Maritime Court, one of five such courts in the state that both passed on the legality of the captures made by privateers and divided the money derived from the sale of condemned vessels between the state of Connecticut and the captors.

Hezekiah Gold commanded a privateer that carried seven guns. His most important capture was an enemy privateer manned by a crew of thirty-five that he took off Stratford Point. Captain Caleb Brewster of Black Rock Harbor attacked the enemy with long, open whaleboats, which could be either rowed or sailed and were usually armed only with a swivel gun. The whaleboats were effective against enemy whaleboats, many of which could be found swarming in the waters of Long Island Sound, and for making hit-and-run raids on Long Island. Brewster was adept at both. On one occasion three of his boats encountered three enemy boats; he and his men killed six of the enemy sailors and took two of the boats captive. In November 1780, he led a fleet of eight whaleboats to Old Field Point on Long Island, where he destroyed a loyalist stronghold and took several captives. Demonstrating his versatility, Brewster also commanded a sloop that he had refitted as a privateer. On February 20, 1783, he and his crew seized a British armed vessel, the *Fox*, his most famous capture.

Probably the single most impressive accomplishment of a Fairfield privateersman occurred in December 1782, when Captain Abraham Cooper Woodhull, who was cruising Long Island Sound in two whaleboats that he had taken out of Black Rock Harbor, captured the *Robinhood*. The thirty-ton schooner was carrying five hundred bushels of wheat, corn, and rye as well as three hogsheads and two barrels of flour, twenty-eight barrels of beef, one hundred pounds of cheese, and one hundred barrels of sea coal. Even after the state of Connecticut had taken its share and he had divided what was left with his crew, this single capture made Woodhull a prosperous man.

Few captains were as fortunate as Woodhull. To run afoul of a British man-of-war probably meant either death or years in a British prison, and some British merchant ships were too much for either whaleboats or sloops to handle. In desperation, some whaleboat commanders took up plundering along the north shore of Long Island. Although the town disapproved "of importing goods into this Town that are plundered from the Inhabitants of Long Island," the practice continued as long as sailors remained unable to participate in peaceful commercial activities. William Wheeler of Black Rock noted in his journal on June 27, 1781, that many Fairfield men "go to Long Island to plunder." With their ocean-borne trade defunct and much of their town in ashes, they had few other options.[35]

Difficult as the years after the raid were, Fairfield men and women attempted to put aside the hatred it had engendered. Some of this hatred could be vented in harmless ways; the town meeting on July 20, 1779, voted "to put about subscriptions to raise a sum of money, as a reward for any person or persons that shall captivate or take prisoner General William Tyron, who commanded the British troops when they burnt this town." The possibility that Tryon would become a prisoner of the Americans was about as likely as Andrew Eliot's joining up with the King's American Regiment, but offering the reward doubtless relieved some of Fairfield's frustrations.[36]

On the other hand, much of the town's rage was misdirected. Fairfield was understandably eager, as stated in a town meeting resolution of April 10, 1783, "to remove all such Persons from this Town who are now in it or may hereafter come into it, who have gone to & joined the enemy." But the town went even further and sought to exclude all former loyalists, even those who had in no way aided the British cause during the war. On August 18, 1783, the town authorized the selectmen to ferret out those in Fairfield "who are Persons dangerous in their political principles to the Town or the state and forthwith to warn every such Person to depart out of the Town."[37]

Such a policy was, at best, shortsighted. Fairfield, reeling from the effects of the raid, needed all the help it could find to recover. Many former loyalists, now thoroughly reconciled to living outside the British Empire, were persons with economic resources, important commercial connections, and genuine talent. By excluding them, the town unnecessarily extended its convalescence at precisely the time when its dominant position in southwestern Connecticut was being challenged. At the end of the American Revolution, one would have had to wonder whether Fairfield could preserve its place of eminence.

## NOTES

1. The most useful studies of Fairfield during the American Revolution are Joy Day Buel and Richard Buel, Jr., *The Way of Duty: A Woman and Her Family in Revolutionary America* (New York, 1984), and Thomas J. Farnham, "The Day the Enemy Was in Town: The British Raids on Connecticut, July, 1779," *Journal of the New Haven Colony Historical Society*, 24 (Summer 1976), 3-63.

2. New Haven *Connecticut Gazette*, Nov. 15, 1765.

3. Ebenezer Silliman to Noah Hobart, Nov. 30, 1765, Hobart Family Papers, FHS.

4. FTR, B, I, Sept. 20, Dec. 29, 1774.

5. Ibid., Dec. 29, 1774.

6. Child, *An Old New England Church*, 83-84.

7. Ellen Lothrop to Nathaniel Lothrop. Sept. 10, 1775, Hobart Family Papers, FHS.

8. Elsie N. Danenburg, *Naval History of Fairfield County Men in the Revolution* (Fairfield, 1977), tells the story of this aspect of the revolution.

9. Buel and Buel, *The Way of Duty*, 105, 106, 109.

10. Oscar Zeichner, *Connecticut's Years of Controversy, 1750-1776* (Chapel Hill, 1949), 203.

11. FTR, B, I, May 18, 1781.

12. William Wheeler's Journal, in Lathrop, *Black Rock*, 34.

13. Beardsley, *Episcopal Church*, I, 242.

14. Ibid. I, 325; Schenck, *Fairfield*, II, 337.

15. FTR, B, I, March 13, 1781; Sept. 25, 1782.

16. Saladino, "The Economic Revolution," 56, 65.

17. FTR, B, I, Aug. 30, 1782.

18. Andrew Eliot, An Address to the First Church. . . July 30, 1779, Fairfield Family Papers, FHS; John Eliot to Jeremy Belknap, March 19, 1777, in the *Collections of the Massachusetts Historical Society*, 6th Series, IV, 107; Buel and Buel, *The Way of Duty*, 132.

19. Andrew Eliot to— — —, March 20, 1781, Fairfield Family Papers, FHS.

20. Saladino, "The Economic Revolution," 62-63.

21. Andrew Eliot to— — —, July 9, 1781, Fairfield Family Papers, FHS.

22. Buel and Buel, *The Way of Duty*, 145-146.

23. Ibid., 164.

24. Ibid., 170.

25. Sir George Collier to Sir Henry Clinton, June 5, 1779, Sir Henry Clinton Papers, William L. Clements Library, University of Michigan.

26. *The Public Records of the State of Connecticut*, ed. Charles J. Hoadly, et al. (Hartford, 1894 and continuing), II, 558-59. Hereinafter cited as *Connecticut State Records*.

27. Ibid. II, 559-60.

28. Samuel Whiting to William Tryon, July 7, 1779, Horatio Gates Papers, New-York Historical Society.

29. Timothy Dwight, *Travels in New England and New York*, 4 vols. (Cambridge, Mass., 1969), III, 361.

30. Schenck, *Fairfield*, II, 392.

31. Samuel Whiting to Jonathan Trumbull, July 9, 1779, in *Collections of the Massachusetts Historical Society*, 7th Series, II, 405.

32. Schenck, *Fairfield*, II, 392; Priscilla Burr to Helen Lothrop, Aug. 10, 1779, in the *Bulletin of the Connecticut Historical Society*, I (Aug. 1936), 3-4; William Wheeler's Journal, in Lathrop, *Black Rock*, pp. 33-34.

33. *Connecticut State Records*, II, 554.

34. Ibid.

35. FTR, B, I, July 20, 1779; William Wheeler's Journal, in Lathrop, *Black Rock*, 36.

36. FTR, B, I, July 20, 1779.

37. Ibid., April 10, Aug. 18, 1783.

# After Independence

U NLIKE MOST large Connecticut
towns, Fairfield experienced a significant growth in population during the
war. Fairfield counted 4863 residents in 1774, a figure that had increased to 5276 by
1782, the date of the next enumeration. But while the population had become larger,
the amount of taxable property had declined, largely because of the raid, from a per
capita average of £10.49 to £7.91. Neither Norwalk nor New Haven, the two other
towns attacked in 1779, experienced such a deterioration of wealth.

Other changes occurred. The heightened awareness of political rights that developed
during the revolutionary period encouraged two Fairfield parishes "to try for town
privileges," that is, to become separate towns. The first was Redding, located a great
distance from the site of town meetings, which took place with considerable regularity
between 1765 and 1789. The people of Redding finally succeeded in convincing the
General Assembly to separate them from Fairfield in 1767. Twenty years later, Fairfield
stated its willingness "that that part of the Parish of Northfairfield and that part of the
Parish of Norfield that lye in the Town of Fairfield be incorporated into a Township
and have all the priviledges and immunities allowed by Law."[1] The General Assembly
proceeded to create the town of Weston, which in 1787 included both modern Weston
and the town now known as Easton. The departure of Redding and Weston reduced
the size of Fairfield by 82.3 square miles.

Other aspects of Fairfield life remained unchanged. Politics remained as conservative as ever, with a heavy concentration of political power in the hands of a few men.
Certainly no new, egalitarian leadership emerged from the turmoil of the revolution.
Although Thaddeus Burr was probably the most important political leader in town during
the revolutionary period, the influence of the Burr family declined somewhat and that
of the Wakemans, the Hubbells, and briefly the Sillimans grew. After the war, Elijah
Abel, Nathaniel Burr's son-in-law, assumed Thaddeus Burr's dominant role.

This same conservatism was evident during the 1780s. At the time of Shays'

*John Warner Barber's engraving of the town green in 1836 showing (from left) the jail, a private house, the rear of the courthouse, and the meetinghouse.*

Rebellion, an uprising of Massachusetts farmers suffering under the yoke of heavy taxes, Fairfield leaders eagerly called for volunteers to contain the rebellion and to keep it away from Connecticut. Lieutenant Daniel Bradley commanded the troops that stood ready to march to Springfield in 1787. When the movement for a revised United States constitution developed, Fairfield endorsed the idea, even though the town had strongly supported the original constitution, the Articles of Confederation, in 1778. Men like Jonathan Sturges and Thaddeus Burr, men whom Fairfield greatly respected, argued that an expansion of federal power would mean a government strong enough to bridle the passions of the "vicious sort," strong enough to prevent such disturbances as the recent uprising in Massachusetts. Once the Philadelphia Convention had completed a draft of the new document, Fairfield was quick to dispatch Sturges and Burr to the Connecticut ratifying convention in Hartford, where Connecticut became the fifth state to approve the Constitution.

During September 1789, Samuel Davis of Massachusetts visited Fairfield. He noted in his journal: "Mr. Eliot's meeting-house is yet unfinished; and the court-house scarcely merits the name, being a temporary building. Fairfield, it is well known, was once a beautiful place. The public buildings, as well as many elegant private dwellings, were burnt down during the Revolution; and men of ample estate yet reside in very humble abodes." George Washington, newly elected president of the United States, visited the following month. He found evidence of the destruction wrought by the British during the war, but was more impressed by "all the farmers busily employed."[2]

Fairfield was at work trying to reestablish the prosperity it once had known. Its

*After Independence*

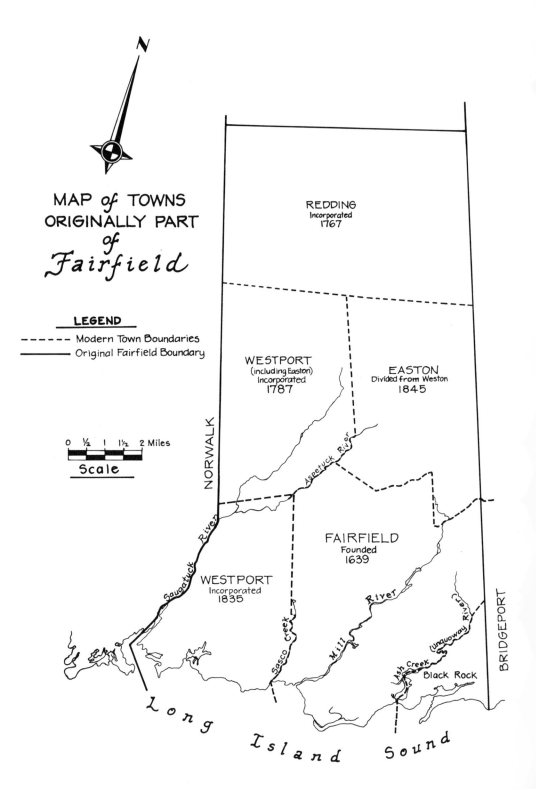

MAP of TOWNS
ORIGINALLY PART
of
*Fairfield*

LEGEND
- - - - - Modern Town Boundaries
———— Original Fairfield Boundary

0   ½   1   1½   2 Miles
Scale

REDDING
Incorporated
1767

WESTPORT
(including Easton)
Incorporated
1787

EASTON
Divided from Weston
1845

FAIRFIELD
Founded
1639

WESTPORT
Incorporated
1835

NORWALK

BRIDGEPORT

Saugatuck River

Aspetuck River

Sasco Creek

Mill River

Ash Creek

(Unquoway River)

Black Rock

Long Island Sound

*Fairfield: the biography of a community*

maritime industry quickly revived, and ships began leaving for Boston, New York, and the West Indies with the agricultural surpluses that Fairfield farmers were again producing. Flax, wheat, dairy products, and meat went to the neighboring states, especially New York. Livestock, corn, barreled meat, and lumber products were dispatched to the West Indies. Black Rock Harbor, out of which thousands of bushels of flax and grain and thousands of head of livestock were exported annually, was so busy that the town meeting established a committee "to lay and bound out the land belonging to the town at Black Rock upper wharf. . . into proper lotts for the building of wharfs and stores upon for the accomodation of such gentlemen as may choose to establish themselves in trade." The shipyards at Black Rock had developed so solid a reputation for quality work that vessels came there from all over southwestern Connecticut to be repaired or fitted out for long voyages.[3]

Samuel Smedley, his military exploits behind him, was the master of the brig *Greenfield*, a West Indian trader owned by Samuel Bradley and his sons, Zalmon and Walter, of Greenfield. Smedley sailed out of Black Rock from 1784 until 1789, carrying horses, barrel staves and hoops, corn, and oats for Hispaniola, St. François, and Turks Island. Molasses, rum, sugar, and salt typically constituted the cargo on the *Greenfield*'s return to Fairfield. Smedley abandoned the West Indian trade only when President Washington appointed him as the first customs collector for the Federal District Port of Fairfield, which included all of Fairfield County.

Mill River, which had languished during the revolution, became deeply involved in the coasting trade. By 1792 the demands on the port's facilites were so great that Fairfield granted to Eliphalet Thorp, Zalmon Bradley, Walter Bradley, and Samuel Cannon "a Water Lot at the Mouth of Mill River . . . for the purpose of building a wharf & Buildings to carry on the business of navigation." Captain Jacob White began constructing a dock on the north side of the river two years later, and in 1799 Fairfield petitioned the General Assembly for permission to establish a lottery "for the purpose of Sinking the channel of mill river harbour."[4]

The sloop *Susanah*, Captain David Banks, master, regularly sailed from Mill River to New York and beyond. On a typical voyage, the *Susanah* carried flax, corn, wheat, and barreled beef and pork to New York and returned with a whole variety of manufactured items, including cotton cloth, pots and pans and pails, nails, and shoes. Occasionally Banks would take on lumber, shingles, and clapboards in North Carolina, leaving there the country produce that Fairfield grew in such abundance.

By the 1790s, Black Rock and Mill River were busier than they had ever been. They were also competing with another port, which, although it had been of no consequence until the American Revolution, was taking more and more shipping away from them. It was located a short distance up the Pequonnock River and was known as Newfield Harbor.

First developed during the 1770s by Stephen Burroughs, Jr., Newfield had enjoyed a distinct advantage over Black Rock and especially Mill River during the revolution: the upper anchorage, three miles from the mouth of the harbor, was completely hidden from British ships that passed on Long Island Sound. Newfield became known as the safest port in southwestern Connecticut. Even so, the community that developed around the harbor, also known as Newfield, included only two stores and two small wharves and was distinctly smaller than either Mill River or Black Rock at the end of

*Engraving of Rev. Timothy Dwight, minister of Greenfield Hill Congregational Church from 1783 to 1795, founder of Greenfield Hill Academy, and president of Yale from 1795 to 1817.*

the revolution in 1783. But in 1789, when the visiting Samuel Davis journeyed to Newfield, he saw "a city in miniature. Streets, docks, and trades denote its future character of commercial importance."[5]

During the 1790s, Newfield—technically part of Stratford—became the fastest-growing community in Connecticut. It developed "a great & constant intercourse" with upper Fairfield County and Litchfield County. A crude system of highways extended from Newfield to New Milford and eventually to Litchfield. In 1797 the road between New Milford and Litchfield became a greatly improved toll road known as the New Milford and Litchfield Turnpike, and in 1801, by which time the Connecticut General Assembly had transformed Newfield into the Borough of Bridgeport, the route that connected the former Newfield with New Milford had become the Bridgeport and Newtown Turnpike. The existence of these roads allowed farmers to ship "vast quantities" of produce to Bridgeport, which in turn became the hinterland's source of a whole variety of goods obtained in New York, Boston, and the West Indies.[6]

Neither Southport nor Black Rock enjoyed the advantage of such extensive trade connections with the interior. Much of the agricultural produce from the Danbury area found its way to Norwalk rather than to either of the Fairfield ports. The Black Rock Turnpike, which eventually connected Black Rock with Easton and later with Brookfield, came into being thirty-one years after the Bridgeport and Newtown Turnpike, and the founders of the Branch Turnpike, a spur of which brought Mill River into contact with Easton, Monroe, and Newtown, only created their road in 1831. The result was that Black Rock and Mill River, which competed with each other as well as with Norwalk and Westport, failed to develop with the intensity with which Bridgeport grew.

But it would be a mistake to believe that Fairfield in 1800 was foundering. On the contrary, Fairfield was again beginning to thrive, its ports busy and its farmers prospering. When Samuel Davis visited the home of Samuel Bradley, in Greenfield, he commented on his host's affluence: "This gentleman is a farmer of opulence and gives us the cordial welcome of abundance." According to Davis, Greenfield, untouched by Tryon's arsonists, was generally a flourishing area. He called upon Timothy Dwight, the minister in Greenfield, and praised his residence: "[It] commands a beautiful view of Long Island" and "his gardens [are] well cultivated."[7]

The fact that Dwight was serving in Greenfield was a sign that the parish was doing well. Dwight, the grandson of Jonathan Edwards, had graduated from Yale in 1769, taught at the grammar school in New Haven and at Yale until 1777, served as an army chaplain until 1783, and then come to Greenfield, where he was the highest-paid clergyman in Connecticut. A man of endless energy, Dwight published two poems of epic dimensions while in Greenfield, one of which he entitled "Greenfield Hill," and, during the same year that he began his pastoral duties, opened a school. "Several Gentlemen having applied to the subscriber to provide instruction for their children, in various branches of knowledge," began his advertisement, "they and others are informed that so soon as Twenty Scholars shall apply, a School shall commence at Greenfield . . . under the direction of Timothy Dwight." He devoted six hours a day to the school, which yearly trained fifty or sixty students, both male and female, from the area and from other parts of the United States at a cost of £30 for room and board.[8]

During the summer of 1786, Dwight oversaw the construction of a school building on the green. A simple one-story structure whose roof sloped upward on all four sides to a cupola, the school contained a single classroom lighted by three windows on each of two sides and heated by a large fireplace at one end. Long boards ran the length of opposite walls and served as desks for the scholars. At these desks toiled the young Henry Baldwin, who would eventually become an associate justice of the United State Supreme Court, and Joel Poinsett of South Carolina, one day to be the United States ambassador to Mexico. (There he would encounter a plant of the spurge family that so intrigued him that he brought several back home, where his fellow Americans honored his discovery by naming it the poinsettia.)

On June 25, 1795, the Yale Corporation elected Dwight president of the college. Unwilling to lose its talented pastor, the Greenfield parish voted on August 5 to deny Dwight permission to leave his post, a decision overruled six days later by the Fairfield County Consociation. Jeremiah Day, who would himself one day be president of Yale, took over Dwight's school.

In April 1781 Samuel Staples, a prosperous North Fairfield farmer and bachelor of seventy-three, invited the Reverend Robert Ross of Stratfield, the Reverend Samuel Sherwood of Norfield, and the Reverend James Johnson of North Fairfield to his home to discuss his plans to establish a free school for Fairfield children, especially those whose parents were unable to afford the cost of public education, to be located in North Fairfield. Andrew Rowland, a Fairfield attorney, prepared the necessary documents, but in doing so, overlooked Staples' request that the school specifically be in North Fairfield; his draft stated only that Staples was making his gift "for the laudable purpose of erecting and supporting a public free school in said Fairfield, in perpetuum, for the instruction of children and youth in useful knowledge and learning, especially such as are sober

*After Independence*

*View of Sun Tavern circa 1870. Built by Samuel Penfield, it was rebuilt after the Revolution, and George Washington did, quite literally, sleep here.*

studious and have not estates sufficient for that purpose &c." Believing the oversight inconsequential, Staples signed the papers.[9]

In August 1781 Ross, Sherwood, and Johnson, the school trustees, chose Greenfield as the location for the school. Staples was furious. The trustees defended their action by asserting that it was in the best interests of the town, Greenfield being more centrally located than North Fairfield. In 1782 the trustees moved the school to the center of Fairfield, and the following year to Stratfield. Ultimately Staples' wish was honored, for in 1792 the General Assembly ordered the trustees to locate the school in North Fairfield; which by that time meant placing the school outside the limits of the town of Fairfield, North Fairfield having become part of the town of Weston.

At the end of the eighteenth century, Fairfield stood as Connecticut's sixth most active urban center. Unlike New Haven, Hartford, New London, Norwich, and Middletown, Fairfield had developed neither direct trade with Europe nor access to a large hinterland. It had fewer stores and a simpler network of streets than any of the five larger communities, each of which the General Assembly had incorporated as a city during the 1780s. But while it did not become a city, Fairfield possessed something of a cosmopolitan air by 1800. Its population included merchants, artisans, mariners, professionals, and laborers, as well as farmers. Thirty stores and shops existed in Fairfield by 1800, seven wharves, and more than a dozen warehouses. The central part of the town consisted of two intersecting streets and two small lanes, around which were located two houses of worship and several taverns, including the Rising Sun Tavern, built in 1780 by Samuel Penfield, where George Washington spent the night of October 16, 1789. Also in the center of town was the courthouse, completed in 1794, an imposing structure where court was held twice a year. Attorneys and their clients from all over the state and occasionally even from New York came to Fairfield, frequented its taverns, and added a sophistication that would have otherwise eluded the town.

The Jonathan Bulkley Tavern, just behind the courthouse, contained the offices of Fairfield's first newspaper, *The Fairfield Gazette*, which began publication in 1786. Stephen Miller, Francis Forgue, Jr., and Jonathan Bulkley operated the paper, which contained as little hard news as any sheet claiming to be a newspaper possibly could. That Fairfield was still largely a country town was indicated by the number of advertisements for lost, strayed, and stolen livestock. Merchants sought to buy "hog bristles" and to sell "Good West India Rum . . . by the Hogshead" for cash or "country produce" through the pages of the *Gazette*. John Squire offered subscribers onions, for which he was willing to "Receive in Payment Wood, likewise Posts & Rails & every other kind of Country Produce." Israel Bibbins informed readers that he "for the purpose of introducing that valuable branch of Stock (Mules) has procured a fine likely Jack Ass, which has been fully proved for his Strength and Vigour."[10] If some advertisements proclaimed the continuing rural character of Fairfield, others showed how cosmopolitan the town was becoming. Anthony Espinosa used the *Gazette* "to inform his Friends in particular and the Public in general, that he carries on the Business of a Baker; — likewise, Hair-dressing, Shaving, Bleeding, and Drawing Teeth: all which Professions he is well versed in." Espinosa, probably as versatile a tradesman as ever did business in Fairfield, established himself in the shop that had previously belonged to William Silliman (the son of Gold Selleck Silliman) and Wright White, located near the meetinghouse of the Prime Society. White and Silliman, who had been retailers, had dissolved their partnership in 1787 after being robbed by "the notorious burglarian Moses Johnson," a local boy gone bad. Hezekiah Nichols notified the *Gazette*'s readers that he would begin manufacturing nails in Fairfield, an activity that would allow local residents to avoid the inconvenience of obtaining nails from either New York or Boston. Joseph Hill, Jr., announced his intention "to Establish a Tobacco Manufactory in the Town of Fairfield; where those Gentlemen in the Mercantile line — Citizens &c. may be Amply Supplyed, with every Species of it."[11]

Fairfield was a post town. Its post office served a large area, residents from as far away as Newtown and Danbury and Redding being compelled to come to town to collect their mail and to dispatch their correspondence. At least one physician was practising in Fairfield all during the 1790s. Dr. David Rogers enjoyed the confidence of town residents and, like the post office, served a wide area. The home of Fairfield resident Jeremiah Jennings acted as a place of confinement for persons who had received a smallpox inoculation and were briefly carriers of the disease.

At the end of the eighteenth century, one could find a variety of skilled craftsmen in the town producing items that earlier generations could have found only in Boston, New York, or England. Gamaliel Bradford Whiting, who was both a watchmaker and a clockmaker, Isaac Burr, a jeweler and a clockmaker, William Burr, and John Bulkley were all making clocks in Fairfield. Whiting had, in 1787, been in partnership with Isaac Marquand, a clockmaker and a goldsmith who had learned his craft from his uncle, Jacob Jennings of Norwalk, and by 1800 had moved to New York. Jonathan Bulkley was carrying on the tradition of John Whitear and John Whitear, Jr. The elder Whitear had arrived in Fairfield by 1736 and had made his living as a clockmaker and a founder of brass bells. His advertisement in the Boston *Gazette* in May 1738 proclaimed his ability

*Cherry desk-on-frame made in Fairfield circa 1740-1760.*

to cast bells as large as 2000 pounds. In 1762 he may have installed one of his bells in the Anglican church in Stratford. John, Jr., carried on his father's business, but died young; Bulkley, his apprentice, probably took over the business.

Other craftsmen were represented in town. Moses Betts was a hatter. Isaac Jennings, a metal worker, produced a variety of tin as well as iron items. In 1800, one notable furniture maker in Fairfield was Jesse Dimon. He came from a rich tradition of Fairfield joiners and turners. Edward and Ozias Budington and David, Nathan, and Ebenezer Bulkley had all built furniture in Fairfield earlier in the eighteenth century. Jacob Leavitt had also been at work at that time. These men, Justin Hobart, Sr., and later Dimon and Justin Hobart, Jr., produced furniture, chairs in particular, for Fairfield households. The few examples of their work that have survived testify to both their practical and their esthetic talent.

There were opportunities for play as well as for work in Fairfield by 1800. Jonathan Bulkley provided entertainment in his Union Hall, adjacent to the tavern he owned.

"The celebrated Mr. Smith & Lady from Europe, but last from Philadelphia" presented to the audience at Union Hall "several Excellent, Dramatic moral lectures, a number of Prologues, Epilogues &c. Also a variety of Songs and Musical Dialogues, performed in the highest taste."[12]

Men, women and children looked forward to the annual party that marked the end of summer, when clams were collected and roasted in the sand. "Age and youth of either sex were of the party, which was very numerous, festive, novel, and agreeable, and closed with a ball in the evening," stated Samuel Davis, who attended the celebration September 4, 1789. He suggested that Fairfielders call it a "feast of Shells."[13]

Once an isolated outpost on the Sound, Fairfield now enjoyed regular stage service along the Boston Post Road, one of the best roads in the early republic. For those not inclined to overland travel, the *Lady of Fairfield*, operated out of Mill River by Captain Stephen Thorp, made frequent trips between Fairfield and New York City. Simpler accommodations could be had on one of the coasting vessels that sailed from either Black Rock or Mill River. A trip to New York or Boston might impress a Fairfielder, with the fact that what passed for sophistication in Connecticut would be thought quite ordinary in these great port cities. James Noyes, the stepson of Gold Selleck Silliman, visited New York when he was twelve. "The houses most all join together; I never see such a fine place in my life," he wrote his grandparents. He could hardly wait to tell his brothers, then in New Haven: "I don't know what they will think when they hear I have been to New York."[14]

Now more than 160 years old, Fairfield provided its residents with a quality of life beyond any expectations of its founders. The Fairfield of Roger Ludlow's time had faced danger on a regular basis; the town's last brush with marauders had been the Tryon raid of 1779. Colonial Fairfield had enjoyed more prosperity than most of its neighbors, but that prosperity could never rival the affluence the town had come to know by 1800. Fairfield men and women also knew a degree of freedom that had never existed during colonial times. The sense of purpose and unity that had prevailed in Puritan Fairfield was gone, but in its place were economic, religious, and, to a lesser degree, political options that allowed Fairfield citizens to make genuine choices and to proclaim, as never before, their individuality.

NOTES

1. FTR, B, I, May 8, 1787. Saladino, "The Economic Revolution," explains the important economic changes of this period after the American Revolution.

2. Journal of Samuel Davis, *Proceedings of the Massachusetts Historical Society*, 1st Series, XI, April 1869, 17; Martha J. Lamb, "Washington as President, 1789-1790," *Magazine of American History*, 21 (Feb. 1889), 100.

3. FTR, B, I, Aug. 24, 1789.

4. Ibid., July 23, 1792, Oct. 21, 1799.

5. Journal of Samuel Davis, *Proceedings of the Massachusetts Historical Society*, 1st Series, XI, April 1869, 19.

6. Saladino, "The Economic Revolution," 350.

7. Journal of Samuel Davis, *Proceedings of the Massachusetts Historical Society*, 1st Series, XI, April 1869, 18.

8. Charles E. Cunningham, *Timothy Dwight, 1752-1817* (New York, 1942), 134.

9. Cyrus Bradley, "A History of the Staples School," Manuscript Collection, Pequot Library.

10. *The Fairfield Gazette*, May 10, Sept. 12, 1787; April 9, 30, 1788.

11. Ibid., Oct. 26, 1786; May 10, 1787; June 17, 1789.

12. Ibid., July 16, 1788.

13. Journal of Samuel Davis, *Proceedings of the Massachusetts Historical Society*, 1st Series, XI, April 1869, 17.

14. Buel and Buel, *The Way of Duty*, 110.

# PART II

Hard times befell Fairfield during the nineteenth century. The most significant town in southwestern Connecticut when the century began, by the time of the Civil War Fairfield had become a small country town and would remain such until the early twentieth century. Fairfield's shipping, commerce, and agriculture suffered as centers for these activities developed in other parts of Connecticut or the United States; manufacturing generally eluded the town. Its sons and daughters fled in numbers to seek economic opportunities elsewhere. Little set it apart from other somnolent New England towns that seemed to have little place in modern America. Only at the end of the nineteenth century did Fairfield begin to develop a new identity, as a suburban community.

# A New Century

PREDICTING WHAT THE new century might hold for Fairfield was too hypothetical for most town residents; they were more concerned with trying to shape that future to their own tastes. They were eager to eliminate any remaining evidence of Tryon's raid twenty-one years earlier, to restore to their town the prosperous look it had had before the attack. They hoped to turn Mill River and Black Rock into important commercial and shipping centers. And they wanted to maintain the affluence that existed in Greenfield and Green's Farms, the town's most important agricultural areas. Fairfield men and women were confident they could, if providence smiled on them, accomplish all these things.

One situation that might have concerned the town's leaders was the decline in population that had occurred since the raid. In 1782, three years after Tryon's visit, Fairfield had had a population of 5276. By 1790 this figure had dropped to 4009 and by 1800 to 3735, a decline of 29 percent. Too discouraged to rebuild in Fairfield, many men and women had abandoned the town to pursue their lives elsewhere. This loss was far more devastating than the destruction of property; houses and barns could be rebuilt, but the lost neighbors would never return.

Even with a population of only 3735, Fairfield remained the second largest town in southwestern Connecticut; only Norwalk was larger with 5246 residents. The composition of Fairfield's population remained essentially as it had been during the colonial period. The vast majority of the residents were white and of English stock. Five percent of Fairfield's people were of African descent and of these about one in four was still a slave, even though Connecticut had instituted a system of gradual emancipation in 1784. Forty-seven slaves resided in Fairfield in 1800; 203 had lived there a decade before. The percentage of blacks remained about the same — there were many more free blacks in town in 1800 than there had been in 1790.

Those who were concerned over Fairfield's smaller population in 1800 could take heart in 1810, when the United States government reported a Fairfield population of

4125 persons, an increase of 10.4 percent since 1800. Fairfield was again larger than Norwalk, which had lost the territory that became New Canaan and Wilton; but had now been surpassed by Stamford, whose population was 4440. Only eight slaves lived in Fairfield in 1810; and still 5 percent of the population remained black.

One factor in the population growth may have been the increased activity taking place at Black Rock and Mill River. The shipping industry by 1805-1806 provided more employment for Fairfield residents than ever before. Samuel Smedley, still the collector at the Customs House, watched the local maritime industry flourish. In 1790, his first year on the job, he calculated that the value of exports from the port of Fairfield (which included all of the coast of Fairfield County) amounted to $50,315.88. By 1795, this figure had nearly doubled. Ten years later Smedley was collecting duties of nearly $30,000 annually at his office in Fairfield, a fourfold increase since he had first taken his assignment at the Customs House, and the value of exports had risen to well over $200,000.

The cause of all this activity was the war that had raged between France and Great Britain since 1793 and that would last, with brief interludes of peace, until 1815. Both these European powers were anxious to take advantage of the United States' position as a neutral, a situation that allowed the American merchant marine to carry noncontraband goods between the ports of belligerent nations. For Fairfield seamen, this meant that trade with both the British and the French West Indies was as open as it had ever been. Even more important, it also meant that the coastal trade was providing unprecedented opportunities. As more and more ships were diverted into the West Indian trade and even into direct trade with Europe, more and more Fairfield ships found work along the coast, work that these larger vessels had abandoned. The result was enormous growth in the shipping business in Fairfield. Tonnage increased; exports increased; trade had never been so profitable, money so plentiful.

But Fairfielders shortly understood that having their prosperity depend upon a war in Europe had its disadvantages. As Great Britain and France altered their policies on the high seas to correspond with the changing circumstances of the war, unsuspecting persons in Fairfield were forced to bear the consequences. France might suddenly decide to close certain ports, or Great Britain to seize neutral ships for alleged violations of arbitrarily imposed regulations. Vast fluctuation in trade was the price Fairfield and other maritime communities had to pay for profiting from the distant war. In 1801, when the war was going full tilt, exports upon which Smedley collected a duty were at an all-time high. But in 1802 and 1803, when a temporary truce was struck between the belligerents, trade dropped by 31 percent. Wild swings in business affairs became a fact of life, but Fairfield learned to live with them. Even the bad times were better than what the town had known for many years.

The war's impact on shipping in Fairfield can best be seen in the Custom House records of tonnage of shipping. These records distinguish between ships occupied in international trade and those involved in coastal trade. In 1794, the Custom House District included about 1400 tons of shipping that transported goods to foreign ports; most of these ships carried cargoes between the United States and various points in the West Indies, rarely to European ports. By contrast, in that same year, about 2050 tons of the district's ships were transporting merchandise along the coast of the United States. In other words, about 40 percent of Fairfield's shipping was made up of ships that plied the high seas and about 60 percent moved up and down the eastern seaboard. By contrast, Connecticut as a whole had committed 68 percent of its shipping to international trade and only 32 percent to the coastal trade.

Between 1794 and 1815 Fairfield's commitment to the coastal trade became even more extensive, and its limited involvement with foreign trade even more restricted; Connecticut, by contrast, continued to send about as large a percentage of its ships to foreign ports and to keep about as many, relatively speaking, of its vessels in the coastal trade. Both in Connecticut generally and in the Fairfield District in particular, more and more shipping vessels were being built; by 1806, Fairfield had more than 7000 tons of shipping, as opposed to fewer than 3500 tons in 1794. But by 1806, 77 percent of all of Fairfield's ships were coastal vessels, compared to 37 percent of all the ships in Connecticut. Because they were so close to New York, which was rapidly becoming the most important port in the United States, literally gobbling up more and more international trade at the expense of small ports, Fairfield sailors had to content themselves with carrying goods between their home port and such places as New York, Boston, and Wilmington, North Carolina.

Of the shipping that did go from the Fairfield District to foreign ports, most was based at Black Rock, still the best natural port in Connecticut except for New London. By 1803, fifteen houses, six stores, and five wharves existed at Black Rock, and the harbor was a hive of activity. The lower wharf that Samuel Squire had built in 1760 became the property of his grandson, John Squire, Jr., about 1805, and young Squire hoped to make more of the wharf than had either his grandfather or father. David Penfield, the son of James Penfield of the Penfield mill and the nephew of Samuel Penfield of the Sun Tavern, began to buy shares in the Middle Wharf in 1805. This was the wharf that thirteen shareholders had acquired in 1767 and that Barlow, Benjamin, and Gershom Sturges owned at the beginning of the nineteenth century. Penfield also foresaw a bright future for his property.

But most of the activity at Black Rock was taking place at the upper wharf. Peter Perry of Mill Plain became the owner of the upper wharf in 1801. His sons, Bradley and Seth, and his son-in-law, Hezekiah Osborn, bought water lots nearby, and in July 1801 the Perrys and Osborn both opened stores at the upper wharf. Hezekiah Osborn, during the same year, also built a simple center-chimney house adjacent to his store. The following year, Terence Riley, who moved to Black Rock from Staten Island, New York, bought the store, warehouse, and wharf that John Wheeler had built, as well as one of the water lots the town had laid out in 1789 but had only recently offered for sale "for the purpose of promoting mechanics and merchants in their various branches with convenient stands for business." By the end of the year he was trying to complete the improvements he had promised the town he would make when he received permission to acquire the lot. Joseph Bulkley and his son Uriah, were engaged in a similar project, also trying to convince the town that they deserved clear title to one of the valuable 1789 water lots. Bulkley had operated a store and tavern in Greenfield until a robbery resulted in the loss of enough uninsured goods to drive him out of the mercantile business; he continued to keep a tavern in Greenfield for many years.

The upper wharf was alive with activity. The town had not only finally stopped procrastinating about selling the water lots but also had decided "to lay out a convenient highway at the upper wharf so called at Black Rock not less than three rods in width for the accomodation of the individuals now settled there in business." The road would provide easy access to the center of Fairfield, something promised many times before but provided only now.[1]

Terence Riley was drowned in July 1805, before he saw the upper wharf fully developed. But the other recent arrivals at Black Rock—David Penfield from Fairfield, the Perrys from Mill Plain, and Joseph and Uriah Bulkley from Greenfield—watched their plans mature into reality. The Perrys added to their property by purchasing Riley's store and vessel from his estate. David Penfield married one of Joseph Bulkley's daughters and owned the Middle Wharf until his death in 1845. The enterprise of J. Bulkley and Son remained one of the most prosperous in Black Rock well into the nineteenth century.

A general store of the type that Joseph and Uriah Bulkley operated was absolutely essential to the economy of Fairfield at that time. The store served as a collection point for country produce—such items as corn, oats, flax, rye, and beef—which the Bulkleys would then send to New York or New Haven or Boston to be sold. The Bulkley store was also the distribution point for all types of goods that could not be produced locally and had to be brought to town, probably from New York or Boston.

The store could satisfy almost any need. It sold sugar for $.25 a pound in 1810; brandy for $2.50 a gallon; rum $.29 a quart; "a set of Knives & forkes," $2.37; nine dog fish hooks, $.12; a pound of chocolate, $.38; or seven yards of calico, $3.50. The Bulkleys sold paper by the sheet and rum and brandy by the glass. If the store did not stock a particular item it would order it. When Daniel Sherwood of Weston came in for iron, Joseph Bulkley told him that iron was not something he kept on hand but agreed to obtain it in New York. With freight and commission, the iron cost $9.30. Sherwood paid for the iron in oats, thirty bushels at three shillings a bushel, which amounted to $11.25. The difference of $1.95 was credited to Sherwood's account.[2]

Probably Bulkley sent the oats to New York. He sent cider there and liked to receive $1.25 a barrel for it. Obtaining $.92 a bushel for flax would have pleased him, as would receiving $.61 a bushel for walnuts. Bulkley usually shipped butter by the firkin (about twenty-eight pounds), and charged $.15 a pound for it. Live turkeys went for $.75 apiece and hams for $.11 a pound, the same price as a dozen eggs.

That J. Bulkley and Son kept its books in dollars and cents during those years before the War of 1812 indicates what a progressive establishment the father and son operated. Most Fairfield businesses were still using pounds, shillings, and pence until after the war, and some businesses that traded only in town kept up the practice until the 1840s. But Bulkley's neighborhood, Black Rock, was hardly a backwater in 1805 or 1810; its involvement with the coastal trade and, to a smaller degree, the West Indian trade, made it a commercial center. It seemed to have a bright future. The Bulkleys, the Perrys, and David Penfield had all testified to this by moving there from other parts of Fairfield. The United States government added its endorsement when in 1808 it authorized the construction of Black Rock Light on Fayerweather Island. In an age of frugality, this was as positive a statement as tightfisted congressmen could make.

Mill River's future also looked promising. The town had paid for dredging the harbor channel in 1799 by raising money through a lottery, and in that same year the road that would eventually become the Connecticut Turnpike was opened to the public. This turnpike made transporting goods to Mill River easier and tied the port to areas to the west. An important link in the turnpike was the bridge that connected Fairfield and Norwalk across the Saugatuck River. Granted authority to build such a bridge and to charge tolls for its use by the General Assembly in 1798, Fairfield and Norwalk had completed the span by the end of 1799. The two towns began to collect tolls the following year. A person on horseback paid three cents; a loaded oxcart or wagon four cents; and a four-wheeled pleasure carriage a full bit, twelve and a half cents. For a farmer's herd the toll was one cent per animal.

The new channel and the new road encouraged merchants to come to Mill River. Isaac Burritt, a sea captain, who had served as the master of the *Liberty*, the *Dolphin*, the *Marietta*, the *Industry*, the *Brilliant*, and the *Anson*, joined forces with William Bulkley to form Bulkley and Burritt, a firm that owned both a store and a wharf in Mill River. Ebenezer Bulkley of Fairfield and William Heron of Redding also formed a partnership and opened a store in Mill River in 1803. By 1806, Mill River could even boast of having a tavern. Left a widow with fifteen children when her husband died that year, Molly Pike decided to convert her home into an inn. Pike's Tavern, just across from the harbor, remained the social center of Mill River for nearly three decades.

Mill River's specialty was the coasting trade. Because the harbor was so shallow, large ships of the type required for the West Indian trade avoided the port. Men like Eleazer Bulkley, probably Mill River's most famous and most successful sea captain, and Walter Perry, who was for a time Bulkley's partner, developed the coasting trade into a fine art. In June 1803 their sloop, the *Juno*, 62 tons, began her career. Walter Perry took her to Boston in September, and this voyage, as the reader will see, indicates how profitable this commerce could be. Perhaps it lacked the romance of Salem's East India trade or Nantucket's whaling industry; but, on the other hand, it was profitable. And profits were more important to men like Bulkley and Perry than romance. Most of Mill River's business was with New York, but ships regularly left the harbor destined for Boston. The *Juno*'s September 1803 cargo of "country produce" comprised 1022 bushels of white corn, 321 bushels of yellow corn, 679 bushels of oats, 102 bushels of superfine flour, 328 bushels of rye, a barrel of pork, a cheese wheel, 10 bushels of buckwheat, and a large supply of feathers, a valuable product in that age of feather beds. The price Bulkley and Perry realized for their cargo and the revenue they derived from freight and passengers amounted to a total of $2359.50. Perry returned from Boston with 80 hogsheads and 260 bushels of salt, 17 quintal of codfish, 2 barrels of oil, one of sugar and one of mackerel, a hogshead of rum, another of molasses, and a box of soap, as well as nails, leather, and "Cantonware." After the ship's expenses were paid the two partners realized a profit of $224.47, and could anticipate making almost that amount again when the items brought back from Boston were sold. In an age when a hogshead (63 gallons) of rum cost $89.24 and a barrel of sugar cost $27.63, a profit of over $400 on a single voyage was large enough to please the most ambitious merchant.

Coastal shippers, storekeepers, and farmers were the three essential components of Fairfield's economy. The farmers produced what the storekeepers collected and sold to the shippers. The shippers delivered these commodities to a market in New York, Boston, or elsewhere. At the other end of the cycle, the farmers bought from the storekeepers those goods the shippers delivered from whatever port they had visited.

Occasionally some refinement might be added to this uncomplicated economic mechanism. Fairfield authorized Edmund Burr to erect a dam and mill on the Mill River in September 1801. What Burr did was mill grain, which was either produced locally or brought from elsewhere, into flour. He then sent this flour — as he did with the *Juno* in September 1803 — to some location where he thought it would demand a good price. Because milling centers had yet to develop in the United States and would not for many years, enterprises like Burr's, small as it was, could be successful.

Beyond such modest refinements, Fairfield men generally declined to experiment with a system that worked well. For the most part, manufacturing was unknown in Fairfield at the beginning of the nineteenth century. To be sure, Eliphalet Lyon did produce rag rugs in his rug "factory" in Greenfield. Lyon was actually a weaver who had been convinced by Timothy Dwight that there was a market for such rugs. Dwight brought him one from New York so that Lyon could examine it to determine how it was woven. The technique was simple, and Lyon set to work making rugs. During his busiest periods, he may have employed one or two apprentices in addition to himself. "Factory" seems a pretty grandiose name for such a modest establishment.

Eliphalet's system of production was no more sophisticated than that used by his son, Wakeman Lyon, also a weaver. Both often worked with materials owned by their customers; both worked essentially alone or perhaps with an apprentice; and both were usually paid in country produce such as corn or rye or cider. The basic difference was that Wakeman wove cloth and Eliphalet both cloth and rugs.

What Wakeman and Eliphalet Lyon did, typical of the manufacturing that took place in Fairfield in the early nineteenth century, was in fact also typical of the manufacturing that had been going on a century earlier. It was what later generations would call cottage industry. Horace Staples, for example, described how the work of spinning was accomplished in Fairfield about 1810: "Generally in time of wool spinning, January and July, our most respectable young ladies used to go about to the neighbors and spin up the wool; two runs a day was a day's work." Staples remembered that "by sunrise in the morning, we were greeted with the hum of the big wheel by young ladies who made it a rule to get their day's work done by noon." The women would be paid in goods, corn or rye, or perhaps a share of the yarn they had made, rather than money.[3]

Even professional men could expect their payment to take the form of barter goods. Samuel Rowland, as distinguished as any lawyer practising in Fairfield, charged $9 for arguing a bill in chancery if the sum in question amounted to $100 or less. If the dispute involved more than $500, his fee went up to $25. But whatever his fee, he knew that payment would rarely be in cash.

With a simple but thriving economy and with both Black Rock and Mill River becoming active commercial centers, the prospects for Fairfield appeared bright. The village of Fairfield, although it would be many years before it again became a commercial center, was an attractive community. Lawyers in particular liked to live and work in the center of town, close to the courthouse. Samuel Rowland lived in the center. Roger M. Sherman, a brilliant young attorney, had been practicing in Norwalk; he decided that his prospects were better in Fairfield and moved to within a short walk of the courthouse in 1807. Two years earlier, another young lawyer of similar abilities had settled in Fairfield. He was Gideon Tomlinson. He would have preferred a home in the center of town, but his new bride insisted on being close to her family in Greenfield. The fact that he and others of his ability were coming to Fairfield augured well for the town.

The town's concern for education also suggested good years to come. In 1795 the Connecticut General Assembly had taken control of the schools away from the ecclesiatical societies and placed it with newly created school societies. This was necessary to allow the distribution of funds recently derived from selling Connecticut's land in the Western Reserve, land that the state—whose original borders extended all the way to the Pacific Ocean—received from the federal government in return for abandoning its claims to land beyond its existing boundaries.

Fairfield complied with the statute and created four school societies, one in the village of Fairfield, one at Greenfield, one at Green's Farms, and one at Stratfield. The schools that had been under the control of the Prime Society, for example, were now the responsibility of the "First Located School Society," which came into existence on October 27, 1797. The society elected Samuel Rowland, Isaac Bibbins, and Nathan Beers "to take care of and manage the prudential affairs" of the society and "to receive the interest of monies arising on the sale of the Western Lands that belong to this School Society."[4] The direct control of the schools was left in the hands of nine—later five and still later four—school visitors, whom the societies selected annually. It was the visitors' task to see that the children learned what they were supposed to and to evaluate and license the teachers. Because of the heavy responsibility they bore, the school visitors, unlike most public officials, received a modest compensation for their work, either $1.00 or $.50 a day depending on the financial condition of the school district they served.

The First Located School Society operated six district schools: Black Rock, Jennings Woods, Middle, East of Middle, Mill Plain, and Mill River. The Greenfield society controlled eight schools: Hull's Farms, Center, Bulkley's, Burr's, Banks's, Sherwood's, Deerfield, and Hoyden's Hill. There was one school under the Green's Farms School Society: the one in Stratfield accommodated pupils from both Fairfield and what would shortly become Bridgeport.

During the 1812-1813 school year, tuition in the First Located Society schools was $.025 a day. The societies also derived income from the Connecticut School Fund, that is, the interest earned on the monies from the sale of the western lands and whatever other sources might be available. The Greenfield School Society owned lands that it was able to lease from time to time. In 1805 Isaac Bronson paid the society $5.00 for the use of the school lot; being both a wealthy man and a banker, Bronson paid cash. The following year, David Hubbell, neither wealthy nor a banker, paid ten and a third bushels of rye for the use of the lot. This was a better arrangement for the society, because it sold the rye for $6.89.

Horace Staples described one of the schools controlled by the Greenfield Society: "The school house . . . [was] 16 x 18, with a stove chimney, probably built in one corner, where the scholars had to take turns to go to warm themselves; often the smoke was so thick as to drive all out of doors." He became a student at the school about 1812 or 1813, attending both summer and winter until he was ten and then winters only until he was fifteen. At sixteen he transferred to the school kept by Bryant Glover who was apparently such a fine teacher that conscientious students from all over Greenfield sought to enroll with him. Staples studied at Glover's school for two winters "of about four weeks each" and then, thanks to the generosity of his parents, finished his "school learning by going to William Belden's Greenfield Academy 40 days."[5]

Staples's education would appear to modern readers to be haphazard at best. A total of eight weeks of school in two years would hardly satisfy current attendance requirements. But Staples was either an exceptional student or the schools were impressively efficient, for after his forty days at the Greenfield Academy, he became a teacher, a profession that he followed with success for the next six years.

The Greenfield Academy was, of course, the school Timothy Dwight founded during his years in Greenfield. When Dwight left to become the president of Yale College, Dr. Jeremiah Day replaced him at the academy. Yale later also called Day to become its president. William Belden, the next principal, managed to maintain the school's quality but was unable to sustain its popularity, which began to decline during the 1830s. By 1835, it had become a "respectable institution for ladies."[6] Another, less prestigious academy existed in Stratfield at the beginning of the nineteenth century and in 1817 still another was in operation at Black Rock. Both of these ventures were short-lived.

Vastly more successful was the academy that opened in the center of Fairfield in 1804. Jonathan Sturges and Samuel Rowland, probably the two most influential men in Fairfield at the time, applied for a charter on behalf of forty-three individuals who had paid $5 a share to own stock in the venture. Sturges, Rowland, the Reverend Andrew Eliot, David Judson, and Nathan Beers, Jr. were the first trustees of the school, which opened with sixty pupils, both boys and girls, under the direction of William Stoddard. Male students who successfully completed the prescribed course of study were, theoretically at least, prepared to go on to college; higher education for females was still only a gleam in Mary Lyon's eye.

School rules were strictly enforced. Some were exactly what one might suspect: "Profanity of every kind to be prohibited at all times." Others provide an insight into the kind of mischief that intrigued the young folks of an earlier time. Firearms were apparently popular: "No gunning to be tolerated at any time and the use of powder to be prohibited." Windows must have been tempting targets for strong-armed youths, then as now, and the hazards of traffic were cause for concern: "The publick Green recommended for place of innocent recreation—where windows are not exposed & and the danger from travelling removed—and no meeting or playing in the streets in the evening after sun down." A student might get into a farmer's watermelon patch or orchard: "No fruit of any kind to be taken from any enclosure without permission of the owner." The rules must have worked, for the school continued to operate, in good times and bad, for eighty years.[7]

College remained out of the reach of most Fairfield young men in the early 1800s, a privilege for the sons of gentlemen. Jonathan Sturges's son, Lewis-Burr Sturges, went to Yale, but Sturges was himself a Yale alumnus, the son of a Yale alumnus, and a prosperous man. Roger M. Sherman also attended that college, as did Gideon Tomlinson, but again, in both cases, well-to-do parents or relatives made their attendance possible. Four years at Yale cost about $900.00. What this meant in 1810 can be partially understood by remembering that farm laborers who provided their own room and board then earned about $.80 a day. Furthermore, expensive as tuition, room, and board were, the cost of losing the young man's labor on the farm for the four years spent in New Haven or Cambridge or New York was certainly as great an expense or greater.

Being without a college education was no real hardship—being poor was. The town looked after its destitute with less enthusiasm than it had fifty or a hundred years earlier. It seemed forever eager to find some device that would help reduce the cost of maintaining paupers. In January 1803, the town voted to look into the possibility of jointly erecting a poorhouse with Norwalk, Wilton, and Weston. The four towns had, by the end of 1804, accepted a provisional plan for the project, the total cost of which was to be about $1000, including land acquisition, a building, and whatever furniture was considered necessary. Each town's share of the cost would depend upon the size of its grand list, and each town was to contribute to operational expenses in proportion to the use it made of the facility. Eight individuals, two from each town, were to be responsible for the poorhouse's operation.

Fairfield liked the plan and voted "that discretionary power be vested in and given to the selectmen to do what is necessary to be done relating to the poor house." The four towns in April, 1805, purchased land in Weston and began to build. By the end of the year, the poorhouse was accepting paupers. Concerned about the legitimacy of the scheme, the Fairfield town meeting voted in April 1806 to petition the General Assembly for enabling legislation to regulate the operation of the poorhouse. At its May 1807 session, the assembly provided the required legislation, preferring to call the poorhouse a "Work-House" and reserving the right to repeal the legislation if conditions at the facility were discovered to be "unreasonable and unjust." The poorhouse proved a satisfactory solution to a perplexing problem; it remained in operation until 1831.[8]

Before 1800, Fairfield had little political life in the modern sense. Candidates ran as individuals. Parties were in their infancy. The idea of seriously campaigning for votes was an idea whose time had yet to come: the office was to seek the individual, not the individual the office. But the pursuit of self-interest was more legitimate in town by 1800 than it had ever been before, and the old ways began to change. After the Fairfield courthouse was destroyed during the Tryon raid, town meetings gathered in the meetinghouse in Greenfield. Once the courthouse was again available for town functions, the residents of Greenfield insisted that meetings should continue to be held at their end of town periodically. Why should they have to do all the walking? they asked. Self-interest also appeared in the tendency of the various parishes to present candidates for public office; Greenfield wanted its point of view represented, as did Green's Farms and all the other areas of town.

Before 1800 political offices were dominated by the same type of men who had been running Fairfield's affairs for decades. Jonathan Sturges was the cultural and intellectual as well as the biological son of Samuel Sturges; both believed that they and men like themselves—the wise, the good, and the rich—were destined to govern and the rank and file were born to defer to their betters. Even Lewis-Burr Sturges, Jonathan's son, would have agreed with his father and grandfather. The perspective of Samuel Rowland and his father, Andrew Rowland, differed hardly at all from that of the Sturgeses.

Thomas Jefferson's election as president of the United States in 1800 horrified men like the Rowlands and the Sturgeses. To their minds, the new president represented the end of old values and the beginning of the reign of anarchy. Benjamin Silliman, the son of Gold Selleck and Mary Fish Silliman, was speaking of the election when he wrote: "It may be true that the Lord reigneth but I think it is also true that the devil has come down having great wrath." Silliman was not engaging in hyperbole; he meant what he said. He asked his mother for the sword his father had worn during the American Revolution: he thought "it not improbable if this atrocious spirit of Jacobinism continues to spread I may be called upon to use it."[9]

If Jefferson's election dismayed some Fairfield men and women, it gave heart to others. Those persons who had had enough of the leadership of men like Sturges and Rowland and who believed that ordinary citizens deserved more of a voice in public affairs saw the election of 1800 as reason to organize and to begin to cast off the domination of the old élite. Walter Bradley and John Hull were the leaders of this new movement, a movement that eventually became the nucleus of the Republican party in town. Those who believed that leadership ought to remain with those who by birth, education, and social position were best qualified to exercise it — persons like Silliman — gravitated toward the Federalist party, the party of George Washington and Alexander Hamilton, the party of Jonathan Sturges and Samuel Rowland, and the party that completely dominated Connecticut at the time.

Before anyone had analyzed what had happened, Fairfield had developed a vital two-party system. That the Federalists were as strong as they were is hardly surprising: it was the party of those already entrenched in power, and it was the party in control in Connecticut. What was surprising was the ease with which the Republicans became an important element. Part of the credit belongs to Bradley and Hull, both men of ability. But part of the explanation came from Fairfield's being more closely tied culturally with New York than with Hartford; Hartford was thoroughly Federalist, but Republicans were strong in New York. Also Fairfield's substantial Anglican and Baptist populations believed, probably with good reason, that the Federalist party was the political wing of the Congregational Church. This in itself was reason enough for dissenters to vote Republican.

As early as 1804, Fairfield sent two Republican representatives, Bradley and Hull, to the General Assembly. They won reelection in 1805 but lost to Federalists David Burr and Ebenezer Banks in 1806. In 1807, Fairfield again selected Bradley and Hull for the legislature. This political dueling carried over to the town meeting, where the Republicans first won control on December 8, 1807, but then lost and regained power depending on the vagaries of political life.

Politics even influenced social affairs. July 4, 1805, was celebrated as usual in Greenfield; the militia marched, and the assembled throng listened to patriotic orations. But when it came time to eat, Jonathan Bulkley noted in his diary, "the Republicans Dined on the Green. Hezekiah Bradley & Mr. Bits cooked for them, . . . . The Federalists Dined at Joseph Bulkley's." Politics had become serious business in Fairfield; the days when the Burrs or the Golds or the Sturgeses or the Rowlands could dominate public life had passed.[10]

But if political life was changing, social life remained a constant. "People in those days were not so much hurried as now," Benjamin Silliman wrote many years later. "There was more leisure in the family, and personal friendship was cherished often through long lives." The people of Fairfield at the end of the eighteenth century and the beginning of the nineteenth, he contended, seemed "to have felt and cherished the social sentiments as a part of their nature." Jonathan Bulkley confirmed Silliman's judgment. Bulkley noted that although the Republicans and Federalists had refused to eat together on July 4, 1805, "both parties appear to be well satisfied with the Celibration & pleasures of the day and to wind up the celibration of the day they had a very Splendid and Grand ball at Joseph Bulkley's ball room attended with Eleven Musiteins and verry excelent Music and about sixty Gentlemen and Ladies." As seriously as Fairfield men and women took their politics, they took even more seriously their traditions of friendship and hospitality. It was one thing to refuse to dine with members of the opposite party, but to miss a party on that account was an act of self-denial too absurd to consider. [11]

Reading diaries from this period in Fairfield's history might give one the impression that life was one long series of social events. Jonathan Bulkley described balls and hops and frolics. Hull Sherwood did the same. Much of it sounded like great fun. Bulkley wrote on August 17, 1808:

> Yesterday Mill River Farms & Mill Plain Company [militia units] went on a party to Long Island but did not land & Returned the same day in the afternoon. . . . After we landed, the company returned to Mr. Able Ogdens . . . and partook of a supper & spent the remainder of the evening in dancing.[12]

There were parties for all. "This day begins the annual Negro frolic which lasts two days at Samuel Beers Jr who cooks for them," was Bulkley's notation for September 11, 1805. "The great folk's had an Oyster Frolic at Mr. Knaps in Fairfield," he wrote on March 15, 1814. And there were locations aplenty where a frolic or a hop could be held—Samuel Penfield's Sun Tavern or James Knapp's Tavern or Molly Pike's Tavern in Mill River or Joseph Bulkley's Tavern in Greenfield. With their sanded floors, oak tables, benches around the room, applejack and "good old brown October ale" on tap, and "good stuff" in the basement, these establishments could always find a fiddler— Moses Sturges was a favorite—and put on a dance.[13] The "good stuff" in the basement was probably West Indian rum, 19,097 gallons of which arrived in the Fairfield Customs House District in the single year of 1810.

But Fairfield's tradition of entertainment and friendship was more important than rum in encouraging good times. As Benjamin Silliman said, "These traits were conspicuous not only among persons in elevated position, but in a good degree also in those gradations in society in which refinement was not dependent on wealth, and limited resources demanded even a frugal hospitality." It was a tradition that Fairfield valued highly, and with good reason.[14]

The beginning of the nineteenth century was a bright period in the town's history. As Silliman proudly pointed out, much of the best from the colonial era was still alive, and some of the good features of the years ahead—such as the appearance of genuine political alternatives—were emerging. If the village of Fairfield had yet to recover fully from Tryon's visit, both Black Rock and Mill River were bustling; and Green's Farms and Greenfield were, as before, home for many prosperous farmers. Fairfield had good reason to be optimistic.

1. FTR, B, I, Dec. 1802. Buel and Buel, *The Way of Duty*, and Peter T. Mott, "The Quiet Revolution: The Triumph of Democracy in Connecticut, 1785-1818," M.A. thesis, Trinity College, 1977, contain useful information about Fairfield in the early nineteenth century.

2. Account Book of J. Bulkley and Son, 1810-1812, Bulkley Family Papers, FHS. The society has a wealth of early account books.

3. Horace Staples, Memoirs, Bradley Family Papers, FHS.

4. Quoted in Elizabeth B. H. Banks, *This is Fairfield, 1639-1940* (New Haven, 1960), 147.

5. Horace Staples, Memoirs, Bradley Family Papers, FHS.

6. John Warner Barber, *Connecticut Historical Collections* (New Haven, 1835) 68.

7. Rules of Fairfield Academy, Fairfield School Records, FHS.

8. FTR, B, I, Dec. 16, 1805; *Private Resolutions and Laws of the State of Connecticut from the year 1789 to the year 1836*, 2 vols. (Hartford, 1837), I, 1521.

9. Quoted in Buel and Buel, *The Way of Duty*, 237.

10. Jonathan Bulkley, *The Journals of Jonathan Bulkley: 1802-1826; December 1844-1858* (Southport, Conn., 1983), 22.

11. George P. Fisher, *Life of Benjamin Silliman*, 2 vols. (New York, 1866), I, 13-14; Jonathan Bulkley, *Journals*, 22.

12. Jonathan Bulkley, *Journals*, 58.

13. Ibid., 123, 36; miscellaneous Sun Tavern documents, Bradley Family Papers, FHS.

14. Fisher, *Silliman*, I, 14.

# The Embargo
## and the War of 1812

IN 1805, Great Britain had begun systematically attacking United States ships in an attempt to stop goods from reaching France, and France had retaliated with abuse of her own to destroy United States trade with England. On December 18, 1807, Jefferson asked Congress for legislation suspending American foreign trade. Within a few hours the United States Senate passed a bill forbidding any American vessels from clearing American ports for foreign harbors and placing coastal ships under heavy bond to prevent their landing outside the United States. Four days later, the House concurred; and Jefferson signed the Embargo Act.

News of the legislation reached Fairfield on December 26 and caused "a great deal of uneasiness in the neabourhood for fear of its fatal consequences."[1] There was good reason for apprehension. All of a sudden business died. Even though Fairfield was involved in foreign trade in only a minor way, the loss of that trade still hurt, in some cases significantly. In 1807, the Fairfield Customs House collected duties amounting to $20,661; in 1808 this figure fell to $1810 and in 1809 to $1599. The drastic decline created havoc.

Compounding that loss was the sudden influx of shipping into the coastal trade. Dozens of ships that had been carrying goods to the West Indies and to even more distant ports now turned to trading within the United States as the only alternative to sitting idle in New London or New York or Boston. Increased competition meant both reduced opportunities and seriously diminished profits.

All whose livelihoods were connected with maritime trade, from seamen to longshoremen and ship's carpenters, found themselves unemployed. General stores discovered that they were oversupplied with "country produce" and sorely deficient in items they usually brought from New York or Boston for their customers. Farmers, however, were too preoccupied with the shrinking market for their products to notice the goods were not available. "The embargo is still on," wrote Jonathan Bulkley in February 1809; "& we have no business on hand nor is it probable we shall have very soon so long as these troublesome times lasts." William Wheeler, who lived at Black Rock, saw the same thing there: "The Embargo had continued a year. Our shipping mostly laid up & Business paralysed."[2]

The only Fairfield organization that benefited from the Embargo Act was the Federalist party. By pointing to the Republicans as the authors of this disastrous legislation, the Federalists recovered from the losses they had suffered earlier in the young century. In addition to denouncing the measure as economically disastrous, they claimed it was part of a Republican plot by which southern slaveholders, like Thomas Jefferson, planned to destroy the economy and therefore the influence of New England. The act was, they argued, one more step in the inevitable march of Jacobeanism across the United States. Having established themselves in control in the rest of the country, Jefferson and his misbegotten band needed only to eliminate the influence of New England to make their control complete, they contended. Lewis-Burr Sturges, who sat in the United States House of Representatives, warned his friends back in Fairfield of the dangers. Jonathan Bulkley, from his vantage point at Mill River, worried about what the future might hold: "dear Bought Liberty I am afraid is in Japurday."

Even Republican support for the embargo had, by the spring of 1809, fallen so badly that Jefferson had to abandon the measure. On March 15, 1809, the Non-Intercourse Act, which allowed for a partial restoration of trade, took its place. Slowly prosperity returned to Fairfield and to the rest of the state and country.

Unfortunately this prosperity was short-lived. On June 18, 1812, totally exasperated with Great Britain's high-handed treatment of the United States and eager to demonstrate that the new nation was truly sovereign and independent, Congress declared war on England. Fairfield learned the news on June 24. Reactions were mixed. Local Federalists viewed the war as an overt attempt by the administration of James Madison to come to the aid of Emperor Napoleon Bonaparte who was also, of course, embroiled in war with Great Britain and who was, in Federalist eyes, the most despotic tyrant since Attila. Republicans, on the other hand, believed that the war was both just and necessary. Fifteen young Fairfield men quickly enlisted in the fight against the former mother country.

Whether the war was right or wrong, its effects on Fairfield's economy were calamitous. In August 1812, William Wheeler noted that "4 vessels nearly 100 tone [sic] each lie nose by nose in Brewster's Cove [in Black Rock] & four more at the wharves by reason of the war." In October he complained "This foolish & unnecessary war goes much against us."[4]

The problem was not government restrictions on trade; the problem was the British blockade of Long Island Sound. Fairfield vessels were at risk whenever they were on the Sound, and even those men and women who remained on land were uncertain about what the British might do. An enemy frigate captured the Mill River schooner *Rising Sun*, bound for Savannah, Georgia under the command of Captain Joseph Perry; the frigate scuttled the schooner and left Perry and his crew in the vicinity of Philadelphia. On September 7, 1813, two British war ships appeared off Mill River. The smaller of the two was the *Atlanta*, a sloop of war that could have entered the harbor, and the other was the *Acasta*, a forty-four-gun frigate. The two ships passed on up the Sound but returned two days later having taken several American sloops. "They were attacked by our gun boats Thursday forenoon," Jonathan Bulkley observed, "& exchanged about 15 or so Guns [i.e., rounds]." The incident put Mill River into a panic; for those who could remember 1779, it seemed like William Tryon's raid all over again. "Moved our Furniture Fryday Sept 10th 1813 the day the English Ships appeared off our place," Bulkley wrote. On September 13, 1813, William Wheeler spoke of an enemy frigate, probably the *Acasta*, "being just back of the bar" and putting Black Rock "into no small trepidation."[5]

Incidents happened almost weekly. Wheeler noted on October 25, 1813, that William Hoyt's "packet was fired upon by an enemy Brig & outsailed her. A grapeshot went thro her sail."[6] The British brig in this case was the *Bover*, fourteen guns. She had recently pursued a sloop almost across Long Island Sound, firing ten or fifteen rounds before giving up the chase. Once again back on normal patrol, the *Bover* encountered a small schooner bound for New York and took her before she had really begun her flight. The commander of the *Bover* apparently decided against sinking the schooner, choosing instead to keep her to sell as a prize. He put two men aboard the smaller vessel and was about to sail away when a gale blew up from the south. The two British sailors lost control of the small schooner in the storm. Her foremast broke before they could get the sails down, and she ran ashore on Fairfield bar. Town officials arrested the two sailors and held them as prisoners of war. It was at this point that the *Bover* came upon Hoyt's packet and sent the grapeshot through her sail, but failed to prevent her escape.

The constant danger almost destroyed the coasting trade. British ships might appear at any time and at any point along the Connecticut coast. In April 1814, two enemy ships threatened Bridgeport. The militia was called out, but after about eighteen hours the two ships sailed away. Black Rock residents awoke on the morning of September 30 to find a British frigate and brig standing off the mouth of the harbor. "The Inhabitants of Bridgeport, Black Rock, Fairfield & Mill River were much alarmed & many sent away their furniture," Jonathan Bulkley recorded in his diary.[7]

Some Fairfield captains were willing to risk capture to take advantage of the profits that could be made during the war. Captain Peter Burr was sailing his schooner, the *Sally*, from New London to New York about October 1, 1814, when he sighted a British war ship. Unable to outrun her pursuers, the *Sally* fell into enemy hands. The British officers ordered part of her crew to be dropped at Montauk Point and part sent to Halifax, Nova Scotia. For some indiscernible reason, they ordered Captain Burr thrown into the sea. His body washed ashore during the middle of November at Branford, Connecticut. How and why he died was unclear. If one can judge from British treatment of other American merchant seamen, he was probably dead when he was thrown overboard, killed because he resisted the British when they attempted to board his ship. Generally the worst one might expect from them was imprisonment in England. Fairfield sea captains Lothrop Burr and Bradley Sturges only managed to return to the United States from a British prison in June 1815, more than six months after the war ended.

Some shipmasters succeeded in avoiding the British patrols and in prospering during the war. In March 1813, Joel Thorp put 165 bushels of rye, 1454 bushels of corn, and 614 bushels of oats onto his sloop, the *Hector*, and sailed to Providence, Rhode

*"Black Rock Harbor Lighthouse, 1808." Mural by Robert L. Lambdin*

Island. His expenses for the voyage to Providence amounted to $106.10, including wages for two crew members and for himself, wharfage, fresh beef and potatoes and bread, and the cost of eleven and a half quarters of rum and a quart of gin. The liquid refreshment doubtless helped the captain maintain his nerve in the face of possible capture. Thorp realized a profit of $216.93 in addition to $36.67 in wages for this short but risky trip to Rhode Island. His account book does not indicate what he made on the return voyage; but even if he made nothing, a $250 profit for the round trip was handsome compensation.

Thorp was a brave man. Foolhardy would be the only way to describe Hull Sherwood and his friends who on August 25, 1814, sailed across "the Sound and beat down to Neat Light and into Cow Harbor. There being about 20 couples, we walk across to J. Scudder and take supper, after which we have a ball with watermelons in abundance."[8] Few Fairfielders in August of 1814 would have found watermelons inducement enough to cross Long Island Sound.

Most of Fairfield's social life during the war was associated with the town's defense. As soon as he realized the extent of the danger the war created for Mill River, Jeremiah

*Fairfield: the biography of a community*

*painted for the Black Rock Bank and Trust Co. in 1948.*

Sturges organized the First Company of Defensive Independent Volunteers. Sturges himself served as captain of the unit, Ebenezer Dimon, Jr., as ensign, Joab Squire as lieutenant, and Jonathan Bulkley (the diarist) as company sergeant. By November 2, 1812, the unit was fully equipped, drilling under "the Willow Tree in Mill River near Mrs. Pikes Inn," and ready for review. Forty-two men served in the unit. During June 1813, the First Company constructed earthwork defenses at Mill River. Sturges and his men formally accepted responsibility for the fort on June 19, an event that occasioned the serving of cake and cheese and the presence of "the ladies." Both the men and their female guests "appeared pleasant & retired in good order,"[9] Jonathan Bulkely declared.

Connecticut governor John Cotton Smith promised to supply a field piece, small arms, and ammunition for the fort. Unfortunately the state found its resources stretched to the limit, and the governor had to renege on his promise. He did, however, come to Mill River on June 21, 1813, and personally inspect the fort and offer words of congratulations to its builders and defenders. According to Bulkley, the governor "was much pleased with our Exertions in Self defence likewise with our new Fort in which he stood & made his communication."[10]

*The Embargo and the War of 1812*

There is evidence that the company managed to salvage two cannon, a twelve-pounder and a six-pounder, and to install them in the fort, and that some men from the First Company were officially enrolled as Connecticut troops from June 27 until November 22, 1814, while they were on duty at Mill River. Governor Smith was particularly anxious about the safety of the coast during the summer of 1814, but when the summer and early autumn passed without incident, he discharged the men. Whether civilian volunteers or Connecticut militiamen, the men of the First Company managed to make every occasion as festive as possible. Usually after drilling, the company "dined at Mrs. Pikes & had a good dinner." On March 6, 1814, Bulkley recorded that "it happened to be training day and all our forces march'd up to Mr. Sam Beer's and had a turkey Frolick, pretty well for war times."[11]

The men who guarded Black Rock may have had as much fun as those who guarded Mill River, but the Black Rock defenders lacked a company sergeant who kept a thorough diary, and their good times are lost to history. The United States government provided two eight-inch cannon and two brass six-inch cannon to be placed in the fort on Grover's Hill. These were expensive and useful weapons of the type that ports all along the coast were demanding. That Black Rock received them while Mill River was unable to convince Governor Smith that it deserved any heavy weapons at all is an indication of the importance attached to Black Rock.

For most of the war, Black Rock was defended by civilian soldiers. During 1814, at the time some men of the First Company were inducted into state service, Governor Smith sent a lieutenant, two sergeants, two corporals, two musicians, and twenty-six privates to Black Rock. The state force at Mill River at the time consisted of only one sergeant, two corporals, and twelve privates. Again Black Rock received priority treatment.

Despite the anxieties of Fairfield residents, little could be done to defend the central part of town. A single fort could protect only a small area of the coast between Mill River and Black Rock. The only positive measure taken in the neighborhood of the courthouse and the green during the war was the construction of a new powderhouse in the fall of 1814, when Fairfield and all the Connecticut coast were feeling particularly vulnerable.

The war was unpopular enough in Fairfield to bring the Federalists back to power. Lewis-Burr Sturges, as staunch a Federalist as lived in town, sat in the United States House of Representatives, and Samuel Sherwood and Samuel Rowland, solid party men, represented Fairfield in the lower house of the General Assembly during most of the war.

The brightest new light among the Fairfield Federalists was Roger M. Sherman. Born in Massachusetts, Sherman had moved to Milford, Connecticut, as a small child, graduated from Yale in 1792, and studied law with Tapping Reeve of the famous Litchfield Law School as well as with Oliver Ellsworth, later a chief justice of the United States Supreme Court. The young attorney opened his practice in Norwalk in 1796 but in 1807, believing that opportunities were greater in Fairfield, the county seat, brought his family to town. He built both a large and elaborate Federal Style house in the center of town and an adjacent law office and set to work building a practice and a reputation.[12]

Sherman believed in orthodox Congregationalism and in orthodox Federalism. While a student at Yale, he had been alarmed by the ideas of David Hume and other

*Roger Minott Sherman, prominent attorney and judge, and his wife Elizabeth Gould Sherman as painted by Nathaniel Jocelyn in 1840.*

deists. He regarded them as underminers of tradition and as propagators of heresy. He found the writings of Jonathan Edwards and the preaching of Timothy Dwight much more to his taste. For the rest of his life he was inclined to view any suggestion for change as a threat to Connecticut's cultural and religious heritage. He saw James Madison as a dupe of Napoleon, tricked by the Frenchman into bringing the United States into the European war on the side of France, irreligion, and despotism.

In 1814 Fairfield sent Roger M. Sherman to the upper house of the Connecticut General Assembly. There he was determined to do all that he could to preserve the New England way — a strong Congregational establishment, a deferential society, and Federalist control. During the autumn of 1814, while Mill River and Black Rock were girding their loins for a possible British attack and Fairfield was busy building a powder house, Sherman believed he had the opportunity to take a major step toward preserving that way of life.

In October, the Massachusetts General Court wrote to Governor Smith inviting Connecticut to appoint delegates to meet with representatives from the other New England states. According to the General Court's letter, the purposes of the meeting were two: to examine the military situation of the eastern states and to consider if "an experiment may be made without disadvantage to the nation for obtaining a convention from all the states of the Union" to consider constitutional amendments guaranteeing equal advantages to all sections of the country.[13]

Smith passed the letter to the General Assembly, where it was referred to a special joint committee of which Sherman was a member. The committee recommended that Connecticut participate in the meeting, which would ever after be known as the Hartford Convention. The principal author of the committee's report was Sherman. In it

*The Embargo and the War of 1812*

he argued that because Madison, obsessed with the idea of conquering Canada, had left the New England states defenseless, the convention had to meet to provide for the security of the northeastern states. When the report was accepted by the entire General Assembly, that body selected Sherman as one of the seven Connecticut delegates to the forthcoming gathering.

By the time the Hartford Convention convened, in December 1814, the United States was facing as dark an hour as it had experienced it its brief history. Its coast was blockaded; its capital had been burned; substantial areas of Maine and New York were in British hands; and a large British army, fresh from the defeat of Napoleon's forces, was on its way to some as-yet-undisclosed invasion point. (Many administration officials believed its target would be New Orleans.) In addition to these problems, President Madison now had to contend with the Hartford Convention, whose proceedings were secret and which was thought by many Americans, including the president, to be plotting the secession of New England.

But before the group in Hartford could decide upon a course of action and present its demands to the Madison administration, the fortunes of the young republic and its president had changed. Word arrived from New Orleans that by some miracle a Tennessean named Andrew Jackson and his ragtag army had defeated the British invaders. On top of that came word of another incredible happening: Great Britain had agreed to terms of peace with the United States. The war was over. It seemed too good to be true. These events made the Hartford Convention look like an assemblage of traitors, selfish, unprincipled men who sought to wring concessions from the federal government at the very moment when the young nation was fighting for its life.

The convention spelled death for the Federalist party in the United States, although it did manage to cling precariously to life in Connecticut, where it was so firmly entrenched, for a few more years. The convention also ended the political careers of the delegates; Sherman held on to his seat in the upper house of the General Assembly until 1818, but would not occupy another public office of importance until 1841, three years before his death, when the General Assembly appointed him as an associate justice of the State Supreme Court.

Fairfield men and women were less concerned about the political fortunes of the Federalist party and Roger M. Sherman than they were about the restoration of peace. The good news reached town on February 20. A committee assembled at James Knapp's tavern to make plans for a celebration. While the committee discussed alternative ways of organizing the festivities, the men at Grover's Hill discharged a volley of cannon fire, the like of which they had never had the opportunity to direct at the enemy during the war.

The celebration began on February 24. A pit had been dug on the Fairfield green big enough to roast a whole ox, an animal so large that the roasting had to begin a day earlier. The official opening of festivities began with the firing of eighteen rounds by Grover's Hill soldiers; this salute was answered by eighteen blasts from one of the Grover's Hill brass pieces that had been moved to the green. In a long procession, Mill River residents towed a boat, with forty boys as crew, on runners all the way to the center of Fairfield. Once all had assembled from Green's Farms and Greenfield and Stratfield and Mill River and Black Rock and Fairfield itself, the crowd entered the meetinghouse to hear remarks by the Reverend Philo Shelton of Trinity Episcopal Church and the Reverend Hemon Humphrey of the Fairfield Congregational Church. "Psalms and hymns were sung, accompanied by instruments of music." Then everyone marched around the courthouse and the Fairfield Academy buildings.

All partook in a "sumptuous repast," men in the academy and women in the courthouse. The Grover's Hill men fired another salute, and then the green was illuminated with the fires from eighteen tar barrels piled in the form of a pyramid. Many then adjourned to Knapp's Tavern on the green or to Pike's Tavern in Mill River for music and dancing. "Thus ended this celebration, the likes of which Old Fairfield has not seen since," wrote a nineteenth-century Fairfield resident who had witnessed the affair as a child many years before. "A barrel of rum had been set up in the morning, with a cup attached, free to all who wished, and . . . among the six thousand who visited the village that day, no one was seen intoxicated." The writer saw this as another victory for propriety.[14]

Fairfield had good reason for jubilation. The war was over, townspeople assumed they would get back to the business of producing farm goods for New York and other markets, some possibly as far away as the West Indies; of building up Fairfield's fleet and expanding its areas of trade; of adding more wharves and stores at Black Rock and Mill River; of completing the reconstruction of the center of Fairfield; and of generally working to become the dominant town in the county once again. As Hull Sherwood and his family dined "upon [an] 18 lb. turkey and puddings" and gave thanks for the "providential deliverance from the calamities of War," he and his neighbors must have felt as confident about their town's future as they had at the beginning of the century.[15]

### NOTES

1. Jonathan Bulkley, *Journals*, 50.

2. Ibid., 65; William Wheeler's Journal, in Lathrop, *Black Rock*, 77.

3. Jonathan Bulkley, *Journals*, 65.

4. William Wheeler's Journal, in Lathrop, *Black Rock*, 79.

5. Jonathan Bulkley, *Journals*, 109; William Wheeler's Journal, in Lathrop, *Black Rock*, 80.

6. William Wheeler's Journal, in Lathrop, *Black Rock*, 80.

7. Jonathan Bulkley, *Journals*, 137.

8. Quoted in Banks, *This is Fairfield*, 231.

9. Jonathan Bulkley, *Journals*, 95, 105.

10. Ibid., 105.

11. Ibid. 106, 123.

12. Little has been written about Sherman. The only biography is Michael V. Bevacqua, "Roger Minott Sherman (1773-1844): Fairfield's Eminent Jurist and Politician," M. A. thesis, Southern Connecticut State University, 1976.

13. Quoted in Richard J. Purcell, *Connecticut in Transition, 1775-1818*, 2d ed. (Middletown, Conn., 1963), 186-187.

14. Quoted in Banks, *This Is Fairfield*, 88; Anonymous 1815 Diary, Bradley Family Papers, FHS.

15. Quoted in Banks, *This is Fairfield*, 226.

*The Embargo and the War of 1812*

# Years of Change

THE RESTORATION of peace brought change to Fairfield. Probably few areas of life felt the impact of new ideas and methods more drastically than did politics. After the War of 1812, more Fairfield men became involved in politics, held public office, and came to feel that their opinions were worthier of consideration than ever before. Consequently there was more rotation in office and, while many of the old names still appeared among the lists of public officials, new names emerged with more regularity than ever.

The Federalists, whose control in Fairfield had been tenuous until the war temporarily revived their ailing fortunes, immediately felt the repercussions of the Hartford Convention. Roger M. Sherman hung onto his seat until 1818, but lesser individuals lost their offices immediately. In the October 1815 session of the Connecticut legislature, John Hull and William Robinson, both Republicans, represented Fairfield. Hull and David Hill, another Republican, won the two seats the following spring, when Fairfield also voted for Oliver Wolcott, the Republican challenger, over John Cotton Smith, the Federalist incumbent, for governor. Wolcott had argued that Federalism was really political Congregationalism and that the time for the disestablishment of the Congregational Church in Connecticut was long overdue. Smith warned voters that the Republican party would squander the values and traditions of Connecticut unless they chose men of steady habits, the Federalists.

Smith survived the election of 1816 despite Fairfield's support for Wolcott, but never again would the people of Connecticut elect a Federalist governor. In 1817, Wolcott defeated Smith. The victory came as a result of a tolerationist platform, which demanded that the Congregational Church be disestablished. The platform possessed great appeal in Fairfield with its substantial dissenting population—Methodists, Baptists, and Anglicans—and with its close economic and cultural ties to New York, where disestablishment had come in 1777. (All the coastal towns of Fairfield County voted for Wolcott and his tolerationist program in the 1817 election.)

*Gideon Tomlinson, the twenty-fifth governor
of Connecticut, lived on Bronson Road.*

The year 1816 saw the end of Lewis-Burr Sturges's political career, although he lived until 1844. The son of Jonathan Sturges, who had himself sat in the Congress of the United States, and a member of Yale's class of 1783, Lewis-Burr Sturges had served fifteen consecutive terms in the General Assembly before serving six consecutive terms in the Congress. But time had run out for men like Sturges. Like Roger M. Sherman, he was a man whose ideas were more appropriate to an earlier time. Suffering from the taint of Federalist involvement in the Hartford Convention, Sturges was too aristocratic, too old-fashioned, too convinced of the infallibility of the wise and the good and the rich, to prosper in the new world of politics.

Gideon Tomlinson belonged to the new era. Born in Stratford, Connecticut, in 1780, Tomlinson had also attended Yale College, class of 1798. After graduation he accepted a position as a tutor on a plantation in Northampton County, Virginia, before returning to Connecticut to study law with Charles Chauncey of New Haven. In 1807, he settled in Greenfield with his new bride, Sarah Bradley Tomlinson, the daughter of Walter Bradley, Samuel Smedley's successor as collector of customs in the Fairfield District and one of the founders of the Republican party in town. Fairfield first sent Tomlinson to the General Assembly in 1817, where he became Speaker of the House in only his second term. He helped draft the Connecticut Constitution of 1818, which did indeed disestablish the Congregational Church and which Roger M. Sherman, predictably, thought would usher in an age of irreligion in Connecticut. Tomlinson served four terms in the United States House of Representatives before becoming the twenty-fifth governor of the state in 1827 and joining the United States Senate four years later. Because of differences with President Andrew Jackson, he eventually left both political life and the Democratic party, the ideological offspring of the Republican party that he and his father-in-law had served so well. Tomlinson believed as strongly in "the intelligence & virtue of the People" as Sturges and Sherman did in the need for common men to defer to the judgment of persons, like themselves, those born to govern.[1]

The dominant role these three men played in political affairs in Connecticut between about 1805, when Sturges first went to Washington, and 1832, when Tomlinson had openly broken with President Jackson, indicated that Fairfield was again a force in the state. Second in influence only to towns like Hartford and New Haven before Tryon's raid in 1779, Fairfield was, for a time at least, again reasserting itself in Connecticut.

By 1820, Fairfield was once more the largest town in the county. The town's fifty-four square miles contained 4151 persons that year. Children could attend any of sixteen common schools and three academies — Fairfield Academy, Greenfield Academy, and Black Rock Academy. The town's grand list amounted to almost $90,000 and included about 550 dwellings and twenty-five stores scattered among Fairfield, Greenfield, Black Rock, Green's Farms, and Mill River. The center of Fairfield included a post office, located in the store operated by Justin Hobart and his sister, Mary, a courthouse, the county jail, the meetinghouse of the Prime Society or Congregational Church, and the academy and was thought to be "considerable of a settlement, although it has never entirely recovered from the devastation which it experienced during the revolution."[2]

Fairfield's economic life remained essentially unaltered after the War of 1812. During the war, when imported products were nearly impossible to obtain, the town had encouraged Benjamin Sturges to build a dam across Mill River to power machinery "for carding & spinning, and weaving and manufacturing cloth."[3] Apparently Sturges and possibly another Fairfield cloth manufacturer prospered for as long as the war lasted; but with the coming of peace and Great Britain's policy of dumping manufactured goods in the United States in hopes of discouraging the Industrial Revolution in this country, Sturges's enterprise as well as whatever local competition he faced collapsed. By 1820, nothing resembling a factory existed in Fairfield. It was still an agricultural town, producing some wheat, more potatoes, and even more corn. These agricultural products continued to find their way to New Haven, Boston, and especially New York.

Walter Bradley replaced Samuel Smedley as customs collector for the Fairfield District on July 6, 1812. He established the customs house in his store in Greenfield, a location that was convenient for him if not for the town's sea captains. The duties he collected during the war had been small because of the danger of British cruisers. The years right after the war were also difficult ones for Fairfield's maritime industry. Great Britain closed its West Indian ports in particular, and other ports generally, to American carriers. European powers began to transport their own goods, thus creating new competition for the American merchant marine. And just as Boston was usurping trade that Salem, for example, had once controlled, so New York was taking more and more foreign trade away from the seaports of Long Island Sound. Foreign commerce and shipping came to center in major ports, New York and Boston, and to avoid the small ones like New Haven and New London and Fairfield.

The West Indian trade, the only branch of foreign trade in which Fairfield was

*The Walter Bradley House built in the 1700s still stands on Bronson Road. It was later owned by the Barzelia Banks family shown here about 1890.*

involved, practically collapsed right after the war. William Wheeler noted on February 24, 1815, the day Fairfield celebrated the restoration of peace, that "West India produce falls to half the price in two or three days, — a great loss to some." Falling prices virtually eliminated Fairfield from the Caribbean traffic. An occasional ship sailed from Black Rock for the islands, to be sure, but infrequently enough to attract attention. William Wheeler wrote that on May 14, 1818, "from the W.I. arrived Capt. G[ershom] Sturges with fruit, molasses & spirits." On January 15, 1820, the departure of the *Chauncey* from Black Rock for the Caribbean merited a comment in his diary. The *Chauncey* returned on July 17 with sixty-one hogsheads of rum. As the 1820s progressed, such voyages occurred less and less frequently. If goods departed from the general area directly for the West Indies, they usually left from Bridgeport; and by 1825 the only foreign trade from Fairfield County originated there.[4]

Fairfield's fleet became a coasting fleet exclusively. Of the four customs house districts in Connecticut — New London, New Haven, Middletown, and Fairfield — Fairfield was by far the least important, that is, generated the smallest amount of money from duties, because its ships rarely left the country. In 1821, 97.3 percent of all the shipping in the Fairfield Custom House District was occupied in the coasting trade. Given Bridgeport's participation in the West Indian trade — limited as that may have been compared to a port like New London — the remaining 2.7 percent of that shipping

*Years of Change*

probably included ships from neither Black Rock nor Mill River. More than a decade earlier, Timothy Dwight had written that "the coasting trade [in Fairfield] is of considerable importance, while that which is foreign is comparatively small."[5]

Mill River harbor, although too shallow for large vessels under any circumstances and able to allow even small vessels entrance to the harbor only at high tide, had several distinct advantages over Black Rock in the coastal trade. Black Rock had access to only a limited hinterland; the Black Rock Turnpike remained in the planning stages as late as 1830. Mill River, on the other hand, was the natural commercial center for both Greenfield and Green's Farms. Its proximity to Bridgeport also hurt Black Rock. Bridgeport already had a sophisticated system of transportation, and area farmers with produce to ship naturally gravitated in that direction. Mill River could hardly afford to ignore the competition Bridgeport offered, but given its ready access to Green's Farms and Greenfield, it certainly was in a far better position to protect itself.

Black Rock might have been able to survive the challenges from Mill River and Bridgeport had not nature intervened in the form of the hurricanes of 1811 and 1821. These storms, which wrought havoc all along the Connecticut coast, demonstrated that Black Rock, while second in the state to New London in terms of the depth of its waters at low tide, provided far less protection for vessels during severe storms than either Bridgeport or Mill River. The storms ended any hopes that Black Rock merchants had not only of being the area's dominant port but of being anything more than its poorest. As of the 1820s, Black Rock's fate, despite the optimism of some local property owners, was sealed.

Mill River, by contrast, became the most prosperous area of Fairfield, "a flourishing maritime village" with a booming commerce that consisted "of a coasting trade with New-York and the southern ports, which is carried on extensively, and generally to advantage."[6] Mill River could, by 1825, claim twenty buildings used in commerce and numbered a brig, five schooners, and twenty sloops in its fleet. The harbor was too shallow to accommodate steamboats, but its sailing ships brought business and affluence to Mill River. Pike and Sturges; Meeker and Sherwood (later W. B. Meeker); Joseph Jennings and then Joseph Jennings and Son and finally Charles Jennings; Banks and Sherwood (later Simon Banks); and Ebenezer Allen would all eventually become major Mill River shipping firms.

The United States government helped where it could. It constructed an inner breakwater in 1815 to provide protection for ships at anchor. Ten years later, in March 1825, it authorized the building of three small beacons to assist captains as they entered the harbor. Congress appropriated $6097 in March 1829 to replace the inner breakwater with one at the mouth of the channel and two years later added another $10,000 to enlarge the harbor's protective system.

This was money well invested in the eyes of Mill River sea captains, because they used the facility to good advantage. David Bradley owned three-eighths of the *Comet*, a Mill River sloop. In July 1817, he made a round trip from New York to Boston, carrying both freight and passengers. After all expenses were paid, Bradley and his partners — the ubiquitous Eleazer Bulkley & Sons and Walter Perry — realized, in three weeks' time, a profit of $356.63, or about a fifth of the value of the *Comet*. By multiplying this voyage by the hundreds that Mill River ships made every year, one can understand how the village flourished as it did.

The good times that some Mill River persons enjoyed during the years after the War of 1812 eluded many Fairfield families. Generally work was scarce and wages down. In addition, the cost of living was up. This perplexing situation arose because for about half a century Connecticut had had too many people. As the population grew larger and larger, as the available land remained constant, and as technology continued incapable of making either workers or the land more productive, more and more Connecticut men and women had to consider the possibility of leaving the state, of seeking prosperity elsewhere.

Shortly after the American Revolution, some Fairfield people began to decide that other parts of the United States, such as western New Hampshire or Vermont, offered more opportunities than Fairfield. Land was cheap and opportunities abundant. By the time George Washington had completed his presidency, discouraged Fairfield families were much more likely to be headed in the direction of New York, Genesee and Westmoreland counties being popular destinations. By the beginning of the nineteenth century, the Western Reserve of Ohio, known to some as New Connecticut, was beckoning Fairfield men and women. The summons became even louder and clearer after the War of 1812; some Connecticut persons said that "Ohio Fever" had entirely taken over their state.

The reasons for the mania were abundantly clear. The life of a farmer in Connecticut was one of endless work and limited rewards. The scarcity of farmland meant that what was available was expensive. In Fairfield, one could expect to pay $60 or $70 an acre for good land — in the Western Reserve, land was selling for $3 an acre, land that was in every way superior to the best farm lands in Fairfield. The Ohio land was more fertile, more productive, and, being relatively free of stones and rich in nutrients, demanded less of the farmer's precious time. Unless one were the only son of prosperous parents and could anticipate inheriting a substantial farm; unless one enjoyed the good fortune of owning part of a Mill River sloop or a store like Walter Bradley's in Greenfield or Justin and Mary Hobart's near the courthouse in Fairfield; unless one had a special skill or an extraordinary education — the idea of pulling up stakes and heading for Ohio was one that a man with his wife would probably at least seriously consider.

Joseph Noyes, the son of Mary Fish Silliman and the stepson of the late Gold Selleck Silliman, decided in the spring of 1800 that "New Connecticut," the Western Reserve, probably had more to offer him than Fairfield ever could, and so set out for Ohio to see if all of the good things that he had heard about the area were true. He returned to the Silliman home on Holland Hill convinced that Ohio was the land of opportunity and immediately put his house and lands and most of his movable property up for sale, in March 1801.

By the morning of June 3, he and his wife and four of their children were ready to leave Fairfield. The departure was as hard for those who stayed behind as it was for those who left. Mary Silliman, Joseph's mother, described the scene: "We all sustained the parting pang with as much fortitude as could be expected . . . so that by standers gave us much credit for our firmness." Mary walked with her daughter-in-law as far as the schoolhouse. "She mounted the carage, I took a lonely seat on the schoolhouse, and looked after them untill the objects by which they past hid them from my sight." Reluctantly she then "commended them to the care of a kind providence, and returned to the vacant mansion."[7]

*Years of Change*

Life in Warren, Ohio was hard for the Noyes family. On May 7, 1802, Joseph's wife died, and after a long and desperate struggle, he ultimately lost all his worldly goods and fell into bankruptcy. Nonetheless, the letters he sent back to his family were filled with exuberant enthusiasm. "Two Days Labour in a Week will afford as good a support as Six in New England," he wrote. This was the absolute truth, he contended, and "if you will take the trouble to visit us, we can cure your unbelief."[8]

Disbelief troubled few would-be pilgrims. A bigger handicap for most was their tendency to believe that Ohio was the answer to all their problems. They traveled west by the hundreds. The vast number of sojourners on the road to Ohio in 1810 prompted Margaret Dwight to write back to Connecticut: "From what I have seen and heard, I think the state of Ohio will be filled before winter." In October 1817, Jonathan Bulkley wrote of persons leaving "this Land of Steady habits to the western world where all the Surplus Inhabitants of N[ew] England are fast drifting." In July 1818 he noted: "Mrs Turney writes she has not had occasion to regret leaving old Fairfield as yet [and that] she was accompanied down the Ohio by a number of Fairfield folks."[9]

Perhaps the most notable man to seek a better life in Ohio was Lewis-Burr Sturges. The former congressman certainly was under no pressure, economic or otherwise, to leave. He moved to Norwalk, Ohio, to oversee the vast tract of land he had accumulated there. As recounted in chapter 6, when Connecticut used part of its lands in the Western Reserve to create a fund to help underwrite the costs of education throughout the state, it employed the remaining portion of that land—called the Firelands—to reimburse Connecticut citizens who had lost property during the American Revolution. Sturges bought up as much of this land as he could. By offering cash to people who were not necessarily poor but generally impecunious, Sturges managed to acquire a great deal of land for a relatively small amount of money. He hoped that by being in Ohio he could obtain a premium price for his real estate. The plan worked handsomely; recent arrivals in Ohio, unfamiliar with frontier prices, were often willing to pay more than the going rate. Sturges found plenty of willing customers. His problem was his fondness for Western corn whiskey, a fondness that eventually consumed both him and his substantial fortune.

For some men and women who found life in Fairfield hard, emigrating to Ohio or western New York was a fine solution. But for others, the idea of moving west had no appeal. The notion of creating a farm out of the Ohio wilderness was too much like trying to do the same thing back home. The whole process involved too much hardship and no guarantee of any reward. Fortunately for these individuals, other alternatives existed.

So while some people were trekking off to New London, Norwalk, or even Fairfield, Ohio, others were going in different directions for the same reasons. A young man might decide to leave his father's farm to go to work in a store in the South, for example. Here was a chance for a man with ambition and a keen mind to accumulate more money than most farmers would ever see. Joseph Earl Sheffield, who was born in Mill River in 1793, saw no future for himself in Fairfield. With his father's reluctant permission, when he was fourteen he moved to New Bern, North Carolina, to take a position as a clerk in a store owned by another Fairfield man, Stephen Fowler, who had also gone to New Bern to seek opportunities he was unable to find at home. Perhaps the elder Sheffields' concerns about their son's leaving home, were eased by the boy's working for a former neighbor and family friend. And they doubtless took comfort in having Mrs. Sheffield's brother, Captain Burr Thorp, in nearby Wilmington, North Carolina.

Joseph learned the mercantile business in New Bern and in 1817 opened his own store in Mobile, Alabama, shipping cotton and other products to New York and using the income to purchase goods for his store. Sheffield made a fortune in the South, used that fortune to invest in railroads in New England and in the West, and retired in 1855 to spend the remainder of his life endowing worthy projects with the wealth he had accumulated. Perhaps he is best known for providing Yale University with the funds for the Sheffield Scientific School.

Jonathan Sturges, a nephew of Lewis-Burr Sturges, was nine years younger than Sheffield. Born in 1802, he went to work in a store his brother, Lothrop L. Sturges, owned in Fredericksburg, Virginia, in 1816. Lothrop was attempting to accomplish there what Sheffield would try in Mobile the following year. Eventually the two Sturges brothers, having found initial success in Virginia, decided to move to New York. Lothrop eventually became the senior partner in Sturges & Clearman, a shipping and mercantile firm, and Jonathan came to head Sturges, Bennet & Company, one of the largest merchant houses in New York. Both men left substantial fortunes, Jonathan's being one of the largest in the country at the time of his death in 1874.

Sheffield and the Sturges brothers were hardly typical of the men who left town to go into business. For every story like theirs one could uncover dozens of others, like that of Nathaniel B. Hill, who left home filled with great expectations but never saw them realized. But because of the stories of success, Fairfield continued for years to provide youngsters trying to emulate the achievements of these men in cities and towns throughout the United States. Even if wealth eluded the young hopefuls, they were happy to have avoided the farm, either in Fairfield or Ohio.

Probably more Fairfield young men went to sea than into business. Here was another way to avoid the drudgery of farm work, and here was the means to accumulate a handsome nest egg in a short time. Working aboard ship meant good earnings. In 1817, a time of low wages, Daniel Bradley was paying ablebodied seamen about $19 a month. (A boy with no particular skills who served aboard ship could count on earning about half that amount.) While both seamen and boys were at sea, they enjoyed the benefits of free board, free room, and in most cases free strong drink.

The best that a farm laborer could hope to make was $20 a month or $.80 a day, from which he had to pay for room and board. This rate remained constant for many years. In Fairfield in 1850, farmers were paying $1.00 a day for laborers who provided their own meals and lodging; ten years later, the figure had increased to only $1.25. If a man had to feed himself and provide his own quarters out of his $.80 or $1.00 or $1.25 a day, the possibility of accumulating enough money to buy a farm or to marry became remote. But a year or two at sea could leave a man with a substantial amount of cash.

The idea of going to sea became even more appealing when one considered the possibilities for achievement. A cabin boy could become an ablebodied seaman. An ablebodied seaman might eventually aspire to be master of a ship. And the most successful sailors—and there were enough examples of these to keep the dream alive—might someday own their own vessel, or perhaps several vessels and a store. The future for

*Portrait of Captain Abraham Gould Jennings, Fair-*
*field native, sea captain, and deacon of the First*
*Congregational Church.*

a farm laborer was more of what he had known from the first—low wages, hard work, little future.

Eleazer Bulkley showed young Fairfield seamen what they might become. Born of poor parents, Bulkley went to sea when he was twelve. He served with Samuel Smedley during the American Revolution and after the war went to New York, where he worked on ships trading with the West Indies and with Nova Scotia. In 1785, he returned to Fairfield and signed on as a mate with Captain Joseph Bartram, who traded up and down the East coast. Bulkley liked the coasting trade and decided to use the money he accumulated during his years at sea to buy a ship with Miah Perry; the two sailed between Mill River, New York, and New Haven. Eventually Bulkley bought out Perry and continued the trade alone. Convinced that he should invest as much of his profits as possible back in the business, he was always looking for larger and more ships to buy. In 1788, he established the firm of Eleazer Bulkley & Sons, a New York shipping company that quickly became as important as any involved in the coastal trade. By 1841, just before he died, he and his sons owned 3790 tons of shipping—more than had existed in all of Fairfield just a few years before.

Bulkley's career served as a guide for others. Wakeman Burritt was a Mill River man who also went into the shipping business in New York, eventually becoming a partner in the firm of Burritt & Cannon, located on South Street near the Peck Slip, where Fairfield ships usually docked. John Gould was the son of Jason Gould and the grandson of Abraham Gold, who had been killed defending Ridgefield during the American Revolution. Younger than Bulkley and Burritt, John Gould entered the New

York shipping business in 1826 when his ships began to travel between New York and Virginia. Later he concentrated on trade between New York and Liverpool, England. Both Gould and Burritt, like Bulkley, died wealthy men. In the years to follow, dozens of young Fairfield men followed this same course with varying degrees of success. Some became heads of major shipping concerns, other spent their lives as clerks; still others were forced to return shamefacedly to Fairfield to pick up once more on the farm.

So many men, in fact, went to New York during these years from Fairfield and towns like Fairfield that by the 1830s the port of New York came to be dominated by New England men and would continue under their domination until after the Civil War. Ports like New York and Boston were growing furiously and smaller ports like Black Rock were finding it more and more difficult to survive. New York attracted New England men by promising them work. Some continued to work aboard ship both as masters and as ordinary seamen. Men like Bulkley and Burritt and Gould headed shipping houses. Somewhat less successful than the heads of shipping houses were the men who became commission merchants, who collected 5 percent on the sales they directed to New York from Mill River, Bridgeport, or some other Connecticut port. Several of Eleazer Bulkley's sons worked as commission merchants as young men. Ship brokers enjoyed about as much status as commission merchants. The ship brokers sold ships, offered them for charter, and located cargoes. A successful ship broker would see that all the vessels in his care were employed constantly. Bulkley's sons also served as ship brokers as they learned the maritime business.[10]

The influx of Fairfield men into New York created an interlocking network of business connections that was almost as tightly bound together as the memberships of the private clubs to which many of these men later belonged. One can picture the scene about 1850, by which time Fairfield men had thoroughly insinuated themselves into the New York port. As Andrew Bulkley, one of Eleazer's sons, walked to his place of business at 88 South Street he must have felt as much at home as he would have in Molly Pike's Tavern. At 40 South Street he came to the offices of Sturges & Clearman, a firm headed by Lothrop L. Sturges; Bulkley had known Sturges since childhood. Forty-eight South Street was the headquarters of John Bulkley & Company, a mercantile business headed by one of Andrew's cousins. Charles Dimon, the son of Captain Ebenezer Dimon, was originally a commission merchant at 73 South Street. Later he became a partner in Dunham and Dimon, a shipping company that maintained its offices at the same address; neither Dimon nor Bulkley could recall a time when they had not known each other. Charles's brother, Frederick D. Dimon, was in partnership with William Webb Wakeman in the shipping company of Wakeman, Dimon & Company. This company traded primarily with the East Indies and China and had its headquarters at 74 South Street. William Webb Wakeman later operated a steamship company—first Wakeman, Gookin & Dichinson and finally W. W. Wakeman & Company—from the same address. Like the Bulkleys, the Wakemans and the Dimons were Mill River people.

By the time he reached his office, the headquarters of Eleazer Bulkley & Sons, his younger brother, George, had probably already arrived at his quarters in the same building. George, who was then working as a commission merchant, found the location convenient in part because much of his business was with Henry J. Beers, formerly of Fairfield, a wholesale grocer doing business at 177 South Street.

Even more entangling than the New York business alliances between Fairfield men were their family and marriage connections. Some of these ties were obvious — their surnames made the Bulkley brothers, the Sturges brothers, and the Dimon brothers easy to identify. Less obvious but no less significant were marriage bonds. Jonathan Bulkley was married to Miranda Thorp, daughter of Captain Walter Thorp. John Gould married Miranda's sister, Mary. Marriage connected two major New York shipping companies: William Webb Wakeman's mother, Esther Dimon Wakeman, was the aunt of both Charles Dimon, of Dunham and Dimon, and Frederick D. Dimon, William Webb's partner. William Webb's sister, Hetty Wakeman Gookin, married Warren D. Gookin, who had been a South Street merchant before joining Wakeman, Gookin & Dichinson.

The Fairfield men and women in New York tended to marry among themselves. Goulds married Thorps, Dimons married Bulkleys, and they all seemed to marry Perrys and Wakemans. The social and business ties among these families led to these connections by marriage; the intermarrying led in turn to even closer social and commercial bonds. And the fortunes that some of these men managed to generate remained under the control of these tightly woven families, remained protected from the grasping fingers of outsiders, voracious persons who were incapable of thinking or acting as a Sturges or a Jennings or a Burr would think or act.

The outward migration of people from Fairfield that lasted from the American Revolution until about 1850 had profound repercussions for the town. It meant first of all the cessation of population growth. Fairfield failed to achieve as large a population as it had had at the time of the American Revolution until after the Civil War. Furthermore, those who left were ambitious, industrious, and innovative. The outmigration left behind a population that was generally content with life as it existed. Some were satisfied because they had either already achieved or were in the process of achieving whatever goals they had set for themselves. Others clung to what they had because they were fearful of change or ignorant of other alternatives.

Content to survive by means of an agricultural system that was becoming more and more obsolete in the face of competition from Ohio and other newly developed areas, and by means of a maritime industry that was at best ancillary to what was happening in the great ports of Boston and New York, the town was entering a slow and long decline during which it was frequently victimized by its neighbors and at the end of which it would be but a shadow of its former self. The period of stagnation was to last for more than half a century.

## NOTES

1. Gideon Tomlinson to Noyes Barber, Dec. 25, 1830, Gideon Tomlinson Papers, Fairfield Family Papers, FHS. Purcell, *Connecticut in Transition*, explains the political changes of these years.

2. John C. Pease and John M. Niles, *A Gazetteer of the States of Connecticut and Rhode Island* (Hartford, 1819), 173.

3. FTR, B, I, Aug. 30, 1813.

4. William Wheeler's Journal, in Lathrop, *Black Rock*, 81, 84. Wheeler noted the decline of Black Rock's role in the West Indian trade.

5. Dwight, *Travels*, III, 359. Statistical information about Fairfield's fleet can be obtained from the *American States Papers, Commerce and Navigation*, vols. I and II, and from the Fairfield Customs District Records, Bridgeport Public Library.

6. Pease and Niles, *Gazetteer*, 174.

7. Buel and Buel, *The Way of Duty*, 236-37.

8. Ibid., 240.

9. Dwight is quoted in Purcell, *Connecticut in Transition*, 95; Jonathan Bulkley, *Journal*, 122.

10. This topic is discussed in Robert G. Albion, "Yankee Domination of New York Port, 1820-1865," *New England Quarterly* 5 (Oct. 1932), 665-98.

# Years of Decline

THE BOUNDARIES of Fairfield had remained constant since the General Assembly had taken the northern part of town to create Weston in 1787. By 1824, another move was underway to separate a section of Fairfield. Ebenezer Jesup and others petitioned the legislature to incorporate a new town from what had been the Green's Farms area of Fairfield and the Norfield section of Weston. Fairfield opposed the move in 1824 and again in 1825 and 1826.

Fairfield's word carried considerable weight in Connecticut at that time. Although a steady stream of Fairfield men and women was deserting town for Ohio or New York or various other points, Fairfield remained the largest town in the county until the late 1820s. Even in 1830 it was second only to Danbury, whose population exceeded that of Fairfield by only 85 persons. Despite Jesup's persistence, Fairfield's opposition to his plan demanded the attention of the General Assembly and meant the end of the scheme.

Barely had that skirmish ended when the town had to face another challenge. Since its creation in 1789, the Fairfield Customs House District had been located in Fairfield. While Samuel Smedley was the collector, until 1812, the customs house was located near the courthouse in the center of Fairfield. When Walter Bradley replaced Smedley, he moved his office to Greenfield, where it remained for twenty years, located in a corner of the Bradley store. In 1832, Bradley lost his position, apparently because of differences that had developed between his son-in-law, Gideon Tomlinson, and President Andrew Jackson. Tomlinson at the time represented Connecticut in the United States Senate and was, like Jackson, a Democrat. Under these circumstances, one would not expect Bradley's post to be in jeopardy. The problem arose when Tomlinson, whose sense of morality was as finely tuned as anyone's in the Senate, broke with Jackson when the president gave his blessing to Secretary of War John Eaton's marriage to barmaid Peggy O'Neale, an affair that should have been of no consequence but that created irreconcilable divisions within the Jackson forces. Jackson retaliated by withdrawing his support of Bradley. Tomlinson hoped his father-in-law's replacement would be a Fairfield man, someone who would maintain the customs house in town. The selectmen—Robert Wilson, Walter Sherwood, Ebenezer Beers, and Abraham D. Baldwin—and the senator, of course, worked hard to see that the new appointee would be a townsman.

Jackson, unwilling to listen to anything Tomlinson might have to say, was compelled to hear Bridgeport's request for the customs house because of that town's growing influence. In the end, Jackson appointed a Bridgeport man, Samuel Simons; he assumed his new responsiblity on July 1, 1832. As was expected, Simons moved the customs house to his town. The change meant little to Fairfield in terms of lost commerce or employment. It did mean a loss of prestige. When George Washington had originally established the customs house district, he would never have considered locating it anywhere else in the county but in Fairfield. But now it was in Bridgeport. Fairfield saw the move as an affront, a slander on a proud tradition.

The town was still smarting over the departure of the customs house when in May 1835 Daniel Nash submitted a petition to the General Assembly asking for the creation of a new town, part of which was to come from eastern Norwalk and part from western Fairfield. The Fairfield town meeting appointed Jeremiah Sturges and David Coley to oppose the petition. At stake was the section of town that had come to be known as Saugatuck, a small community built on the eastern side of the river of the same name just opposite a somewhat larger village where industry was just beginning to take hold; the community on the western side of the river was in Norwalk. Saugatuck was too remote to be of vital importance to Fairfield, but the town saw the move to take it as another challenge. Unfortunately this challenge, like the one over the customs house, was one against which Fairfield was unable to defend itself; during its May 1835 session, the General Assembly created the town of Westport, in the process taking both population and territory from the already beleaguered Fairfield.

Almost immediately after its creation, Westport began to cast covetous eyes on Green's Farms. Some Green's Farms people, notably Joseph Hyde, wanted to join the new town. In 1839, Hyde petitioned the assembly for the annexation of Green's Farms to Westport. Fairfield appointed Jeremiah Sturges to fight the petition. Sturges was successful in 1839 and again in 1840, when Moses Taylor offered an almost identical memorial. Thomas Robinson replaced Sturges as the town agent in 1841; he too managed to stave off the Westport challenge.

But by this time Fairfield had less ammunition than it would have had just a few years before. By 1840, Fairfield had fallen to fourth place in population in the county. For the first time Bridgeport was the largest town in southwestern Connecticut. Danbury was second and Norwalk third. Bridgeport, Danbury and Norwalk were all becoming industrial towns; the vast majority of Fairfield's population of 3654 made its living in agriculture. Jobs in manufacturing were as rare in town as they were plentiful in Bridgeport. In fact, in 1840 the brand-new town of Westport boasted $97,600 invested in manufacturing while Fairfield could claim only $53,400.

Recognizing Fairfield's position of weakness, those urging the annexation of Green's Farms to Westport refused to abandon the fight. In 1842, Moses Taylor came back with his petition. Moses A. Sherwood represented the town in opposing Taylor, but he failed to prevent what many saw as inevitable. The General Assembly voted in May 1842 that Green's Farms should be separated from Fairfield and joined to Westport. Again Fairfield lost population and territory, including some of the best farmland in town.

*John Warner Barber's engraving of the Borough of Southport viewed from the south in 1836.*

By 1850 the town included only 3614 persons, and had it not been for the arrival of the first large contingent of immigrants (most of them from Ireland) the population would have been close to 3300. In fact, since 1820 Fairfield's population had fallen 13 percent, while that of Connecticut had grown 35 percent; that of the United States, 141 percent; and that of Bridgeport, 278 percent. Compared with the time of the American Revolution, Fairfield's population decline was even more dramatic—a 32 percent reduction. Part of this was attributable to the loss of Green's Farms and Saugatuck, but more important in explaining how Fairfield lost 32 percent of its population while the United States as a whole grew by 560 percent was the migration of men and women out of town.

The population decline that had occurred by 1850 could easily have been even greater. In 1842 the Fairfield town meeting received a petition "signed by a large number of the Inhabitants of the said Town of Fairfield to be presented to the next General Assembly . . . praying for a division of the said town of Fairfield into two towns." The object of this petition was to make Mill River into a separate town. By far the most prosperous section of Fairfield, that village probably could have survived as an independent entity.[1]

Talk of independence for Mill River had begun many years before. Back in 1831, the Connecticut General Assembly had officially changed the name of Mill River to Southport when it created the Borough of Southport. Many Southport people believed that this was the first step in independence for the village. They remembered that Bridgeport, before the General Assembly transformed it into a full-fledged town, had started life as a borough, and they understood that a borough functioned much like a town except that it lacked the authority to send representatives to the General Assembly.

Jeremiah Sturges, who had fought to change the name of Mill River to Southport and had been responsible for wrestling funds from Congress for the improvement of Southport harbor, and Jonathan Bulkley, the first warden or chief executive officer of the Borough of Southport, were the driving forces behind the creation of the borough. Sturges was also the first president of the Connecticut Bank, Mill River Branch, which was chartered by the General Assembly at the same time that it created the borough, and Bulkley was the bank's first cashier. (The Mill River Branch became the Southport National Bank in 1851.)

During almost the entire nineteenth century, Southport was the commercial center of Fairfield. By the 1830s, it contained about seventy dwellings, eight stores, an academy, a post office, and an Episcopal church, besides the bank. It also was the most important port between Bridgeport and New York. A glance at the *New England Mercantile Union Directory* for 1849 demonstrates how complete Southport's domination of commercial life in Fairfield had become. Of five groceries in Fairfield, all were in Southport. The only coal dealer was in Southport, as was the only manufacturer — Sherman and Hawley, which produced saddle trees. Also in Southport were Fairfield's only stove dealer, only dry goods dealer, and only bank.

In 1854 a second bank opened in Fairfield. It too located in Southport. In fact, this new bank, the Southport Savings Bank, did business in the Southport National Bank building for eleven years; in 1865 it opened its own building. Frederick Marquand, born in Fairfield in 1799, organized the bank. The son of Isaac Marquand, a silversmith, Frederick grew up in New York, where his father had gone to find a wider market for his wares, and learned his father's trade. But as good a silversmith as he became — and he apparently was one of the best in New York — he was an even better financier. In 1832, he returned to Fairfield, specifically to Southport, built a Greek Revival mansion for himself and his family, and devoted the rest of his life to enhancing his fortune, endowing theological schools, and obliterating any evidence that he had once been a craftsman. The bank was certainly more avocation than vocation.

By the time Marquand moved to Southport the village could boast of its many palatial residences, the homes either of Fairfield men who had done well in the local shipping business or of Fairfield men who had returned home after successful careers in New York. Building an elaborate home was an acceptable way of demonstrating to friends and neighbors the extent of their success; and by constructing a home that reflected the latest trends in architecture, they could show that they possessed the good taste with which men of wealth surely ought to be endowed.

Rarely were such individuals content to purchase an existing structure and make do with it. Wakeman B. Meeker bought the old center-chimney colonial house that William Bulkley had built back about 1770 and used it as his home for many years, but few of Meeker's friends and associates followed his example. They were more inclined to do as Charles C. Perry, a wealthy shipowner and merchant, did when, about 1825, he built his Federal style home — that is, construct a dwelling that deviated dramatically from earlier traditions, a dwelling that reflected their new status. By building such a house, Perry set himself apart from those Southport persons who were not so fortunate as he and surrounded his wife and children with luxury and convenience. He also made an investment that he was sure would hold its value.

Actually Charles Perry's home in Southport was one of the last built with the delicate Adamesque details that characterized it as Federal. Even by the 1820s, the Neo-

*The Frederick Marquand House, which stood on the site of the Pequot Library, circa 1870.*

Classical style was coming to dominate American architecture. Walter Thorp and Paschal Sheffield both built houses just after Perry did, both of which, although modest in scale and vernacular in execution, bore the details of classical buildings. They portended things to come in Southport architecture.

Henry Perry and his brother, Francis D. Perry, each built Greek Revival homes complete with five-column porticos in 1832. By the 1840s, when Austin Perry added a Corinthian portico to his home, the five Perry dwellings of Henry, Francis, Gurdon, Austin, and Oliver H. Perry were stately examples of Greek Revival architecture at its finest. They created as impressive a collection of wealthy merchants' homes as existed in southwestern Connecticut—a modern Athens right in Southport.

But because these men were so eager to remain abreast of current architectural trends, the Neo-Classical style shortly lost its appeal also. By 1850, when Wakeman

*Years of Decline*

B. Meeker decided that it was time that he proclaim the extent of his success, he chose to erect an American Italian villa. Meeker had no other choice if he was to be in vogue. His new home had the details of a villa — the low-pitched and widely overhanging roof and an ample veranda. It also had a pretentiousness that Southport's Greek Revival mansions had managed to avoid; apparently Meeker hoped no one would underestimate the extent of his achievements.

Southport's public buildings were almost the equal of its private dwellings. The Southport National Bank, built in 1833, marked the transition from Federal to Greek Revival style, and the Southport Savings Bank, which was constructed thirty years later, heralded the passage from Greek Revival to Italianate architecture. Trinity Episcopal Church moved to Southport in 1828 but suffered the loss of one building to a fire and another to a tornado before it built the Carpenter's Gothic structure that opened in 1862. The Congregationalists built their first church in Southport in 1841, a simple but well-proportioned Neo-Classical building, and the Methodists, thanks to the generosity of Joseph Wakeman, erected an equally modest and equally distinguished meetinghouse in 1854. That Southport could support three churches and two banks and that the Southport Episcopalians could recover so quickly from a succession of disasters indicated, no less than the presence of the village's mansions, the degree of its prosperity.

If Southport suffered from any circumstance that might have restricted its prosperity, it was its limited access to Connecticut's agricultural hinterland. The Connecticut Turnpike, to be sure, served the village, but that road never lived up to the expectations many Southport persons had for it. At best, because it stretched along a coastline that was rich with ports, it brought goods from only as far west as the Saugatuck River. Farmers who lived on the other side of the river generally sent their goods to Norwalk for transfer to New York. Green's Farms, which was served by the turnpike, Mill Hill, Mill Plain, and Greenfield were the only farming areas that consistently relied on Southport. The Branch Turnpike, which originated at Bennett's Bridge in Newtown and which passed through Monroe and Easton on its way to Westport, attracted some business to Southport, but probably less than it brought to Norwalk. Certainly Fairfield's most prosperous village would have been even more affluent if it had possessed a road system that came even close to that which had served Bridgeport so handsomely.

Southport's problems with roads reflected Fairfield's general indifference toward transportation. Perhaps because traveling and shipping by water had been so easy for so long, throughout the first half of the nineteenth century Fairfield remained uninterested in spending money on its roads. When Henry Sherwood first proposed the idea of the Branch Turnpike, Fairfield agreed to allow the road to pass through town but only if its share of the construction costs remained under $200. When it appeared as if Fairfield might have to spend more than that, the town meeting voted to oppose Sherwood's petition to the General Assembly for incorporation.

Fairfield's highway surveyors found the task of collecting the highway taxes in their district the most arduous part of their jobs. As a consequence, in 1847 the town voted "that the Select Men be authorized to let out the highways... for the term of three years to be kept in repair during sd. term to such contractors as they may think best for the Interest of the Town." This scheme failed, and the following year Fairfield went back to using highway surveyors to maintain the roads.[2]

Fairfield did support Walter Thorp's 1832 petition to the General Assembly "for the laying out of a turnpike road to commence . . . in Black Rock . . . and to terminate near the house of David Williams in Weston."[3] Worthy as it was, the idea for the Black Rock Turnpike came thirty years too late. Bridgeport had already established itself as the port for that hinterland which Black Rock hoped to serve. From the first the turnpike failed to live up to the expectations of its stockholders. In 1842, within a decade of its founding, the Black Rock Weston Turnpike Company was asking the General Assembly for permission to discontinue the road. By 1847, those sections in Fairfield had been abandoned to the care of the town, a responsibility that the town accepted, albeit reluctantly.

The construction of the turnpike did initiate a flurry of activity in Black Rock. David Smith, a builder from Greenfield, moved to the harbor in the 1830s and built eight dwellings and a carriage factory, all in the transitional Federal-Greek Revival style. Encouraged by the growth of the carriage industry in Bridgeport, Thomas Ransom, a Black Rock merchant, had located backers in Bridgeport and had commissioned Smith to build the factory. By 1840 Ransom and his partners had invested $27,000 in the carriage works, were employing more workers than any other establishment in town, and were annually producing more than $50,000 worth of carriages and wagons. Before the decade was over, Black Rock residents, enjoying their newfound affluence, constructed a church of their own, the first one in the port's two-hundred-year history.

The harbor also became the site of shipbuilding again. The Bridgeport *Republican Farmer* reported on November 14, 1856: "A fine ship, called the Charles Cooper, was launched in good style, this forenoon, at Hall's Ship Yard, in Black Rock. She measures about ten hundred tons, and is designed for the Antwerp trade."[4] The Hall referred to was William Hall, who moved to Black Rock from Maine about 1855. At the time of his arrival, four shipyards were in operation at Black Rock, although three of them — Captain John Britten's, Verdine Ellsworth's, and the one operated by Sturges & Clearman of New York — occupied themselves exclusively with repairs. Only Samuel Wilson's yard, the one Ichabod Wheeler had originally established, actually built ships. Wilson, in 1853, had built the largest ship ever constructed at Black Rock until Hall laid the keel of the *Charles Cooper* — the *Black Hawk*, launched on September 17, 1853, and, unfortunately for Wilson's reputation, lost at sea during her maiden voyage. Hall came to Black Rock because he thought it could become a shipbuilding center. Apparently a man of means, shortly after his arrival he built an elegant Italian villa for his family and bought out Wilson and the others.

He was well on the way to fulfilling his ambitions for the harbor when he died suddenly in 1860. His business became the property first of Hilliard & Rew and then of Rew and Walker; and under the management of both, it degenerated until it became nothing more than a chandlery and a graving yard, a nautical junkyard that disposed of unrepairable and unwanted ships.

A similar fate befell the rest of Black Rock. The carriage works had declined to such a point that Thomas Ransom gave up the business and moved to Bridgeport, where he opened a store. The carriage plant became a bellows factory. The Middle Wharf, the one that David Penfield had owned, became a coal yard, run by Woodruff Burr, and the lower wharf, which Samuel Squire and his progeny operated for so many years, became the pier for the George Hotel on Grover's Hill, a favorite spot for wealthy summer residents, where the sons and daughters of former shipwrights could now find

*Years of Decline*

employment as groundskeepers and maids. Speaking in 1887, William B. Glover, perhaps Fairfield's most prominent civic leader at the time, stated that by the end of the Civil War Black Rock "was a very immaterial and inconsequential part of the town of Fairfield." This was hardly the fate that Thomas Ransom and William Hall had had in mind for the harbor.[5]

The railroad arrived in Fairfield even before Black Rock's decline. The town reacted with indifference. In fact, Fairfield was suspicious of the innovation from the first. When in 1839 the Connecticut General Assembly was considering a petition to bring rail service to Fairfield, the town refused to support the memorial in any way. Five years later, it fought an attempt by the Housatonic Railroad, which already connected Bridgeport with Sheffield, Massachusetts, to come into town.

The Connecticut General Assembly chartered the New York and New Haven Railroad in 1844. Town residents appear to have ignored the possibility that the railroad might bring new life to their community. They seemed more concerned with how much it would pay for the lands it needed. William Burr's 1846 letter to his brother, David, explaining their father's negotiations with the railroad was typical of existing attitudes. "Some think that those that stand out [for a high price] will not do so well, but father is obliged to as he cannot get his price, which is 1000 dols," William wrote. "At first he asked 800, but everyone said it was not enough."[6] Besides getting as much as possible for their land, Fairfielders worried about what the railroad might do to the town's streets and roads. The town meeting regularly directed the selectmen to examine the railroad crossings to see that they were in as good condition after the railroad arrived as they had been previously.

The first train passed through town on its way to New York from New Haven on December 27, 1848. Two days later the same train—consisting of an engine, coal car, and four passenger cars—made the return trip. Regular service began early the following year. One could board the train in Fairfield (there was also a station in Southport) and arrive at 34th Street in New York City two hours and ten minutes later, or remain on the train for another fifteen minutes and reach Canal Street, all the way downtown.

The coming of the railroad brought change, often in ways that were totally unanticipated. The opening of service probably killed any thoughts that Southport residents still had about their village becoming a separate town, because the trains threatened to take more business away from Southport than they would bring. This unfortunate situation arose when railroad officials designated Bridgeport and Norwalk as market terminals and made Southport only a passenger and freight station. The village now faced the discouraging prospect of seeing part of the produce that had once come to it for shipment to New York going to either of the two designated terminals. Residents of Southport, still the most prosperous and commercially active part of Fairfield, decided, privately and unobtrusively, that separation offered no advantages to them. In December 1854, the Southport borough meeting adjourned sine die.

Certainly the railroad failed to make Fairfield any more sanguine about manufacturing than it had been. In 1840, Fairfield ranked seventh among the county's towns in terms of capital invested in industry, and the carriage factory in Black Rock accounted for more than half of the total investment in town. Most of the "factories" in Fairfield were like the one in which Samuel Wilson produced firearms. Wilson—who should not be confused with the Black Rock shipbuilder—employed one man besides himself, had invested about $600 in his plant, and in a typical year produced $600 worth of guns, more or less. Sherman & Hawley, the saddle tree manufacturers in Southport, operated on a similar scale. After the railroad arrived, in 1850, by which date the Black Rock carriage works had fallen on hard times, the biggest employer in town was the Wilson shipyard, where ten men worked. During that year the yard built one schooner, worth $13,000. Fairfield at the time included a venetian blind maker, James E. Beach; a patent medicine agent, Jacob B. Toucey; a "Daguerrier artist," William Naramore; and more than four hundred farmers, but it had nothing that could pass for a factory.

Fairfield was a farming community. According to the census of 1840, it produced large quantities of corn, oats, rye, potatoes, and flax. John Sherwood remarked many years later that he had seen as many as five thousand bushels of corn at one time going out of Southport harbor in 1840.

Before the 1840s, little had changed in the routine of farmers' lives since the early years of the century. April began the busiest time of the year; that was the month that farmers and their oxen would begin plowing. It was also the time they spread fertilizer, perhaps manure but probably seaweed because local animals failed to produce manure in the quantities demanded by their owners and the idea of importing stable manure from New York was one that was just beginning to take hold.

Farmers collected seaweed along Fairfield's beaches, usually in June, and then allowed it to dry and decompose before spreading it the following April. Collecting the material was about as hard as any work faced by farmers and their oxen. The seaweed was wet and heavy—frequently a single yoke of oxen was unable to pull a full cart out of the sand at McKenzie's Point, a favorite collecting location, and then up Sasco Hill. In these situations, two farmers would work together, teaming their animals to move a single load. Because the kelp and other weeds were so highly prized, farmers would sometimes try to claim all the seaweed found on an entire stretch of beach. To prevent this the town meeting on December 2, 1839, voted that no person could own any seaweed "other than that which he puts into cart or other Vehicle of conveyance and removes from said beach."

May was planting time for most crops, and in June, when they were not gathering seaweed, the farmers started mowing, a task that would probably last into July. July was also the month to pull flax and begin harvesting potatoes. Potatoes were still being dug in August, when Fairfield farmers also mowed their salt meadows, cradled their oats, and began collecting corn. They had more corn, along with rye, to gather in September, and that month and October were also the months of planting wheat and picking apples and making cider. In November, December, and January farmers broke and cleaned their flax, threshed oats and rye, and butchered animals for the dinner table. February was lambing time, also the month for the farmer to prune his fruit trees. March meant more lambs, brush to be cut, and hayseed to be sown. April was once again time to plow.

In addition to their seasonal chores, farmers had a whole array of tasks that must have seemed never ending. They had to care for their stock, milk cows and collect eggs, maintain buildings and fences, cut and haul and split mountains of firewood, repair machinery and tools that seemed forever to be breaking, train working animals, deliver products to market, and try to keep abreast of the new agricultural innovations. Angeline Morehouse was impressed when one of her neighbors used equal parts of "plaster &

*William B. Meeker's dock at Southport circa 1872.*
*The warehouse held onions and other farm produce.*

guano" on his potatoes with good results. She learned of this technique by chance, but farmers living near Southport formed themselves into the Green's Farms Agricultural Club in 1861 in order "to advance the knowledge of Agriculture and Horticulture in this Community." The group met every Monday evening to hear of new ideas and also operated a library where members could borrow books on most aspects of farming.[7]

The most revolutionary agricultural innovation that came to Fairfield during the 1840s was the commercial cultivation of onions. Farmers had grown onions in Connecticut since colonial times, but only with the development of the globe onion did the product become important in Fairfield. The Southport Globe onion, which could be white, red, or yellow and was the favorite of Fairfield farmers, required regular attention but provided an amazing yield. Planting took place as early as possible in hopes of getting onions to market while prices were still high. Only a small area could be cultivated by a farmer working alone, because the fields had to be prepared with meticulous care and the plants required constant weeding from the time they emerged from the soil until they were ready to be harvested. Lewis Burr in 1850 raised 750 bushels of onions on one and a half acres and realized a $483 profit. By that time, most Fairfield farmers were growing at least some onions, the typical farmer probably producing about one-seventh as many onions as Lewis Burr and the town's total crop being about 15,000 barrels (two and three-quarters bushels to the barrel).

The price of onions varied from season to season and from year to year. Assuming he paid a consignment fee of about 10 percent, Lewis Burr sold his 750 bushels of onions for about $535, or $1.96 a barrel. In November 1867, yellow onions were bringing $3.00 a barrel; in March 1868, yellow onions of the same quality were selling for $9.00 a barrel. In December 1869, wholesale grocers in New York were paying between $1.30 and $1.60 a barrel, depending upon the quality of the onions.

Fairfield farmers could ship their onions either by train or by boat, but the vast majority chose to ship them on the market boats that served Southport for several reasons. Because the shipping season occurred during autumn and winter, farmers had to consider the possibility that their onions might freeze. If they did, they became essentially worthless. The railroad tried to eliminate this problem with speed; during cold weather, it attempted to move the onions to New York within two or three hours of loading. Aware that speed was a service they could not offer, the market-boat captains packed the barrels of onions between layers of salt hay and canvas. Fairfield farmers, who probably had been storing their onions in their cellars or in heated barns to keep them out of the cold, believed this was a better way of guaranteeing the safety and value of their produce.

Shipping by boat was also more convenient. It meant driving to Southport instead of to the railroad market terminals of Norwalk or Bridgeport. As Bacon Wakeman later recalled: "It was customary for farmers in the hills to watch the shores and when the boats were sighted, to spread the word and immediately drive down to Southport so as to get as near the head of the line as possible. The line extended for many blocks on four different streets." It must have been a fascinating sight: the ox carts and wagons loaded with onions filling the streets of the village, roughly dressed farmers using the occasion to catch up on the news.[8] Just as interesting must have been the efforts to clean the streets after many dozen well-fed animals had spent the better part of the day waiting their turn to reach the docks. Frederick Marquand and Oliver H. Perry probably could muster little enthusiasm for a stroll through their neighborhood on the mornings after the market boats had visited.

Fairfield farmers also liked to ship their onions by boat because they believed this was the most economical way of getting their produce to New York. The boat owners took the onions on consignment, transported them to New York, and sold them, and kept a commission for their trouble. In 1859 Wakeman Hubbell sent forty-one barrels of onions to New York aboard the *Sarah B. Bulkley*. Hubbell's onions brought $1.59 a barrel or $65.25, of which the master of the *Sarah B. Bulkley* kept $6.15, or 9 percent, and returned $59.10 to Hubbell. Munson Perry sent sixteen barrels on the same voyage. New York wholesalers paid $1.33 a barrel for his onions, or $21.25, of which the owners of the *Sarah B. Bulkley* kept $2.40, 11 percent, returning $18.85 to Perry. These were typical transactions. Perry paid a higher percentage than Hubbell because his shipment was smaller, but a charge of about 10 percent was usual. Farmers considered this reasonable. Also they usually knew and trusted the shipowners and shipmasters.

The market boats were usually sloops of fifty tons burden or more. Probably the most famous was the *Mary Elizabeth*, owned by Joseph Jennings and Son. For most of her life the *Mary Elizabeth* was an eighty-one-ton sloop, but in 1884, her master, Richard Reed Elwood—who spent forty-nine years at sea, thirty-six of them as master of the *Mary Elizabeth*—delivered her to Cos Cob, where Palmer and Duff refitted her as a schooner. The *Mary Elizabeth*, which remained in service until the coastal trade ended in Southport in 1904, could carry up to 1500 barrels of onions and usually made one round trip a week to New York, departing Southport on Saturday evenings.

*Years of Decline*

*Onion harvest on Mill Hill late in the nineteenth century.*

The two most important Southport shipping companies were the various Jennings firms and the succession of businesses involving Wakeman B. Meeker, the first being Meeker and Sherwood (a partnership with Simon Sherwood) and the last being W. B. Meeker & Sons. Meeker's boats left the village on Tuesday evenings for their weekly trips to New York. In addition, various other companies, both from Southport and elsewhere, carried onions to New York from time to time.

The masters of these boats, like Captain Elwood, were accomplished seamen even though their ships were small and usually had only a crew of three. Elwood had sailed between New Haven and the West Indies before coming to Southport. Captain Levi W. Burr, master of the *Ganges*, had also had a deep-water career before turning to the coastal trade. Captain Seth Bulkley proved his skill as a sailor when he managed to get his sloop, the *Merchant*, owned by Meeker & Sherwood, out of Southport harbor in the teeth of a furious gale to come to the assistance of the *Lexington*, a steamship that exploded and burned off the coast of Fairfield in January 1840. One hundred and twenty persons lost their lives in the disaster; the only three who survived were rescued by Bulkley and his men.

The masters hated to return in ballast to Southport and so were always eager for a cargo that would sell back in Fairfield. After leaving New York, they would occasionally sail over to Perth Amboy, New Jersey, to pick up a load of coal for one of the coal yards in town. They might also take on lumber that had been transported down the Hudson River from Albany. But the masters eventually found one item for which there seemed to be an inexhaustible market: stable manure from New York, which Fair-

*Fairfield: the biography of a community*

field farmers would buy and spread on their fields. Bacon Wakeman describes how the returning boats, filled with their odiferous cargo, would wait for high tide and ride up as far as possible on the beach. When the tide went out, farmers would drive their wagons right up to the boats to get the manure. "We would work like Trojans to unload the boat on one tide," he remembered. If a farmer's sons worked especially hard, they could count on their father's rewarding them by letting them ride back to Southport on the empty sloops. "We derived a great deal of pleasure on boat rides on these boats," said Wakeman.

Because Fairfield was a farming town and because the farmers' prosperity was susceptible to so many variables, Fairfield learned to live with great economic fluctuations. The year 1840, for example was a prosperous one. Fairfield crops were abundant and the market for them good. Farmers were happy, as were the owners, masters, and crews of the coasting vessels and the proprietors of stores and shops. But 1842 was a hard year. The market for agricultural goods fell, and all of Fairfield suffered.

Erratic as Fairfield's economy was, it remained amazingly simple. Barter continued the way of life for most families. William Bradley of Greenfield was a farmer who kept detailed accounts of his affairs from 1812 until 1846. When his family needed shoes, he arranged with William Williams, a cobbler, to provide them and compensated Williams by carting brush for him, plowing his corn, "Sledding Load wood from Catamount Swamp," and delivering quantities of flax, rye, straw, and "whitewood boards" to him. Hezekiah Bradley's bull serviced one of William Bradley's cows, and his boar one of William's sows; William paid for the breedings by "Carting 1 load Ship planks from Job Perry mill to Black rock." On the other hand, William received "1 pint rum & pound Tobacco" from Walter Bradley for "help killing your hogs." Sarah White, an unmarried woman who lived in the center of Fairfield, must have had some productive hens, because she used eggs to buy everything from "Hyson tea" to cloth to molasses.[10]

Even professional men contined to collect their fees in country produce. During the 1840s Dr. Rufus Blakeman of Greenfield charged $.19 for extracting a tooth, $1.25 for two house calls and medicine, $.625 for vaccinating a child, $.125 for "7 blue pills," $2.00 for setting a broken leg, $.63 for "a visit, bleeding, &c.," and $2.50 for "visit to child from bed and spending night." Regardless of what a particular fee might be, the doctor probably had to settle with his patients by accepting a load of wood, a day's work at carting stone or manure, corn, potatoes, or "a quarter pig."[11]

Actually many of Dr. Blackman's impecunious neighbors considered his services a luxury, something of which they would avail themselves only under the most desperate circumstances. Given the wages of the time, the attitude is easy to understand. A female servant, like Catherine Barry who had just arrived in Fairfield from Ireland and who worked for Walker Lyon, earned $1.00 or $1.25 a week with room and board. In 1860, Angeline Morehouse paid a recent arrival from Ireland $14 a month and his board to work on her farm. He agreed to provide his own lodging and to do his own laundry. Angeline might have offered him a bit more to start, perhaps $18 or $19 a month, had he been a native American and not a Catholic. A skilled worker, perhaps a carpenter, could have made about $1.75 a day if he provided his own room, board, and other necessities.

Given the scarcity of money and the competition for what existed, many merchants and craftsmen traveled from house to house to sell their wares or services. Angeline

*Years of Decline*

Morehouse bought many of the items she was unable to produce on the farm from one "Mr. Roe, who comes around every week with groceries."[12] Shoemakers, such as William Williams, also visited local homes and normally used leather produced on Fairfield farms to make or repair shoes. Tailors made similar rounds, as did butchers, who would slaughter hogs and cattle for a share of the meat.

While some Fairfielders continued to live like their parents and even their grandparents had before them, others kept themselves abreast of all that was modern in the United States. These were the Fairfield residents who maintained close ties with New York. Even before the coming of the railroad, travel between Fairfield and New York had been both convenient and inexpensive. During the 1840s one could travel by steamboat from New York to Bridgeport in three hours and twenty minutes. The same trip by steamer as far as South Norwalk and the rest of the way to Fairfield by stage was even faster. The Southport market boats carried passengers as late as 1856, by which time the railroad made this slow form of travel obsolete.

During the 1840s Fairfield became a summer resort for New Yorkers. Its original summer people were principally former residents who had moved to the city to make their mark and, having done so, yearned for the peace and solitude of country life. Frederick Marquand built his home in Southport in 1832. Jonathan Sturges built his "cottage" in 1840, the same year that John Gould returned. The sons and grandsons of Eleazer Bulkley liked to live at least part of the year in Fairfield.

Not all the earliest seasonal residents had had Fairfield connections. Isaac Bronson was born in Middlebury, Connecticut in 1760, studied medicine with Dr. Lemuel Hopkins of Waterbury, and gave up medicine for a career in banking in New York before purchasing Timothy Dwight's former residence in Greenfield as a summer home in 1796. Bronson liked Greenfield so well that he made it his permanent residence, organizing the Bridgeport Bank in 1806 to provide himself with something to do in addition to maintaining his business interests in New York and being a country gentleman. His son, Frederic, an even wealthier New York financier, inherited the Greenfield estate in 1838. Although Frederic used the house only as a country home, he expanded it greatly in 1862, six years before his death. His son, also Frederic, inherited the estate. Under the younger Frederic's countrol it continued to be one of the most elegant summer homes in all of Connecticut.

With individuals like Frederick Marquand, who also maintained residences at Newport, Rhode Island, and Tarrytown, New York, and Jonathan Sturges, the father-in-law of J. Pierpont Morgan, and either of the Frederic Bronsons living in Fairfield for at least part of the year, other affluent New Yorkers began to think of the town as a fashionable place to maintain a second home. Nine new houses were constructed in Fairfield in 1840 at an average cost of $4389, which would have built a mansion even by John Gould's standards. In 1850, the Reverend Samuel Osgood, minister of the Church of the Messiah on Broadway, built Waldsteen, an eighteen-room summer home. Although not a businessman, he was typical of the summer residents who were arriving by the middle of the century, persons who had in common wealth and a winter home in New York.

Among the first individuals to understand that money was to be made as a result was John B. Steenbergen, a New York entrepreneur who arrived in town about 1846

*The James B. Thompson House built circa 1847 by John B. Steenbergen
still stands on the corner of Old Post Road and South Benson Road.*

or 1847. Steenbergen came to Fairfield both to build homes for wealthy New Yorkers who wanted a summer residence away from the confusion of city life and to construct a hotel. "Steanbergen [*sic*] is turning over the town," William Burr informed his brother, David. "He bought Elisa Hulls place for 5000 and Mr. Pecks for 9000, with every inch of ground he owned in Fairfield. He is now going to saw the Bellows factory [the former Black Rock carriage works] in t[w]o, and move it to Pecks for wings on each end of that house and then construct it for a *regular* hotel with ball and bar rooms, billiard tables and an nine-pin-alley."[13]

The town buzzed with talk about Steenbergen's activites. Elizabeth Hull (the "Elisa" William Burr mentioned) wrote to a friend in New York on December 1847: "You have doubtless heard of the great improvements in our Village, taking down our venerated homes and erecting fine tasteful mansions in their places. Mine still stands firm with its solid timbers, but it is to be razed to the ground the present week to show the most beautiful house of the four that had been built in the row." The four houses of which she spoke were located on the south side of Main Street, now Old Post Road, extending from Benson Road toward the town green.[14]

The new hotel stood on the north side of Main Street, diagonally across from the green, where Knapp's Tavern had once reigned. "The hotel exceeds every thing else in size," William Burr declared. Elizabeth Hull called it "monstrous big," and Jonathan Bulkley said that he had heard it was "the Largest Public House in the State of Connecticut."[15] Initially operated by a Mr. Thomas, formerly the manager of the United

*Years of Decline*

States Hotel at Saratoga Springs, New York and more recently of the Howard House in New York City, the hotel came to be known as the Fairfield House and was as popular as any resort hotel on the Connecticut shore.

Elizabeth Hull referred to Steenbergen as "our Bonaparte through whose agency the great works are accomplished. . . . He is a wonderful man, forms great plans and accomplishes all. With the telegraph [which had just arrived], railroad [which was about to come] and Mr. Steinbergen's [*sic*] efforts this is made *New Fairfield*."[16]

Some Fairfielders lacked Miss Hull's enthusiasm; they resented outsiders intruding in their affairs, rebuilding their town to offer it for sale to other strangers. William Burr told his brother about the vandalism that some town residents had directed against Steenbergen: "I forgot to write that Steanbergen [*sic*] had 116 of his iron pickets bent last week. They have been bent once before and he had them straightened." The most recent incident occurred while Steenbergen was in New York, Burr said, and "he came up in a terrible rage and offered 200 dols to the one who would detect the rogue and called up one of his Irishmen [and] asked him if he would take a double-barrelled gun and shoot the first man that laid his hand on the fence that night." The worker refused the assignment; Steenbergen fired him and found a man who would stand guard with the gun. When this second employee, also an Irish immigrant, told his employer that he was incapable of shooting anyone, he too found himself without a job. Finally Steenbergen ordered one "Richard Mason to take the gun, and Richard stands as a sentinel every night."[17]

The vandalism should have surprised no one. By the time Steenbergen arrived in town a wide gulf had developed between Fairfield's rich residents and those who were less fortunate. During earlier times, the differences between well-to-do and ordinary citizens were not so large as to create serious social tensions. But about the same time that Steenbergen was trying to make over Main Street to the tastes of rich New Yorkers, many young Fairfielders—native-born Americans as well as immigrants, persons of both thrift and industry—found that buying real estate in town was beyond their means. Although too deferential to voice their anxieties except through futile and surreptitious acts of vandalism, these persons resented the influx of newcomers who inflated property values and whose life-styles they could never hope to emulate. It was one thing to welcome home a native son like Jonathan Sturges, who had uncovered the secret to success in New York; it was quite a different matter to tolerate the arrival of pretentious men and women who had never heard of Fairfield until it became an address they could use to impress other ostentatious persons.

Fortunately life offered enough diversion, enough simple pleasures, to prevent Fairfield's ordinary people from becoming bitter. Sleighing was probably the town's most universally acclaimed activity, and balls and hops attracted young persons to the local taverns. The first Mondays in May and September, when the militia gathered for drill, were filled with fun. Uncle Kit and Aunt Dinah, "colored folks formerly with Mr. Samuel Rowland," furnished root beer, cakes, and cookies from the steps of the Congregational Church after the soldiers had performed their duties; a glass of root beer cost three cents and a cookie one. Zike Pair, a Bridgeport resident who was the only Indian left in the area, used a bow and arrow to knock pennies from a wooden split. If he hit the penny it was his; if he failed, the person who had risked the copper got to keep it. Fairfield's young women were sure to be there "hanging on the fellows and taking in the sights and amusements." Before drill day was over, those who were particularly fond of rum found that "their legs got tangled pretty well."[18]

Annual events like the strawberry festival also attracted large audiences. Angeline Morehouse said that at the festival of 1859 she got home after eleven o'clock in the evening. "We passed a very pleasant evening very similar to last year's party," she wrote. "A table was set with the good things & the men occupied that room the most of the time carrying out filled plates & returning with empty ones. . . . The ladies were dressed splendidly. Ma thinks that Mrs. Holly was dressed the most of any."[19]

Weddings were occasions for major celebrations. Jonathan Bulkley spoke of a wedding party where many of the guests stayed all night and then came to his home the following day. "We had music vocal and instrumental, and played accuse the criminal, brake the popes neck and every play that appears simple in moments of reflection." All had a wonderful time.[20]

Official holidays were few. The biggest was probably the Fourth of July, a time to celebrate the nation's independence with "National salutes, baked pigs and wine, with merry songs and music." Then as later, Thanksgiving, more a religious than a secular celebration, was a great time for eating. Christmas tended to be recognized primarily by Episcopalians. Congregationalists still believed that it smacked too much of Popery, but even they would indulge in a special dinner, perhaps "roasted and boiled turkeys, pies of chickens, pudding and pies of vegetable kind, pumpkin and mince and tarts."[21]

Work and play were not mutually exclusive. In 1816, Hull Sherwood reported that "today I raise the main body of my house with about 40 men." Once the house was in place, Sherwood provided "a field for ball playing until supper is ready — we have a good Pot Pie made of veal and turkey sufficient for a plentiful supper. The principal part tarry in the evening and drink grog and sing by the spirit of it until 9 o'clock." Sarah White spent many afternoons and evenings quilting with friends or perhaps sewing "garments for the Greeks" during that nation's war for independence.[22]

Sarah White's interest in the plight of the Greeks typified the town's concern with moral and social issues. The two decades after the War of 1812 were years of renewed interest in religion. Not since the Great Awakening had Fairfield men and women been so preoccupied with saving their souls and working for the church. Hardly a month went by when the faithful could not visit a revival meeting in either Fairfield or Bridgeport. Fifty or a hundred persons might renew their commitment to Christ at a single gathering. Church membership soared.

The zeal for religion carried over into areas of social concern. When a Mr. Yale delivered a peace lecture in 1832, Fairfield residents flooded to hear him. The town enthusiastically supported a hospital for the care of sick and disabled seamen during the 1840s. The Reverend Nathaniel Hewitt, who came to the First Church in 1818, encouraged residents to endorse the temperance movement, but it was not until 1829, two years after Hewitt left town to devote his efforts to the work of the American Temperance Society, that the Fairfield Temperance Society began meeting every month "to forward the cause." The members all agreed to abstain from the use of alcoholic beverages and to urge others to do likewise; they believed "that the use of intoxicating liquors is, for persons in health, not only unnecessary, but hurtful & that the practice is the cause of forming intemperate appetites and habits."[23]

The society's golden years came in the 1840s when its members pushed a motion through the town meeting stating that any purveyor of strong drink had to pay $5.00 to the treasurer of the town and give bond for $100 "that such person shall not sell any Wines or Spiritous Liquor to be drank in his or her house, shop, or dependencies nor suffer any so sold to be there drank and shall not at any time sell a less quantity than one pint." Even the town's tavern owners — George Peck, George Burr, Samuel A. Nicholas, Charles Nicholas, Abraham Benson, Aaron Burr, and Lyman Banks — had to abide by the regulation.[24]

The first organized efforts to improve the lot of Fairfield women appeared at this time. The Young Ladies Educational Society provided diversion as well as an opportunity for Fairfield women to expand their learning by meeting once a week for "a prayer, reading a portion of the sacred Scriptures, singing and the perusal of some good and entertaining book." Many women from the society enthusiastically supported Sarah A. Sherwood during her ordeal. Sarah had been a spinster for many years, living on the dividends from a substantial estate that she had inherited from her parents. In June 1858, she married Jessup Sherwood in Greenfield, who at once demanded control of all her assets. When she refused, Jessup obtained a court order forcing her to comply, Connecticut law at the time stipulating that a woman's property became her husband's at the time of marriage. Sarah answered the court the same way she had answered her husband and quickly found herself in jail for contempt. Jessup remained ensconced in the comfortable home that she had owned before the two were married. At this point, Fairfield women began a campaign to bring the plight of Sarah Sherwood to the attention of the Connecticut General Assembly. After numerous delays, the assembly finally, on July 7, 1865, declared Sarah to be "sole, single and unmarried with as full right to her property as if she had ever remained sole and unmarried." She and the women of Fairfield had won; they rejoiced together as she emerged from her long incarceration.[25]

Neither women nor men showed similar concern for the predicament of blacks, either in town or elsewhere in the United States. Although slavery was dead in Fairfield, discrimination was not. In 1822, the local court found a black man guilty of rape and ordered his execution. The General Assembly intervened and reduced his sentence to life imprisonment. William Wheeler explained that the legislature had seen fit to alter the sentence because "there were some doubts whether he committed the Rape or not"; reasonable doubt was apparently insufficient cause for acquittal of a black man.[26] The extent of antislavery activity in town seems to have been limited to support for the American Colonization Society, which was more concerned with returning blacks to Africa than it was with freeing them from slavery.

By 1850 the Irish had replaced blacks as the largest ethnic minority in Fairfield. Impelled to leave Ireland because of the terrible famines of the 1840s, many had arrived in the northeastern United States in time to be included in the census of 1850. Bridgeport's Irish population by that date was 15 percent, many of them coming to take advantage of the employment opportunities in the city's new factories. Fairfield also felt the effects of the immigration. By 1850 its Irish population constituted 7 percent of its total population, and by 1860, 13 percent. The only employment Fairfield had to offer to these people, individuals largely without either skills or education, was work as farm laborers or domestic servants.

The Irish felt the harshness of discrimination. They suffered more because they

*Fairfield Academy shown here in the 1860s was built in 1804
between St. Paul's Church and the Burr homestead. It was moved
to its present site in the 1950s.*

were Roman Catholics than because they were foreigners, uneducated, and poor. Fairfield had a tradition of anti-Catholicism that dated back to the time of Roger Ludlow; it died a long and lingering death. Angeline Morehouse in 1859 attended a prayer meeting at the Greenfield Congregational Church at which the speaker discussed regeneration, showing "what our belief is & then the absurdities of the belief of the Romish Church."[27] Three years earlier Fairfield had shown strong support for William T. Minor for governor. Minor, the candidate of the Know-Nothing party, a party openly dedicated to nativism and anti-Catholicism, served as governor from 1855 to 1857.

After what the Irish had endured in their native land and on their journeys to the United States, they could survive anything they encountered in Fairfield. By 1852, the Reverend Thomas J. Synott, a native of Ireland and one of the priests at St. Augustine's Roman Catholic Church in Bridgeport, was conducting services for Catholics in private homes in Fairfield. By the following year, he and his parishioners had purchased a lot on what was then Mechanic Street, now the Post Road, and begun work on a simple wooden chapel large enough to seat three hundred worshipers. Fairfield's Catholic population — which totaled only slightly more than one hundred families, the overwhelming majority Irish but including a few German immigrants as well — raised $2400 for the project, a king's ransom when one considers that many of these families were surviving on barely $20 a month. Despite the hostility they faced, relatively few immigrants in Fairfield became paupers. In 1860, for example, the town supported forty-two paupers, thirty-three of whom were American-born and nine immigrants. The new arrivals must have learned quickly that "being on the town" was a humiliating experience.

"Being on the town" had meant, before 1831, being in the poorhouse that Fair-

*Years of Decline*

field, Norwalk, Wilton, and Weston operated in Weston. Having abandoned this joint project in 1831, Fairfield once again began farming out its poor, that is, boarding them in the homes of persons who offered to take them in for a sufficiently low fee to satisfy tightfisted town officials. In 1837, the town appointed Roger M. Sherman and Jeremiah Sturges, two of its most distinguished citizens, to meet with other Fairfield County towns in an effort to revive the idea of a joint poorhouse. Nothing came of this or of several other schemes, including one to buy the John Wakeman farm in Greenfield and use it as a poor farm; the practice of boarding the poor with individual families therefore continued. The only positive aspect of this plan was that it was cheap; the town paid an average of about $80 a year to keep each pauper.

If that figure sounds paltry, one must remember that the town and state were together, at that time, spending about $2 per pupil per year to educate Fairfield's children. In 1860, for example, 1204 students were attending the seventeen common schools in town. The state of Connecticut contributed $1505 toward the operation of these schools and the town $948. Fortunately other sources of revenue existed. The First Located School Society, in the center of town, operated the cemetery and used the funds derived from it to supplement the budget for the society's schools. In 1837, the United States had granted surplus funds from its budget to all of the states, and in Connecticut these funds had found their way to the towns. Fairfield received $8763.17, money it placed in the Town Deposit Fund to earn interest, which the town then distributed among the school societies.

Under the circumstances, it is not surprising that the schools in town were less than a great source of pride. Some teachers had real ability; others should have found another profession. The schoolhouses were often in bad repair and some, according to the Board of Visitors of the First Located School Society, "are destitute of those out buildings which are so essential to the decency, health, good manners and good morals of the pupils."

Private schools offered the best education in town. In 1860, Augusta A. Smith of Southport opened the Seaside Seminary, which was at various times a boarding school for girls and a day school for both boys and girls. For more than twenty years it provided a broad curriculum and an abundance of moral and religious instruction for the young persons whose parents could afford its tuition.

Fairfield Academy continued to be the educational pride of town. The teachers were well trained, usually young Yale graduates. School was in session six days a week, forty-eight weeks a year, with only a few holidays—Thanksgiving, Fast Day, the Fourth of July, and New Year's Day. Teachers drilled the students daily in Latin, Greek, geometry, and geography, and at the close of the school year they conducted rigorous examinations of the students, during which the youngsters were required to deliver declamations before the entire school population. If some young miscreant had neglected his studies, the whole school would know.

Those who attended the school seemed to recall violations of the rules more than the rules themselves. Arthur D. Osborne eventually became the president of the Bank of New Haven after finishing at the academy in 1845. He remembered most vividly sprinkling red pepper on the school's wood stove to create a cacophony of coughing and sneezing. Tormenting the geese that lived around the academy pond by feeding them apples with strings and pieces of papers tied to them was another of his favorite pranks. Osborne also had fond memories of stealing cider out of the casks at the local cider mill and of skinny-dipping in Ash Creek. He would never, he later claimed, forget the time that Theodore Turney, a student, chased Joseph A. Benton, the principal, around the school with a gun.

Mrs. Jane Kippen recalled how Arthur Bennet, in 1839, had achieved immortality in the minds of his fellow students by borrowing Ellen Morehouse's horse and, sitting astride facing the animal's tail, raced it around the courthouse green to the pleasure of all except James Tufts, the teacher at the time. Tufts interrupted Bennet's ride and then unintentionally added further to the young equestrian's renown by imposing a punishment, the exact nature of which has been forgotten, but which classmates claimed was more fit for a convicted felon than a mischievous adolescent.

The antics of children like those at the academy and the day-to-day activities of farm men and women, most of whom endured what must have appeared to the town's wealthy social set as dreary lives, constituted what was vital in the small country town that Fairfield had become before the Civil War. Women cooked Indian pudding, salted porgies, prepared scallop potpies, boiled doughnuts, made elderberry and currant wine. Husbands weeded onions and collected seaweed and discussed with their wives the relative merits of burning oil or kerosene in their lamps. Unlike their more affluent neighbors, ordinary Fairfielders seemed forever to be walking, from the courthouse to Black Rock, from Greenfield to Southport. The town even required Sturges Ogden to preserve the giant oak tree near his barn "for a shade for public use" where overheated walkers might find refuge.[28]

Beyond the grand homes that John D. Steenbergen and others were building, the cycle of life continued, work that never seemed to be done and the small pleasures that made it tolerable, occasionally the great joy of children being born or the crushing sorrow of relatives and friends dying. When Sarah Shelton's mother lay dying in New Haven, where Dr. Jonathan Knight, perhaps the most competent physician in Connecticut, had operated on her for a blocked intestine, the daughter wrote: "Death had come and she must go. On Monday she was quite comfortable but Tuesday afternoon her hands began to mortify. I could not then believe she was dangerous nor did she." But her mother did speak about dying, saying that "if it was the Lord's will she felt resined [and] she thought she had a good hope through Christ and was not afraid to die." The following day she died. Sarah brought her mother's body back to Fairfield, and life continued as it had before and as it would again, ordinary people enduring with dignity the warp and weft of Fairfield's existence.[29]

## NOTES

1. FTR, May 7, 1842.

2. Ibid., Dec. 6, 1847.

3. Ibid., April 30, 1832.

4. Bridgeport *Republican Farmer*, Nov. 14, 1856.

5. William B. Glover, The Town of Fairfield's Appeal from the Railroad Commission, argument for the appellant, 1887, FHS.

6. William Burr to David Burr [1847], Theodosia Burr Lyon Collection, FHS.

7. Angeline Morehouse to Samuel Morehouse, June 27, 1859, A. E. Jennings Collection, FHS; Charter of the Green's Farms Agricultural Club, Volunteer Associations Collection, FHS.

8. Judge Bacon Wakeman, talk before the Fair-

field Luncheon Club, May 11, 1927, Fairfield Scrapbooks, FHS.

9. Ibid.

10. William Bradley, Account Book, 1822-46, Bradley Family Papers, FHS; Sarah White, Diary, April 25, 1825, White Family Papers, FHS.

11. Dr. Rufus Blakeman, Account Book, 1822-1844, Rufus Blakeman Papers, FHS.

12. Angeline Morehouse to Samuel Morehouse, Nov. 22, 1858, Jennings Collection, FHS.

13. William Burr to David Burr [1847], Lyon Collection, FHS.

14. Elizabeth Hull to Mrs. Thomas L. Callendar, Dec. 19, 1847, *Annual Report of the Fairfield Historical Society* (1922), 21-22.

15. Ibid.; William Burr to David Burr, Nov. 28, 1847, Lyon Collection, FHS; Jonathan Bulkley, *Journals*, 197.

16. Elizabeth Hull to Mrs. Thomas L. Callender, Dec. 19, 1847, *Annual Report of the Fairfield Historical Society* (1922), 21-22.

17. William Burr to David Burr [1847], Lyon Collection, FHS.

18. William Burr, *Early Recollections of Fairfield Life* (n. p., n. d.).

19. Angeline Morehouse to Samuel Morehouse, June 20, 1859, Jennings Collection, FHS.

20. Jonathan Bulkley, *Journals*, 190.

21. Quoted in Banks, *This Is Fairfield*, 223, 226.

22. Sherwood is quoted in Banks, *This Is Fairfield*, 232; Sarah White, Diary, March 21, 1828, White Family Papers, FHS.

23. Fairfield Temperance Society Papers, Voluntary Associations Collection, FHS.

24. FTR, Jan. 13, 1840.

25. Hon. Curtis Thompson on Mrs. Smith Case, July 7, 1865, Bradley Family Papers, FHS.

26. William Wheeler's Journal, in Lathrop, *Black Rock*, 93.

27. Angeline Morehouse to Samuel Morehouse, May 7, 1859, Jennings Collection, FHS.

28. FTR, B, I, Feb. 19, 1818.

29. Sarah White, Diary, May 25, 1844, White Family Papers, FHS.

# The Courthouse

IN 1800, when the Connecticut General Assembly first created Bridgeport, the new community was little more than an arrogant brat striving for an identity of its own, separate from those of its two older neighbors, Fairfield and Stratford. But Bridgeport, only a borough in 1800, refused to be ignored. In 1800 it established ties with a vast hinterland by means of the Bridgeport and Newtown Turnpike. Bridgeport had its first bank in 1806, and the fact that Isaac Bronson, an astute businessman from Greenfield, organized the Bridgeport Bank instead of establishing one in Fairfield indicated that Bridgeport's future must have been bright even at that early date.

Just after the War of 1812 the production of saddlery became an important aspect of Bridgeport's economy. About the same time Fairfield shoppers began trading at Bridgeport stores in large numbers. Its harbor had advantages over both Black Rock and Southport. A writer in 1819 described it in glowing terms: "The depth of water on the bar [at the mouth of the harbor] at high water . . . is thirteen feet; within the bar the water is much deeper, and has a muddy bottom, so that, at low water, loaded vessels lie at ease on the flats, while those in the channel . . . have sufficient depth of water, as ships of 200 tons can conveniently load at the wharves." Moreover, he pointed out, "vessels, when once within the bar, are at all times safe from dangers of the sea," which was certainly not the case at Black Rock.[1]

The same writer predicted "that it will not prove altogether an illusion, to calculate, that at some future period [Bridgeport] will become a considerable town." Almost 2000 persons lived there in 1820 and worked in a factory making saddles and saddle trees, three printing plants, two book binderies, fifteen large warehouses, twenty-eight stores, and a bank. Still only a borough, Bridgeport already was home to two newspapers.[2]

The General Assembly made it a town in 1821, about ten years before it became a major center for the manufacture of carriages. Steamboats began to travel between New York and Bridgeport in 1824, and daily service began in 1834. Two steamers were daily making the round trip by 1846. Fairfield travelers could ride or walk to Bridgeport, catch the steamboat there, and still be in New York many hours sooner than they would have been had they taken passage on one of the boats that sailed from Southport to New York.

Bridgeport became a city in 1836. Four years later the Housatonic Railroad Company had connected the new city with New Milford and all the towns between, and by 1842 the same line extended all the way to Sheffield, Massachusetts. The Naugatuck Railroad, completed in 1848, went from Bridgeport to Naugatuck, Waterbury, and Winsted; in 1849 the New York and New Haven Railroad linked Bridgeport with the cities on the coast.

By 1850 Bridgeport had clearly become the most important community in southwestern Connecticut. By Connecticut standards, its rise had been meteoric. In 1830, Fairfield's population was still one and a half times as large as Bridgeport's. But in 1850, the vastly younger community was twice as populous as its venerable neighbor, and in 1860 it would be three times as large.

Its prestige had grown as rapidly as its population. Even in 1824, when Lafayette traveled through Connecticut on his way to Boston, the revered Frenchman stopped in Fairfield only to take "a cold bite" at Knapp's Tavern before proceeding on to Bridgeport to spend the night. President Andrew Jackson, when visiting southwestern Connecticut in 1833, ignored Fairfield altogether and greeted well-wishers only in Bridgeport. Far from resenting the slight, many Fairfielders journeyed to the neighboring community to get a glimpse of their president.

By the 1850s, Bridgeport surpassed Fairfield in terms of wealth, population, and influence. Commercial property in Bridgeport was worth about $1,120,000; in Fairfield, about $21,000. Bridgeport's dwellings were worth almost $3,000,000; those of Fairfield, $869,000. More than $735,000 was invested in manufacturing in Bridgeport; Fairfield had no factories after the carriage works folded at Black Rock. An average acre of land in Fairfield was worth about $50; in Bridgeport, more than $230. Fairfield did exceed Bridgeport in two categories: thanks to the recent influx of wealthy persons into town, Fairfield men and women owned slightly more stock than did Bridgeport residents; and because most of the ships that used Bridgeport harbor were owned elsewhere while those that sailed from Southport were moored there, Fairfield's fleet was much the larger.

Given its importance in Fairfield County and in the state, one might expect that Bridgeport would covet certain remnants of Fairfield's former glory. Bridgeport had already campaigned hard to win the customs house. But the prize that Bridgeport really sought was the Fairfield County Courthouse and the designation "shire town."

The courthouse had resided in Fairfield since the General Assembly had first authorized its establishment. It had been one of the reasons for Fairfield's importance during the colonial years; and even well into the nineteenth century, its presence added an element of refinement and sophistication the town otherwise might have been without. During the months that the court was in session, it met during business hours from Monday morning until Saturday at noon. Except for the lawyers who lived right in Fairfield, most attorneys found lodging in town for the duration of the session, usually traveling home only on weekends. Erudite and socially prominent, these men were welcome guests in many Fairfield homes.

Over the years the presence of the courthouse had meant that Fairfield was relieved of the responsibility of maintaining a town hall, because the courthouse contained a room, called the town room, that served Fairfield as a meeting place for town meetings as well as gatherings of town committees and town officials. Care of the room was charged to the town, while the building as a whole, which was the property of the county, was kept up by that government.

As early as 1830, Bridgeport leaders began to consider how they might capture the county seat for their town. On December 28, 1833, the Bridgeport town meeting created a committee to examine the courthouse question. It recommended that Bridgeport petition the General Assembly to seek the transfer of both the courthouse and the jail from Fairfield to Bridgeport. This early attempt, which Fairfield fought through its agents, Jeremiah Sturges and Ebenezer Jesup, had no chance of success, but it did stimulate Fairfield to offer to bear some of the cost of refurbishing the neglected courthouse. Bridgeport tried and failed again in 1840 and yet again in 1841. That year Norwalk entered the fray as well, claiming that its position near the geographical center of the county made it the logical location for the county court. Fairfield held Norwalk at bay as it had Bridgeport.

Bridgeport refused to be denied. In 1850, it again delivered a petition to the assembly asking to become the shire town. Bridgeport officials argued that Fairfield lacked adequate facilities to lodge and board the lawyers who attended the court. Thomas B. Osborne, who with Horace Banks was chosen by the Fairfield town meeting to oppose the Bridgeport petition, assembled a delegation of Fairfield's fattest men to demonstrate the folly of Bridgeport's contention, presenting them as living evidence of how one might prosper on Fairfield cooking. Whether because of Osborne's unorthodox technique or in spite of it, Fairfield prevailed once again, as the General Assembly denied Bridgeport's petition yet another time.

Two years later Bridgeport and Norwalk were again before the legislature, and Fairfield was once more preparing for the onslaught. The General Assembly, acting as if it had devoted enough time to this matter and expressing its annoyance with what had come to be a perennial request, accepted a committee report that denied the two towns' request in the most emphatic terms. The report stated that "the court house situated in Fairfield, though ancient, is a commodious and good building for the transaction of the business of the court," and admonished Bridgeport and Norwalk: "There is no want, nor ever had been, of suitable and proper accommodations at Fairfield, for those who resort there during the sessions of the Courts; and if the most ample accommodations have at any time been unprovided there, its has been owing to the fact, that for many years past it has been the settled policy of a portion of the people of both Bridgeport and Norwalk. . . to keep this question in an unsettled state."[4] The report *then* continued by asserting that Fairfield was a better location than either of the other two towns because it was more centrally located relative to the population of the county.

This report, which was accepted by the entire legislature, would, most members of the General Assembly hoped, put the matter to rest. When the jail at Fairfield burned in 1852, the commissioners of Fairfield County voted to rebuild on the same location, and several prominent Fairfield men, including Judge Osborne, began looking into the possibility of constructing a new hotel—one that would specifically cater to the needs of lawyers, witnesses, and jurors.

*The Courthouse*

But Bridgeport continued to press the matter. On April 21, 1853, it again voted to petition the General Assembly for transfer of the courthouse, but this time also offered "to provide a suitable place for the necessary public buildings, and to erect the same for the use of the County." Bridgeport even agreed to assume any contracts the county had signed to rebuild the jail in Fairfield and "save the County harmless from any tax on account of the same." Bridgeport's offer of a new courthouse, built without expense to the county, would be hard for the legislature to refuse.[5]

Fairfield selected Oliver H. Perry, George B. Kissam, and John Gould to oppose the Bridgeport petition, Perry and Kissam then representing Fairfield in the General Assembly and Gould having become active in town politics after his successful career in New York. Of the three, Perry assumed most of the responsibility for presenting Fairfield's side of the matter and spent weeks carefully preparing his case. He contended that there existed no reason to move the courthouse: Fairfield was centrally located, possessed transportation facilities that were entirely adequate, and offered accommodations that few attorneys saw fit to criticize. He documented each point with detailed statistical information and with testimony from individuals involved with the courts.

Oliver H. Perry also spoke with passion. The scion of a shipping family, he discussed the loss Fairfield experienced when Bridgeport wrested the customs house away from the town. He compared the promoters of the Bridgeport scheme to take the courthouse with William Tryon, who had led the British attack on the town in 1779: "Like this hostile foe wd. you again raze to the ground these buildings & remove them forever from our midst. Then will the ghost of our departed prosperity haunt your unquiet hours in after life & leave you the uncomfortable reflection that you joined hands with the oppressor!"

He appealed especially to representatives from other country towns, like Fairfield. "To those of my fellow members who come from rural towns which like my own have sacred associations connected with the past & perhaps around whose history old memories cling. . . , to them wd. I make a last appeal in behalf of right & justice and time honored associations," he said. "As you love your native soil & the domestic altars your fathers have erected theron—as you cherish the hallowed memories of its past. . . , I conjure you to withhold yr vote for such an unjust & cruel despolation of that which is so dear to me." In his mind, as in the minds of many of his neighbors, Perry was fighting for two hundred years of Fairfield history and what that history meant. His overblown rhetoric reflected his understanding of the gravity of the contest as much as it did his own taste for hyperbole and drama.[6]

The outcome of the issue depended less on anything that Perry might have said or done than on whatever action the joint select committee that considered the Bridgeport petition might take. That committee included nine men, none from Fairfield County, and was chaired by John S. Yeomans of Columbia, which was in Tolland County. On two separate occasions, the committee voted 5 to 4 to leave the courthouse undisturbed in Fairfield. Yeomans, using his powers as chairman, refused to accept either of these votes as final. When he ordered a third ballot on the question, Danford Morse, a representative from Union, also in Tolland County, changed his vote, giving the committee a new majority in favor of transferring the courthouse to Bridgeport. Perry was certain that Yeomans, a Democrat, had made some kind of corrupt bargain with Morse, also a Democrat, to get him to change his mind. The Fairfield spokesman even suggested privately that Bridgeport money had mysteriously found its way into the pockets of both Yeomans and Morse, but had no way of proving such allegations.

The committee's report was almost a paraphrase of the Bridgeport petition. It stated that Fairfield did not "afford sufficient accommodations for the parties, witnesses, jurors &c., having business at the court" and contended that it was "comparatively inconvenient and difficult of access" and that the courthouse, itself, was a "considerable distance from the Railroad depot." As if to add insult to injury, the report concluded by referring to Bridgeport as an important business center and asserting that "this is, of course, not true of the location at Fairfield, which is a small village, inhabited to a considerable extent by people from New York city, and almost destitute of business and of business relations with other parts of the county."[7]

The Bridgeport petition and the committee's report next went before the full legislature. There the vote fell along party lines. Eighty-four Democrats and ten Whigs in the lower house voted in favor of moving the courthouse, thirty-one Democrats and fifty Whigs votes against. In the Senate, twelve Democrats and one Whig voted to move it, and three Democrats and five Whigs voted to keep it in Fairfield. Of the few Democrats who voted against the Bridgeport petition, many were western Fairfield County representatives who saw the move to Bridgeport as creating additional inconvenience for their constituents; for them, constituent concerns outweighed party discipline.

The General Assembly, by legislation enacted on June 30, 1853, removed the court from Fairfield and established it in Bridgeport, required that city to erect a courthouse and a jail, and demanded that Bridgeport pay the treasurer of Fairfield County "the amount of all expenses and liability incurred in the erection" of the new jail in Fairfield, and impose a special tax to cover these expenses. Bridgeport complied happily.[8]

The removal of the court traumatized Fairfield. On August 20, the town meeting passed a resolution that reflected Fairfield's bewilderment and hurt: "It is the sense of this meeting that the procurement of the Public Act removing the County buildings from Fairfield to Bridgeport is on the part of Bridgeport unprecedented in its circumstances and unjustifiable in its character and should be resisted to the last by every citizen of the town of Fairfield who had pride enough to feel or moral sense enough to estimate a public outrage and a public wrong." The meeting then vowed "that the town of Fairfield will never submit quietly to this act of pain and violence and will use every exertion to obtain its repeal and to procure . . . a restoration of its ancient privileges."[9]

The loss, many Fairfield men and women believed, amounted to a public declaration of their town's diminished status. The General Assembly had, or so it seemed, relegated Fairfield—once the proud hub of southwestern Connecticut, an urbane and sophisticated center—to the status of an inconsequential country town, barely more important than Redding or Weston or Easton or Westport, communities that had been spawned from Fairfield, communities that always functioned on the periphery of the important business that had until now transpired in Fairfield.

Bridgeport's arrogance made the loss even harder to bear. On October 4, 1853, a Bridgeport poet paid homage to his city:

*Child of the Sound—Pequonnoc's pride,*
*On every sea thy gallant coursers ride,*
*No Court House graced Connecticut's shore,*
*Till thou, brave Bridgeport, furnished one,*
*Till thou, brave Bridgeport, with view divine*
*Furnished the wherewith from thy well stor'd mine;*
*Beautiful City! who shall know—*
*The height to glory thou shall go.*
*Child of the East, what tongue shall name*
*In after years thy splendid fame;*
*Pregnant are coming years to thee,*
*Big with thy future destiny.*

Under different circumstances, Fairfield might have found consolation in knowing that the author of this doggerel lived in Bridgeport and not Fairfield; but at the time, this attempt at poetry was one more burden to bear. The Bridgeport *Republican Farmer* referred to Fairfield when it editorialized "that in mechanical, manufacturing, merchantile and trading operations, she is as a 'desert waste'." The Bridgeport *Standard*, just three days later, reported that the courts were originally held in Fairfield "because it was the most important town in the County. For a long period it held that dominant position. It began to decline," the paper arrogantly continued, " at or about the time of the conflagration, more than seventy years since, and for a score of years, or longer, the old village has had nothing in the way of business to distinguish it from a dozen other places in the County."[10]

Bridgeport even became the owner of the partially constructed jail on the Fairfield green, by paying $6384 to offset what the county had spent reconstructing the building. Clearly Bridgeport had no use for the incomplete structure, and so in September 1854 sold it to St. Paul's Episcopal Church. The following March, St. Paul's received permission from the Fairfield town meeting "to use the ground lately occupied as the jail site for the purpose of erecting a church edifice thereon."[11]

The former courthouse became the property of the town of Fairfield and was henceforth known as the Town House. Having more space than it needed to conduct its business, Fairfield voted to lease the upper part of the building to the Fairfield Female Seminary, "provided the trustees [of the seminary] keep the building insured to the benefit of the town." What Fairfielders had called the town room continued to be used for town meetings.[12]

Seven years later, on October 26, 1861, an unknown arsonist set fire to the Town House. Despite the reward of $500 offered by the town, the culprit went undetected, but his crime finally forced Fairfield to remodel the building, once an imposing structure but one that since 1853 seemed to confirm Bridgeport's notion that Fairfield was nothing more than just another country town. The Civil War interrupted the rehabilitation, which was finally completed in the early 1870s when workmen, at a cost of more than $6000, transformed the ancient structure into an ornate Second French Empire building, complete with a mansard roof. At the same time Fairfield decided to modernize the Town House, it also ordered that all official business be conducted in that building and that all town officials remove all town papers from their own possession and deposit them in the appropriate offices there. Fairfield even went so far as to insure the refurbished building—although only for two-thirds of its value—and agreed to pay half the cost of filling in the nearby Academy Pond, property owners in the vicinity to bear the other half. The area that had been a pond was, the town ordered, forever to be unencumbered by buildings and to "remain as a part of the Public green."[13]

This outburst of civic pride lasted only a short time. Within a few years, farmers living near the Town House were using the lawn to pasture their horses and cows. The Fairfield *Advertiser*, which was vastly more tolerant of the abuse of the town's properties than modern Fairfield newspapers would be, was so outraged by the neglected condition of the Town House grounds that it called them "an eye sore to residents and visitors." Shortly after the *Advertiser*'s denunciation, the town ordered the selectmen to "take all necessary action in abating the nuisance in the cellar of the Town House." The nuisance was specifically a "Privy nuisance," which was rapidly rendering the entire building uninhabitable for all but the most olfactorily insensitive residents. It was almost as if Fairfield were trying to confirm the arrogant slanders of the Bridgeport press and to assume the bucolic role to which, many townsmen believed, the General Assembly had assigned it by taking away the courthouse.[14]

## NOTES

1. Pease and Niles, *Gazetteer*, 195.

2. Ibid., 198.

3. Jonathan Bulkley, *Journals*, 249; William Wheeler's journal, in Lathrop, *Black Rock*, 97.

4. Connecticut General Assembly, *Report on the Fairfield County Court House Case*, May session, 1852.

5. *Petition of the Town of Bridgeport to the Connecticut General Assembly*, April 21, 1853, May session, 1853.

6. Oliver H. Perry, notes for a speech, 1853, Courthouse Relocation File, FHS.

7. *Report of the Joint Committee on the Petition of the town of Bridgeport for the removal of the county seat from Fairfield to Bridgeport*, May session, 1853.

8. An act in alteration of "An Act relating to Courts" and of "An Act concerning Prisons," *Public Acts of Connecticut, 1851-1859*, 85-87.

9. FTR, Aug. 20, 1853.

10. Bridgeport *Gazette*, Oct. 4, 1853; Bridgeport *Republican Farmer*, Aug. 30, 1853; Bridgeport *Standard*, Sept. 2, 1853.

11. FTR, March 13, 1855.

12. Ibid., Sept. 15, 1855.

13. Ibid., Nov. 17, 1869.

14. Fairfield *Advertiser*, June 10, 1886; FTR, Aug. 22, 1887.

# The Civil War Era

FRIDAY, APRIL 12, 1861, was a cold and stormy day in Fairfield. The wind blew unceasingly, sending sheets of rain across the town. About 4:30 that morning, while most residents were still asleep, news arrived that Fort Sumter, a United States military installation at Charlestown, South Carolina, had been the target of an artillery bombardment launched by troops of the secessionist government of South Carolina. Despite the cold and the increasingly severe storm, crowds of apprehensive Fairfield men and women, eager for more information, gathered at the telegraph office. The townspeople were uncertain both about what was happening in South Carolina and about how to define their duty in this crisis.

Fairfield held mixed emotions about the Civil War. The town had recently aligned itself with the Republican party. In 1856, Fairfield had supported the first presidential candidate that party ever nominated, John C. Fremont; he easily carried the town over James Buchanan, the Democrat, who some Fairfield voters believed was indifferent to the expansion of slavery. In 1860, when Abraham Lincoln was a presidential candidate for the first time, he won 63 percent of the Fairfield vote; but many men in town refused to vote in the presidential election that year. The fact that Lincoln won so handily was less a reflection of the town's enthusiasm for him than of its hostility or indifference to his opponents. William Buckingham, the Republican candidate for governor and a man closely identified with Lincoln, carried Fairfield, but only by ten votes.

Lincoln's election, in retrospect one of the great turning points in the history of the country, competed with other questions for the attention of Fairfield men and women, some of whom regarded the election as less than crucial. Angeline Morehouse was apparently more interested in the price of onions than in national politics. In November 1860, the month of the election, she revealed where her priorities lay: "Wakeman Meeker says that Lincoln's election had cut off the onion market in the south. It is a pity he was elected before we sold our onions."[1] Some parishioners complained that the Greenfield Congregational Church was uncharacteristically silent on the great issues then facing the country; what could have been absorbing the church's attention is hard to imagine.

The support Lincoln received in Fairfield came not because of his general opposition to slavery but because of his specific opposition to the addition of any new slave territory to the United States. Having regularly sent sons and daughters West for nearly a century, Fairfield detested the idea, demanded by the South, of opening Western lands to slavery, detested the thought of seeing its progeny forced to compete with slave labor in Kansas or Nebraska. When Lincoln vowed to prevent the addition of any slave territory to the Union, Fairfield applauded.

But the town's antagonism to the expansion of slavery and the town's stand on slavery where it already existed were two totally different questions. The fight against slavery interested few Fairfield men and women. Fairfield's indifference about the slavery issue was part of a lack of concern about blacks in general. In 1857, Connecticut conducted a referendum on the question of extending the franchise to blacks in the state. Eight of every ten voters throughout the state opposed the extension; in Fairfield County, the vote was nine to one against.

Fairfield's black population had declined steadily since the American Revolution. Throughout the colonial period and even as late as 1820, one person in twenty in town had been black; by 1860 only 3 percent of the population fell into this category. Certainly the decline in the town's black population reflected the diminishing economic opportunities in Fairfield. To what extent it indicated an unfriendly atmosphere for black residents cannot be ascertained from so great a chronological distance. Those blacks who lived in town were generally domestic servants or agricultural laborers. A few exceptions existed, of course. Edwin Bulkley was a black farmer who owned sixteen acres, land he must have maintained meticulously because it was worth $2500 in 1860, far more than similar small farms owned by his neighbors. His farm produced rye, corn, oats, butter, and hay and allowed him to enjoy a middle-class standard of living, a claim few of his fellow blacks could make.

How and to what extent Fairfield might contribute to the war effort was a question the town pondered. It possessed no industrial capacity. The carriage works at Black Rock was totally defunct, and the biggest industrial employer in town currently was Meeker & Pike, a tanning company that barely kept four workers busy throughout the year. Fairfield's farmers could help, and did. Much of what they produced during the war went ultimately to army kitchens. Onions were in short supply throughout the conflict because medical officials believed them useful in preventing scurvy; local farmers did all they could to meet the demand.

Fairfield's greatest contribution to the Union cause was the number of men it sent to battle. During the earliest months of the war, when most Northerners believed the conflict would be brief, enlistment provided enough men to fill the Union ranks; but as the war dragged on and people came to comprehend its horror, finding enough troops developed into a major problem. On July 2, 1862, President Lincoln called for 300,000 men to serve for three years. Governor Buckingham organized Connecticut into recruiting districts in order to provide the 7145 men needed to meet Connecticut's quota. Supporting the governor's efforts, on July 24, Fairfield authorized the selectmen to pay $25 to "each man who shall enlist in this Town in the United States Service" before August 20.[2] On August 5, realizing that this pittance would engender little patriotism, Fairfield increased the bounty to $125.

*The Civil War Era*

In August, Lincoln called for another 300,000 men. Knowing that his state could never provide additional volunteers in such numbers, Buckingham instituted a draft that would go into effect on September 10. Even before the draft became law, Fairfield extended the bonus of $125 "to any resident of this town who has or shall enlist under the last two calls of the President . . . provided that the town shall be credited with such enlistment on its quota in case of a draft."[3] But something even more alluring than $125 had to be found if the town was to meet its quota before the draft went into effect. On October 20, Fairfield increased the bounty to $200 and on October 23 raised it again, to $275. The bounty paid draftees rarely enticed them to serve; usually they used the money to hire substitutes, a practice that was fully condoned by both the state and federal governments.

But even the draft failed to guarantee that Fairfield would meet its quota. On September 10, the first day of the draft, the first selectman, Simon Sherwood, took sixty-two Fairfield draftees to New Haven for physical examinations. All of the men were found sufficiently healthy to serve, but before they had returned to Fairfield, five of them paid between $300 and $500 to obtain substitutes, and the other fifty-seven discovered that there was an even easier way to avoid military service — they could buy medical exemptions in New Haven for more or less $75, depending upon the fees of local physicians. Only the five substitutes entered the service, and probably at least two of them deserted before actually being mustered into the infantry.

When a New Haven newspaper reported how the fifty-seven had avoided the army, the town of Fairfield, feeling slandered, appointed Oliver H. Perry, Benjamin Pomeroy, Sherwood Sterling, and Edward I. Alvord to refute the story and restore Fairfield's patriotic image. A week later, it instructed the selectmen to "inform the Governor . . . of the progress this town is making in filling its quota of Volunteers and make such explanation as may be required."[4]

Although Fairfield paid fewer bounties than it anticipated, thanks to the willingness of Connecticut physicians to find some flaw in even the fittest of men, it still incurred a substantial debt by the end of 1862. In February 1863, the town voted to issue $35,000 worth of bonds to cover the indebtedness it had contracted for war purposes. Fairfield planned to appropriate $4000 each year to cover the interest on the debt and to repay part of the principal, a scheme that required an immediate tax increase of two and a half mills. Unexpected costs cropped up as never before in the town's history. In December 1862, for example, Fairfield added $90 to its budget by voting "to pay the sum of ten Dollars per Month for nine Months to the Family of Eugene Slason commencing from the date he was drafted, the said Eugene Slasons family being destitute." War was an expensive business.[5]

On March 3, 1863, Congress passed the first federal conscription act, a dubious piece of legislation that allowed a drafted man to avoid serving by paying $300, which the government could either use to hire a substitute or merely accept as a commutation fee, that person's contribution to the war effort. The draft in Connecticut took place on July 18, and on August 4, Fairfield appropriated $20,000 purportedly "to take action and provide Measures of relief for such of our Citizens as may be Drafted." What the town really did was appropriate the money in order to provide each draftee with $300, which he could use to provide relief for his family in the unlikely event he did actually enter the service or which he probably would use either to procure a substitute or to pay "the proper officer of the United States" the commutation fee.[6] Clearly Fairfield, like dozens of other Connecticut towns, preferred to surrender the equivalent of many fortunes rather than send its young sons and husbands off to war.

By January 1864, Fairfield had paid the commutation fees of forty-five men and had also spent $2550 to hire substitutes for eight draftees: G. H. Bradley, W. B. Ogden, R. B. Jennings, F. E. Burr, William Burr, David Sherwood, Benjamin R. Dimon, and Eugene Slason. Neither during nor after the war were Fairfield men reticent about admitting that they hired substitutes or paid the $300 commutation fee to avoid military service.

When the president sent out additional calls for men in the autumn of 1863 and in the spring of 1864, Fairfield appointed agents, usually Alba D. Wood and Samuel Pike, to find men to fill its quota. Wood and Pike managed to get the bodies they needed by hiring whatever substitutes were available, by taking men, as the Bridgeport *Republican Farmer* reported sarcastically, "from different sections, of all conditions and colors." The two agents charged the town $5 a day for their services, and the town paid up to $200 for each substitute. In August it raised this figure to $300 and further stated that, if this amount proved insufficient to obtain enough men, the selectmen were authorized "to take such other measures as they may deem expedient, and at their discretion to pay any sum or sums of money necessary to secure said quota."[7] Fortunately Governor Buckingham was able to convince the War Department at the end of 1864 that Connecticut had provided more than its share of men for the conflict, and consequently the pressure on the town ended; but not before saddling Fairfield with an enormous debt that would require many decades, several bond issues, and numerous tax increases to repay.

Most of the Fairfield men who served in the Civil War were part of the Seventeenth Regiment, Connecticut Infantry, a unit of Fairfield County residents that William H. Noble of Bridgeport organized in July 1862. Mustered into service on August 28, the Seventeenth departed for the front on September 3 to the cheers of thousands of relatives, friends, and neighbors who gathered at Seaside Park to send them off.

The men of the Seventeenth Regiment were introduced to combat at Chancellorsville, Virginia. Part of General O. O. Howard's Eleventh Corps at Chancellorsville, the Seventeeth occupied the extreme right of the flank that Howard's command was protecting. The regiment was facing south on the evening of May 1, 1863, when General Thomas J. Jackson, better known as Stonewall, struck from the west with 24,000 men. Two companies of the Seventeenth were on picket duty when the initial onslaught came, overwhelming them, but not before they managed to retreat to the regiment lines. Noble then succeeded in getting his men to swing to the west and to fire several volleys before they too retreated in confusion. Jackson's soldiers inflicted 120 casualties on the regiment; Colonel Noble was severely wounded. But by holding on as long as it did, the Seventeenth delayed Jackson and allowed Adolphus Bushbeck's brigade to shift its front and fortify itself well enough to hold the Confederates for thirty minutes. That half-hour gave General Howard and General Joseph Hooker sufficient time to organize their defense, a line that eventually held against Jackson's force.

After the engagement at Chancellorsville, the Seventeenth rested until the Army of the Potomac began to follow General Robert E. Lee's advance into northern territory, a pursuit that culminated in the battle of Gettysburg. Arriving on that battlefield the first day of the fighting, the Seventeenth, under the command of Lieutenant Colonel Douglas Fowler, found itself pushed forward to the extreme right of the Union position, where it was assigned the task of testing Confederate defenses on Oak Hill. It had barely begun to probe the Confederate positions when Jubal Early's force struck, inflicting 198 casualties on the Fairfield County men and forcing them to retreat to Cemetery Hill, where Howard's Eleventh Corps checked any further Confederate advance. At the cemetery, the Seventeenth established its defensive lines behind a stone wall where, the following day, July 2, 1863, it held the famous Louisiana Tigers until those Confederate troops broke and retreated in the face of Union reinforcements.

The men of the Seventeenth endured the same emotional and physical discomfort as most Civil War soldiers, Union or Confederate. Allen Smith, of Company G, wrote back to Connecticut just about a week after the Seventeenth departed from Bridgeport: "I am well but homesick. . . . When I come to think of my Wife & Children & think that if killed in battle they will be thrown on the cold charity of the world then I feel bad & sometimes cannot contain myself so but that I weep in spite of all my efforts to prevent it."[8]

After surviving Gettysburg, George Hale, who was then in the West Philadelphia Hospital, wanted to share his exhilaration over that Union victory with his neighbors back home. He wrote to Francis D. Perry: "We have had a hard battle and suffered a good deal but the old flag still waves where the rebel flag waved on the first of July. We have drove them in confusion before us . . . I was hit by a musket ball in the left hip . . . [but] I think I shall be ready to fight them rebs again in a couple of months."[9]

Following their distinguished service at Gettysburg, the Seventeenth, camped on Folly Island, South Carolina, participated in the siege of Charleston. From South Carolina the unit went to St. Augustine, Florida, where it remained until the end of the war, guarding convicted Union deserters.

Allen Smith survived both the battle of Chancellorsville and the battle of Gettysburg without injury. He found life at Folly Island both good and bad. The Folly River, he happily reported, "is completely lined with oysters so if the Government dont furnish us rations we can live on oysters & be independent." On the other hand, "there is the musquitoe with a bill like a barn owl & flies in abundance with fleas & lice in any quantity from a single one up to a gross." But what he found even more disheartening was being wet day after day; dry clothes were nonexistent for enlisted men. "I am nearly used up. Now how I wish this war would end or that I were out of it. It is killing business this being exposed to the weather." Smith's fellow soldier George Hale, who had more of a stomach for military life, found duty on the island tolerable: "We are not anxious to get home untill we whip the infarnel rascals."[10]

Christmas on Folly Island was celebrated in fine fashion. The men ran foot races, climbed a greased pole, and tried to catch a suspended ring with a sword while riding bareback at a full gallop. Once the contests were over, they sat down to a dinner of boiled ham, codfish balls, mashed potatoes, onions, pickles, bread and butter, pies, and coffee. After dinner those who smoked enjoyed cigars provided by the government. Hale called the meal "the best dinner we have had since we have been in the service."[11]

Life in St. Augustine, even the life of a jailor, was an improvement over anything the men of the Seventeenth had known earlier during the war. Hale told Francis D. Perry that "it is rather the nicest place we have been in yet. I am in hopes we shall stay

*Major John B. Morehouse, Fairfield native
and Civil War hero.*

here the remainder of our time. I think we ought to see some easy times; we have seen hard times enough." Even Allen Smith had to admit "this is a real healthy place but as old almost as time." Born and bred in Connecticut, Smith encountered sights in St. Augustine unlike anything he had ever seen back home. "The houses are mostly built of sea shells matted together so that it has the appearance of stone," he wrote. "The inhabitants are nearly all Spanish or Spanish descent." Most amazing of all, "They can all speak the Spanish language, little children and all." He liked the Spanish people he encountered — "They are very clever & sociable" — but was surprised to find "they are nearly all catholics." Smith was less enamoured of the black Floridians: "Darkies are plenty, all free now & saucy; they have a notion they are a little better than white folks but I rather think they are a little mistaken."[12]

Probably Fairfield's greatest Civil War hero was John B. Morehouse who, on October 16, 1861, enlisted in the First Connecticut Cavalry, a unit that engaged the enemy over ninety times, saw 15 percent of its number killed in action, 22 percent captured, and more than 50 percent casualties of one sort or another. Often a member of patrols that raided behind enemy lines, Morehouse was captured twice by Confederate troops, the first time on June 8, 1862, at Cross Keys, Virginia, and the second time on June 20, 1863, at Frederick, Maryland. In each instance, he served as a prisoner of war before being paroled. He was also wounded twice, once at Ashland, Virginia on June 1, 1864, and at Reams Station, Virginia, just twenty-eight days later. Promotion came quickly for him even in a unit where candidates worthy of promotion were numerous. Originally a sergeant, he was promoted three times in 1863, to second lieutenant, to

*The Civil War Era*

first lieutenant, and to captain. He became a major on February 16, 1865, the rank that he held until the end of the war.

Morehouse and the men who served with him were indeed "fighting fools." They covered themselves with glory. Toward the end of the war they were serving under the command of General Philip H. Sheridan. At Waynesboro, Virginia, on March 2, 1865, the Confederates were so well entrenched that Sheridan himself doubted they could be dislodged. He sent the First Connecticut Cavalry and two other regiments against the enemy. The First initiated the charge. In the face of a driving ice storm, struggling through mud that was so deep the horses could barely walk, the Connecticut men struck the Confederate flank, diverting the defenders' attention long enough to allow General George A. Custer to move against the center of the enemy line. Before the day was over, the Union army had taken the position, along with 1303 prisoners.

When Sheridan attempted to give chase to the Confederate force, General James Longstreet moved his men forward to cut off the Union pursuers. Sheridan sent the First Connecticut Cavalry against Longstreet's troops to open the route for his main force. The cavalry routed the Confederates and allowed Sheridan to cross the North Anna River, but not before seventeen Connecticut men had lost their lives.

At Five Forks, Virginia, on April 1, after two unsuccessful charges and terrible losses, General Custer and his men finally broke through the enemy defenses and captured six thousand Confederate troops. Later Custer reported: "In this memorable battle, the First Connecticut achieved the honor of being the first to leap the enemy's breastworks, seize his cannon, and turn them on the retreating foe." Six days later Major Morehouse led an attack on General Robert E. Lee's wagon train near Harper's Farm, Virginia. Morehouse came away with several Confederate prisoners and many horses and mules from the train.[13]

By April 9, Lee's forces faced certain destruction if they continued to fight. General Ulysses S. Grant requested that Lee surrender, and Lee agreed to meet with Grant to discuss the terms of capitulation. To recognize the bravery of the men of the First Connecticut Cavalry, Grant selected that unit to escort him when he went to Appomattox Court House to receive Lee's surrender. One can only imagine the emotions experienced that day by Colonel John Morehouse or Captain Marcus Sterling or Private Charles W. Thorp or Private Charles A. Nichols or any of the other Fairfield men, the joy of ultimate victory and the grief of knowing that half their comrades were missing or had been killed or wounded.

Morehouse, Sterling, Thorp, and the other men from the First Cavalry were not the only representatives of Fairfield serving in Virginia that day. John Perry, for one, was there as well; he was recovering from wounds he had received when he and the other members of his company had been the first Union infantrymen to enter Richmond. During the autumn of 1864 and the spring of 1865, his unit, the Twenty-Ninth (Colored) Regiment, Connecticut Volunteer Infantry, had seen heavy fighting and had suffered outrageous losses. Commanded by white officers, denied firearms until they were about to meet the enemy, regularly assigned menial duty, the men of the Twenty-Ninth fought bravely and won the praise of their division commanders both at Richmond and at Kell House, Virginia.

Monday, April 10, 1865, was cold and rainy, nearly as miserable a day as April 12, 1861, had been. But the news was better. On the tenth, Fairfield learned that the war was over, that Lee had surrendered. Lee's capitulation meant the end of searching for recruits among a population that was unswervingly reluctant to go to war. It meant also that the town could reduce its budget to traditional levels; except, of course, for the expense of carrying its substantial debt. It meant welcoming home the men who had served, who had endured bad food and filth and incompetent officers and pain. Eighteen Fairfield men would never return; they had given their lives for the Union. But for most residents, the end of the war was a chance to get back to the way things had been.

The conflict, in fact, brought little change to Fairfield. Between 1860 and 1870, to be sure, its population grew by almost 29 percent, but this was caused by the abrupt decline in movement to the West, not the war. The last significant migration took place in the 1850s, when some Fairfield men and women went either to the gold- and silver-producing areas of the West or to the new territories of Kansas or Nebraska. By the time of the war, Fairfield persons were finding greater opportunities in Bridgeport than in the West. That city's population increased almost 50 percent during the 1860s, and the assessed valuation of its property grew by 43 percent. Although getting back and forth to work in Bridgeport was a chore for all Fairfielders except those living in either Stratfield or Black Rock, the opportunities for employment were so great that individuals were more likely to tolerate that inconveneince than to head west.

Fairfield's increase in population also came as the result of the continued influx of European, especially Irish, immigrants. By 1870, more than 20 percent of Fairfield's population was made up of immigrants, the overwhelming majority of whom were from Ireland. The town's black population also increased slightly during the decade, reaching nearly 4 percent by 1870. For both black Americans and the recent arrivals, few employment opportunities existed in town except for household servants, many of whom worked in wealthy homes, or for farm laborers, hired men.

Fairfield's assessed valuation had failed to increase as significantly as had its population or Bridgeport's. The 1860s witnessed only a 10 percent increase in the value of Fairfield property. The decline in the size of Fairfield's fleet was one reason for the slow growth. Because more farm goods were going to New York by rail than ever before and because local farmers were facing more and more competition from Western producers, the market fleet began to shrink. Except during the busiest season, as of 1870 only two or three sloops made the round trip between Southport and New York each week. Fairfield's fleet, valued at more than $375,000 in 1855, was worth only about $110,000 in 1870.

Manufacturing failed to compensate for the loss of shipping. To be sure, the war years and the years right after Appomattox saw more industrial activity than Fairfield had experienced before, but even this growth was slow. The backers of the Copper & Sulphuric Acid Company, located on Ash Creek, invested $80,000 in their plant, but it survived only a few years before L. F. Curtis, a Bridgeport druggist, bought the whole operation for $8500 and turned it into what eventually became both the Fairfield Chemical Company and the Manhattan Fertilizer Company. Under various owners, both companies lasted into the twentieth century. Hubbell, Walker, & Gill established a malleable iron works in the same part of town, but this foundry remained in Fairfield only a short time before becoming part of Bridgeport's industrial establishment. In 1870, Augustus Jennings and his brother, Isaac, set up a small plant in Southport where they manufactured Japanese paper ware, light but durable dishes and pails made by hydraulically pressing hemp fibers into various shapes. The factory served as a branch for their main plant, which was located in New York until 1892 or 1893, when Charles B. Jennings, who had come to head the company, consolidated his manufacturing operations in a single mill in Fairfield. He continued to manufacture a variety of products until 1910, when his firm ceased operating.

More important than the Jennings plant was the Mott Manufacturing Company. James S. Mott moved to Fairfield in 1868 or 1869, bought land, and constructed a factory where he planned to build carriages made largely of rubber, a substance Mott believed to be infinitely superior to wood and leather, the materials normally used in the manufacture of such vehicles. Convinced that his ideas would revolutionize the carriage industry, Mott planned to use traditional materials only for the chassis, axles, and wheels. By 1879, he was facing economic problems, and he was looking for a buyer for his plant. Fortunately the Fairfield Rubber Company, headed by Nathaniel Wheeler, bought the plant and began to produce a variety of carriage accessories such as back buggy boots, buggy aprons, and carriage covers. Wheeler, who also ran the gigantic Wheeler & Wilson Sewing Machine Company in Bridgeport, turned Mott's failure into success. The rubber company employed 180 workers by the 1880s and would remain the largest employer in Fairfield for many years.

This factory was unique in town. Other industrial enterprises were either so small that they employed only four or five hands at most, or survived only a few years. In fact, with the exception of the rubber works, the biggest financial enterprise in Fairfield was probably Thomas T. Moody's icehouse, which produced—that is, cut, on local ponds—and sold $30,000 worth of ice in a good year. Moody employed fifty men during the cutting season and ten during the months when ice was in great demand.

Almost all of Fairfield's commercial activity occurred in Southport. Aside from a scattering of grocery and dry goods stores in Greenfield, Fairfield, and Black Rock and a few businesses that catered to tourists in Fairfield, all the town's enterprises were in Southport. That village was also the scene of most of the business construction in town. In 1865, the Southport Savings Bank opened its new office, probably the most important commercial structure built between the Civil War and the end of the nineteenth century.

Agriculture, while not thriving, remained Fairfield's major industry. With 13,740 acres under cultivation or in pasture, the town produced agricultural products worth about $360,000 in 1870. Onions accounted for about one-third of that amount, with potatoes, oats, and milk and butter also important. Much of this production took place on large, by Connecticut standards, and carefully managed farms. Joseph Jenning's 122-acre farm yielded $3200 worth of onions and $1000 worth of potatoes as well as 250 pounds of butter and thirty tons of hay. In 1870 alone, Jenning's agricultural products brought in $5957. W. B. Morehouse, on his hundred acres, was only slightly less prosperous. His crops that year were worth a total of $5490, $4000 of which came from onions alone. More typical of Fairfield farmers was Arthur Sherwood, whose crops sold for $1500; he realized $750 from his onions and $250 from his potatoes, all produced on thirty-six acres. Living on the edge of poverty, Philip Shay, a recent arrival from Ireland, was surviving on eight acres of land from which he obtained goods worth $260 in 1870, most of which were consumed right there on the farm.

*Fairfield: the biography of a community*

*Residence of James Mott, founder of the Fairfield Rubber Co. and selectman, was built circa 1870. This view was taken in the 1940s when it was a hotel for summer visitors.*

During the years right after the Civil War, Fairfield suddenly took an interest in the Black Rock and southern Stratfield sections of town. Generally areas that Southport, Greenfield, and Fairfield ignored, they became the object of the town's attention and of the town's largess in the form of new roads. On October 1, 1866, the town authorized the selectmen to lay out Iranistan Avenue. West State Street, from Division to sixty-six feet beyond Iranistan, was a concern the following year and Black Rock Avenue the next. During 1868, Fairfield also agreed to extend Iranistan Avenue to Beach Road and to straighten Division Street. The town lavished the same kind of attention on this long-neglected area during 1869, by which time it had even finished its part of Seaside Park.

So much money was going to Black Rock that in September 1868 the Southport *Chronicle* felt compelled to speak out, calling attention to the favorable impression that "broad and straight" streets generally made on visitors to a community. "Do we ever realize when walking through our [Southport's] narrow, crooked, zigzag streets, filled with obtuse angles, what the effect must be on a stranger?" demanded the paper. "Our town is called upon, year after year, to lay taxes to make improvements in the eastern portion of it, adjoining the city of Bridgeport, which city derives most of the benefits of such improvements." It was high time, the *Chronicle* argued, that Southport began to get a share of this money.[14]

What the *Chronicle*'s editor undoubtedly understood but refused to acknowledge was that there was a reason behind the town's consistent favoritism of Black Rock. Bridgeport had its eye on both Black Rock and southern Stratfield, and Fairfield, eager

*The Civil War Era*

to make up for past neglect, was willing to build all the parks and roads that area residents wanted to keep them happy. On November 17, 1869, the town meeting appointed a "Committee of Observation" to "watch the action of the City of Bridgeport in relation to conveying a part of this town to and forming a part of Bridgeport." Now three and a half times the size of Fairfield, Bridgeport was an even more formidable opponent than it had been when it took the county seat and the courthouse in 1853.[15]

Fairfielders believed that their town had already contributed more than enough to Bridgeport's success. Not only had Fairfield lost the courthouse and the customs house, it had also sent hundreds of young men and women to Bridgeport to work in its factories, banks, and stores. Furthermore, Fairfield spent thousands of dollars each year in Bridgeport, for several decades now the commercial center of the entire region. The relationship seemed entirely one-sided; Bridgeport did all the taking, and Fairfield, at least in the eyes of its residents, all the giving.

Probably Greenfield, in particular, presented the greatest contrast between bustling, prosperous Bridgeport and sleepy Fairfield. Greenfield, long the center of farming in town, testified to the decline of Connecticut agriculture more than any other part of town. Southport's commerce and weaithy seasonal residents helped maintain its prosperity. Fairfield also had its summer people, both residents and visitors. Black Rock and Stratfield were close enough to Bridgeport to bask in some of that city's reflected success. But Greenfield had only its farms, and they were unable to meet the competition from upstate New York and the Middle West. In 1868, Jonathan Sturges, who resided in New York but had been born in Fairfield and had maintained a cottage in town since 1840, wrote that he had "lived to see the Rise & Fall of Greenfield." A few years later, the Newtown *Bee* contrasted Greenfield as it had existed before 1830 with the village nearly half a century later and called the difference one more "striking instance of the decline of Connecticut hill towns."[16]

But Bridgeport was relentless. Advocates of the plan to annex Black Rock and southern Stratfield argued that property values in the area would increase dramatically once annexation occurred, that they were foolish to remain a part of Fairfield. The editors of the *Chronicle* urged Fairfield residents to attend a special town meeting on March 17, 1870, to consider a proper response to Bridgeport's threat: "Look out for the interests of the town at the meeting tomorrow afternoon. Down with the division." The *Chronicle* prepared for a fight: "Bridgeport is all well enough in her way, but let us show her that she cannot, without a bitter struggle, tweak the nose of old Fairfield."[17]

Fairfield's voters gathered at the town meeting in large numbers and agreed to inform the Connecticut General Assembly that they were "against the granting by your honorable body of the petition of the City of Bridgeport... for the extension of the limits of said City into the town of Fairfield." The meeting appointed John Gould and Orland B. Hall to argue the town's case before the legislature.[18]

In May Bridgeport presented a petition to the General Assembly requesting authority to annex that part of Fairfield east of Ash Creek and Division Street, now Park Avenue. Gould and Hall countered with Fairfield's opposing memorial, and both documents went to the Standing Committee on Incorporations for consideration. Apparently Gould and Hall did little to win support for their town's position among the nine members of the committee. The *Chronicle* complained about "the inactivity of those who have the matter in charge" and wondered if they were "being caught 'napping'!"[19]

Fairfield found the prospect of further dismemberment alarming. "Old Fairfield has already been sufficiently sliced. We don't want to be shaved down into nothing." One letter to the *Chronicle* contended that "this division would leave us nothing but a long narrow strip, a peninsula, as it were, and all this, after we have expended more from the town treasury, for that part of town, than all the rest put together."

Rumors began to circulate about Bridgeport's unscrupulous efforts to win support at the General Assembly. According to observers who claimed to know about such matters, Bridgeport was prepared to use any means to win, even if it meant appealing to the basest instincts of the least ethical element in the legislature. "The whisper of 'Champagne' in the ears of the red-nosed, voluptuous-lipped, rustic tipplers will at any time gain their votes, and such are the men who will be found to vote in favor of this annexation scheme," asserted the *Chronicle*.[20]

Whether or not that was an accurate description of those who did vote for annexation hardly mattered; what did matter was that the General Assembly dealt with the question expeditiously. On June 30, the Committee on Incorporations reported in favor of the Bridgeport petition; and within a day, both houses had passed a bill transferring the territory in question to Bridgeport. The legislature demanded of Bridgeport only that it refrain from taxing its new residents to pay for the acquisition of the area and that it should tax them to pay off their share of any existing debts that Fairfield might have. Almost before Fairfield realized it, it had lost slightly more than three square miles to its eastern neighbor.

The tendency in Fairfield was to place full blame for the loss onto the allegedly deplorable tactics employed by Bridgeport advocates of the scheme. The town resounded with stories of legislators, victims of strong drink, happy to do Bridgeport's bidding. In fact, Black Rock and southern Stratfield stood ready to leave even before the legislature acted. Owners of 1340 of the 2000 acres Bridgeport annexed favored joining the city; the owners of about 269 acres expressed their opposition, while the other property owners were indifferent. If proponents of annexation behaved unethically during the months before the legislature acted, they did so by claiming that land values would, without question, increase once the area was within Bridgeport; no basis for such an assertion existed, and it proved to be absolutely incorrect.

James S. Mott, the rubber carriage manufacturer, handled the details of the transfer with Bridgeport. Although he had arrived in town only a year or so before, Mott already had created a place for himself in Fairfield political life. In fact, he revived the Democratic party in Fairfield after it had fallen into disfavor, a result of the tendency of townspeople to associate it with the South and secession. By the 1870s, the Democrats and Mott— who had no interest in seeking public office himself—controlled the political scene in town. Under their leadership Fairfield attempted, for the first time in many years, to modernize and improve town government. Mott had initiated this effort by refurbishing the Town Hall. He made possible the expenditure of $6000 to transform the ancient structure by spreading the word among his fellow Democrats that they should appear at seven o'clock for an eight o'clock town meeting. Because the hall could hold only about 20 percent of those eligible to participate, many Republicans were therefore

*The old Fairfield town hall, formerly the Fairfield County Courthouse in the early 1900s.*

excluded, and the meeting authorized the $6000 whereas it had initially approved only half that amount.

At Mott's urging, Fairfield also abandoned the costly practice of holding elections for certain town offices, offices that had become positions of little or no importance but which the town refused, for reasons of nostalgia, to forsake totally. The selectmen subsequently appointed haywards, fence viewers, and pound keepers. On the other hand, the town began to elect certain other officers whose responsibilities had grown: the registrar of births, marriages, and deaths; the registrar of voters; the assessors; and the treasurer of the school fund.

Fairfield began to pay closer attention to the collection of town taxes as well. It combined the offices of first constable and tax collector into a single position to facilitate the collection process, approved an elaborate plan "for the Speedy and proper Collection of the taxes of the Said Town,"[21] and agreed to print annually one thousand copies of the report of the Committee on the Collection of the Taxes. To assure the collector's honesty, Fairfield required him to obtain a surety bond for ten thousand dollars.

The town's concern with financial matters also expressed itself in new town regulations that required the selectmen to honor only claims for which the town had received a full and complete bill, to pay only those bills that had the endorsement of a majority of the selectmen, and to issue a complete statement of the town's financial condition by September 15 of each year, a statement that was to be available to the public in the town clerk's office. To guarantee that the selectmen performed their new responsibilities in a professional manner, the town agreed to pay each one $4 a day when on town business, the total each official might earn annually being limited to $250, not an inconsequential sum in the 1870s or 1880s.

Fairfield had to be concerned about money. During the recent war, the town had accumulated a debt of almost $50,000, an astronomical amount for a traditionally frugal town that avoided debt altogether. In February 1877, the town meeting, in an effort to fund a portion of its floating debt, agreed to "issue bonds to the amount of Thirty-Eight-thousand dollars" and to pay "interest at the rate of Six per cent. per annum."[22] The cost of servicing its debt was so overwhelming that Fairfield became embroiled in the necessity of borrowing more and more money to meet current expenses. It issued $30,000 worth of 4 percent bonds again in 1884 and $40,000 worth of 3.5 percent bonds in 1889. In a typical year, interest and principal payments cost the town about one dollar of every four it spent. In 1891, for example, the town's estimated expenses were about $35,000. Of this, $10,325 went to the schools, $4800 for care of the poor, $4000 for roads and bridges, $2350 for salaries, $4320 for election expenses, military tax, and sundries, and $9140 for interest charges and principal repayment.

With the Civil War almost thirty years in the past, Fairfield continued to be enmeshed in debt. By 1894, it owed about $112,000, of which $42,000 was floating debt. Faced with such a burden, it resolved to pay off $5000 a year until the amount was reduced to a manageable level. Entering the twentieth century, Fairfield still owed well over $50,000 but was finally committed to reducing its obligations where possible.

In these measures, many engineered by James S. Mott before he returned to Pennsylvania, Fairfield attempted to catch up with the times. Fundamentally unchanged by the Civil War and still relying on an outmoded economic foundation that had less and less place in the late nineteenth century, Fairfield could at least try to make its government more efficient, more rational, better able to serve the needs of its people.

## NOTES

1. Angeline Morehouse to Samuel Morehouse, Nov. 22, 1860, Jennings Collection, FHS. Persons interested in Connecticut's part in the Civil War should examine John Niven, *Connecticut for the Union: The Role of the State in the Civil War* (New York, 1965).

2. FTR, July 24, 1862.

3. Ibid., Aug. 15, 1862.

4. Ibid., Oct. 27, 1862.

5. Ibid., Dec. 1, 1862.

6. Ibid., Aug. 4, 1863.

7. Bridgeport *American Farmer*, Jan. 8, Feb. 5, 1864; FTR, Aug. 9, 1864.

8. Allen Smith to – – –, Sept. 28, 1862, Wakeman Family Papers, FHS.

9. George Hale to Francis D. Perry, July 9, 1863, Wakeman Family Papers, FHS.

10. Allen Smith to – – –, Sept. 16, 1863, and George Hale to Francis D. Perry, Dec. 26, 1863, ibid.

11. George Hale to Francis D. Perry, Dec. 26, 1863, ibid.

12. Same to same, May 3, 1864, and Allen Smith to – – –, July 8, 1964, ibid.

13. *Report of the Service of the Connecticut Men in the Army and Navy of the United States During the War of the Rebellion* (Hartford, 1889), 56, 57, 59.

14. Southport *Chronicle*, Sept. 11, 1868.

15. FTR, Nov. 17, 1869.

16. Jonathan Sturges, Memoirs, and undated clippings from the Newtown *Bee*, Bradley Family Papers, FHS.

17. Southport *Chronicle*, March 16, 1870.

18. FTR, March 17, 1870.

19. Southport *Chronicle*, May 11, 1870.

20. Ibid., June 15, 1870.

21. FTR, April 19, 1879.

22. Ibid., Feb. 17, 1877.

Chapter 13, bottom page 378-end of 380, end of chapter 13

# A Resort Community

**B**RIDGEPORT'S example of material success was too dramatic, too impressive not to encourage some Fairfielders to want to reproduce it in their own town. Probably the Southport *Chronicle* spoke for many residents when it urged the development of manufacturing in Southport and other areas of Fairfield. The editor of the *Chronicle* was particularly enthusiastic about a plan that William A. Pitt of Stamford was developing to locate a coal-gas plant on Southport harbor. This could be the first step in transforming Southport into an industrial center, the editor exclaimed, one that would offer employment for hundreds of Fairfield residents, one that would bring the same kind of wealth to that village as had come to Bridgeport. It can be done, the editor urged: "Look at Bridgeport!"[1]

A few years later, when it appeared as if steam packet service would be established between Southport and New York City, the *Chronicle* again sounded off about the advantages of industry. The packet service could be the beginning of a new day. Raw materials would arrive from distant locations to be transformed into manufactured goods in Southport. The time for action was now. "Prospects are cheering. Step aside, croakers, and let the wide-awake try their hand." Bridgeport was again the example the *Chronicle* would have Fairfield follow.[2]

Given Fairfield's circumstances in 1880, ten years after the loss of Black Rock, such a point of view made sense. Agriculture, the activity that still supported most of the town's residents, already suffered from an illness that would prove terminal—Western competition. The town's population had fallen to 3748, down from 5645 in 1870, thanks in part to the loss of Black Rock but also because of the dearth of economic opportunity in town. Bridgeport was now almost eight times the size of Fairfield in population.

In 1880, the likelihood of circumstances turning around in Fairfield was at best dim. To be sure, some industrial development during the late 1870s had created a few jobs. The Manhattan Fertilizer Company, which would become the National Fertilizer Company in 1895, remained on Ash Creek. It employed about seventeen workers, who worked only irregularly and who collectively earned barely $3600 in 1880. The Fairfield Chemical Company, also still on Ash Creek, paid its twenty-four hands almost $15,000 in the same year; it produced goods worth about $120,000, as opposed to the $45,000 worth of fertilizer its neighbor manufactured. The Fairfield Rubber Company was the only other industrial establishment in town. One-third of its employees were women and children, which allowed it to keep wages to a minimum. It paid fifteen hands $6000 to produce about $120,000 in goods. Fairfield's manufacturing base obviously remained unimpressive and offered jobs to few residents.

The failure of industry to take hold in Fairfield resulted from the town's hostility toward manufacturing and the social consequences that inevitably accompanied it. The editor of the *Chronicle* could exclaim forever about the advantages of factories, but the argument convinced only a handful of townspeople. Most of Fairfield's ordinary residents, while acknowledging Bridgeport's great success, refused to follow their neighbor's lead. Those who were dissatisfied with their lot in town usually left. Earlier they had moved west or south or to New York; now they were likely to find themselves in Bridgeport or some other industrial city. The residents who remained in town were either content or too bound by their own fears, indolence, or inertia to try anything new. They either liked or were willing to tolerate what was available in a small country town.

This population was joined by a group of men and women who had consciously sought rural life. These were Fairfield's seasonal or retired residents, of whom the town had an abundance. Having passed years in urban areas, usually New York, these individuals, eager to live among persons like themselves and filled with nostalgia for an age that survived only in a town like Fairfield, wanted nothing to do with factories and tenements and urban workers who more than likely had little education and spoke with strange accents. This was what they had left behind.

These retired and seasonal residents were only a minority in the population, to be sure, but an influential one. Their presence accounted for most of the jobs available in town. And when they combined with those ordinary folks who contentedly remained in Fairfield, they constituted an almost impregnable barrier to any new factories that might want to come to town. The Southport *Chronicle* complained endlessly about the unwillingness of Fairfield residents to sell land to industrial developers. They were, the paper contended, holding back progress; certainly, they were keeping industry at bay.

Whether the *Chronicle* wanted to accept it or not, Fairfield's future seemed to be as a resort community, not as a mill town. Former Fairfield residents who had gone to New York or elsewhere to find success continued to return. Men like Charles Dimon and Henry J. Beers became the neighbors of men like Moses Bulkley and Benjamin Pomeroy and Zalmon Wakeman, who had remained in town and prospered. The New York *World* correctly assessed the situation when it stated that "the beginning of the popularity of Southport and Fairfield as a summer resort was when the sons and daughters of these towns who had wandered far to gather wealth came home to spend in the quiet of their native villages a portion of the heated terms [i.e., summer]." These people, the *World* continued, then attracted others, friends and business associates.[3]

Fairfield was full of wealthy retired persons by 1870. The census of that year lists person after person—along with an estimate of his or her assets—who fit into this category. Frederick Marquand described himself as a "real estate broker" and judged his fortune to be worth about $900,000. John C. Sanford suggested that his occupation

*View of Old Post Road and St. Paul's Episcopal Church from the town green looking west in the 1880s.*

be described as "at home" and said his assets totaled $400,000. Neziah Bliss called himself a "broker"; he owned about $300,000 worth of property. Oliver B. Jennings told the census enumerator he was a "merchant" who was worth about $100,000, and the forty-five-year-old Dwight Morris, whose fortune totaled about $275,000, described himself as a "retired lawyer."[4]

The wealthy found three areas of Fairfield especially attractive: Southport, Main Street (now Old Post Road), and Mill Plain. Main Street was home to Oliver Burr Jennings. Born in Fairfield in 1825, he left town to enter the dry goods business in New York. He went to California in 1849, where he wisely decided to sell dry goods rather than prospect for gold. He accumulated his first fortune in the West. By 1862, he was back in New York, where he became involved with William Rockefeller (his brother-in-law) and John D. Rockefeller in the organization and management of the Standard Oil Company. In addition to his Main Street residence, Jennings also maintained a home at 48 Park Avenue in New York. In Fairfield he was surrounded by neighbors who were more or less as wealthy as he: Samuel Glover, Gardner Weatherby, Henry L. Mills, Charles Phelps, O. W. Jones, and William Nichols. Jennings also had an American Indian neighbor, Ely Parker, an Iroquois who had served as General Grant's assistant adjutant-general during the Civil War and who had since become a successful Wall Street investor.

Mill Plain was, in particular, the home of the Sturgeses, Jonathan, who originally established the family fortune, and his sons, Frederick and Henry C. Dr. Samuel Osgood's estate, Waldsteen, was located a short distance from the Sturges cottage. Beyond both, on Greenfield Hill, the younger Frederic Bronson occupied his family's estate on weekends and during the warm weather, often traveling between New York and Fairfield with The Coaching Club of New York, four-in-hand driving being one of his great passions.

Southport was the home of the Wakemans, the Bulkleys, the Perrys, the Sherwoods, as well as Frederick Marquand and his son-in-law, Elbert B. Monroe. Monroe, a New York banker, was successful in his own right. Southport was in great demand among New Yorkers. "Enquiries for desirable houses are being made by city people who have heard through the papers of the desirability of Southport as a Summer residence," reported the Southport *Chronicle* in 1892.[5] Similar statements appeared in the paper almost every summer. By 1893, New York developers were willing to pay as much as $1000 an acre for farmland in Southport and on Sasco Hill.

The most complete contemporary report on Fairfield as a resort community appeared in the New York *Commercial Advertiser* in September 1885. The paper, offering its own interpretation of how Fairfield had become so popular with "dozens of families of wealth and culture of New York," contended that many New Yorkers had visited the town on summer vacation and become so enamoured of it that they had subsequently built homes there. Many of these homes "they keep up the year round, steaming down to the city daily or frequently." After a day at business, the men returned to Fairfield to be "met at the station by the female contingent in stylish vehicles and becoming apparel, and whirled thence in a twinkling to their pretty homes on either side of the long, wide, shady main street."

The *Commercial Advertiser* described Main Street in as glowing terms as it did the tired businessmen's homecoming. Along the street stood "about twenty-five residences surrounded by extensive grounds, which are laid out in the best style of landscape gardening, with delightful lawns, gardens, trees and shrubbery, winding walks and driveways, statuary, conservatories, tennis courts, etc." The houses themselves were usually wooden, modern, elaborate, and imposing.

Other parts of Fairfield had neighborhoods that rivaled Main Street. The paper mentioned Mill Plain as the home of the Sturges family, and clearly held both the home and the family in great awe. It also praised the estate of Dr. Osgood and referred to the Bronson home as "one of the richest and most complete estates in the country." Actually Frederic Bronson thought that the house in Fairfield, the one his grandfather had originally purchased from Timothy Dwight and which his father had expanded to include a cavernous ballroom on the second floor, was a bit too rustic. In 1891, six years after the *Commercial Advertiser*'s report, he ordered the old house demolished and commissioned Richard Morris Hunt to design a three-story, forty-two room brick mansion.

The *Commercial Advertiser* was as flattering in its account of Southport. The residences there certainly could stand a comparison with those on Main Street and Mill Plain. The home of Frederick Marquand which would be demolished after his death, seemed to be the paper's favorite in that part of town.

Fairfield's two hotels, the Fairfield House (which became the St. Marc Hotel when Louis Cleveland, brother of President Grover Cleveland, bought it in 1872) and the Allen House, which had earlier been the Benson House, both received high praise for

*Engraving of Fairfield House, located on the corner of Old Post Road and Bench Road, from the June 4, 1864 issue of "Frank Leslie's Illustrated Newspaper."*

the accommodations they offered to "summer boarders." The Fairfield House, located on Main Street, contained more than one hundred rooms, an immense ballroom, a dining room nearly as large, and a bowling alley. Its promoters described it as "beautifully situated amid scenes that charm the eye, its excellent drives, attractive walks, freedom from all restraints, combine with its healthful and invigorating atmosphere to render it one of the most homelike of all summer resorts."

The people who visited the hotels were men and women of means. In 1891, an observer reported that "the St. Marc Hotel is well filled with a cultured class of guests, such as one finds at Cooperstown & Richfield Springs; they are mostly from Boston, New York, and Philadelphia." The hops that the hotel sponsored were grand events. "On Friday evening last a hop took place; a number of the guests from the Black Rock Hotel came over, which added much to the enjoyment of the occasion," a Fairfield resident reported. "The American Band (sixteen pieces) of Bridgeport furnishes the music for St. Marc's this season, and also gives a concert on the village green every Friday evening."

The *Commercial Advertiser* noted that "no summer in the country would be complete without its church fair, and the ladies of St. Paul's have recently achieved theirs." It must have been a grand occasion: "The tables were profusely strewn with fancy articles of all sorts, the work of many fair diligent fingers, while across one end of the room was a bower of lovely natural flowers, and in convenient corners various edible and partable goods." This was precisely the kind of diversion the city people wanted, a brief journey back to what the United States had been just a few years before.

Almost all of those who came to think of Fairfield as a resort spoke favorably of its assets. "The view from the beach, out upon the Sound, on a clear moonlight evening, with Black Rock light on the left, the Penfield Reef red-flash light in the middle distance, and the electric lights of passing steamboats still farther off, is one not easily surpassed or forgotten." Another nineteenth-century evaluation concluded: "Horseback riding, lawn tennis, boating and bathing on a beach that cannot be surpassed, the charming rambles on the banks of the lovely Mill river, and excursions not only through delightful scenery but also to regions rich with historic interest, Fairfield is surely a most delightful place to visit."[6]

In 1870, six trains a day arrived from New York and six a day from New Haven. Ten years later, the number of daily trains from each direction had doubled. The fare to New York one way from Southport was $1.40, and one could purchase a round-trip excursion ticket from Fairfield for $2.40. For those who preferred to travel by water, the *Nelly Green* left South Norwalk for New York each morning at 7:45, ten minutes after the train from New Haven arrived, providing plenty of time for passengers to take the free omnibus from the depot to the wharf. The boat reached Pier 37, at the foot of Market Street, at 10:30. It departed for Connecticut at 2:45 in the afternoon, arriving in Norwalk at 5:45, just in time to catch the train that would get into Fairfield at 6:35. Round-trip passage on the *Nelly Green* was $1.25, a bargain even in those times.

Fairfield's proximity to New York was revealed in innumerable ways. William H. Johnson, who ran a funeral parlor in Southport during the 1860s and 1870s, advertised "interments procured in any Cemetery either in this State or New York." When William Webb Wakeman died in New York in 1869, as many New Yorkers as townspeople attended his Southport funeral; his family chartered a special railroad car to bring in New York mourners. Fashionable Fairfield weddings were catered by New York firms. In 1885 Benjamin Pomeroy's daughter, Mary Francis, married Brooks Hughes Wells. "The supper was furnished by Pinard of New York, the music consisting of six pieces was also from New York."[7]

Fairfield was a resort for Bridgeport as well as New York. The Southport *Chronicle* worried that Bridgeport capitalists might buy up most of Fairfield and turn it into a country seat for themselves. Dr. I. DeVer Warner, the inventor of an amazing array of undergarments for women and a major Bridgeport industrialist, purchased several tracts of land in Fairfield, including the Fairfield House; many believed he would divide the land and encourage his Bridgeport neighbors to move to town. Eventually he sold much of his land but kept enough for his own residence. His decision to settle in Fairfield came at the same time that other Bridgeport entrepreneurs were arriving, such influential men as Treat Campbell and Clapp Spooner.

Although Fairfield's beach was one of its greatest attractions, both permanent and seasonal residents avoided living there. Most nineteenth-century Fairfielders would never have considered the idea. Even disregarding the dangerous storms that struck the area and overlooking the swarms of mosquitoes that patrolled the coast, one would have avoided the area because the roads to the beach were suitable only for pedestrians. An 1880 map of Fairfield prepared by Samuel Glover, a New York realtor, discloses no development either along the beach or in the wet areas immediately behind it.

Real estate development of the beach area waited until people of moderate means began to seek out the town's advantages. Unable to afford elaborate summer homes, these individuals could buy only the least attractive land in Fairfield—the beach—and could build only flimsy cottages, buildings that they probably planned to rent for part

*Action at the Fairfield Beach Club in the 1890s.*

of each season, at least, to help defray the cost of maintaining them. These were not New Yorkers. The first beach dwellers were from right in Fairfield County, specifically from Danbury, headquarters of the American hat industry.

Francis M. Pike, William B. Glover, and Glover's mother, Mrs. Emily Glover, owned much of Fairfield beach. They began to carve their property into lots and offer them for sale in the early 1890s. In 1891, only one modest cottage stood on the beach; it was called the Danbury Cottage, after the home of its owner and of his summer tenants. By 1897, fifteen cottages surrounded the original structure, and the whole area came to be called Little Danbury. Reef Road, built in 1895, connected the humble settlement with Fairfield. Once the road was in, E. W. S. Pickett, who operated a grocery store in town, began to send his wagon, loaded with provisions, to the cottage community every day during warm weather.

Bridgeport people of moderate means, following the example of Danbury, also established second homes in Fairfield. They too built inexpensive cottages along the beach. In 1897, a contemporary observer noted that "at Pine Creek is a pretentious beach set-tlement, that aspires to the somewhat ambitious title of 'Little Bridgeport.'" Fragile and unimpressive as some of the homes at Little Bridgeport appeared, even affluent Fairfielders acknowledged that the area "has delightful views, fine fishing, while the opportunities for bathing and yachting cannot be excelled along the Connecticut shore." Both Little Bridgeport and Little Danbury remained important, if unassuming, settlements in Fairfield.[8]

*Fairfield: the biography of a community*

Fairfield's humble summer residents attracted much less attention than their affluent counterparts. The anonymous residents of Little Danbury did ordinary things, boring things. The Bronsons and Jenningses and Perrys, forever the objects of the town's curiosity, entertained famous guests at lavish parties, lived on a scale beyond the comprehension of most townspeople, were persons of large affairs. They were constantly scrutinized, usually admired, often envied, and occasionally resented.

At times affluent individuals seemed to go our of their way to encourage resentment. W. B. Van Wagenen, a prosperous resident of Sasco Hill, sued the New York *Herald* for $15,000 for libel in 1897. The *Herald* had reported the arrest of Van Wagenen and his wife for assaulting their cook and coachman, a Mr. and Mrs. Cookson. Apparently Van Wagenen was taken with Mrs. Cookson and on several occasions made advances toward her. When Van Wagenen became insistent in his amorous intents, the cook told her husband, and the couple decided to resign. Mr. Cookson went to Mrs. Van Wagenen, who he thought would be understanding of his wife's predicament, and explained that they were leaving because of her husband's refusal to leave Mrs. Cookson alone. While they were packing, the Van Wagenens came to their quarters and first verbally and then physically attacked their former servants, forcing them to flee without collecting the wages that were due them. Eventually the Cooksons obtained their pay, and still later a jury required only fifteen minutes to decide against the Van Wagenens in their suit against the New York *Herald*.

Agnes Murray was a thorn in the side of many Fairfield residents for years. Clearly unbalanced, she took endless delight in whatever misery she could create for the individuals whose lives she touched. In 1887, she threw the village of Greenfield into a turmoil by allowing her "large and remarkably pugnacious ram," an animal that had already committed "many a deed of violence that should have earned him the butcher's knife," to wind up "a long career of crime" by attacking Adelia Hummell. Usually it was Miss Murray's dogs who terrorized the neighbors.[9]

The following year, Miss Murray shocked the entire town by kidnapping her blind brother from his Washington Place home in New York and bringing him to Greenfield. The brother, John B. Murray, who was seventy, had recently married Felicia Marianne Leiss, then eighteen, against the wishes of his sister. On the pretence that she was taking him to see a physician who could restore his eyesight, Agnes tricked her brother into coming to Greenfield. There she held him for three weeks before another brother, Bronson Murray, learned what had happened and returned the confused but happy septuagenarian to the family residence on Murray Hill, where his adolescent bride impatiently awaited his return.

The rank and file of Fairfield's population was constantly aware of the differences between their own situation and that of their rich neighbors. In most instances, this awareness created a sense of awe among of the town's population, a willingness to defer to the wishes of the wealthy and powerful. Usually the majority of Fairfield residents, who certainly were not wealthy people, tried to accommodate their more affluent neighbors whenever possible.

Fairfield's willingness to share its beach was a case in point. The beach was one of the town's most important assets. In 1879, changes in the flow of Ash Creek caused the beach to erode. Despite a huge debt, the town voted $500 to construct a "Bulkhead or such other work as may be found necessary to restore the current of said creek to

*A Resort Community*

its natural course, channel, and to protect Fairfield Beach."[10] Yet seven years later, when a group of twenty-six of Fairfield's most affluent citizens devised a scheme to operate part of the beach as a private club, the town willingly acceded. Frederick, Edward, and Henry C. Sturges, Walter and Oliver B. Jennings, Frederic Bronson, and twenty of their friends organized The Fairfield Beach Company. The purchase of a share of stock in the company ($50) entitled one to a bathhouse either within the forty-by-sixty-foot, two story pavilion the company built or in one of the adjacent smaller buildings. Fairfield residents could purchase annual memberships that entitled them to the same privileges for $10. The club's facilities were only available to residents of more than moderate means—$10 was clearly beyond what many families could afford—and control of the private section of the beach was a privilege monopolized by the few.

This arrangement apparently satisfied most of Fairfield's population. But when Henry S. Glover, Oliver G. Jennings—the son of Oliver B. Jennings—and Frederic Bronson formed The Fairfield Beach Improvement Company to extend the same group's control over an even larger area of the shore, the people of Fairfield reacted. They were willing to share this important natural resource, but they were unwilling to turn its control over completely to their more prosperous neighbors. At a town meeting held on April 22, 1895, the voters decided, 45 to 26, "that our Representatives be and hereby are instructed to use every effort to prevent the granting of a charter to the promoters of the Beach Improvement Company." The scheme died that evening.[11]

Such friction between Fairfield's seasonal and year-round residents was rare. Fairfielders not only welcomed their more affluent neighbors (and the employment they provided), but took pride in the fact that they had chosen the town as their home for at least part of the year. If Frederic Bronson or another such magnate supported a particular point of view on an important issue, most folks listened. But the ordinary people of Fairfield refused to abandon their pride and independence; although their town had seen better times in the past, times when its prosperous yeomen had kept a whole fleet of vessels busy carrying produce to New York, before New York and Ohio farmers had come to dominate the market quite so completely, these people ultimately saw themselves as the guardians of Fairfield's heritage and the guarantors of its future.

NOTES

1. Southport *Chronicle*, Feb. 1868.
2. Ibid., Nov. 29, 1871.
3. Quoted in ibid., June 28, 1892.
4. 1870 Census, Manuscript Schedule I, Fairfield, Connecticut State Library.
5. Southport *Chronicle*, June 30, 1892.
6. Quoted in the Fairfield *Advertiser*, Sept. 10, 1885.

7. Southport *Chronicle*, Dec. 15, 1868; Fairfield *Advertiser*, Oct. 15, 1885.
8. Fairfield Scrapbooks, 1897, FHS.
9. Fairfield *Advertiser*, May 20, 1887.
10. FTR, Nov. 3, 1879.
11. Ibid., April 22, 1895.

# The Private Town

FAIRFIELD MEN AND WOMEN of the nineteenth century sometimes questioned whether technological change necessarily meant progress. Certainly they were less than enthusiastic about bringing manufacturing to town. Talk of the railroad's coming failed to produce the kind of excitement that one might have expected, and once construction had begun the town did little to facilitate the building of the lines within its boundaries. It even made life difficult for the telegraph company by frequently complaining about the appearance and location of poles and other equipment.

Fairfield wondered if the railroad and the telegraph improved or impaired the quality of life in town. Speaking before the Connecticut Railroad Commissioners in 1887, William B. Glover, a member of the law firm of Perry & Perry, which represented the town at that time, maintained that, after the New York and New Haven Railroad arrived, Fairfield went into a decline. It had once been a commercial and political hub, Glover argued; "then the operation of the railroad changed all that and in making Bridgeport a centre transferred to it, the county-seat and all of Fairfield's former business." The result was a complete transformation of Fairfield; "from a place of importance and business in the county it has become a simple country town, a place of residence and of quiet summer resort."[1]

At the end of the Civil War, when the idea of a street railway system first came before the town, Fairfield people had problems making up their minds. Certainly the advantages were obvious. The railway, which the Bridgeport Horse Railroad Company planned to construct, would make working and shopping in Bridgeport easier and would make travel between Black Rock and Fairfield and Southport more convenient.

But disadvantages existed as well. The line might attract undesirable outsiders to Fairfield. While the town lacked any legal power to keep out unwanted persons — as it had possessed in colonial times — its residents used various means to restrict newcomers from coming to Fairfield. One device was to keep industry out; this meant employment

*Car 275 of the Connecticut Co. on the Post Road and Riverside Drive circa 1914.*

opportunities remained limited. Another was for property owners to sell their lands discriminately. The Southport *Chronicle*, always the spokesman for "progress," tried to explain why Fairfield was not growing after the Civil War: "Many of our citizens who have plenty of unoccupied land in the village, will not sell at any price; and second, others who will sell, hold their lots at far too high figures." The *Chronicle*, of course, had an answer: "Build up the village gentlemen! Those of you who have its interests at heart, and you can do so in no better way than by putting your lots at moderate figures, thereby inducing others to come and settle in our beautiful village." Residents, however, continued to ignore the paper's advice.[2]

Eventually Fairfield endorsed the Bridgeport Horse Railroad Company's petition to the General Assembly to establish service in town. The charter the legislature granted in 1866 allowed the company to build from Bridgeport to Black Rock and on through Fairfield center to Southport. The company succeeded in constructing the line only as far as Black Rock, however; patronage was low, and the company, barely able to maintain service on existing lines, failed to build all the routes it had originally planned.

By the late 1880s, electrified street railways began to replace the horse railroads in the United States. Not all interests were enthusiastic about the trolleys' connecting urban centers and the areas around them. Steam railroads, in particular, fearing the loss of business, tried to restrict the development of this new form of transportation. In Connecticut, the New York, New Haven and Hartford Railroad led the fight to prevent the chartering of trolley companies. The railroad's efforts to block electric streetcars were entirely successful until the May 1893 session of the General Assembly. At that time, the legislature granted thirty-five charters to trolley companies but also provided various forms of protection against competition for the steam railroads. The new and complicated legislation even granted towns the power to regulate both new and existing street railway corporations. Fairfield, for example, now possessed complete authority to determine the location of tracks and equipment within its borders.

The Bridgeport Traction Company, formed in 1893 by the merger of several horse railroad companies operating in the Bridgeport area, was one of the thirty-five companies the General Assembly originally chartered. It possessed the exclusive right to build from Bridgeport through Fairfield to Southport but could do so only after it satisfied whatever requirements the town might impose.

The first question the company and the town had to resolve was the route the line would take in Fairfield. The company hoped to construct the line down Main Street (now Old Post Road) to Benson Road, diverting north on Benson to Mechanic Street (now the Post Road) and then west on Mechanic to Southport. Some residents, however, wanted the line to continue out Main Street all the way to Southport.

The debate over the trolley route came to have broader implications than the company's management had ever anticipated. In August a carefully conceived and executed campaign in favor of the Mechanic Street route began to unfold. Letters to the editor of the Southport *Chronicle* appeared arguing for that route. Prominent citizens began speaking out in favor of locating the track on the less prestigious avenue. Frederic Bronson, Henry C. Sturges, Oliver Buckley, and several of their similarly affluent friends distributed a broadside, "Facts for Citizens to Consider," that presented the same point of view.

These men emphasized the harm that could be done to Main Street more than they did the advantages of having the tracks on Mechanic Street. "Main street is kept at great expense by the residents there, always in perfect order," was a fact of utmost importance in their minds. That the trolley would mean the loss of Main Street's magnificent trees and the destruction of the street's "macadamized" surface was another. "There is a moral obligation on the part of the town to preserve the street as it now is," they argued, after reminding their readers that Main Street residents had themselves paid to "harden" the street.

Main Street was also, of course, the location of the Congregational church, and "those who gave the most of the money subscribed for the building of the new Congregational Church, are very much opposed to having the cars on Sunday, unloading noisy excursionists for the beach in front of their very doors." The possibilities were terrible to contemplate, the authors of "Facts for Citizens to Consider" warned. "A noisy, boisterous, drinking crowd of 3,000 persons went to a less attractive town than Fairfield the first Sunday the cars began to run there." Many of the 3000 devoured their dinners "on the church steps and strewed the grounds around with empty beer bottles, lunch boxes and refuse matter of all kinds." The authors hoped that no unthinking Fairfield resident would "be so unkind as to vote to have the quiet of the Sunday in Fairfield now preserved for over 200 years broken up, and church services seriously disturbed there, in this manner."

One should be assured, they continued, that a town vote in favor of the Main Street route would drive "nearly everyone on the Main street" out of town, "because in Fairfield they could no longer have the quiet and rest for which they come there, in the summer time, on purpose to enjoy." This was a frightening prospect, because

*The Private Town*

the residents of Main Street paid one-tenth of all the taxes paid in town. But please remember, the broadside concluded, "it is not to save the property of the rich or poor that we ask you to vote for the Mechanic Street route. No one will probably be individually injured on either street, whichever way the road is built."[3]

Nothing that the advocates of the Mechanic Street route did was done subtly. Bronson, Bulkley, Sturges, and the others were so obvious that the whole town understood that the vote would be between the wealthy town residents and those obligated to them, and the rest of the town.

Emotions were high when the voters assembled to decide this issue on September 4, 1893. Many persons spoke in favor of one or the other of the routes, but probably what Samuel Morehouse said made more sense to more voters than anything anyone else suggested. He spoke in favor of locating the tracks down Main Street. "I do not see why the people on Main Street should make fish of one and foul of another," he said in reference to the argument that having the tracks on Main Street would hurt property values but placing them on Mechanic Street would have no corresponding impact. "Our homes on the back street are as dear to us as are those on the Main street to their owners although ours are not so costly or so elegantly maintained. Yet to avoid their personal inconvenience they wished to crowd the road from Main street to Mechanic street."[4]

Fairfield voters, many of whom felt insulted by the blatant demands of Main Street residents for special treatment, listened intently to Morehouse. When the vote was counted, 284 individuals agreed with him that the trolley should run down Main Street and only 240 voted that it should be located on Mechanic. As would be the case during the discussion over the Fairfield Beach Improvement Company, the town's ordinary citizens respected their affluent neighbors, but they refused to confuse diffidence with servility.

Once the town had decided on the trolley route, the next step was construction. The cars were already in operation in Bridgeport when Livingston George Smith arrived in that city for the first time in 1894. Coming from New York, he was impressed by the simplicity of the system. "There was no conductor," he noted. "The passenger entered the rear door and if he had the right change dropped his fare in a box in the front." But if he had neither a nickel nor five pennies, he would pass whatever coin or bill he had forward, and the driver would send the change back in an envelope in which the passenger would find the five cents for the fare box.[5]

Had Smith visited Fairfield, he would have had to walk, because the town repeatedly rejected—as by state law it could—the company's construction proposals. Colonel N. H. Heft, president of the traction company, met with the selectmen to obtain final approval of these plans in September 1894, more than a year after the town voted on the trolley route. He even brought a forty-four-foot-long map with him to explain the proposed system of tracks and accompanying equipment. When he left the meeting, he and the selectmen were still at odds. A special town meeting held on September 17 considered the restrictions that it should place on the company. Heft attended this meeting, and again he left without reaching an agreement with the town.

Finally, in October 1894, the company acceded to the town's demands. The trolley was to run through Fairfield to Southport on a single, rather than a double, track "on the side of the street, with turnouts and ample room for the hitching of horses between

*Postcard view of Brooklawn Country Club's original clubhouse circa 1911.*

the tracks and the side of the road; there are to be wooden poles (as opposed to iron). . . ; the tracks are to be laid to the post office in Southport, unless the selectmen stop them at the blacksmith shop." Both parties finally satisfied, construction began in Fairfield on October 29.[6]

The first piece of track was barely in place when the company encountered labor problems. The Italian workers who were building the line went on strike because the company, certain that it could take advantage of immigrants so unfamiliar with American ways, was charging each of them ten cents a day to ride the trolley from Bridgeport to the construction site in Fairfield; they would go back to work when the company stopped cheating them, they said. Bridgeport Traction, embarrassed that its meanness had been publicly revealed, dropped the practice.

The line was completed in just over two months. On December 9, the first streetcars traveled from Bridgeport to Fairfield and Southport. But the next day, trouble intervened again; the company had to terminate service because of an act of mass sabotage. Apparently the New York, New Haven and Hartford Railroad, unable to prevent the trolley from operating by legal means, hired a gang of New Haven toughs, also recent immigrants, to cut the wires that powered the trolley. "Officers were detailed on the case, but of course without avail," the newspaper reported.

Bridgeport Traction restored operations quickly, and several days of normal service followed. Every fourteen minutes, beginning at 6:43 in the morning and continuing until 12:47 the following morning, a car arrived in Fairfield from Bridgeport and another car departed Fairfield for that city.

*The Private Town*

Then worse misfortune struck the ill-starred line. On December 21, 1894, Harry Wildman Roscoe, a three-year-old child, was killed in an accident involving a trolley. Little Harry and his father, Frederick Roscoe, had been riding in a wagon near the trolley tracks. As the streetcar approached, the horse panicked and bolted across the tracks, throwing both father and son out of the vehicle. The boy's father held on to the reins and was dragged clear of the tracks, but Harry was crushed by the trolley. "I cannot say that anyone was to blame," said the grieving father, "but they have killed my boy."[7]

The public responded to the accident as Harry's father had. Most residents held Bridgeport Traction to blame for the boy's death, the *Chronicle* reported. Had the killer trolley been equipped with fenders, many Fairfielders suggested, it might have knocked the boy aside rather than crushing him. A medical report postulating that the lad had died when his head struck the tracks and had not been killed by the car failed to silence the critics.

Young Harry Roscoe's death came just as the company was seeking to expand its operations in Fairfield. Bridgeport Traction wanted to extend its lines into various sections of town: into Stratfield to the Stratfield Baptist Church; from Main Street down Beach Road all the way to the shore; and throughout Southport by means of a loop. In addition, the company also hoped to construct a line from Southport, along the shore route, through Green's Farms to Westport.

Never bursting with enthusiasm for the trolley and still horrified by the death of the Roscoe boy, Fairfield saw no advantage in having more streetcars in town. More cars would mean more outsiders. Convinced that the company intended to exploit Fairfield's natural resources, especially its beaches, town residents denounced in particular the company's "traction and picnic enterprises." Why should the town grant the company access to its beaches so that it could provide "for the amusement of our Bridgeport neighbors" and for the continued prosperity of traction company stockholders? they asked. Furthermore, why should the company take advantage of Fairfield roads, built and maintained with scarce tax dollars, without compensating the town in some way? "Why should we tax ourselves to build new roads and make valuable improvements and then hand them over to outsiders?" asked one indignant citizen. "Let the town get some of the benefit — or at least keep what it has."[8]

Fears that Bridgeport people might obtain easy access to Fairfield's beaches and anger at what many perceived to be the company's economic exploitation of the town finally spurred action. At a special town meeting on February 23, 1895, the town instructed the selectmen "to oppose *all* laying of trolley tracks on *all* streets of the town not now occupied by them." After the trolleys had been in operation only ten weeks in Fairfield, the town decided that it had had its fill of the newfangled device, an invention that seemed to create more problems than it solved.[9]

The biggest problem the streetcars created resulted from their depositing unwelcomed outsiders in town. Southport residents complained that too many Bridgeporters came to town every Sunday; they were not as respectful of the Sabbath as Southporters thought they ought to be. The *Chronicle* reported that townspeople were "in favor of doing something to restrict the people who came to Southport and behave in an unseemly manner."[10] — but doubted that the town would bar the sale of ice cream on Sunday as a mean of keeping these unwanted people out.

Fairfield did refuse to eliminate the sale of ice cream but went out of its way to make life difficult for the Bridgeport Traction Company. The selectmen in July 1896 imposed new regulations on the trolleys. At no time and under no circumstances were they to travel through Fairfield at a speed in excess of ten miles per hour. Furthermore, the town required each motorman to turn off his car's power one hundred feet before each intersection and to pass through these crossings on only the momentum from the car's "own motion prior to the shutting off of such power."[11]

In December 1896, Bridgeport Traction was again trying to expand its operations. It planned to build a new line into Fairfield from Bridgeport, a line that would come into town along the King's Highway, connect with the Main Street line, and then proceed down Beach Road and eventually to Little Danbury. The company also again tried its plan to build a loop through several streets of Southport—East Main, Water, West Main, and Pequot Avenue—and then on to Westport.

The General Assembly dispatched a committee to Fairfield on January 23, 1897, to meet with local residents and to consider the route extension requests. Representative Howard N. Wakeman was willing to compromise with the company. He would allow the extension of service if the company would guarantee a five-cent fare for passengers traveling from Fairfield to any location in Bridgeport. (At that time, trolley riders had to pay five cents to reach the Bridgeport line and an additional five to travel to any point within the city.) A. E. Rowland wanted the town to insist that the company run its tracks only on property that it owned and that it pay a tax for the privilege of crossing town roads. He complained that the quarter-mile-long road to Little Danbury had cost the town $3000 and argued that Bridgeport Traction had no right to cheat the taxpayers by using the road for its tracks.

The company countered this opposition by offering a reduction in fares in return for Fairfield's support for its planned extensions. If the town allowed the trolleys to go to the beach and if it allowed the company to "secure a plot suitable for a park," the company would reduce the fare charged to ride from Southport to Bridgeport from ten cents to five. Fairfield wanted nothing to do with the plan. Granting Bridgeport Traction access to the beach and the right to build a park there would destroy the beauty and serenity of the shore by "dumping upon our borders, a noisy, irresponsible crowd of hilarious pleasure seekers that would disturb the quiet of the town." The possibility of the company's opening a resort at Pine Creek, though less objectionable than an amusement park directly on the shore, was still "bad enough" to stimulate outspoken opposition.[12]

The town meeting of February 20, 1897, rejected the company's plan to build a line to Little Danbury, and the meeting of May 23 agreed to allow the company to build from Southport along the Connecticut Turnpike to Westport; but under conditions that would have made the line an almost inevitable financial liability to Bridgeport Traction.

Despite all the complaints about the traction company's use of Fairfield streets without compensation to the town, the real issue was not the use of these roads but the necessity of keeping outsiders at bay. Throughout 1898 and 1899, the traction company resumed its efforts to secure access to Fairfield's beaches and to fulfill its plan to build either a hotel or an amusement park on the shore. In 1899 the company was at last able to obtain a right of way to the beach through private land. As an individual and not on behalf of his company, Andrew Radel, president of Bridgeport Traction, bought the William R. Jones estate in the spring of 1898, a property of ninety-six acres

*The Private Town*

that extended from Main Street all the way to the beach and for about seven hundred feet along the shore. In February 1899 Radel sold most of the Jones estate to Treat Campbell, a business associate, retaining about three hundred feet on the beach as well as a sixty-foot-wide strip of land that ran from Main Street to the shore. The following month, the traction company petitioned the legislature for authority to extend its lines to the beach through Radel's private property.

Fairfield was as vehement in its opposition to this scheme as it had been to any of the other company plans to reach the waterside. The use of public roads was not an issue here; the more important concern was excluding that class that might use the streetcars to reach the beach. Radel's plan collapsed when Colonel N. H. Heft, the former president of the Bridgeport Traction Company but now chief of electrical operations for the New York, New Haven and Hartford Railroad, accused Radel and four other Bridgeport Traction Company stockholders of using the company for their own private advantage. Unwilling to sanction possibly fraudulent activities, the General Assembly, at the conclusion of a hearing in Hartford in April 1899, rejected the company's request.

The legislature in 1897 had made it relatively easy for streetcar companies to construct new lines so long as they were lateral to existing steam railway routes. This gave the Bridgeport Traction Company the opportunity to extend its tracks into the interior of Fairfield. The section of town that seemed most enthusiastic about trolley service was Stratfield. Residents of that area, many of whom worked in Bridgeport, hoped for a line that would connect their neighborhood directly with the streetcar routes in that city.

Comprising the eastern section of Fairfield, Stratfield was a sleepy rural area until the mid-1890s. The community had remained such a backwater that it lacked even a general store. Residents as late as the early twentieth century were closer to the Bridgeport Public Market than to any other grocery. But then southern Stratfield began to undergo the process of becoming a Bridgeport suburb. This process began when the North Avenue trolley in Bridgeport made Stratfield more accessible for persons working in the neighboring city. Although a mile from the streetcar's terminus, Stratfield grew rapidly. New streets as well as new houses made it the site of most of the building in town. In fact, its development largely accounted for Fairfield's population growth between 1890 and 1900, a period that saw the number of town residents jump from 3868 to 4489. For the next three decades, eastern Fairfield would experience more growth than any other part of town.

The area's new accessibility attracted the attention of a group of wealthy men from Bridgeport, Dr. I. DeVer Warner in particular. Warner and his friends had been looking for a rural setting where they could establish a private sports facility, a club much like the one that Bostonians had built in Brookline in 1882. They were eager to find a spot away from the din of the city, a place that would remind them of the rural setting in which most of them had grown up. Stratfield provided the ideal location; by using the trolley, any member could travel to the proposed location of the club in fifteen minutes from Bridgeport's railroad station.

They organized and incorporated the Brooklawn Country Club in 1895. "The object of this Corporation shall be to promote outdoor and indoor sports in the City of Bridgeport," stated the club's charter. Although it was located in Stratfield, it was a Bridgeport organization, as its charter indicated. In 1913, for example, of the more than four hundred members of the Brooklawn Country Club, only eleven were from

Fairfield. Initially the club's most important activities were tennis and baseball; $300 was allocated to construct six tennis courts and $250 for a baseball field; the Golf Committee was "authorized to expend not more than $100 in laying out golf links." The following year, the club became one of the first twenty-five members of the United States Golf Association, and golfing became its members' principal interest.[13]

The growth of the area and the creation of the club led to a movement to separate Stratfield from Fairfield and to make it, like Black Rock, part of Bridgeport. The plan enjoyed the support of many Stratfield residents. They were unhappy about the failure of Fairfield to deliver a variety of civic improvements that were already available in Bridgeport, such as gas and electric service, sidewalks, and sewers. Annexation by Bridgeport would mean access to such facilities, they believed. It would also mean lower taxes—Fairfield's tax rate was ten mills, Bridgeport's only four and a half. In addition, by joining Bridgeport, Stratfield hoped to attract a spur line of the Bridgeport Traction Company. The North Avenue line stopped a mile short of the center of Stratfield, which residents hoped would become a streetcar terminal. One Stratfield man was especially frustrated because "the would be representatives of the town are at the present time in the legislature opposing 'any further extension of the trolley lines in the town of Fairfield.' "[14]

One of the most visible advocates of separation was Moses Banks, a prominent citizen and a school committeeman. Although Banks later explained that his primary interest was bringing trolley service to Stratfield and that he saw the annexation scheme as a means to that end, he, like other Stratfield residents, believed they had been neglected by Fairfield too long. "It is the prevailing opinion that we are left out in the cold and of 'no consequence' as some of our people express it except to pay taxes and vote," wrote Banks. "It is no wonder that some of us see no other recourse except to fall into the 'open arms' of Bridgeport."[15]

Opponents argued that the plan was a scheme concocted by a group of Bridgeport real estate developers, especially W. E. Seeley, who was also one of the incorporators of the Brooklawn Country Club. Opponents also pointed to the lessons to be learned from Black Rock's experiences. Proponents of annexation in 1870 had assured Black Rock property owners that the value of their real estate would increase once the area became part of Bridgeport. This proved to be wishful thinking, because no significant increase in values took place until the 1880s, when the area came into demand for the construction of new housing. In fact, several of the speculators who bought Black Rock property just before annexation lost money because they found themselves compelled to sell before the appreciation took place.

The annexation scheme fizzled. Earl Porter, the attorney in charge of presenting the separatists' petition to the General Assembly, failed to do so until late in the legislative session; and although hearings were held in March 1897, action was deferred until the next meeting of the General Assembly. In the meantime, Stratfield attracted Fairfield's attention. The selectmen clearly understood that the departure of Stratfield would mean the loss of the Fairfield Chemical Works, whose assessed value was $51,925 and which in 1896 had paid $553.80 in taxes to the town. They decided that perhaps some of Stratfield's problems were worthy of consideration. Moses Banks, on the other hand, claimed that he never really wanted to leave the town of his birth; once Fairfield decided to make some overdue improvements to Stratfield Road, Banks's devotion to his original home grew even more intense. He and others eventually began to wonder themselves if the whole plan had not been a scheme of Bridgeport real estate people after all. By the time of the next legislative session, separation was a dead issue.

While most of Stratfield's early development occurred in its southern neighborhoods, the establishment of the Brooklawn Country Club and the annexation debate pushed real estate activity toward the north. In 1895, James Seeley, William's brother, began buying land close to the club and dividing it into building lots. But this early activity was premature. Intense development, such as had taken place adjacent to State Street, had to wait for the construction of a trolley line on Stratfield Road, one that reached as far as the Stratfield Baptist Church. This, the first extension of trolley service in town, came in 1911, seventeen years after the Bridgeport Traction Company had begun operations there.

Six years before the Stratfield trolley began taking passengers, the Brooklawn Company, a real estate investment firm formed by a group of Bridgeport businessmen, bought the former estate of Clapp Spooner, who had been president of the Adams Express Company, an important antecedent firm of the Railway Express Company. The Brooklawn Company, which later became the Brooklawn Park Association, divided the Spooner property into sixty-nine lots in 1911 and began to sell these lots to wealthy Bridgeport businessmen, many of whom had earlier lived either on affluent "Golden Hill" or near Park Avenue in that city. The association demanded that each purchaser sign an agreement by which he or she was bound to the regulations and restrictions of the association, rules that dealt with the price of the homes (a minimum of $5000 or $7000, depending upon location), land use, and property maintenance.

In time Brooklawn Park became an almost private community of Bridgeport men and women who had retreated from the hurly-burly of the city to the pastoral countryside of Stratfield. Membership in the Brooklawn Country Club was never a requirement for living in the park, but the club generally served as a common source of identity for area residents, as an antidote for the loss of social intimacy that came with suburban life, and as a means of asserting one's position within an impersonal and industrial society.

Throughout World War I and in the years immediately after, Stratfield was a favorite location of real estate developers, although few could afford to construct homes as elaborate as those built in Brooklawn Park by Horace Merwin, president of the Bridgeport Trust Company, or Webster Walker, head of the City Ice and Coal Company. Webster reportedly spent more than $250,000 on the construction of his home at a time when the association required only that $7000 be spent.

Stratfield also developed a sense of community pride in the early years of the twentieth century. In 1910, when the town of Fairfield voted "to provide street lights for the Villages of Fairfield and Southport," Judge Elmore S. Banks amended the resolution to insert the word "Stratfield" into the resolution; suddenly the community had become assertive.[16] In 1911, the Stratfield Improvement Association began its efforts to bring a volunteer fire department, sidewalks, a new school, and street signs to the area.

But while the coming of the trolley encouraged community pride, it also confirmed and accentuated Stratfield's orientation toward Bridgeport rather than toward Fairfield. Even before the trolley, Bridgeport had been more accessible than Fairfield; once the trolley was in operation, the ties with that city became even more intimate. The future physical evolution of Stratfield, the first area of Fairfield to become a genuine suburb, would reflect the diverse urban and suburbanizing forces emanating from Bridgeport more than it would any impact from Fairfield.

The trolley also brought change to Southport. It caused the business center of Southport to move away from the harbor and onto Pequot Avenue, a street that had been merely a byway until after the arrival of the streetcars. The trolley stop on Pequot Avenue, called Carey's Corner, became the nucleus of the new commercial area. The business that eventually came to be Switzer's Drug Store had originally been located on the waterfront. Probably J. Frederick Jennings was its first owner, but sometime before 1885, Harding B. Rieffestahl bought the store. He in turn sold it to K. J. Damtoft, who in 1895, the year after the trolleys arrived, sold it to Luin B. Switzer, who moved it to Carey's Corner. The corner was also the site of Fred Disbrow's Grocery Store and later of the telephone exchange. When the Jelliff Manufacturing Company, which made various wire products, decided to build its own quarters, it too left the harbor for Pequot Avenue.

The coming of the trolley also encouraged some Southporters to think again of separating from Fairfield. In 1895, individuals began talking about a new town, to be called Southport, that would include Southport, Greenfield, and Green's Farms. The idea appeared too late in that year for its advocates to present it to the General Assembly, but, said the *Chronicle*, if "it were properly agitated, and the right kind of bill drafted, I think there would be little difficulty forming the new town."[17]

In 1895 such an idea might have seemed viable; certainly Southport remained the commercial hub of Fairfield at that time. But in retrospect, one can see that the timing was entirely wrong. By 1895, Southport had already become less important than it had been just a few weeks before. It had begun to lose population; more people lived in the village in 1880 than in 1900. Business was also down. During the 1880s, more than a ship a day arrived and departed from the harbor. Maritime traffic had fallen off sharply by the middle 1890s. The area's onion crop in 1896 was devastated by cutworms, a problem for which that generation had no remedy. The year before, both in Connecticut and elsewhere, farmers had produced onions in such quantities that prices fell to record lows; upstate New York was by this time already growing vastly more onions than Connecticut. And in 1894, Fairfield's crops were so bad that farmers had no onions to sell despite the prevailing high prices — 1892 was the last good year for the area's onion farmers.

The coastal shippers suffered as much as the farmers. One hundred thousand barrels of onions departed from Southport harbor in 1895; in 1896 only about thirty thousand barrels went out of that port. The United States government was no help to shippers. It spent thousands of dollars on Bridgeport's harbor but refused to widen or dredge the channel in Mill River, which provided less than ten feet of water at low tide and was so narrow that even the small market boats could navigate it only with difficulty. Many fully loaded boats had to wait for the next tide before they could leave the harbor. These inconveniences were expensive for shipowners, and more and more of them began to avoid Southport. Even yachtsmen often chose Black Rock or Westport over the Mill River harbor.

The trolley combined with the decline of the onion-market-boat industry to alter Southport's position within Fairfield. The trolley transferred the commercial center of

Fairfield from Southport back toward the center of town. Instead of riding the trolley west to trade in Southport, Fairfield shoppers tended to travel east toward Bridgeport, the commercial mecca of southwestern Connecticut. As a consequence, Southport, Green-field, and even Green's Farms people passed through Fairfield; some even stopped. Significantly less traffic passed through Southport.

In the ten years after the opening of the trolley, Fairfield center became the site for new commercial construction. When Hall's Block was built in 1894, Southport seemed the logical place to locate it. But of the four major buildings erected in town in the years immediately after the trolley made its presence felt, three were in Fairfield—the Freeman Building, Perry's Block, and Saum's Building—and only one, the new Southern New England Telephone Company Building—was in Southport. Even the newspaper moved; the Southport *Chronicle* ceased operations and was replaced by the Fairfield *Review*.

The only new religious institution, and the fastest growing, also located in Fairfield. This was St. Thomas Roman Catholic Church, which became a parish church in 1876 and moved to its permanent location in 1880. When fire destroyed the church in 1892, the Reverend Thomas Coleman and his congregation rebuilt on the same site, the dedication of the new facility taking place at the end of 1894. Perhaps Fairfield Catholics had little choice but to build in the center of town. Certainly this was generally where the Catholic population settled, and probably Catholics encountered less hostility there than they would have in Southport, where the citizenry remained strongly Protestant well into the twentieth century.

If nativism and anti-Catholicism were problems in Fairfield at the end of the nineteenth century, the prejudice must have been expressed subtly. Irish Catholics re-mained by far the largest immigrant group in town, and while their lot in life certainly had been difficult initially, little evidence of obvious antagonism toward them existed by the end of the century. The town's public press was virtually free of it. The papers complimented St. Thomas on its activities and reported on the willingness of old Fairfield families to contribute to such causes as Irish famine relief. Fairfield's Catholic residents encouraged townspeople to recognize Christmas, Easter, and other such days in the ecclesiastical calendar as holidays; whereas Fairfield would have certainly resented such Roman practices just a few years before, the town tended "to see the appropriateness of making special efforts on these joyful occasions."[18] The American Protective Association, which sought to exclude immigrants and especially Catholic immigrants from American life, failed to win any appreciable number of converts when it came to town in 1894. In part the A. P. A. foundered because Fairfield had itself rendered its Irish Catholic population politically impotent, unable to threaten the town's Protestant establishment. The election of Daniel Moloney as tax collector in 1877 should not be taken as evidence that Irish-Americans generally held positions of political responsibility. On the contrary, they were generally as excluded from political leadership as they were from the social life of native-born Americans. On the other hand, economic opportunity was frequently available to the Irish, and antagonism between Protestants and Catholics, natives and immigrants, was not strong enough to encourage such groups as the A. P. A. to prosper in town.

Without question having St. Thomas in the center of Fairfield helped to swing the commerical balance back in the direction of the old village. More and more new businesses realized that this was the place to locate. By the early twentieth century,

*Lithograph of St. Thomas Aquinas Roman Catholic Church built in 1893-94 on the site of the present church. It was demolished in 1956 but the rectory still stands.*

twenty-eight grocery stores existed in town. Not only were twenty of these in Fairfield, but so was the one that represented the wave of the future in food shopping and the one that had chosen its location most scientifically: this was the Great Atlantic & Pacific Tea Company, Store Number 820, located on Eliot Street (now the Post Road). At the same time, eleven saloons were operating in town; of the eleven, nine were in Fairfield and only two in Southport.

The coming of streetcars to Fairfield altered some aspects of town life; it accelerated the change in Stratfield that Bridgeport's proximity had begun, moved the center of Southport from one part of the village to another, contributed to that community's decline as a commercial hub, and focused the town's attention once more on its ancient center. What the trolleys were unable to do was to alter Fairfield, except Stratfield, in fundamental ways. Residential patterns remained unchanged. The trolleys failed to bring large numbers of new immigrants from eastern and southern Europe to town, although these people already lived in large numbers in Bridgeport. By the same token, industry refused to follow in the path of the streetcars; as late as 1900 Fairfield's factories employed only 130 workers. Life before 1894, when Bridgeport Traction began operations, and life after 1894—even a decade or more after—remained basically unchanged.[19]

The reason for this limited impact was the determination of Fairfield to control, as far as possible, its own destiny. Fairfield would accept the trolley for the sake of convenience. But it made admission by either manufacturers or by southern and eastern Europeans as difficult as it could. It not only refused to make any concessions to manufacturers to attract them to town; its citizens consistently declined to sell their property

*The Private Town*

to factory owners. And if Fairfield wanted no undesirable industries, it certainly wanted no undesirable residents. When I. DeVer Warner sold Grasmere, one of his Fairfield properties, to the Bridgeport Land and Title Company, town residents were frightened that it would be divided into small lots and sold "on easy payments." If this should occur, "the chances are a very undesirable class of residents would be attracted to the spot, much like those on Lenox Heights," a section of Stratfield with a substantial immigrant population. The best that Fairfielders could do was hope that "Grasmere is not destined to become a settlement for tar paper houses and all nationalities huddled in together." Both ordinary citizens and affluent residents, despite the differences that separated them, saw Fairfield as theirs, their private town.[20]

## NOTES

1. Glover, Fairfield's Appeal from the Railroad Commission, 1887. Copy in the FHS.

2. Southport *Chronicle*, Feb. 15, 1869.

3. *Extracts from an Article, as to why the Double Track Trolley Railroad Should not Go through the Main Street of Fairfield Village* (n.p., n.d.). Copy in the FHS.

4. Southport *Chronicle*, Sept. 4, 1893.

5. Livingston George Smith, Autobiography, FHS, 383.

6. Southport *Chronicle*, Oct. 15, 29, 1894.

7. Ibid., Dec. 24, 1894.

8. Ibid., Dec. 24, 31, 1894.

9. FTR, Feb. 23, 1895.

10. Southport *Chronicle*, June 13, 1895.

11. FTR, July 15, 1895.

12. Southport *Chronicle*, Feb. 15, 1897.

13. Brooklawn Country Club, Verticle File, FHS.

14. Southport *Chronicle*, Feb. 1, 1897.

15. Ibid., Feb. 11, 1897.

16. FTR, Oct. 3, 1911.

17. Southport *Chronicle*, Feb. 25, 1895.

18. Southport *Times*, April 1, 1880.

19. Sam Bass Warner, Jr., *Streetcar Suburbs* (Cambridge, Mass., 1962), describes the development of three towns that became streetcar suburbs of Boston. Fairfield clearly did not follow this same pattern.

20. Bridgeport *Times*, Jan. 1, 1909.

# PART III

At the end of the nineteenth century, Fairfield was beginning to awaken after decades of repose. Convinced of the need of both change and continuity, town residents began to adjust to the coming of a new century. The growth of the eastern areas of town initiated the transformation of what as late as 1900 was still a small rural community. Thanks to two world wars, a national economic catastrophe, a burgeoning federal government, and a revolution in transportation and communications, Fairfield lost the parochial system of loyalties that had always characterized its existence and, while yet retaining a uniqueness of its own, became a suburb, a part of America's interdependent and monolithic society.

# A New Fairfield

THE LATE nineteenth and early twentieth centuries witnessed the stirring of a new vitality in Fairfield. After decades of somnolence, the pace of life was beginning to quicken. Some of this occurred as a result of the country's growing technological sophistication. In 1915, F. E. Lane still built and repaired carriages in his Southport shop. But there were also six garages in town that repaired automobiles, five located in Fairfield itself, the new commercial center, the new hub.

Industry made some substantial gains in town during the first years of the twentieth century. E. I. DuPont de Nemours and Company bought and enlarged the Fairfield Rubber Company in 1916. Francis B. Perry and his partners had invested $100,000 in the Fairfield Underwear Company by 1915. Originally established as the Eastern Underwear Manufacturing Company, it employed about 150 workers at its plant on Sanford Avenue. The Fairfield Aluminum Foundry Corporation, which later became the Aluminum Castings Company, began production in 1906 in response to the growing demands of the automobile industry. The C. O. Jelliff Manufacturing Company of Southport produced wire netting, wire cloth, screen, and riddles. Incorporated in 1902, the company built modern facilities on Pequot Avenue in 1907 after having operated out of Charles Jelliff's store on the Southport waterfront since the 1870s.

In 1915 both the Handy and Harmon Company and the Max Ams Machine Company moved to town. Max Ams manufactured automatic canning machinery, and Handy and Harmon produced items for the silversmithing industry. Both businesses located in the Grasmere section. The Kilborn-Sauer Company, manufacturers of both automobile and marine accessories, opened on the Post Road in 1914. More in keeping with Fairfield's agricultural heritage was the Kennel Food Supply Company. Simon C. Bradley, a breeder and trainer of hunting dogs, developed a recipe for dogfood, which he originally baked in his own kitchen. Advertising at field trials eventually created enough demand

211

*The last of the market fleet at Southport. "The Hummocks,"*
*present country club site, are in the distance.*

for the food to justify constructing a plant; by World War I it was shipping between five and six tons of the mixture daily.

These new industries were essential for Fairfield. The onion business was nearly defunct, the market boats entirely so. Even the resort trade had fallen on hard times. The St. Marc Hotel was now a private residence. In fact, the only two hotels in town were the Ash Creek Hotel, operated by Casper Schick, a well-known Fairfield bartender, and the Unquowa Hotel, which Arthur Lee Donovan ran in the former residence of James S. Mott. Neither hotel made any pretence of being what the Fairfield House had once been. The only other businesses in town were establishments that served the ordinary needs of the population, businesses like E. W. S. Pickett's grocery on the corner of Sanford and the Post Road or the Fairfield Hardware Store, where Edgar Riker worked, or the Unquowa Garage, Joseph Russo, proprietor.

The growth of industry and the corresponding increase in employment opportunities meant a sudden surge in population. Fairfield's population increased 37 percent during the first decade of the twentieth century, from 4489 in 1900 to 6134 in 1910. Many of the new residents were either immigrants or the children of immigrants. In 1900, 47 percent of the town's population had either been born outside the country or were the children of foreign-born parents. By 1910 these categories accounted for 56 percent of the population, most of them Irish-Americans. The town's black population continued to drop to 1.4 percent in 1910 from 1.9 percent ten years earlier.

The growing population kept builders and developers busy. Holland Hill and Tunxis Hill were the scenes of particularly intense activity, especially after the announcements that Max Ams and Handy and Harmon were building factories nearby. These areas—unlike Stratfield, also a rapidly developing section—became working-class neighborhoods characterized by dense development and even multifamily housing. A glance at the 1912 map prepared by the Fairfield Realty Company shows the beach to be generally built up from Penfield Road to Pine Creek Road, a phenomenon of the

*The Fairfield Rubber Co. plant on Mill Plain Road in the early 1900s,*
*now occupied by the Fairprene Co., makers of coated fabrics.*

last decade and a half. Another busy section was the center of Fairfield, where factories as well as commercial establishments and residences had appeared in the past ten years as the area around the old village reasserted itself. But eastern Fairfield, in part an industrial community in its own right and in part a Bridgeport suburb, was the area where builders found more work than in any other part of town.

The sudden awakening of Fairfield in terms both of its growing population and of its expanding industry forced the town to undergo a period of self-examination. On the one hand, much about the community seemed hopelessly out of date; but on the other, too much of what was perceived to be good about the old town and the "old days" seemed in danger of being lost. The result was that Fairfield, like most of the United States, was caught up in a frenzy of self-improvement in the late nineteenth and early twentieth centuries. At the same time that Progressives were attempting to revitalize the country's cities and states and eventually even to refine the national government, Fairfield men and women were busy trying to make their town a better place to live. They sought to accomplish this both by making the town more modern and by reviving the qualities of an earlier, and perhaps better, age. No problem was too small to attract the attention of some residents, their ultimate objective being a Fairfield without flaws, a paragon on Long Island Sound.

This work was started by individuals associated with the Democratic party but completed by persons who identified closely with Theodore Roosevelt and his particular brand of Republicanism. For the most part, Fairfield had been a Democratic town since the time of James S. Mott. Republicans would occasionally win control of the town government, but the Democrats would be back the following year to recover what they had lost. This began to change in 1896, when the Democratic party ran William Jennings Bryan as its candidate for president of the United States. The "boy orator of the Platte" was too radical, too inclined toward such wild ideas as an eight-hour work day, to win the support of Fairfield voters. William McKinley thoroughly trounced Bryan in 1896 in Fairfield and carried with him to victory virtually all state and local Republican candidates as well. Although the Democratic party remained a force in town until 1910, Fairfield's affinity for the Republican party grew steadily during the decades after McKinley's election. Even when the party abandoned the conservative philosophy of McKinley for the progressive one of Theodore Roosevelt, Fairfield stayed with the Grand Old Party.

Town government was the first target for improvement. To encourage professionalism among elected officials, the town began to pay almost all its officeholders. The salaries would not have allowed one to live on Main Street, but they were an indication that Fairfield expected professional performance from the men it elected. The new position of first selectman, created in 1888 to make one man essentially responsible for the administration of town government, paid $200 a year. The other selectmen earned $150. Most officials were compensated by the day; $2 was the standard rate. Small as these salaries appear, the payment of town officers became the fifth largest item in the town budget, costing the taxpayers about $2300 a year at the turn of the century.

Fairfield wanted its government to be as modern and efficient as possible. In 1895, it began the massive task of indexing its land records, an expensive undertaking, but one that made life simpler for anyone buying or selling real estate. In 1888, the town established a Board of Health, an agency that was long overdue. In an age when sewers were unknown in Fairfield, the town health officers were among the busiest town officials. Dr. Valery Harvard, one of these officers, must have enjoyed writing graphic citations to health offenders. "Privy nearly full and overflowing or leaking, the overflow or leakage running and forming pools in rear of said engine house," he informed Nehemiah Jennings of Southport. "Nearby, in connection with lodging-house also owned by you, is an open privy, or privy without seat, wide open to flies, malodorous and a danger to neighboring houses." Harvard also noted "in connection with said lodging-house, a large pile of rubbish very repulsive to eye and nose, and very attractive to flies."[1]

Fairfield created a Town Oyster Committee "with power to designate suitable places . . . for planting or cultivating oysters, clams or mussels." Few issues had received more attention during the nineteenth century than the protection of the town's oyster population. As early as 1806, the town meeting had voted strict regulations governing the circumstances under which oysters and clams might be taken. Any outsider caught digging clams or oysters in Fairfield was to be fined "in a sum not exceeding 17 dollars for each offense." Only a foolish or desperate oysterman would have risked such a fine.[2]

Even with strict regulations in effect, shellfish became more and more difficult to find. In 1826, the town stipulated that oysters could be taken only on Tuesdays and Saturdays and encouraged the enforcement of the law by authorizing that any penalties imposed on offenders "shall belong to any person who shall sue for and prosecute the same to effect."[3] As of the 1840s, town officials assigned specific oyster beds to individuals who had the exclusive privilege of oystering within the limits of their grounds.

But Fairfield's appetite for the bivalves continued to jeopardize the shellfish population. Sixty or seventy bushels might be required for an oyster frolic, and to see fifty or so persons digging on the clam flats at one time was routine. The problem became more acute when boats from other towns began coming to Fairfield to participate in the harvest. The Southport *Chronicle* denounced "those piratical crafts from neighboring ports, who scoop up and carry off, right from under our very noses, seed oysters." By 1870, the paper was advising local residents to make citizens' arrests of the interlopers: "If they come again this year, let us see to it that they are taught a lesson which will secure us, hereafter, from their piratical visits." But stopping the poachers was nearly impossible when they could sell oysters for $5.50 a barrel.[4]

Those oysters that escaped local gourmands and outside poachers came under attack by starfish at the end of the 1880s. Professional oystermen used special dredges in attempting "to subdue the pests and save the oysters" but met with little success.[5] So in an attempt practically to reintroduce an oyster population in the waters off Fairfield, the selectmen appointed a Town Oyster Committee in 1906, hoping to find ways to guarantee that shellfish would continue to survive.

Sidewalks and flagpoles—the first a statement of Fairfield's desire to be modern and the second an expression of its reverence for the past—seemed to concern as many Fairfield men and women as did the plight of the oyster. Private citizens raised money to construct sidewalks. When the sidewalk went in between the Fairfield railroad depot and the post office residents hailed William H. Donaldson, who organized the effort, with such enthusiasm that one might have thought he had brought the courthouse back to town. One could find no easier way to incur Fairfield's wrath than by riding a bicycle or horse on its sidewalks; such an offense was punishable by a substantial fine.

Flagpoles were regarded as essential town improvements. Greenfield dedicated its pole on September 6, 1892. More than eighteen hundred persons witnessed the celebration. A month later a similar ceremony in Southport attracted a slightly smaller crowd, but the *Chronicle* saw fit to approve the event: "Admirably planned and perfectly executed, the entire occasion was most happily observed."[6]

Residents ultimately measured the extent of their town's refinement in terms of the miles of "macadamized" road that it possessed. The process of "hardening" the roads began in the 1880s, when Frederic Bronson, Frederick Sturges, Oliver Burr Jennings, and other wealthy residents began paying to pave the roads in front of their homes or the roads between their homes and the depot. The town became involved in 1888 when it guaranteed whatever additional money would be needed to complete a macadamized road from Black Rock Bridge to Meeker Dock in Southport on the condition that its citizens privately subscribe $8000. In 1894, it purchased its own stone crusher in hopes of reducing the cost of hardening even more roads.

As the nineteenth century ended and the twentieth began, Frederick Sturges and Oliver Gould Jennings seemed almost to vie with each other to see who could "macadamize" more feet of road. Frederic Bronson dropped out of the competition about 1889, by which time he had paved most of what officially came to be called Bronson Road on August 13, 1884. He had reached a private understanding with the town that if his taxes were forgiven he would spend twice their amount on the roads. He did this each year between 1884 and 1889, although in 1886 he spent far more than he had promised. By 1904, the town's streets looked so exquisite in the eyes of the proud citizenry that it seemed appropriate to the town meeting to assign names to those roads that had not yet been so honored and to mark all the principal avenues with street signs.

Care for the poor was a more perplexing problem than building roads. An 1879 report in the Bridgeport *Standard* on the plight of Fairfield's paupers embarrassed both officials and residents of the town. When the *Standard*'s correspondents arrived at the home where the poor were being kept, they encountered a woman of about sixty "gazing away into vacancy." The strangers' presence elicited no response from her. Working near her was an old man who caned chair seats. He was crippled, as was the old woman who sat beside him. These three were then the only persons living at this home. Another old woman was usually there but was visiting her daughter, and an insane woman had been removed to another home, where her bizarre behavior could be more closely monitored.

When asked if they were well cared for, the one woman who was coherent replied that they were not. "We have been obliged to live during the past winter on hams alive with maggots and so offensive that only hunger induced us to try to eat them," she reported. She also complained about the lack of firewood. The old man confirmed what his companion had said about the hams. His sister, he revealed, had written the selectmen about the conditions that existed there, and some improvements had followed before things returned to normal.

The biggest problem for the poor was the lack of medical attention. The elderly man—whose anonymity, like that of his female companion, was preserved—said that he had been seriously ill during the previous winter but no physician had called to see him. The visitors also learned of another man who had been boarded by the town at Hulls Farm for $3 per week. He was then moved to another family where he received inadequate food, became ill, was denied access to a physician, and died. What appears to have outraged the *Standard* in particular about this incident was the fact that the town interred the man without benefit of Christian burial.[7]

Aware of these unfortunate circumstances, the town attempted to find someone who would provide better and consistent care for its paupers. Frank L. Sherwood of Greenfield took on the responsibility from 1880 until 1892, years that saw the elimination of the worst conditions that had previously existed. During the following decade, the selectmen again moved the poor from the home of one low bidder to that of another, but continued to provide better medical care. Finally in 1902, the town meeting authorized A. P. Wakeman and Rufus B. Jennings to pay as much as $3000 for a poor farm. They found a suitable property, the management of which became the responsibility of the selectmen, and the town transferred its paupers there. Under the direct care of the selectmen, they probably received better care than they had at any time during the previous century.

The quality of education provided by Fairfield schools was a matter of little concern until almost the end of the century. In the 1870s the town provided thirty weeks of common school education, the quality of which varied not only from school to school and teacher to teacher but, more importantly, from district to district, each district being essentially autonomous. This lack of consistency prompted the town in 1887 to consolidate the administration of the schools under a single school committee, eliminating the school districts that had existed in various forms since the town's founding.

By 1895 fifteen schools served the children of Fairfield; the East Long Lots School accepted Westport youngsters as well. The schools ranged in size from the Southport School, with 210 pupils, to the tiny Hoyden's Hill School, where Miss Minnie T. Lewis administered discipline, education, and an example of morality and uprightness to seven young scholars.

The town offered education through grade six. Persons seeking additional education might have attended Miss Augusta A. Smith's Seaside Seminary, still operating in Southport, or the Fairfield Academy. The Academy had fallen on hard times and closed in 1887 but had been revived by F. H. Brewer, the former principal of the Home and School for Boys, a residential school that actively sought New York boys who could, " while enjoying a happy life in the country," be "under the influence of a Christian home."[8]

In 1899, the School Committee, eager to establish a uniform curriculum, adopted a course of study "to the end that the work of the departments in all schools throughout the Town may in some degree correspond."[9] The committee, in 1903, ordered a complete evaluation of the physical condition of the schools in hopes that the town would follow up with an effort to remedy whatever defects were uncovered. The Middle School and the Southport School seemed to be in the greatest need of repair, probably because they had by far the greatest amount of use. The town agreed to make the necessary repairs and appointed an inspector of the schools whose responsibility it was to see that they were adequately maintained. The town agreed to pay him $3 a day, up to $45 a year.

Now fully involved in the drive for better schools, the School Committee hoped to hire a superintendent who would spend part of his time supervising the schools in Fairfield and part of his time doing the same thing in Easton or Westport or Stratford. None of these neighboring towns was interested in the idea, unfortunately. Later Trumbull also declined. Finally Fairfield was able to hire William A. Wheatley, who had been superintendent of schools in Poughkeepsie, New York. He worked exclusively in Fairfield for a year; then Branford agreed to share his services and the expense of his salary. When Branford suddenly abandoned the arrangement, Westport joined with Fairfield to keep Wheatley.

The first superintendent brought a variety of changes to Fairfield education. He persuaded the town to spend more money annually for each pupil; by 1907, the per pupil cost was up to $20.15 a year. The School Committee changed the school names in 1905: Southport School became Pequot School; Centre became Sherman; Mill Plain became Lafayette; Greenfield became Dwight; and other names were similarly altered. That same year, Fairfield added an eighth grade, hired a truant officer, and adopted another, more elaborate, unified course of study. The School Committee had decided by 1907 to hire only graduates of the Connecticut Normal Schools to teach in Fairfield.

Fairfield had briefly considered providing high school education for its youngsters in 1885. The voters turned down the idea but did urge the several districts—still in operation at the time—to consider the matter and to bring their thoughts back to the next town meeting. Apparently little support existed for high school education, because nothing more was done at the time. Fifteen years later, on June 9, 1900, the School Committee voted to send twenty students from Fairfield "who shall pass the best examinations for entrance to the Bridgeport High School."[10] The committee later agreed to pay the tuition of any student who passed the examination.

In February 1914, the high school question was again demanding the town's attention. The Board of Education on February 18 asked wealthy Fairfield residents for contributions to create a high school. At that time seventy-eight adolescent scholars from town attended the high school either in Bridgeport or in Westport. Later in the year, the board voted to establish the first year of a high school course that it hoped to have in place in four years. The course would offer "everything and as much of everything as is needful for the admission to any university or technical school including Yale, Harvard, Vassar, Mt. Holyoke, etc." The forty-six freshman students and their teacher, Miss Florence Townsend, met in the Sherman School, a new grammar school that the town had been able to construct thanks to a generous gift from Samuel H. Wheeler.[11]

Having high school students in an elementary school was only a temporary arrangement, the town hoped. But Fairfield, still struggling with a substantial debt, lacked the funds for another building. At this point Annie B. Jennings, the daughter of Oliver B. Jennings and the sister of Oliver G. Jennings, intervened to force Fairfield to forsake this makeshift arrangement and establish a separate high school of its own. After listening to seemingly endless discussion of the merits and difficulties of creating such a school, she purchased a house on Unquowa Road and gave it to the town to use as a high school; it opened in 1916.

Town improvement included public utilities. The telephone was the first to arrive. In January 1879, the town "accepted the Telephone placed in the Town House by 'the Southport, Fairfield and Bridgeport Telephone Co.' for the use of the town for public and official business." The company, organized by Ebenezer Burr, Jr., had actually begun operations the previous year. It remained in business until 1882, when it sold out to the Southern New England Telephone Company. The new company installed additional service in Fairfield in 1896, making it possible to call Bridgeport for ten cents and other parts of the state for twenty-five. The Southport *Chronicle*, which never had a kind word to say about the railroad or the trolley, was uncharacteristically complimentary about the activities of the phone company: "The company have set some eight or nine poles and they are unusually comely as telephone poles go. They are of chestnut, good proportions and shaved."[12] By 1904 there were 124 telephones in Fairfield and by 1912, 513.

Electrical, gas, and water service arrived much more slowly. Street lights illuminated downtown Southport by 1870, but these lights were merely kerosene lamps. Electric lights and public water were not even promised until more than twenty years later, and before either water or power was delivered, the General Assembly had to choose from a variety of would-be providers. The Fairfield Electric Company, the Southport Water Company, the Uncoway Light & Water Company, The Fairfield Gas & Electric Lighting Company, and the Unquowa Water and Light Company all wanted, at one time or another, to serve parts of Fairfield. The town found the situation so confusing that it established a committee "to consider the best means of protecting the Town interests in the Legislature in relation to the various applications for charters for street railways, Electric lights, water and other Companies in this town."[13] Fairfield was well advised to create such a committee, because some of these companies never intended to provide the town with service. They hoped only to acquire the right to provide service and then sell that right at a handsome profit to a business that legitimately intended to furnish water, gas, or electricity. The Southport Water Company and the Fairfield Gas and Electric Lighting Company were both owned by the same group of New York men, men who believed there were quick profits to be made in Fairfield.

At the end of the century, the Unquowa Water & Light Company, a locally owned company, had won the town's endorsement to furnish Fairfield with water, sewers, and electrical service on the condition that the company be in operation by July 1, 1903,

*Fairfield: the biography of a community*

invest $25,000 in its water service plant, and receive final approval from the town. The company hired Albert B. Hill, a civil engineer from Bridgeport, to determine the best location for a reservoir. He decided upon the Hemlocks, a location that Herbert E. Smith, a chemist from the State Board of Health, also regarded to be as good as any in Fairfield. In 1900, the town meeting authorized Unquowa Water & Light to operate in Southport and Mill Plain.

The Bridgewater Hydraulic Company began operations in Fairfield in 1901, the town having granted it the right to extend its lines into town and to supply the central village with water in that year. The management of Unquowa—Simon C. Sherwood, Oliver Gould Jennings, and O. T. Sherwood—decided in 1902 that their interests would be best served by selling whatever rights the company owned to Bridgeport Hydraulic. After several delays caused by confusion over assessments and service areas, Bridgeport Hydraulic purchased anything of value that belonged to Unquowa. Bridgeport Hydraulic's pipes were in the ground and water was flowing through them to some Fairfield homes by 1905.

Electric lights were even slower to arrive. After several companies had reneged on promises to furnish power, the Bridgeport Electric Company agreed in 1900 to deliver service in Fairfield and charge the same rates there as it did in Bridgeport. Again nothing happened. In 1906, the selectmen, exasperated with the failure of the electric companies, arranged for the lighting of Main Street from Ash Creek to Sasco Creek by means of gasoline lights. Four years later, most of the town still lacked electricity, and the select-men purchased new gas lights to be installed in the villages of Fairfield, Southport, and Stratfield. Gas lines, the work of the Bridgeport Gas Light Company, were in place in the more congested sections of town by June 1910. The United Illuminating Company actually began delivering electrical power to parts of Fairfield in September 1908. The company was providing much more extensive service by 1913 when it replaced the three-year-old gas street lamps with modern electrical fixtures; the distribution of electrical power to many homes in the southern part of town was well under way by then as well.

One reason for all the interest in street illumination was civic pride. Another consideration that was even more compelling was the crime wave that had struck Fairfield. By 1905 burglaries were an everyday event. The typical victims were stores, although some "yeggmen" were audacious enough to enter and rob private homes, even homes that were occupied.

Crime had existed in Fairfield before the beginning of the twentieth century, of course. It had appeared irregularly as a problem in the colonial period and during the nineteenth century. On June 8, 1813, thieves broke into Salmon Sherwood's store in Mill River and made off with almost $500 worth of "the Lightest & most Valuable Goods" in the store. In 1880, the town installed two cells on the first floor of the Town Hall and hoped to fill them with the burglars who had recently begun breaking into homes up and down Main Street. Six years later, Fairfield offered a reward of $250 "for the apprehension of the late burglars in the town."[14]

As the 1890s opened, crime began to blossom into a major community problem. A new "lock-up," built in 1891, demonstrated the town's concern with the issue, but according to some residents that concern was inadequate. Strong action was needed, they argued; but Fairfield, with no police force, was unprepared. When the economic crisis of 1893—really a major depression—sent large numbers of unemployed men

*A New Fairfield*

wandering through Connecticut, fearful town residents started to panic. Back in 1869 when tramps were a problem, "an impromptu vigilance committee" organized and "armed with horse-whips" took care of the problem.[15] The same solution appeared appropriate again.

Fairfielders formed a citizen's committee to consider possible solutions for ridding the town of crime. The committee hired its own police to patrol the town streets at night. How long this practice continued is uncertain; the names of those who financed the operation are likewise lost. By 1895, the town also periodically hired individuals, usually burly fellows from Bridgeport, to maintain law and order. These measures seemed to deter thieves for a time, but by 1905 burglaries had reached epidemic proportions again.

Despite both private and public attempts to eliminate this persistent problem, it refused to disappear. During the early morning of September 6, 1907, four "cracksmen" broke into E. W. S. Pickett's store, which also contained the post office. Awakened by strange noises, Pickett dressed, found his shotgun, and walked the short distance from his home to his store. He discovered the four men in the process of taking $400 in cash and stamps. Pickett opened fire, and the robbers answered in kind. Fairfield had not witnessed so much gunfire since it had celebrated the end of the War of 1812. The four escaped, but not before the whole town was aware of the magnitude of the problem. Pickett's valiant defense of his property apparently failed to intimidate the criminal element, because the following night thieves broke into the home of Mrs. Harry Mills on Main Street. These two events, coming in succession as they did, generated enough reaction among the law-abiding population to again alleviate the problem. Eventually Fairfield turned the issue of police protection over first to Deputy Sheriff Wallace M. Bulkley and later to Deputy Sheriff Hezekiah R. Elwood, both essentially untrained but competent and resourceful lawmen.

By the first years of the century, Bulkley or Elwood and the constables who assisted them were spending more and more of their time keeping automobile drivers under control. "Scorchers" (whom later generations would call "speeders") were the particular problem. In 1902, Fairfield resolved "to regulate the speed of automobiles on the highways in town." Deputy Sheriff Bulkley found the high-speed drivers particularly irritating, especially because they often refused to stop when he ordered them to and he had no means by which to chase the offending "automobilists."[16]

In May 1904, he found an answer to his dilemma; he "had strong iron chains, fit to hold a boom across a river, placed at convenient points and then waited for the fly to walk into his parlor." The first "fly" to appear was a certain Mr. Green—a New York man who gave Bulkley a pseudonym. Green "was speeding it up to the tune of 30 miles an hour, according to a stop-watch" when Bulkley yelled to him to stop. The deputy later reported that "the machine looked like a yellow streak as it went whizzing through Main Street, Fairfield." Instead of stopping in response to Bulkley's summons, Green drove on and, at the same time, "dexterously applied his thumb to his nose and extended the remainder of his hand in regular order so as to present a very annoying gesture." Taking advantage of a nearby telephone, Bulkley called ahead to another deputy, who pulled one of the heavy chains across the road and into place. Before he realized what had happened the disgruntled Green was in the hands of the law, forced to pay $200 bond to guarantee his appearance in court (a bond that he later forfeited). Fairfield consistently sought "to prevent unlawful speeding of automobiles . . . and particularly to

*Section of E. W. S. Pickett's grocery store on the corner of Post Road and Sanford Street in the 1890s. It burned in 1911.*

endeavor to prevent speeding of automobiles in races and in so called hillclimbing contests."[17]

By 1910, town residents were complaining about the amount of automobile traffic on Fairfield's streets. These complaints prompted officials to measure the flow of traffic on Spring Street, now the Post Road. Between 7 A.M. and 6 P.M. on August 6, 1912, 1077 cars drove through the center of town. This meant almost one and a half cars a minute traveling along Spring Street. From the perspective of 1912, this was a problem needing attention.

In their efforts to make Fairfield a better town in which to live, residents created a vast number of societies, clubs, board, companies, and associations. Some of these were desperately needed; certainly the fire companies were.

The Fairfield Hook and Ladder Company had its origins back in 1890 when the Fairfield Congregational Church burned. After the fire, Oliver B. Jennings offered the town a hook and ladder truck. The gift inspired about 150 men to form a firefighting company. Unfortunately, once the excitement of the new truck wore off, most of the men lost their interest in public service. Another religious institution, St. Thomas Church, burned in 1893. This event prompted Otto Jacoby, a Fairfield barber, to set about forming another unit. He called a meeting for September 11, 1893, to take place in his shop. There Jacoby and W. W. Hull, Isaac N. Bock, E. W. S. Pickett, and I. N. Gray organized the company. The following year, the town donated land on Spring Street for a firehouse, and in 1895, the General Assembly chartered the company, which remained entirely self-supporting for the first seventeen years of its life. Not until 1910 did it make any demands upon the town, when it needed "an auto chemical combination fire fighting apparatus" that was beyond its means.

The story of the fire-fighting companies in Southport is a more complicated one. In December 1894, a terrible fire destroyed three structures, one of them being the old

*A New Fairfield*

Pike's Tavern building on Main Street. Having no fire company of their own, village residents had to depend on the Fairfield company to contain the blaze. This was the first of a series of suspicious fires in Southport. When the livery stables owned by Charles Mills and three warehouses belonging to C. O. Jelliff burned in September 1895, Jelliff and Robert Mallette, editor of the *Chronicle*, called for the creation of a village fire department. Jelliff, Mallette, and others met on October 3 and 14 and established the Southport Fire Department. But apparently these original members refused to welcome all the Southport men who wanted to join the company. As a consequence, on October 17, some of those disappointed firefighters formed the Pequot Fire Department.

Until 1900 the two companies, except at the time of an actual fire, functioned independently. Eventually, after protracted negotiations that would have strained the patience of a seasoned diplomat, a majority of the members of the Pequot Fire Company agreed to transfer the company's property to the Southport Fire Department, and some of the Pequot firefighters themselves joined with Southport. When a new firehouse opened in January 1915, it opened to provide quarters for Southport's one and only fire company.

Improvement societies attracted an amazing amount of attention. These organizations served as catalysts for the development of specific projects, such as sidewalks or flagpoles or the enforcement of speeding laws. Originally the societies in Fairfield, such as the Mill Plain Mutual Improvement Society, were women's groups that sought to improve the minds of their members through organized study. By the time the Sasquanaug Association for Village Improvement was formed in 1887, the direction of these groups had changed. The Sasquanaug Association sought "the general improvement and beautifying of the village of Southport." Rebecca Pomeroy Bulkley, the wife of Henry T. Bulkley, was the driving force behind the association, which raised almost $17,000 in the first decade of its existence and which brought everything from streetlights to sidewalks to Southport.[18]

The Village Improvement Society of Greenfield, organized by Sarah King Bronson, Frederic Bronson's wife, during the summer of 1897, sought for Greenfield what the Sasquanaug Association was bringing to Southport. One of Mrs. Bronson's group's most lasting accomplishments was probably its promotion of the use of the name Greenfield Hill instead of the simpler traditional appellation, Greenfield. (Greenfield Hill, the reader will recall, was the title of Timothy Dwight's poem about the area.)

The Fairfield Association for Village Improvement came into being in 1899, and the Stratfield Association, already mentioned, twelve years later; both hoped to accomplish the same kinds of improvements sought by the other groups.

The Improvement Association of Fairfield and Vicinity was a slightly different organization. It was conceived by Oliver Gould Jennings to attack a single problem, the mosquito, probably the single least attractive feature of Fairfield. For years it had been the cause of discomfort and of illness. Livingston George Smith, who worked for the Sturges family in Mill Plain during the 1890s, accused mosquitoes of being "the cause of so much malaria in that neighborhood."[19] The Improvement Association of Fairfield and Vicinity probably enhanced the quality of life in town as much as any improvement organization by spending the money it raised to drain suspected mosquito breeding grounds, thereby reducing the population of that troublesome insect.

Two town societies existed to serve the social and professional needs of farmers.

*Fairfield Fire Department No. 1 in the 1920s. The firehouse on
Reef Road is now the site of the Sherman Green Firehouse Deli.*

One was the Patrons of Husbandry, the Grange, established in Greenfield in 1893. The other was the Greenfield Country Club, formed in 1901 "for the purpose of affording opportunity for the study of agriculture, music and literature and promoting good fellowship and social improvement." The club had a baseball team and a whist team. From 1901 until 1911, it operated one of the largest agricultural fairs in the area. As agriculture faltered in Fairfield, so did the club and the public's interest in its fair.[20]

Service clubs abounded in town. The Fairfield Fresh Air Association, established in 1893, existed to provide "short vacations in the heated season of the year to the poor children of the crowded districts of cities . . .; also to relieve distress and suffering by the establishment of a permanent home for poor children and their parents, and other unfortunate persons throughout the entire year."[21] During the Spanish-American War, the Fresh Air Association converted its home into a hospital for seventeen convalescing soldiers, most of them suffering from malaria. Three other Fairfield associations assisted in this effort: the Red Cross Auxiliary, which had only come into existence in Fairfield in 1898; the Dorothy Ripley Chapter of the Daughters of the American Revolution, of Southport; and the Eunice Dennie Burr Chapter of the same organization, established in Fairfield in 1894.

The Gould Homestead, created in 1910 by the will of Elizabeth B. Gould, daughter of shipping magnate John Gould, provided a free vacation home for "any white unmarried Protestant female between the ages of 18 and 50 who may be dependent wholly upon her own labor for support and residing within the county of Fairfield."[22] The

*A New Fairfield*

Wakeman Memorial, established by Frances Wakeman and Cornelia Wakeman Grapo, the daughters of William Webb Wakeman, offered plenty of books and a room in which to read them to the young men of Southport.

The myriad of organizations established by this generation included associations that were both useful and self-serving. Annie B. Jennings helped in 1914 to establish the Birdcraft Sanctuary after the Connecticut Audubon Society, originally founded in 1898, was reorganized and empowered to operate such a facility. Miss Jennings was also the driving force behind the Fairfield Anti-Suffrage Society, which tried to convince the town's women that they were better off with men controlling the nation's political life. The Visiting Nurses Association began to serve the town in 1917; it made 656 nursing calls, 247 instructional visits, and 165 business and inspection calls during its first year. The B. C. & M. M. R. Club aspired to provide nothing beyond bachelor's comfort and married man's relief to its members in Southport beginning in 1894.

Libraries, in the form of book collections that were available to dues-paying members, had existed in Fairfield since before the American Revolution. On occasion they might have lasted for ten or twenty years before their members, having read all the books, lost interest. In 1877 a group of Fairfield's most prominent citizens, including Oliver B. Jennings and Henry W. Curtis and Morris W. Lyon, met together to form a company "to provide and maintain a Public Library in the town and county of Fairfield."[23] Originally located in the old Fairfield Academy, the Fairfield Memorial Library enjoyed the substantial financial support that its predecessors had never had. By 1879 it employed a paid librarian, and by 1899 its directors were planning a permanent building, which opened to the public on June 11, 1903, after a dedication ceremony that brought dignitaries from around the state and from New York and Massachusetts.

Mr. and Mrs. Elbert Monroe, who had lived in Southport for several years before moving to Tarrytown, New York, built the Pequot Library as a memorial to the Fredrick Marquands, Mrs. Monroe's uncle and aunt and parents by adoption. Completed in 1893 and formally opened on February 28, 1894, the library stood on the site of the Marquand home and contained a reading room, an auditorium, a general collection, and a specialized collection of Americana.

Given the town's rapidly growing immigrant population, one might expect native-born Americans to be especially interested in asserting their connections with the establishment of colonial America and the founding of the republic. The creation of two separate chapters of the Daughters of the American Revolution in Fairfield within a single decade clearly indicated the desire of native women to distinguish themselves from the town's more recent arrivals. Similar concerns also help to explain the creation of the Fairfield Historical Society in 1903. Founded largely because of the efforts of Reverend Frank S. Child, minister of the Fairfield Congregational Church, the society began collecting information, manuscripts, and artifacts relating to Fairfield even before it had a headquarters of its own. By 1915 it was situated in a modest facility, a room on Broad Street, and a growing membership assured its future.

Sarah Banks, the wife of Horace, kept a diary during the early twentieth century. Reading her entries might lead one to believe that life in Fairfield at this time was too dull for modern tastes. Aunt Sally, as most of Mrs. Banks's friends and relatives knew her, still did many things her parents and grandparents had; she and her family salted hams and pork, took corn to the gristmill—four mills survived into the twentieth cen-

# SHERWOOD HEARS LOVE LETTER READ IN COURT

## Dec. 13 - 05

## Bank Wrecker Betrays No Emotion When His Epistle to Miss Stivers is Made Public.

Side Lights Upon Career of Criminal Brought Out In Superior Court To-day, It Appears He Was Much Interested in Fashionable Mililners.—How He Was Captured at Panama.

me interesting sidelights on the
nce that Oliver T. Sherwood was

Sherwood was interested in mobile garage in New York w

*Headline from December 13, 1905 issue of the Bridgeport "Daily Standard" reporting some of the more racy aspects of Oliver Sherwood's trial.*

tury in Fairfield. But she could also do something as modern as taking the trolley to Bridgeport (after, of course, walking all the way from Greenfield Hill to Southport).

Certainly enough went on in town to keep conversation lively. People talked for weeks about a shocking railroad accident on the morning of July 12, 1911, when fourteen people were killed in the worst train wreck in the area's history. Likewise when Abbie Jane Barnes Barlow sought a divorce from her husband, John Barlow, because he had become overly affectionate with his widowed sister, Hannah Barlow Baker, residents had some real issues to consider.

No subject, however, received more attention than Oliver T. Sherwood, cashier of the Southport National Bank. Sherwood, a Yale graduate, seemed to have all he could ever want in life, a fine wife, an impressive Shingle style home in Southport, the respect of his neighbors, one of the oldest and most influential names in Fairfield. On May 1, 1903, Charles S. Perkins, a federal bank examiner, stopped by the office of the Southport National Bank for a routine inspection of the books. When he left later that day, he departed in his usual manner. But he returned on May 5 and again on May 6 and once more on May 7. Clearly something was wrong.

On May 12, Oliver T. Sherwood was in New York City trying to convince one Elizabeth Stivers of 5 East 27th Street to accompany him on an extended trip to Central America. Sherwood, it seemed, had embezzled $200,000 from the bank and used much of the money to keep Miss Stivers in a style which he thought befit her and to maintain a second life for himself. Sherwood had been practicing medicine—without a licence—

*A New Fairfield*

*"Mailands," home of Oliver Gould Jennings on North Benson Road, was built in 1906. It is now McAuliffe Hall of Fairfield University.*

in New York for some time. He found that maintaining two identities, as well as both a wife and a mistress, was expensive.

Elizabeth Stivers turned down Sherwood's invitation to see Panama. He was disheartened but could not linger. Off he went to Canada and San Francisco and Columbia, and eventually Panama. He lived and ineptly treated patients there until Joe Priest, a Secret Service detective from Texas, awakened him one morning in July and brought him back to Connecticut to answer for his actions. The Southport National Bank went into receivership, its depositors eventually obtaining a bit more than half of what they had placed with Sherwood for safekeeping, and the wayward cashier went to prison. This bizarre episode kept the town buzzing for many months.

The town's wealthy residents continued to provide excitement. Greenfield Hill people followed the construction of DeVer H. Warner's new summer residence with great interest. Who could ever have guessed there was so much money in corsets? Warner's new home was hardly as spectacular as Oliver Gould Jennings's. In 1906, Jennings had decided to take a wife and also had come to the conclusion that his present home, while adequate as a bachelor quarters, was much too humble for a married couple. "Only a millionaire of the most expensive taste would ever think of destroying a dwelling which was remarkable as one of the finest from New Haven to Greenwich," said the Bridgeport *Daily Standard.* As the son of Oliver Burr Jennings, Oliver G. apparently believed that his taste qualified him to destroy any building he owned; he razed one mansion in order to spend $1,000,000 to build Mailands, a French chateau set on seventy-six acres. This, together with his principal residence at 882 Fifth Avenue, New York, and his cottage, Belacre, at Newport, Rhode Island, were sufficient even for him and his bride.[24]

Compared with him, his sister, Annie B. Jennings, lived in relative simplicity at Sunnie-holme, a residence containing thirty rooms, ten fireplaces, and fifteen baths that she had had created in 1910 by combining two of the houses that John B. Steenbergen built back around the middle of the century. Oliver's other Fairfield sister, Emma, Mrs. Hugh Auchincloss, also preferred a plainer life-style than her brother's. The home she later built on Sasco Hill was situated on a mere six acres, and the residence itself contained only fifteen rooms and five baths, not including, of course, the servants' quarters or the gatehouse.

The young men of Fairfield, while not so impressed with the comings and goings of their rich neighbors as their parents might have been, were as enthusiastic as any of their contemporaries about baseball and football. Baseball began to be popular in Fairfield right after the Civil War. Two men's teams existed in town by then, and few young men from town would miss an opportunity to go to New York to see the Brooklyn Atlantics play. Almost as good was a contest between the Greenfield Resolutes and the Westport Rip Raps. The Fairfield Rubber Company had a team; William Granville, "the Fairfield Giant," was the team pitcher who threw "a very strong ball few can hit." The Fairfield Baseball Club maintained a field near Pickett's store. Most Connecticut towns refused to allow baseball games to be played within their boundaries on Sundays; Fairfield even tolerated Sunday baseball. DeVer Warner, Dr. Warner's son, "was a great baseball enthusiast," said Livingston George Smith, who managed the Warner estate in the 1890s. "We skimmed off the humps on a large level place in one of the meadows, sowed some grass seed, kept it mowed with a horse lawn mower, and they played ball there every Saturday afternoon all summer, when the weather permitted." At times, Smith asserted, "there would be a thousand people there watching the game."[25]

By the 1890s, baseball had to share its premier position with football. The Fairfield eleven suffered humiliation at the hands of Bridgeport on August 30, 1892, the final score being 34-0, but on September 1, the Fairfield baseball team made up for the loss by defeating Bridgeport 5-2. By 1897, the revitalized Fairfield Academy had a football team, although it was not until 1914 that the frugal taxpayers of Fairfield were willing to sponsor a team for the Sherman School.

If the material for gossips was thin and if the wealthy folks were not building new houses or leaving again for Europe and if the baseball and football teams had been idle, Fairfield was always willing to discuss the weather. The big topic of climatological interest in the early twentieth century remained the blizzard of 1888. Franklin Bulkley noted in his diary on March 12, 1888: "A terribly snowy time also very cold at night.... The greatest snow storm I ever saw." Four days later thirty men with five yoke of oxen were trying to dig through the drifts in front of Bulkley's house: "It is twenty feet deep in the street by our garden." On the same day Frank L. Sherwood merely noted that it was "fearful hard traveling." The Fairfield *Advertiser* confirmed the stories of twenty-foot drifts, but concluded that "the excitement of the novel experience has kept up all spirits and the holiday . . . has been kept with considerable fun and jollity, despite the antagonism of the elements." In the years after 1888, as the story of the blizzard was told and told again, the elements became all the more antagonistic, the snow all the deeper, the wind all the stronger.[26]

Thanks to the efforts of many residents, Fairfield was a nicer place in 1910 than it had been in 1900 or 1890. The schools were better. Various organizations were attempting to address specific Fairfield problems, from streetlights to care for invalids and summer vacations for poor youngsters. Telephones and electricity and gas and public water made life easier for many. There were more jobs in town, and it was more convenient to travel to work in Bridgeport. Even the lowly oyster now had some official friends in the Fairfield Town Hall.

Fairfield men and women of the time naïvely believed that all things were possible, that a solution existed for every problem. The turn of the century, like the nineteenth century as a whole, was a time of innocence, an innocence that Fairfield would never know again. World War I and the changes it would bring would guarantee that.

## NOTES

1. FTR, June 13, 1916.
2. Ibid., June 26, 1908; April 10, 1806.
3. Ibid., Dec. 11, 1826.
4. Southport *Chronicle*, Sept. 12, 1868; Sept. 14, 1870.
5. Fairfield *Advertiser*, Nov. 4, 1886.
6. Southport *Chronicle*, Oct. 11, 1892.
7. Bridgeport *Standard*, May 23, June 13, Sept. 22, 1879.
8. Home and School for Boys Collection, Fairfield School Records, FHS.
9. Quoted in Banks, *This Is Fairfield*, 168.
10. Ibid., 169.
11. *Annual Report of the Town of Fairfield*, 1914, 85.
12. FTR, Jan. 6, 1879; Southport *Chronicle*, Dec. 24, 1896.
13. FTR, Jan. 16, 1893.
14. Jonathan Bulkley, *Journals*, 106; FTR, April 3, 1886.
15. Southport *Chronicle*, April 1, 1869.
16. Quoted in Banks, *This Is Fairfield*, 121.
17. Bridgeport *Daily Standard*, May 23, 1904; Banks, *This Is Fairfield*, 121.
18. Charter of the Sasquanaug Association, Voluntary Associations Collection, FHS.
19. Livingston George Smith, Autobiography, 447.
20. Charter of the Greenfield Country Club, Voluntary Associations Collection, FHS.
21. Charter of the Fairfield Fresh Air Association, ibid.
22. Charter of the Gould Homestead, ibid.
23. Charter of the Fairfield Memorial Company, ibid.
24. Bridgeport *Daily Standard*, July 28, 1906.
25. Livingston George Smith, Autobiography, 405, 407.
26. Quoted in Banks, *This Is Fairfield*, 115, 116; Fairfield *Advertiser*, March 16, 1888.

# World War I

WORLD WAR I catapulted a reluctant Fairfield into the twentieth century. The war accelerated those forces—suburbanization and industrialization—that had begun to appear in the early 1900s and pushed them forward with such velocity that the town changed more between 1914 and 1918 than it had during the previous quarter-century.

The changes came by accident, not design. Generally satisfied with their community, the town's residents were unenthusiastic about altering it. The *Fairfield Review* in April 1913 surveyed the town and found it to be "an excellent example of a well balanced community not often seen even in busy New England." What pleased the *Review* in particular was the presence in town of three different sources of employment: farms, "the few manufactories," and "the few large estates." This particular combination was ideal from the paper's point of view, for it resulted in general prosperity, "the best roads in the State," a tax rate that was "lower than in most towns," and a population that was "well fed, happy, and law abiding."[1] Even if the *Review*'s objectivity was suspect, the town's grand list proved Fairfield was doing well. By the end of 1913, the list exceeded $6,000,000, nearly double what it had been in 1898.

Fairfield paid little attention to those events that carried Europe to the brink of war. Townspeople refused to believe that what was happening on the other side of the Atlantic could have any significance for them. Even when war came, in August 1914, they found it difficult to grasp how it might influence their lives. With few exceptions, their perspective was local, not national, and certainly not international. News that Mr. and Mrs. Frederick Sturges had been on the *Kronprinzessin Cecile* of the North German Lloyd Line while the British navy pursued it and its cargo of gold from Ireland to Bar Harbor, Maine, created a flurry of excitement, but most of the Sturgeses' neighbors believed that this encounter brought the war about as close as it would come to their town.

Although Fairfield men and women denied that the conflict might alter their existence in any significant way, they reacted strongly to the horror of the war. Where they could help, they were eager to do so. The Red Cross was as busy as any group in town. In the autumn of 1914, two and a half years before the United States entered the war, the local Red Cross chapter mobilized the domestic skills of Fairfield women to provide socks, gloves, scarves, and hospital garments for British and French soldiers and European refugees. The *Fairfield Review* suggested that these efforts, while laudable, should really be directed toward making life easier for poor people living in town. The Red Cross volunteers disagreed. Meeting at the home of Mrs. William B. Glover, who oversaw the production of these goods, they continued to knit and sew for the people of war-ravaged Europe. Probably as many as half the women in Fairfield took part in this program in one way or another.

From time to time, the possibility of American entry into the war demanded Fairfield's attention. Residents in May 1915 wondered what the sinking of the *Lusitania* off the coast of Ireland might mean for American neutrality. The United States government could hardly ignore the loss of 124 American lives, but the crisis passed without disrupting relations between the United States and Germany. So did a whole series of other, less dramatic events. But in February 1917, when Germany announced a policy of unrestricted submarine warfare, most Fairfield people understood that war was more than just a possibility. Only a matter of days after the German announcement, the national Red Cross instructed all its chapters to organize first-aid classes and prepare for assembling hospital equipment and surgical supplies.

The State of Connecticut was determined to be ready when and if war came. As soon as he learned that German submarines would attack neutral as well as belligerent ships, Governor Marcus H. Holcomb asked the General Assembly to authorize a military census in Connecticut. The legislature, eager to flaunt its patriotism, had a bill ready for the governor's signature by February 6. The new law required all males over the age of sixteen to register for the draft. Unwilling to appear any less enthusiastic about preparedness than the governor and the legislature, Fairfield's first selectman, Charles A. Rowe, immediately appointed thirty-six military census agents; they completed their enumeration by the end of March.

Governor Holcomb, like many of his constituents, believed that the danger facing Connecticut emanated both from Germany and from the state's foreign-born population. Foreigners were unlikely to have developed any real loyalty to the United States, he contended, and Connecticut Yankees, having for decades regarded immigrants as either too simple or too indolent to be feared, suddenly began to take a closer look at their unfamiliar neighbors, suddenly were inclined to see deferential and industrious men and women as potential saboteurs and incendiaries. The greater the likelihood of war, the more suspicious and fearful the native population became. On March 9, 1917, the General Assembly created the Home Guard, a ten-thousand-man force that would protect Connecticut from subversion.

Fairfield, no less susceptible than the rest of the state to antiforeign hysteria, had already taken steps to secure vulnerable installations. Eleven days after the German proclamation of unrestricted submarine warfare, Deputy Sheriff William H. Gould assigned special deputies to guard the Bridgeport Hydraulic Company reservoirs at Samp Mortar and the Hemlocks. Each deputy carried either a Winchester rifle or a shotgun and an automatic pistol. Laden with bandoliers, they were, the Bridgeport *Telegram* reported, "walking arsenals."[2] Many Fairfield residents presumed that German operatives sought to disrupt Bridgeport's and Fairfield's water supply in an effort to undermine industrial production.

Once the legislature authorized the Home Guard, Fairfield's leaders promptly set about finding recruits. On March 29, 1917, the Bridgeport *Telegram* reported that "Fairfield's recruiting officers for the Home Guard are starting work in earnest now." Town officials hoped to enroll every man between the ages of sixteen and forty-five who was not a member of one of the Bridgeport militia companies. (Technically any man between sixteen and sixty was eligible to join, but the town was especially eager to encourage younger men.) To make enrolling as easy as possible, recruiters accepted applications at the Handy and Harmon plant on King's Highway, the town clerk's office, and the Southport Bank. "Fairfield has much territory to guard if war is declared and a Home Guard organization will be found of great use," the *Telegram* contended.[3]

The Home Guard was still organizing when the United States, unable to convince Germany to abandon its attacks on American ships, declared war on that country on April 6, 1917. The nation's involvement in the war necessitated, according to Connecticut officials, even more diligence in the fight against potential sabotage. On April 12, Benedict Holden, a member of Connecticut's Military Emergency Board, came to Fairfield to encourage enlistments in the Home Guard. Apparently the failure of local aliens to rise up against the Hemlock Reservoir or the United Illuminating Company had cooled the enlistment ardor of local men. Holden planned to convince Fairfielders that the danger was real, despite the lack of actual attacks. He was only partially successful: when the Home Guard began its drills on April 28, only eighty men showed up, despite hopes for two hundred. Even after Captain William E. Smith took command of what became Company M, Fourth Regiment of the Connecticut Home Guard, and even after the men were equipped with Springfield rifles and regular uniforms, no more than sixty or seventy men ever reported for drill. To Fairfield's credit, after the initial antiforeign hysteria passed, the town remained more concerned about the Central Powers than about any imaginary threat that might arise from Tunxis Hill, the home of most of the town's recent arrivals.

America's declaration of war prompted the state to establish war bureaus within each Connecticut town and city. Judge Bacon Wakeman became the chairman of the Fairfield War Bureau, an organization that included many of the town's most influential individuals and families. Frederick Sturges, having survived his ordeal aboard the *Kronprinzessin Cecile*, was a board member. Charles A. Rowe, the first selectman, and Joseph I. Flint, the town clerk, were also part of the organization. Several women were members, including Mrs. William B. Glover, Mrs. DeVer H. Warner, and Mrs. Samuel H. Wheeler. The War Bureau's principal function was to see that all town assets useful to the nation's defense were "duly husbanded and its energy, products and financial resources . . . efficiently and economically administered." Any efforts by the Red Cross, the Y. M. C. A., the Knights of Columbus, or similar organizations to further the war effort had to receive the bureau's approval.[4]

Other Fairfield citizens decided which local boys were to be drafted. On June 6, 1917, when Fairfield men began registering for conscription at the Town Hall, 1035 men enrolled. On July 9, these same men returned to learn which of them were eligible for conscription and the order in which they would be called. Once summoned, each

*Patrick Leo Carroll, who served in World War I, poses with his parents.*
*He became a building contractor after the war.*

candidate could expect to appear before the Thirteenth Exemption Board, headed by Dr. William H. Donaldson of Fairfield, for a determination of his fitness for service. In August, the Exemption Board examined the first 188 Fairfield men called. Of this group, it exempted all but 36; these men became Fairfield's first draftees.

On September 19, 1917, this contingent left for Fort Devens, in Ayer, Massachusetts. Town offices, schools, banks, and stores closed at noon on that day to allow Fairfield to give the men a proper sendoff. A public subscription provided wristwatches for every man, and the Fairfield Red Cross gave each of them a comfort kit, which included soap, shaving equipment, and a Bible. Judge Alfred B. Beers of Bridgeport, former Connecticut commander of the Grand Army of the Republic, shook each draftee's hand, spoke a few words of encouragement, and directed the group toward the trolley that would take them to Stratford; there they would meet the "Fort Devens Special."

Dr. Donaldson barely had time to bid the recruits farewell before he was again attending to the work of the Exemption Board. Finding enough men to meet the board's quota took more time than Donaldson could really afford. In late September, he and his colleagues examined 1900 men to find 132 who could be inducted into service. The clerical work generated by the board was more than a paid staff of three could manage; Donaldson frequently had to ask for volunteers in order to meet the government's deadlines.

Some Fairfield men went to war without being drafted, and some of these were among the first members of the American Expeditionary Force to reach France. As early as July 1917, two Fairfield brothers, Bartholomew and Arthur J. Bennett, were already familiar with trench warfare, with lice and trenchmouth, and with casualty lists that grew faster than the work of the Thirteenth Exemption Board. Dr. W. T. Nagri was a lieutenant in the 1st Connecticut Ambulance Company, a unit that included five other Fairfield men, and John Carroll was in the United States Army Signal Corps.

These and more than four hundred others who would later join them were involved in an enterprise unlike any their Fairfield forbears had ever known. Dispatched by a nation that had recently emerged as a world power, they traveled to a distant continent to fight in a war whose meaning few of them probably understood. Unfortunately other young people from town would have to endure similar ordeals in other wars; this became part of living in the twentieth century.

As more and more Fairfield men entered the service, a new responsibility fell onto the War Bureau. It began maintaining a list of Fairfield servicemen and their immediate families. Using this list, the bureau hoped to monitor the conditions of these families and to prevent the kind of suffering that soldiers' relatives had had to endure during the Civil War. Where it was found that any family was in need, the bureau would call upon the town for assistance, and because Judge Wakeman had astutely appointed First Selectman Charles A. Rowe as chairman of the bureau's relief committee, Wakeman had reason to believe that whatever assistance was required would be forthcoming.

Besides those on the Thirteenth Exemption Board and the War Bureau, dozens of other Fairfield civilians were busy fighting the war from home. In addition to her other work with the Red Cross, Mrs. William B. Glover supervised the Fairfield Canning Kitchen. During the late summer and autumn of 1918, the kitchen operated in the Sherman School from Tuesday through Friday. The purpose of the kitchen was to preserve for the coming winter all that had been produced on Fairfield farms during the recent growing season. For ten cents the kitchen would can a quart jar of string beans, corn, peas, or beets; householders were responsible for providing the produce and the jars, and the kitchen supplied rubber rings, salt, and labor. If a Fairfield family produced more fruit and vegetables than it required for its own use, the kitchen would sell the surplus and use whatever profit was realized for war relief or to purchase sugar for the jam it sent to military hospitals.

Supplementing the work of the Canning Kitchen were the efforts of the Fairfield Garden Club, the Fairfield schools, and Mrs. Glover to encourage young residents to cultivate gardens. Since by 1917 few Fairfield children still lived on farms, the schools provided lectures and demonstrations about gardening. The town contributed a four-acre plot where children could stake out gardens if there was no available land at home. Those children who did live on farms were encouraged to join pig clubs, the ultimate object of which was to make Fairfield self-sufficient in pork.

Those who had no inclination for gardening or canning or keeping a hog in the back yard could help the war effort by observing "meatless Tuesdays" and "wheatless Wednesdays." Guaranteeing that men in the service had enough food required Fairfield men and women to sacrifice. President Woodrow Wilson spoke about the war as one "to make the world safe for democracy" and as one "to end all wars." If it took Tuesdays without meat and Wednesdays without wheat to accomplish those noble objectives, Fairfielders were willing to go without.

In the fall of 1917, Judge Wakeman asked his neighbors to endure an additional privation, one that really tested their commitment to the dream of a world safe for democracy. As chairman of the War Bureau, Wakeman opposed granting any licenses

*Ladies of the Fairfield Chapter of the American Red Cross in front of their headquarters at 289 Beach Road during the World War I era.*

*Fairfield: the biography of a community*

for the sale of alcoholic beverages in town. He took this stand not out of zeal for the temperance or antisaloon movement but rather to conserve badly needed national resources, resources that he believed could be better used to defeat the Central Powers than to alter the moods of Fairfield men and women. Each year, as part of the town election, Fairfield, like other Connecticut towns, decided whether it would be "dry" or "wet." In 1917, more than half of Connecticut's 168 towns excluded alcohol. The judge wanted to add his town to that list.

Wakeman had a wealth of allies. He enjoyed the support of all those persons who believed that the production of whiskey and beer was a waste of vital resources. He also had the backing of the antisaloon element in town, who were convinced, that "the searchlight of truth is driving King Alcohol from his throne."[5] Voters, even those who rarely bothered to go to the polls, insisted on expressing their opinions on the question. A typical town election at that time would bring between 500 and 600 residents to the polls. In October 1917, 987 persons cast their ballots. Of these, 433 voted with Wakeman against licensing, but 554 voted to keep Fairfield's saloons open. "Meatless Tuesdays" were one thing, but a dry Fairfield was quite another.

The winter of 1917-18 was so cold that frozen harbors prevented the regular delivery of coal. This problem was compounded by shortages created by government demands for fuel. In January 1918, First Selectman Rowe reported that Fairfield had only enough coal for thirty days, even assuming that residents were conservative in its use. The cold weather and the scarcity of fuel resulted in frigid homes and the spread of infectious diseases, a situation that made the months of February and March seem interminable.

The following winter was even worse. The weather was less severe, and coal more abundant; but illness became a problem of life and death. The winter of 1918-19 was the winter of the great influenza epidemic. In the United States as a whole, more than 500,000 persons died. The Holland Hill section of town was the most severely affected. The Red Cross and local physicians decided that only the establishment of an isolation hospital could prevent illness from engulfing the entire population of the area, but finding a suitable building seemed to be impossible until Frank S. Child and Frederick Sturges, Jr., the two managers of the Fresh Air Home, offered their facilities on an emergency basis. The Red Cross provided a trained nurse who supervised the dozens of volunteers who actually cared for the sick. The town paid the salaries of a matron and a cook and purchased whatever supplies the Red Cross was unable to obtain as donations from Fairfield families.

Despite the hard times, Fairfield continued its generous support of Red Cross and Y. M. C. A. efforts to provide for the needs of servicemen and participated enthusiastically in Liberty Loan campaigns. During the spring of 1918, in particular, hundreds of Fairfield men and women attended rallies to raise funds for the Red Cross or to encourage the sale of bonds. Held at the Greenfield Hill Congregational Church or Sherman's Hall or some other location that would accommodate a large crowd, these rallies followed a standard format. Speakers related "tales of the courage and heroism of the men of the Front," one of the town's three liberty choruses sang patriotic songs, the Unquowa Band or the Order of Red Men's Band played a rousing concert, and then, as the audience sat in solemn reverence, Judge Wakeman or some other dignitary would read the honor roll. Following the end of the formal meeting, Red Cross, Y. M. C. A., or Liberty Loan volunteers would solicit contributions from the audience. Their love of country aroused, most citizens gave as much as they could.[6]

Each of the major fundraising and Liberty Bond campaigns in Fairfield was an enormous success. The Red Cross, in its first drive, sought to raise $8000; Fairfield contributed $17,000. In its second, it hoped for $15,000 and realized $27,400. The Y. M. C. A. set the modest goal of $5000 for its one drive of the war and came away with $24,000. Each of four major Liberty Bond rallies in Fairfield vastly exceeded its quota; in total the town's residents bought about $800,000 worth of bonds.

Fairfield women continued to make items for the Red Cross. Their total production was astonishing: more than 250,000 gauze dressings, 15,000 muslin bandages, 12,000 surgical shirts, 1000 flannel night shirts and 1000 flannel pajamas, 1800 hospital shirts, 900 sweaters, 1700 pairs of socks, and 1300 comfort kits. The local chapter also sent $32,892.23 to its Washington headquarters to be used for national and international work.

But while all this good work was going on in Fairfield, more important events, both in terms of the war and in terms of Fairfield's future, were happening in neighboring Bridgeport. That city became one of the principal sources of munitions for both the United States government and for the allied countries of Europe. Two-thirds of all the small arms and ammunition produced in the United States for the Allies were manufactured in Bridgeport. The Remington Arms Company, which had moved its headquarters to that city in 1912 when it merged with the Union Metallic Cartridge Company, was one of the main reasons for this production. In November 1915, a year and three months after the start of the war, Remington employed 3000 workers. By the following May, this figure had jumped to 16,000, and by May 1917, a month after the United States entered the war, Remington had 36,000 workers on its payroll. Remington's sister company, Union Metallic Cartridge, had employed 2000 workers in November 1915; by May 1917, it had increased its work force to 7000, and before the end of the war, 12,000 men and women worked for the company. These two firms alone, of the dozens of manufacturers in Bridgeport, added nearly 40,000 employees in the eighteen months from November 1915 to May 1917.[7]

Because of such employment opportunities, Bridgeport exploded with new population, rising from fewer than 50,000 people in 1890 to more than 140,000 in 1920. Between the outbreak of the war in Europe and the entry of the United States into the contest, Bridgeport grew by more than 50,000 persons. No greater problem faced the city than finding places for its new population to live. In an attempt to solve this dilemma, the Bridgeport Chamber of Commerce in 1915 formed the Bridgeport Housing Company, a public corporation. With the assistance of funds from the United States Housing Corporation, an agency created by Congress to provide housing for workers who moved to industrial areas to manufacture war goods, the Bridgeport Housing Corporation built one thousand new dwellings in eight locations in greater Bridgeport. One of these, the Grasmere Apartments, "modest brick structures built facing a bit of park land," was located in Fairfield.[8]

The Grasmere development was merely the most obvious evidence of how Bridgeport's growth caused Fairfield to expand as well: filled to the brim, Bridgeport was spilling over into Fairfield. Stratfield, which in the early part of the century had become the first section of Fairfield to feel the effects of suburbanization, developed into an even more obvious suburb of Bridgeport; Brooklawn continued to be one of the

*Typical unit of the Grasmere housing development erected in the Meadowbrook Road-Grasmere Avenue neighborhood during World War I.*

neighborhood's most sought after by successful Bridgeport business and professional men. In fact, in 1917 a group of Stratfield parents acknowledged what they perceived to be their anamolous situation—certainly not within Bridgeport but, likewise, not emotionally part of Fairfield either—by organizing an independent elementary school for their children, the Unquowa School. For years the officers of the school were either Bridgeport businessmen or wives of Bridgeport businessmen.

The growth of Holland Hill and Tunxis Hill was even more furious. Also suburbs of Bridgeport, they developed differently from Stratfield, providing homes on small lots, often in multifamily structures for working-class families; these sections became the most densely populated areas of Fairfield, more populous, in fact, than parts of Bridgeport.

In 1910, Fairfield contained 6134 persons; by 1920 that number had grown to 11,475, an 87 percent increase. The population expansion came almost entirely from the influx of new residents. Most of the newcomers arrived from Bridgeport. Attracted by low taxes, moderate real estate prices, an abundance of outdoor space, and the opportunity to escape the noise and congestion of an industrial city, people flocked into town. Dr. Frank S. Child—the pastor of the Fairfield Congregational Church, a leader in many civic organizations in town, and certainly one of the keenest students of life in Fairfield—observed in 1918 that "the staid and quiet village is a memory." He noted with regret that the Post Road "is now one of the liveliest throughfares in New England—jitneys, trolleys, trucks and automobiles making a hurly-burly of noise and movement distracting and perilous to our people." Perhaps Child was a bit pessimistic, not surprising given his Calvinistic perspective. Another eyewitness who wrote in 1917,

George C. Waldo, painted a happier picture of the town: "But the pride of Fairfield is in its cozy homes and the beautiful grounds which surround them, making it one of the most desirable residence districts along the shores of the Sound."[9] Perhaps the difference in point of view between Child and Waldo arose because Child lived in Fairfield, while Waldo was a Bridgeport man. From Waldo's perspective, Fairfield was a town of residences, a place for persons employed in Bridgeport to live and to raise families, while Child saw Fairfield in terms of what it had been—a quaint but self-sufficient community—and what it had lost—its old-fashioned character and its independence.

Fairfield was so preoccupied with its own growth that the end of the war came almost by surprise. Celebrations were quickly organized. In Southport, residents arranged both a victory festival in the assembly hall of the new Pequot School and a huge bonfire rally which consumed an effigy of the Kaiser, much to the delight of all who attended. The men, women, and children who gathered in the center of Fairfield attended a victory parade that featured an Aluminium Castings Company float, a contingent of schoolchildren and their teachers, the local Boy Scouts, probably more automobiles lined up one behind the other than most Fairfielders had ever seen, and the ladies of the Degree of Pocahontas dressed in Indian garb.

Because of the haste with which these events were organized, many Fairfield residents believed that other, more carefully conceived ceremonies were essential if the end of the war was to be properly celebrated. In February 1919, the newly organized American Legion sponsored a memorial service for the Fairfield men who had died in the war. Relatives of the dead veterans received certificates of appreciation from the French government.

But the big celebration came a year after the war ended. On November 8, 1919, Fairfield acknowledged its 450 sons and daughters who had served in the war. Red, white, and blue bunting adorned the centers at Southport, Fairfield, Holland Hill, and Stratfield. One hundred and fifty veterans gathered to march from Southport to Benson's Switch (where the trolley turned around) and back to the Town Hall. The Unquowa Band, several local worthies, including Judge Wakeman and Dr. Donaldson, and a platoon of soldiers accompanied the veterans. At the Town Hall, Jennie Watmough, an army nurse who was every bit as much a veteran of "over there" as any of the male marchers, presented to the town a purple flag bearing twelve gold stars, each representing a Fairfield resident who had died in the war. Judge Wakeman, on behalf of the veterans, honored Mrs. William B. Glover with a silver loving cup in appreciation for all the thousands of socks and surgical dressings and hospital shirts and flannel pajamas that she had worked to deliver to American servicemen. More than three hundred people then gathered at Sherman's Hall for dinner, songs by the Southport and Greenfield Hill liberty choruses, and an evening of dancing.

Those persons who organized the November 8 celebration expected the events of that day would be described in history as the closing of Fairfield's participation in the World War. From the point of uniforms, battles, heroes, and pomp and circumstance, there could hardly have been a more fitting conclusion. No celebration, no matter how moving or well attended, could mark the end of the war's impact, for the direction that conflict set for the town would become the one it would follow for decades to come.

1. *Fairfield Review*, April 2, 1913.

2. Bridgeport *Telegram*, Feb. 12, 1917.

3. Ibid., March 29, 1917.

4. Quoted in Banks, *This Is Fairfield*, 125. The atmosphere in Connecticut during the war is skillfully analyzed in Bruce Fraser, "Yankees at War: Social Mobilization and the Connecticut Homefront," Ph.D. dissertation, Columbia University, 1976.

5. Bridgeport *Telegram*, Sept. 18, 1917.

6. A typical rally is described in the Bridgeport *Standard American*, April 23, 1918.

7. On the growth of Bridgeport, see Mary Proctor and Bill Matuszeski, *Gritty Cities* (Philadelphia, 1978), 71-74.

8. Frank Samuel Child explained the wartime changes in the *Annual Report of the Fairfield Historical Society* (1918), 7-9. The activities of the United States Housing Corporation during the war are the subject of Miles L. Colean, *Housing for Defense: A Review of the Role of Housing in Relation to American Defense* (New York, 1940).

9. Child, *Annual Report of the Fairfield Historical Society* (1918), 7; George C. Waldo, Jr., *History of Bridgeport and Vicinity*, 2 vols. (New York, 1917), 270-1.

# Fairfield in the 1920s

AMERICANS HAD GIVEN little thought to what the end of the war might mean. Certainly both Fairfield and Bridgeport were totally unprepared for peace. Economic dislocations developed immediately. Within a year after the cessation of hostilities, Remington Arms employed only 300 production workers—down from a wartime high of 36,000—and was desperately seeking a buyer for the 1.5-million-square-foot factory it had built to handle military orders. Union Metallic Cartridge Company dismissed 8500 workers during approximately the same period of time. Bridgeport Brass furloughed most of its employees while it reorganized and reopened with a work force that was fifty percent smaller. Few of Fairfield's industries were so drastically affected, but those closely associated with defense production, like the Aluminum Castings Company, certainly were; Aluminum Castings survived because the giant Aluminum Company of America bought it. Hamilton & DeLoss, which only began operations in 1917 when it managed to secure several government contracts, failed to survive the transition to a peacetime economy. Its owners closed the plant on Grasmere Avenue and offered it for sale. Bought and operated for a time by the Hawthorne Company of Bridgeport before closing again, it sat empty for several years, a stark reminder of a vanished prosperity.

Workers responded to the impossible combination of more and more layoffs and a constantly increasing cost of living with a rash of strikes. The American Graphophone Company, Bridgeport's third largest employer, was shut for several weeks in 1919 as the result of a walkout. Except for a strike that eventually closed the Connecticut Lock Company, Fairfield had to endure little of the labor unrest that troubled Bridgeport, but the threat of strikes at local establishments and the consequences of Fairfield men and women boycotting their Bridgeport employers created both tension and economic hardship in town.

The demands placed on Fairfield by unemployed workers during the postwar years far exceeded any the town had known earlier. In 1920 it appropriated $11,000 for its

240

charity fund, which provided care for needy residents. The $11,000 was gone in two months. Charles A. Rowe, who served as first selectman until 1921, anticipated that the town might have to spend as much as $55,000 during that year on its poor—one-fifth of Fairfield's entire budget.

Distress existed in all parts of the town, but again Holland Hill and Tunxis Hill, as had been the case during the influenza epidemic, suffered the most. Conditions within those neighborhoods reminded many Fairfield residents of what they imagined existed on New York's Lower East Side: town officials found a widow attempting to support eight young children on $8 a week; several former servicemen, unable to locate work after returning from Europe, were destitute, incapable of caring for their families.

Such problems seemed to be beyond the competence of the selectmen, a point of view confirmed by Charles A. Rowe when he decided in October 1921 to retire from politics. Frederick A. Burr, a farmer, a Republican, and a selectman since 1913, replaced Rowe as first selectman.

Burr and other leading residents believed that some of the distress in town could be relieved by establishing a private agency that would identify cases of genuine need for local charitable organizations. Dr. William H. Donaldson liked the idea, as did Arthur Perry, Harold C. Bullard, the ubiquitous Mrs. William B. Glover, and several other influential persons in town. During the first three months of 1922, the town had spent more than $20,000 assisting 174 different families, and the Visiting Nurses Association had distributed record amounts of food and milk to malnourished infants and tuberculosis victims. The necessity for professional management of the town's welfare problems was obvious to Burr and the others.

Created as the Fairfield Family Welfare Society, the new organization hired a trained social worker, Mary E. Dennis, who immediately began the tasks of identifying families in need, furnishing necessary relief either from town or private sources, and coordinating the chairtable efforts of various organizations. The society also expected Dennis to provide social and financial counseling to distressed families and to discourage among them any indefinite dependence on charity.

Although the hazing of immigrants never became the popular pastime in Fairfield that it did in many Connecticut communities, the native population did believe that foreigners were the source of most of the poverty in town and that a good dose of Americanization would ease their economic distress far more than Mary Dennis's charity. In 1919 the Fairfield schools introduced an Americanization course for adult foreigners. The object of the course was to assist foreign-born residents to become productive citizens of the United States by offering them instruction in English, the history of the United States, and "American Ideals and Customs." Three Americanization schools existed in town, one at Nicholas Terrace, one at Holland Hill, and one in the center. A total of 157 students were enrolled in the program. At the conclusion of the course at Holland Hill, the Board of Education presented the students with certificates of attendance, and the students demonstrated how well they had learned their lessons. Several who had had little understanding of the language of their adopted land at the beginning of the year conducted a conversation in English; another student read a composition entitled "Why I Became a Citizen of the United States"; and a Mr. Csulik delivered an oration on the life of Herbert Clark Hoover. This was followed by a performance of Hungarian folk dances and the singing of "The Star-Spangled Banner." A similar program held at the Sherman School was highlighted by the presentation of an original composition by George Parchimowicz in which he explained the proprietary interest he had come to take in the factory where he worked. Many of Fairfield's most prominent citizens attended these exercises "and expressed themselves as having been highly entertained, and delighted at the apparent progress made by the students."[1]

Mary Dennis endorsed these efforts at Americanization but refused to accept the nativist idea that Fairfield's immigrant population was to blame for the hardships that it endured. She took it upon herself to provide a little education for the native-born men and women of Fairfield. She was, for example, careful in her reports to show how many "Americans," that is, native-born persons, required the services of the Family Welfare Society. In 1924 she noted that 20.5 percent of all the cases that came to her involved native Americans and that this was "in contrast with our usual belief that practically all the socially incompetent who need our help are foreign." She went on to warn against thinking that "some deliberate form of sinfulness such as shiftlessness, intemperance, neglect, etc., is the single factor at the root of family misfortunes." The real problem, she declared, was usually illness.

She hoped to alleviate tensions between families that had lived in the United States for many generations and those that had just arrived. Most of her work, she acknowledged, was with "these simple ignorant, foreign people, who, after all, do most of our heavy and least pleasant industiral work." She would have no one underestimate these people: "They are simple and unlettered, but direct and unconscious in their hospitality and generous gratitude. Few are so poor that they do not wish in some measure to make return for service."[2]

Fortunately the heavy case load that Mary Dennis carried when she first came to the Family Welfare Society was eased by the end of 1922, when prosperity began returning to southwestern Connecticut. In 1920 the General Electric Company purchased the huge plant that Remington had been trying to sell in Bridgeport. Within a short time, the company had transformed the former gun factory into the sixth largest General Electric facility in the United States. By the end of the decade nearly four thousand individuals, hundreds of them Fairfield residents, worked at the plant.

Fairfield's economy also benefited from the tendency of industry to follow its employees to the suburbs. The Bullard Machine Tool Company had been in Bridgeport since 1880. The descendants of Edward P. Bullard, the company's founder, began making their homes in Fairfield in the late nineteenth century. In 1920 the company moved most of its production facilities to Fairfield, where it continued to produce vertical turret lathes as well as the Fairfield Mult-Au-Matic, a multispindle machine that could automatically perform several machining functions. The company retained its Bridgeport address, obviously believing that the name Bridgeport meant more in industrial circles than Fairfield. The G. Drouve Company, which manufactured skylights and windows, also relocated from Bridgeport to Fairfield, and followed Bullard's example by continuing to receive its mail in Bridgeport.

The Bridgeport Rolling Mills arrived in Fairfield four years after the Bullard Company and took over what had been the Connecticut Lock Company on Sanford Avenue. The Aluminum Company of America, a Pittsburgh firm, came to Fairfield in 1922, when it bought the Aluminum Castings Company of Southport. Before the decade was over, it had moved into a new facility on the Post Road. In 1923 Girard and

*Fairfield Center in the 1920s looking west on the Post Road from Unquowa Road.*

Company, a manufacturer of chemicals, moved to Fairfield from New York; three years after its arrival, its president, F. Donald Coster, merged it and McKesson and Robbins, Incorporated, of New York, a pharmaceutical company, to form McKesson and Robbins, Incorporated, of Connecticut, a business that became vitally important to both Fairfield and the pharmaceutical industry.

By 1922 Fairfield even had a newspaper again. Having been served for many years by the Southport *Chronicle*, which went out of business in 1909, and then by the short-lived *Fairfield Review*, Fairfield went almost a decade without a paper of its own. In June 1922, Edward M. and Lillian Brennan moved to Fairfield from New York. Edward Brennan had worked for both *The New York Times* and the *New York Tribune*. On July 1, 1922, he began publication of the *Fairfield News*, which he and his family would control for almost thirty years.

Life in Fairfield in the 1920s was taking on a more and more modern aspect. As early as 1922, 1100 telephones were in service in town, and residents were making about 5000 calls each day. By the end of the decade, the number of phones had doubled and the number of calls almost tripled. Many Fairfield families owned radios as well as telephones and enjoyed listening to Bridgeport's radio station, WICC, as well as the New York stations. Not everyone in town had electricity, of course, but enough homes either had electrical service or were having electricity installed to keep three Fairfield electrical contractors in business.

Motion pictures were also part of the town's life in the 1920s. The Community Theatre had all the latest releases; Rudolph Valentino and Theda Bara visited town regularly, thanks to celluloid film. The Great Atlantic & Pacific Tea Company had been the first chain store to appear in Fairfield; others came in ever-increasing numbers during the twenties. By the end of the decade, there were two A&P stores in town in addition to two First National stores, an outlet for Consumer Food Stores, a Great Union Tea Company store, a Logan Brothers Company store, and a Rexall drugstore. Not all the

*Fairfield in the 1920s*

old merchants were forced out of business. Mercurio's, which opened in 1900, maintained itself on the basis of its reputation for quality food, and William McGarry, who operated a blacksmith shop across the Post Road from the Sherman School, still held his own along with four other blacksmiths in the face of increasing numbers of gasoline stations.

No modern devices intruded on Fairfield's existence more than the automobile. It changed virtually every aspect of life in the town. The automobile created new ways of making a living; by 1925 Fairfield included an automobile body shop, two automobile dealers, two painters of cars, nine businesses that sold automobile parts and supplies, nine garages that offered repairs, and one firm that rented cars. The coming of the automobile forced Fairfield to hire more policemen and to look to other, more modern, means of traffic control; in June 1927 the town installed its first "automatic signal to regulate traffic." Until then motorists had had to drive to Bridgeport to see a genuine traffic light. By the time the light was in operation, nearly twenty-six hundred cars were registered in town. This number would have been slightly smaller except for Oliver G. Jennings, his sister, Annie Burr Jennings, and his neighbor, Walter B. Lashar, president of the American Chain and Cable Company of Bridgeport: among them, these three residents owned thirty-four automobiles.

More than anything else, the automobile gave Fairfielders the opportunity to live where they wanted, regardless of where they might work or shop or attend religious services or movies. When the trolley first began carrying workers to jobs in Bridgeport, commuters had to reside within walking distance of the Bridgeport Traction Company lines. The result was clusters of settlement in Stratfield, Holland Hill, Tunxis Hill, and the Oldfield section. But with a car, a commuter could live, without any real inconvenience, in the remotest areas of town, sections that even as late as the world war were thought to be the exclusive domain of the town's few remaining farmers. Cars were more expensive than trolleys, to be sure, but for many Fairfielders the convenience was well worth the added cost.

As automobiles made remote areas more accessible, the price of land for development in these sections began to increase. At the same time, the value of Fairfield lands for agriculture was declining. Connecticut farmers had been facing economic ruin for decades. Between 1890 and 1920, they had forsaken more than 40 percent of the state's agricultural acreage. In 1920, 215 farms still survived in Fairfield, and these farms supported 8.6 percent of the town's population. By 1930, only 165 farms were still operating, a decline of 23 percent, and a mere 4 percent of Fairfielders lived on them.

There was other evidence of the collapse of agriculture. The Greenfield Country Club, established in 1901 to encourage the study of agronomy, had sponsored one of the most successful agricultural fairs in Connecticut. In 1911 the club discontinued the fair because of declining interest, and in January 1925 the club itself was ready to expire; its membership had fallen off drastically. In August of that year, it sold its real estate to the Greenfield Hill Country Club, an assemblage of golfers and socially prominent men and women who wanted to build "a real country club" complete with an eighteen-hole golf course, a clubhouse, and exclusive membership regulations.

Unlike departing manufacturers, when farmers abandoned an area they left no decaying carcasses behind, no unsightly piles of scrap, no hulking factory buildings that were both too expensive to restore and too costly to demolish, no deserted railroad sidings. As agriculture died in Fairfield, it left behind land, land so attractive that developers spent long hours devising ways to acquire it. The combined effects of the passing of the farmer, the opening of his lands for development, and the coming of the automobile meant a building boom unlike anything Fairfield had seen before, even during the frenzied days of World War I.

Subdivisions appeared one after the other. In 1926 the Fairfield Land Improvement Company — owned by Oliver G. Jennings, Horace B. Merwin, and E. Ellis Dillistin — announced plans to build nineteen houses off Mill Plain Road. Almost two hundred houses were built in town in 1927. Approximately the same number went up in 1928. The Guaranty Building and Mortgage Company, O. C. S. Ziroli, president, began to develop forty acres in Jennings Woods in 1929. Sasco Park, which included sixty-eight lots, each with about sixty feet of frontage, took shape that same year; so did the Knollwood development in Stratfield. Rural Greenfield Hill experienced more growth than any other part of town, while Tunxis Hill and the King's Highway area, already densely populated, saw little activity.

With additional housing and additional population came an increased demand for goods and services. This in turn created a market for more commercial space. When Robert D. Goddard and Theodore E. Steiber built a retail building on the Post Road between the Sherman School and the Fairfield Trust Company, their project so impressed the officers of the trust company that they decided to begin work on a new building. The center of Fairfield was transformed during the 1920s. So was the commercial center of Stratfield, when two Tudor style shopping centers appeared there.

The result of this activity was a constantly growing grand list. In 1921 the list amounted to about $21 million; ten years later, it had reached $40.5 million, a 92 percent increase. In terms of dwellings alone, Fairfield added slightly more than nineteen hundred new structures during the decade, a figure that represented a 79 percent increase and almost twice the number of houses that had existed in Fairfield at the beginning of the century. This increase was necessary to accommodate a population that grew from 11,475 to 17,218 during the 1920s and that was living in slightly smaller households in 1929 than it had at the beginning of the decade.

By 1930 Fairfield's residents were both ethnically and religiously mixed; in fact, two of every three persons living in town then was either born outside the United States or was the offspring of foreign-born parents. For decades Irish-Americans had constituted the only numerically important immigrant group in Fairfield; it was the Irish who had brought Catholicism to the town, and it was they who still in 1930 made up the bulk of the membership of St. Thomas Roman Catholic Church.

As the twentieth century unfolded, new nationalities began to appear in town. A casual observer might make the mistake of associating the coming of these new ethnic groups with the development of the electric streetcar. A convenient chronological parallel exists between the era of the trolley and the massive influx of eastern and southern Europeans into Fairfield. While the streetcar certainly made areas adjacent to Bridgeport easier to reach and while one cannot deny the importance of geographical mobility, the arrival of these new groups in town had less to do with the trolley than with their carefully considered decisions to take advantage of the opportunities Fairfield offered.

Contending with both fluctuating prosperity and ethnic discrimination, these immigrant groups insisted upon preserving family solidarity and ethnic ties. They thought of home ownership more as a way to maintain the family than as a means to privacy and relief from urban life, those considerations generally uppermost in the minds of native-born Americans as they moved to town; but these new groups made no less a conscious choice to come to Fairfield than did the owners of the factories where many of these same immigrants worked.

Ethnic leaders often played a crucial role in their countrymen's decisions. The migration to Fairfield of Hungarians, the largest new ethnic group to come to town between 1900 and 1930, presented a dramatic example of the part leaders took. Hungarian entrepreneurs encouraged the movement of their brothers to town. By blending their personal economic ambitions with their desire to maintain solidarity with their kinsmen, these leaders significantly altered the face of Fairfield's population. Their strategy was simple but sound, given the obstacles they faced; they purchased tracts of land in Fairfield, subdivided these tracts into small and inexpensive lots, and offered them for sale to their fellow Hungarians.[3]

Frank Timko was a pioneer among Fairfield's Hungarians. In 1906 he purchased Winona Park, a wooded area in the vicinity of present-day Fiske Street, between State Street and the New York, New Haven and Hartford Railroad. He divided the land into seventeen lots and sold the parcels to his compatriots, many of whom stretched their budgets to the limit to purchase the land and many of whom intended, at least for the present, to use the property only as garden space or for weekend retreats. A short distance away, he developed another plot, this one also between State Street and the railroad tracks. Today his influence on that area is memorialized by a street that bears his name.

John Dezso, John Renchy, and Samuel Greenbaum operated in a similar fashion. Dezso was prominent in the Bridgeport Hungarian community. As president of the West End Coal Company, the West Side Furniture and Music Company, and the Bridgeport Publishing Company and as vice-president of the West Side Bank, he had established his reputation as an astute businessman. In addition he served for sixteen years as president of the Hungarian Aid Society. John Renchy, who operated a tavern in Bridgeport, sat on the board of the West End Bank, performed as an officer of the Hungarian Aid Society, and was a member of the Board of Aldermen in his adopted city. Their friend and associate Samuel Greenbaum was the treasurer of the West Side Bank, a member of the Jewish Hungarian community, and a man highly regarded by other Bridgeport bankers.

Prior to the outbreak of World War I, these three men bought a large tract of land north of Jennings Road, east of High Street, west of Black Rock Turnpike, and south of Greenfield Street. This particular property lay at the western end of that section of Tunxis Hill that had been developed during the recent war. Dezso, Renchy, and Greenbaum named their property Karolyi Park in honor of Count Michael Karolyi, a Hungarian national hero. Between 1915 and 1920, the three developers divided the park into small lots, usually 25 feet by 100 feet. They then established streets in the park and also named them for Hungarian heroes; Andrassy, Hunyadi, and Rakoczy existed by 1920, and shortly thereafter the partners established Apponyi and Baros. John Dezso then began to lure his fellow Hungarians to Karolyi Park by offering them lots for $250 each and monthly payments of only a dollar. These buyers, like those who bought from Timko, usually used their lots to grow vegetables and flowers and dreamed of the day when they could afford to build on them.

Another Hungarian immigrant, George Vecsey, had come to Bridgeport to work at the Bridgeport Malleable Iron Company. Just before World War I, when large numbers of Hungarians were coming to Bridgeport, Vecsey left Bridgeport Malleable Iron and entered the real estate business. He bought several parcels of land and built small homes on them, homes that he sold to his countrymen. One of his developments was located in northern Stratfield, where he bought a large tract from the Wheeler family.

Andrew Veres brought the first substantial group of Hungarians to the central section of Fairfield. He owned land off Reed Road that had originally been a marsh. Interested in farming, he drained the land and raised both vegetables and animals on the property. As the demand for residential lots grew during the 1920s, Veres subdivided his land and encouraged Hungarians living in Bridgeport to become his neighbors in Oldfield.

Other Hungarian entrepreneurs followed this same strategy. Many Hungarian families, of course, bought land from non-Hungarians, but these pioneering businessmen did establish focal points for the settlement of their countrymen, neighborhoods that provided social warmth, a shared identity, and a sense of security, all of which were essential to the goal of preserving the family in a strange land.

During the 1920s, homes appeared on the lots the Hungarians had purchased. Many Hungarians had anticipated the time when, after accumulating savings in the United States, they might be able to return to their native country. For many this dream died in 1919 when the Treaty of Trianon divided the kingdom of Hungary into several different countries. For many Hungarians, returning home would be returning to a foreign land, to nations like Czechoslovakia and Yugoslavia, which were only created after World War I. Remaining in the United States was the only alternative open to them, and home ownership became an important priority.

Some of the Hungarians who came to Fairfield were Catholics; others were Protestants; still others were Jews. Encouraged by the First Hungarian Church of Bridgeport, the Fairfield Magyar Reformed Church, a Protestant church located on King's Highway and dedicated on November 21, 1925, became the first uniquely Hungarian religious institution in town. The second, St. Emery's Hungarian Roman Catholic Church, was located in a small, converted clubhouse, where the Reverend Benedict Biro said the first mass on January 1, 1932.

Jews, whether from Hungary or elsewhere, lived in Fairfield during the early twentieth century, but only in small numbers. Mrs. Elizabeth Barsky Nickowitz later recalled her family's moving to Stratfield in 1905. Her father, Morris Barsky, had worked as a tailor for many years before entering the real estate business. It was through his real estate ventures that he became friendly with Henry Jones, a Bridgeport businessman who maintained a summer home on Valley Road in Stratfield. When Jones decided to sell the property, Barsky expressed an interest and eventually bought it and moved his family there. Mrs. Nickowitz remembered the neighbors as "gracious towards us" but also noted that her parents were "the only Jews who dared to come to Stratfield" for many years.[4] In fact, Fairfield's Jewish population remained too small to justify the establishment of a synagogue until after World War II.

Besides Hungarians, Poles were the largest of the other new immigrant groups. Again coming by way of Bridgeport and encouraged to settle in Fairfield by various ethnic leaders, such as Stanley Ryzak, Poles tended to make their homes initially in the Oldfield and Tunxis Hill sections. Despite the fact that the trolley passed through the Oldfield neighborhood as early as 1893, that area failed to develop into a residential suburb because it was marshy and because local property owners insisted upon maintaining the vicinity's bucolic character and landscape until the 1920s. By 1927 enough Poles lived there to support their own church, St. Anthony's Polish Catholic Church, which stood on Pine Creek Road. The Poles on Tunxis Hill, like their Russian and Slovak neighbors, probably continued to attend church in Bridgeport.

The Italian-Americans who lived in Fairfield were, unlike the Hungarians, the Poles, the Russians, and the Slovaks, scattered around the town. The largest single contingent was located in the Southport area, encouraged to move there by Philip Pepe and William Garofalo, the organizers of the Pequot Political and Athletic Club and men interested in real estate development. But Italian families also lived in Tunxis Hill and in Oldfield. In 1926 St. Thomas Church established a mission in Tunxis Hill because many Italian-Americans in the area were converting to Episcopalianism in order to join St. Michael's Episcopal Church, where an Italian clergyman was serving. In 1938 the mission broke its formal ties with St. Thomas and established a separate identity as Holy Family Roman Catholic Church.

The patterns of discrimination encountered by these new immigrants were much like those that Irish-Americans had found. Fairfield's native population was more willing to excuse economic ambition among their ethnic neighbors than they were to accept either political or social aspirations. For pharmacist and real estate developer John E. Boyle, or grocer and commercial property owner Charles A. Wyrtzen, or Benjamin E. Plotkin, the founder of the Fairfield Masons Supply Company and a real estate entrepreneur, to achieve financial success met with the approval of the town's establishment. But with few exceptions, this same group retained control of the important political offices in town until after World War II. They managed this through their total domination of the Republican party. (In both Fairfield and the state, the Democrats were generally impotent between 1910 and the election of Governor Wilbur L. Cross in 1930.) Local Republicans emasculated such efforts to influence town politics as the Pequot Political and Athletic Club or the Independent Political Club located in Tunxis Hill, the "international section of Fairfield."[5]

The Yankees also refused to permit incursions into their social domain. Benjamin E. Plotkin was one of the thirty-six individuals who in 1925 provided funds to allow the Greenfield Hill Country Club to purchase the property of the old Greenfield Country Club. Plotkin thought that he, like the other thirty-five, would become a charter member of the club. Instead he was asked to submit a formal application for membership and later learned that, despite the protests of Simon C. Bradley and J. Nelson Hutchinson, his application had been rejected because he was a Jew. Other town clubs similarly excluded individuals because of their religion and nationality.

One group that found new opportunities developing for them during the 1920s were the town's women. Despite the valiant efforts of the Fairfield Branch of the Connecticut League Opposed to Women Suffrage, Annie B. Jennings, chairman, the XIX Amendment to the United States Constitution went into effect in August 1920, just in time to give women the right to vote in the presidential election of that year. Barely two years later, Fairfield elected to public office the first woman in its entire history. She was Anna L. Bulkley, and she became a member of the School Committee. During that same year Joseph I. Flint, who was serving as both town clerk and tax collector, died; his wife, Clara M. Flint, assumed the offices her late husband had held.

Before the decade was over Edna F. Elwood had become the town's first female justice of the peace, Gertrude Donaldson had been appointed assistant prosecutor of the Fairfield Town Court, and Finette B. Nichols was vice-president of the Fairfield Republican Town Committee. In 1931, Nichols won election to the General Assembly from Fairfield, an office she would hold for many years.

Women advanced outside the political field as well. In 1924 the *Fairfield News* incorporated a column on "Women in Business." While few of the women featured held positions of great responsibility, the type of work they were doing indicated that middle-class women could, if they were so inclined, lead independent lives, answerable to neither a father nor or a husband.

Fairfield also had to make its peace with the XVIII Amendment, which made illegal the manufacture, sale, or transportation of intoxicating liquors. Prohibition inconvenienced Fairfield's drinking population—which certainly represented a majority of the town's adults—by forcing them to pay exorbitant prices for illegal whiskey, and created one more task for Fairfield's haphazardly organized law-enforcement system. Judge Bacon Wakeman was the prohibition enforcement officer in town, but the day-to-day job of constraining local bootleggers fell to Hezekiah R. Elwood, a constable and the chief law enforcer in town, Thomas Shaughnessey, a constable, and Arthur J. Bennett, a constable and a traffic officer. None of them received a salary, their only compensation being the fees they received for performing various functions: making arrests, giving traffic tickets, and the like.

These men apparently made a conscientious effort to enforce prohibition. In November 1923, Bennett was on his way to direct traffic at the Sherman School when he noticed a truck that seemed to have a suspicious look about it. The driver claimed his cargo consisted of sausage casings, but, when Bennett inspected the barrels the truck was carrying, he discovered twelve hundred gallons of bootleg beer. Three months later Bennett and Shaughnessey raided and destroyed a hundred-gallon still on Hoyden's Hill; the illegal operation was the property of John Matz of Grasmere Avenue.

While the local bootleggers were a tame group compared to those who operated in New York or Chicago, they still took their business seriously. When Bennett arrested Thomas Gray for selling liquor illegally, Gray's cohorts decided to teach the Fairfield constables a lesson. Just a few week after Gray went to jail, Thomas Shaughnessey was on duty in Southport when a car approached him, purportedly to ask directions. As Shaugnessey walked toward the car, the driver pointed a gun at the constable and announced that he was about to pay for the arrest of Gray. Fortunately the gun misfired, and Shaughnessey, with the help of several Southport pedestrians, was able to arrest the driver before he could escape. He turned out to be Edward Gray, Thomas's brother and business partner.

Almost a year later, Bennett, who was the commander of the George Alfred Smith Post of the American Legion, left the post headquarters after a turkey dinner and drove to his home on Grasmere Avenue. On his way to work the next morning, the officer noticed that his car was running badly. When he stopped to look for the problem, he found two sticks of dynamite wired to the car's ignition system. Edward Gray, who had just emerged from prison for his ill-fated effort to kill Shaughnessey, was arrested about a week later for the attempted murder of Bennett.

Prohibition and the increase in crime that it brought was one reason for the eventual

*Fairfield in the 1920s*

establishment of a regular police department in Fairfield. The *Fairfield News* began endorsing the idea during the autumn of 1922. In 1925 problems created by a youth gang that loitered around the Delbuono Store at Tunxis Hill Road and Old Stratfield Road again focused the town's attention on the need for a professional police force. Three years later constables Elwood and Bennett were both wounded by David Hazay after Elwood was summoned to the Hazay home to quell a domestic disturbance. This incident, the likes of which Fairfield had never seen before, prompted the town to hire these two wounded officers and William T. Burr and Charles R. Gandorf on a regular, salaried basis.

Another attempt at modernization came just a short time later. As soon as he recovered from his wound, Elwood, who had patrolled the town at night in his own vehicle, became the operator of the town's first and only police car. It took the officer less than an hour to demolish the new cruiser and nearly kill himself. Apparently his foot accidently slipped off the accelerator rest and hit the accelerator, which he mistook for the brake. Officer Elwood, his broad-brimmed Stetson hat, and the patrol car all ran headon into one of Greenfield Hill's sturdiest trees. A subsequent investigation revealed that the embarrassed Elwood had never driven a gear-shift car before, his personal vehicle being a "flivver."

At the end of the decade, Fairfield established a full-fledged police department. In 1929 it hired a fifth officer, Eugene R. Burns, and adopted regulations for the operation of the force, and the following year the town voted in favor of formally establishing the Fairfield Police Department. Arthur J. Bennett became its first chief.

The town hired its first paid firefighter, James Brown, in October 1918, almost exactly twenty-five years after the formation of the Fairfield Volunteer Fire Company, by then known as Fairfield Hook and Ladder Company No. 1. Ten years later, it created a five-member Fire Commission. Each of four commissioners represented one of the four volunteer companies in town—Fairfield, Southport, Tunxis Hill, Stratfield—and one, Greenfield Hill, which still had no unit of its own. The commission was to provide and maintain all fire-fighting apparatus, which was the property of the town, and to employ one caretaker and one fireman or driver for each district. The volunteers would continue to supply the bulk of the personnel and to retain their autonomy within each company.

The demands for other town services also grew. By the early 1920s, Fairfield already had a Town Plan Commission that oversaw the establishment of new roads in town. Steps were also under way to create a building code, primarily the work of architect O. C. S. Ziroli, and a plumbing code, eventually devised by William M. O'Dwyer, the third selectman, who also happened to be a plumbing contractor. In 1924 Nelson R. Pearson became the town's first building inspector.

Bacon Wakeman began raising support for his plan to bring zoning to Fairfield in 1922. Various organizations endorsed his scheme. The Fairfield Improvement Society, the Luncheon Club of Fairfield, the Stratfield Improvement Association, and the Improvement Society of Fairfield and Vicinity all worked for zoning. The Improvement Society in 1924 hired Robert Whitten, a city planner from Cleveland, to prepare a preliminary town zoning report. When Whitten's report was completed, the society held a public meeting, conducted by Albert E. Lavery, at which the planner presented his ideas. He urged the immediate creation of a zoning commission to establish and enforce zoning regulations in town.

During the course of the meeting Annie B. Jennings—like her brother, Oliver G. Jennings, an advocate of zoning—expressed her concern that the Town Plan Commission had grown too powerful and should be made subordinate to the proposed zoning commission. Generally convinced that Fairfield residents ought to pay careful attention whenever she spoke, Miss Jennings was taken aback when Dr. William H. Donaldson, the chairman of the Town Plan Commission and a man who was as universally admired in Fairfield as any, arose and demanded the audience's attention by beginning his remarks: "Miss Jennings displays her ignorance as to the state of affairs."[6] Donaldson's refusal to be intimidated kept the issue of the town plan and the issue of zoning separate and forced Fairfield to think not only in terms of zoning but also in terms of long-range planning.

In November 1924, the town meeting created a zoning commission; and the following year, the commission, with the assistance of the Technical Advisory Corporation, a New York firm, divided the town into five different zones: Residential A—single family with yard space on all sides; Residential B—one- and two-family homes; Residential C—apartments and tenements; Business; and Industrial. Basically designed to maintain existing land-use patterns and to prevent damaging intrusions into residential neighborhoods, the zoning regulations went into effect in August 1925.

Because of the rate at which Fairfield was growing, Andrew L. Riker, who replaced Donaldson as chairman of the Town Plan Commission, began suggesting during the summer of 1929 that Fairfield develop a comprehensive master plan. Such a plan was essential, argued Riker, if the town was to control its own growth. When Henry B. Stoddard took over for Riker, he and First Selectman Burr and Andrew S. Huntington, a civil engineer, continued to push for a comprehensive plan.

Simultaneously Dr. Lawrence E. Poole and Dr. Valery Harvard, both of whom, like Dr. Donaldson, served as town health officers, led a drive for the construction of sanitary sewers in Fairfield. Poole contended that unless sewers were built, the town ran the "danger of a serious epidemic."[7] Rebuffed again and again, Poole refused to abandon the idea. Finally, in 1929, he convinced the town to appropriate $10,000 to hire William Gavin Taylor and Gerald W. Knight, engineers from New Jersey, to conduct a sanitary survey of the town. Taylor and Knight's report argued that Fairfield must install a sewer system despite the projected cost of $1,729,000. This was more money than the town was willing to pay, and so the following year, on instructions from the newly created Fairfield Sewer Commission, Knight came back with a revised plan that would have cost about $900,000 and would have concentrated on only the most congested areas of town.

Unfortunately both sanitary sewers and a comprehensive town plan were many years in the future. The Great Depression and the Second World War lay ahead, and both would be over before either of these two projects was ever begun.

Fairfield's effort to create a government capable of coping with the problems of its growing population was orchestrated by First Selectman Frederick A. Burr. During his tenure, which lasted from 1921 until 1931, the town added a Police Department, a Fire Commission, a Parks Department, a Building Department, a Zoning Commission, a Board of Zoning Appeals, and a Sewer Commission. The town's budget increased from less than $600,000 to approximately $2,000,000; and although its debt grew from $400,000 to $1,441,000, the 1931 debt was equal to only .67 times the annual property

*Fairfield in the 1920s*

tax collected, while that of 1921 had equaled .87 times the tax collected. The vast bulk of the debt had been incurred trying to build schools, including the 1925 Roger Ludlowe High School, fast enough to keep up with increasing enrollment. Burr was the last farmer ever to serve as first selectman and one of the most able persons to hold the town's highest office.

Throughout the 1920s, Fairfield's beaches remained the center of warm weather activity. During the early years of the century, private pavillions, likes the ones owned by John Boyle and by the Fairfield Pavillion Company, had catered to the "trolley crowd" from Bridgeport. But by the autumn of 1917, this often rowdy contingent was undermining the quiet of the Fairfield Beach Company, soon to become the Fairfield Beach Club. Henry C. Sturges, president of the company, complained on October 27, 1917, that "a large portion of the beach controlled by one of our members has been a source of great anxiety to all of us this summer and has at times proved a very serious public nuisance." The owner of the property was none other than Oliver G. Jennings, who had bought three hundred feet of beachfront shortly after the Fairfield Beach Company had come into existence. When he and others failed to win the town's endorsement for their plan to control much of the beach through the vehicle of the Fairfield Beach Improvement Company, Jennings let his property sit idle for several years. But just before World War I, he leased it to the Fairfield Pavillion Company, about which Sturges was complaining.

In response to these criticisms, Jennings sold the property to his friend Joseph I. Flint, the town clerk, tax collector, and chairman of the Republican party in town. Flint in turn sold the property back to the Penfield Reef Corporation, which was run by Jennings, DeVer H. Warner, Horace B. Merwin, and E. Ellis Dillistin. Jennings and Warner, of course, require no introduction; Merwin and Dillistin were the president and secretary-treasurer, respectively, of the Fairfield Trust Company. These men guaranteed that the Penfield Reef Corporation would allow none of its bathers to cause problems for the beach club and that it would provide bathing facilities for those Fairfield families who had recently been excluded by the beach club when it discontinued the public use of its facilities. From the point of view of Jennings, Merwin, and Mrs. DeVer H. Warner, all of whom served on the board of the club during the 1920s, this arrangement solved two annoying problems.

Farther west the beach was considerably less exclusive. Boyle's pavillion eventually became the property of Charles J. Collins and certainly attracted few visits by members of the beach club. Judge Bacon Wakeman hoped that the town would ultimately buy the Collins and Penfield Reef properties and turn them into public beaches to supplement the limited town facilities that existed at Sasco Beach, at the foot of Sasco Hill, and at the ends of Pine Creek, Beach, and Benson roads. The Depression vanquished that suggestion.

The cottages that stood beyond the Collins pavillion were unattractive and relied on outdoor toilets in an area that regularly flooded, posing a danger to the well-being of the community. The Zoning Commission and the Building Department combined forces to prevent additional construction in the area, but the unsightly cottages that already existed remained both a visual and a health problem.

The waterfront in Southport might also have become a problem after the shipping industry left except for the fact that the harbor was so easily converted from commercial

*Fairfield High School circa 1920, present site of the Tomlinson Middle School.*

to recreational use. Interest in racing had grown in Southport as the market boats disappeared. Local yachtsmen had popularized the sport even before the World War, and the pumping of thousands of yards of fill from the bottom of Southport Harbor to complete the Fairfield Country Club in 1916 vastly improved the port's facilities. In November 1920, Frederick T. Bedford, Laurence Craufurd, Harold Lloyd, and Johannes Schiott formed the Pequot Yacht Club. The thirty charter members included eleven from Fairfield, eleven from Green's Farms, and eight from Bridgeport. The club acquired the old Harris Hardware Company building in 1926 and remodeled it as a clubhouse, and in 1933 leased the Wakeman Memorial Building to add to its facilities. The cost of maintaining a boat and the annual dues of $65 placed the Pequot Yacht Club beyond the means of most Fairfield families.

Many Fairfielders satisfied their sporting appetites by following the fortunes of the high school football team or of the Fairfield Tigers, a semiprofessional football team sponsored by the American Legion. Baseball continued to be a great favorite. The industrial league included teams from the DuPont plant, the Aluminum Company, Handy & Harmon, and the Porcupine Company, a construction firm. The town team, made up of the best players from Fairfield, traveled to games in both New York and Connecticut and was usually accompanied by a bus filled with zealous fans.

Four golf courses flourished in town by the beginning of the 1930s. The Brooklawn Country Club, the Fairfield Country Club, and the Greenfield Hill Country Club all maintained private courses. But any Fairfield resident could play at Fairchild Wheeler Park, the Bridgeport municipal golf course, which was located in Stratfield.

The variety of recreational facilities in town reflected Fairfield's mixed population. Unlike most of the communities of southwestern coastal Connecticut, Fairfield included individuals who represented every social and economic class. Harold Gray, the creator

*The Fairfield High School football team of 1923.*

of "Little Orphan Annie," could stroll about his estate on Sasco Hill and see the homes of other town residents, some of whom were officers of major New York firms, others of whom managed Bridgeport factories, and still others of whom were the production workers who toiled in those and other plants.

Such diversity within the town was hardly evidence that all residents enjoyed an equal say in local affairs. Those who owned seats on the Southport Club Car, for example, insisted upon having their say about town matters. Oliver G. Jennings and his sisters, Emma Jennings Auchincloss and Annie B. Jennings, owned seats on the car which made daily round trips to New York City. So also did Witherbee Black, of Black, Starr & Frost, Jewelers; George P. Brett, the president of the Macmillan Publishing Company; Charles S. Munson, the president of National Carbide; Carleton H. Palmer, the president of Squibb & Company; and Frederick Sturges, Jr., whose grandfather and father had made so much money that he could either take or leave corporate titles, depending upon his inclinations.

For years these men, or people like them, had guaranteed that their voices would be heard on public affairs by personally funding community projects: paying to macadamize roads, providing schools for the town, guaranteeing the upkeep of this or that institution. But by the 1920s, the town's needs had outgrown even the pocketbooks of persons as wealthy as these. Annie B. Jennings gave the town its first high school, but its second, Roger Ludlowe, cost hundreds of thousands of dollars.

By the time that school was built, Fairfield's wealthy residents had discovered less costly methods of maintaining their influence. In the first place, they kept a close rein on the town Republican party, either running it themselves, as Oliver G. Jennings did after the death of Joseph I. Flint, or assigning the party leadership to loyal associates such as Albert E. Lavery. They also controlled the Board of Finance, which the town had created in 1918 after borrowing substantial amounts of money to build schools. This board enjoyed enormous power because it submitted the budget that ultimately went to the town for adoption; no public monies could be expended without the board's approval.

From its inception until World War II, the Board of Finance represented the well-to-do of Fairfield. Wealth had been a prerequisite for selectmen during colonial times and was now essential for members of the Board of Finance. In 1921, when Frederick A. Burr began directing town affairs, neither he nor his two colleagues were men of great influence, but on the Board of Finance sat Oliver G. Jennings; John C. Lobdell, a large landholder in Greenfield Hill; Frank E. Morgan, a retired New York broker; Simon C. Bradley, president of both the Southport Savings Bank and the Kennel Food Supply Company; Elmore S. Banks, an attorney; and Jonathan Godfrey, president of the Compressed Box Company. Twenty years later, the occupations of the three selectmen were patternmaker, electrician, and steamfitter, while the seven members of the Board of Finance included the president of Southport Savings Bank, the president of the Mitchell Dairy Company, a man who was both secretary-treasurer of the C. O. Jelliff Manufacturing Company and vice-president of the Southport Savings Bank, a lawyer and a stockbroker and an engineer who were all employed in New York, and Oliver G. Jennings's son.

This arrangement apparently satisfied the people of Fairfield, for the Board of Finance was elected, not appointed. Certainly no one ever accused the board of any improprieties, and one would be mistaken to think that this group's insistence upon having a large voice in running the town indicated any desire on its part to subvert the best interests of Fairfield. Determined to protect what they found most desirable in town, the members of this group enjoyed the luxury of being able to do so without oppressing others.

The end of the 1920s witnessed the death of Dr. William H. Donaldson, who had come to town in 1885 just after completing his studies at Bowdoin College and the College of Physicians and Surgeons in New York. During his years in Fairfield, he helped organize the Fresh Air Home, the Fairfield Memorial Library, the Fairfield Trust Company, the Town Plan Commission, and the Luncheon Club. He also delivered more than twenty-five hundred babies and never refused a patient because that person was unable to pay for his services. He died of a heart attack after unsuccessfully attempting to save a drowning victim at the beach off Benson Road.

On the day of his funeral, all business, both public and private, stopped in town. Hundreds of men and women surrounded his home, unable to enter because of the throngs already inside. Outside his house, the *Fairfield News* observed, "there were notable and distinguished citizens of Fairfield and Bridgeport, familiar to everyone, and there were humble citizens from far flung sections of town, some of them women attired in the European manner with shawls over their heads."[8] A man as comfortable rebuking Annie B. Jennings for her ignorance of the Town Plan Commission as he was caring for a sick child or a pregnant woman in any of Fairfield's humblest homes, Donaldson symbolized the townspeople's commitment to their community, a commitment that allowed them, despite their diversity and despite the velocity with which their town was growing, to live in harmony.

## NOTES

1. *Annual Report of the Town of Fairfield*, 1920, 86-88.

2. *General Secretary's Report to the Family Welfare Society of Fairfield*, May 20, 1924; May 4, 1925. Copies in the FHS.

3. The role of ethnic leaders in encouraging particular immigrant groups to settle in particular areas has been carefully documented by John Bodnar, *The Transplanted* (Bloomington, Ind., 1985). Magdalene Havadtoy, *Down in Villa Park: Hungarians in Fairfield* (Fairfield, 1976), describes an important aspect of Fairfield's history and does it well. See also "Racial Groups in Fairfield," RG 33, WPA in Connecticut, 1935-44, Ethnic Group Survey, Box 69, Connecticut State Library.

4. Greater Bridgeport Regional Planning Agency and Connecticut Preservation Office, *Stratfield Historic Resources Inventory* (Jan.-June 1979), I, 16-18.

5. *Fairfield News*, May 19, 1923.

6. *Ibid.*, Sept. 27, 1924.

7. *Ibid.*, July 15, 1922.

8. *Ibid.*, Aug. 18, 1928.

# The Great Depression

LIKE THE REST of the country, Fairfield watched and worried when disaster struck the New York Stock Exchange on Thursday, October 24, 1929. By the weekend, local experts were predicting that the worst had passed and that the following week would bring a return to business as usual. It was a busy time of the year, and few spent the weekend agonizing over the stock market. C. Buckingham and Company, distributors of fuel oil, and the Bridgeport Gas Light Company were reminding customers to examine their furnaces in preparation for the coming heating season. The Women's Guild of the First Church of Christ met on Saturday to make plans for its forthcoming Harvest Supper. Both the DuPont Bowling League and the Fairfield Mason Supply Company Bowling League were in full swing. And many town residents wanted to see the Marx Brothers in *The Cocoanuts* at the Community Theatre; it looked like great fun, lots of laughs; and it was a "talkie."

Anyone who missed out on a carefree weekend would have to wait for some time before having another. On October 29, the stock market collapsed completely, and within two weeks $30 billion in the market value of stocks had disappeared. For some residents the impact was immediate. Livingston George Smith, who lived diagonally across from the Town Hall, observed how some "people who lived in luxury with lots of servants and fine cars, were reduced to penury and had to radically change their way of living."[1] Walter B. Lashar, whose life-style rivaled even that of the Jenningses, was already on a slide that would eventually cause the town to seize his mansion for the non-payment of taxes.

More important for the town was the impact of the crash on ordinary individuals. These were residents whose fortunes were tied less directly to the stock market and who came to understand the dimensions of the disaster only as business people and consumers, their economic confidence shattered, began to curtail expenditures. Eventually reductions in spending led to lay-offs in volatile industries, such as construction; the building boom was dead in Fairfield by the middle of 1930. Other businesses began general cutbacks. By the fall of 1930, between 175 and 200 people were out of work—enough to create a crisis in town.

By Connecticut law, each town was responsible for its poor. This was a situation that had remained basically unchanged since the days of Roger Ludlow. Fairfield had to muddle through as best it could. In November 1930, the Board of Finance authorized additional money for the care of unemployed persons and their families. To do so, it had to withdraw the funds already allocated for a comprehensive town plan. It refused to authorize more money for relief without also suggesting the town put all ablebodied, unemployed men to work either on the roads or in mosquito control. The Fairfield American Legion established a clearinghouse for anyone offering employment, even odd jobs, and for individuals looking for work. The Family Welfare Society began a drive for funds, and in Southport and Barlow Plain, volunteers went door to door asking householders to hire the unemployed to do painting or gardening or other chores.

By March 1931, the town budget was reeling so badly that for a time the selectmen began making loans rather than grants to needy persons. The grants were costing the town about $10,000 a month and were providing relief for approximately 165 families, or about 750 individuals. A typical family on relief might expect to get about $38.50 a month—barely enough for even the most frugal family, but that money was worth much more than it had been just a few years before. Economists estimated during the summer of 1931 that the 1926 dollar had increased in value to about $1.43, and prices reflected this increase. Shoppers at any of Fairfield's six A&P stores could purchase two packs of Old Golds, Lucky Strikes, Chesterfields, or Camels for $.25; small wonder that cigarette smoking was increasing. For less self-indulgent customers, the A&P offered 2.5 pounds of Quaker cornmeal for $.13 or a pound of Gorton's codfish for $.23. At Devore's Bakery, cupcakes sold for $.19 a dozen and bread for $.05 a loaf. At Mercurio's, a careful shopper could buy a can of Campbell's baked beans for a nickel and a gallon of cider for $.30.

Just as low prices provided little relief for the unemployed, they also provided little relief for the town budget. Fairfield was running out of money. To increase taxes made no sense because residents were already frequently unable to pay their levies on schedule. Frustration levels rose among town officials, the unemployed, and the overburdened tax payers. Residents wanted a scapegoat, and the most likely candidate was Frederick A. Burr, the first selectman.

Burr's political enemies began to organize within his own party during the summer of 1931. At the head of this group was John Ferguson, the leader of the newly formed Fairfield Republican Club. On September 7, in "the biggest political meeting in the history of Fairfield," Ferguson and his followers won control of the Republican party and nominated Edward L. Barlow, president of the E.W. Carpenter Manufacturing Company of Bridgeport, to replace Burr as the party's nominee for first selectman.[2] The weapon with which Ferguson attacked Burr was Nicholas Matiuck, a town labor foreman who had used town workers to make improvements on his own land. Certainly no one even hinted that Fred Burr was dishonest, only that he had failed to stay aware of Matiuck's activities, activities that eventually sent the foreman to prison for a year and forced him to make restitution of $12,750 to the town.

Clearly Ferguson's attack on Burr had less to do with Matiuck's crime or Burr's competence that it did with either Ferguson's ambition or the town's frustrations. Arthur

J. Bennett, the popular chief of police, with whom Burr had publicly clashed and who was rarely reluctant to involve himself or his department in political affairs, strongly supported the Ferguson contingent; this also hurt Burr.

The whole affair became even nastier when, about a week after the Republican caucus, Bennett and two other officers were arrested on charges of illegally disposing of confiscated liquor. The three had allegedly seized 213 bottles of beer and over 110 gallons of whiskey which they themselves either consumed or shared with friends. Although all three were cleared of the charges and returned to duty, Bennett lost his former position as chief. That post went to Hezekiah Elwood, a Democrat but a man close to Burr and a man less inclined to involve the Police Department in politics.

Once in office, First Selectmam Barlow turned over the detailed work of caring for the poor to the Family Welfare Society and established Fairfield Emergency Relief, Incorporated, to try to raise relief money from private sources. The organization's first campaign failed to reach its goal of $75,000; it gathered only $42,000. By that time one person in seventeen in Fairfield was on relief.

In the early months of 1932, Fairfield was going broke. Tax Collector David H.S. Huntington used all the reasonable means at his disposal to try to collect the $140,000 that was due the town. If the Fairfield Trust Company and the Black Rock Bank and Trust Company had not provided the town with emergency credit at a rate below that which they were currently charging other customers, the town would have been unable to meet its obligations.

The Family Welfare Society was overwhelmed with work. It and the Visiting Nurses Association had already moved into larger quarters on Reef Road in a building that had briefly housed Fairfield's only black church. In addition to screening all applications for relief, the Family Welfare Society also labored to prevent lending agencies from foreclosing on even more Fairfield homeowners. Fairfield was a town of owner-occupied homes; in 1930 about 90 percent of its housing units were the residences of their owners. Now foreclosures were threatening to change this. One developer alone, Joseph Wakeman, foreclosed on 240 mortgages. As a result of both loan foreclosures and economic necessity, cars were also disappearing—disappearing so rapidly, in fact, that the grand list fell in both 1931 and 1932.

The demands for relief refused to subside. By the beginning of 1933, nine hundred families in town were receiving assistance, and the town was again facing bankruptcy. Town leaders debated the idea of cutting the average rent allowance from $16 a month to $10 and lowering the average food allowance, which then stood at $.85 a week for a child, $1.50 a week for a woman, and $1.60 a week for a man. Cutting the rent allowance alone, they estimated, would save $30,000.

More pressure meant more frustration and the search for additional scapegoats. During the spring of 1933, residents directed more and more criticism toward Mary E. Dennis, the executive director of the Family Welfare Society. She personally investigated every relief claim submitted to the town, and she became the target both of persons whose claims she denied and of rugged individualists who believed she was too soft-hearted. Her valiant service to the community failed to silence those who needed someone to blame. Despite the protests of First Selectman Barlow and of Albert E. Lavery, the president of the Family Welfare Society, Mary Dennis resigned. If anything, her resignation further complicated the town's difficulties.

*The W. P. A. at work constructing storm drains in Fairfield in the 1930s.*

Ultimately the federal government saved Fairfield from a situation it could not manage. Elected president in 1932, despite Fairfield's preference for Herbert Clark Hoover, Franklin Delano Roosevelt intervened in the problems faced by towns like Fairfield. In August 1933 the first federal money began to arrive in town, and before the year was over almost six hundred unemployed Fairfield persons were at work for the federally funded Civil Works Administration. The Roosevelt administration refused to assume the total burden for Fairfield's unemployed. Generally the federal government provided three out of every five dollars needed to assist them. In a typical Depression year, Fairfield could count on receiving between $250,000 and $300,000 either directly or indirectly from Washington.

Most of the federal dollars sent to Fairfield came as wages for workers employed by the CWA or the PWA or the WPA or some other agency created by the New Deal. Fairfield had to provide the necessary tools for the workers and also whatever materials the various projects required. As a consequence of the work these agencies did, Fairfield's public facilities improved vastly during these years. A new post office, a restored town hall, several new playgrounds, school libraries, and a far superior road system were the tangible legacies of this era.

The New Deal failed to bring sewers to Fairfield. Despite the continued agitation of Dr. Poole, the Board of Finance was unwilling to appropriate any funds for sewer work except $2600 to conduct another sanitary survey. The town's lack of interest in sewer construction resulted primarily from its precarious financial situation, but also important was the opposition expressed by certain individuals who feared that installing sewers would give federal bureaucrats another opportunity to intrude into Fairfield affairs. The United States government seemed to be everywhere. On November 23, 1936, Fairfielders, for the first time, found themselves assigned Social Security numbers and carrying Social Security cards. While the federal presence reassured some residents, it frightened others. Annie B. Jennings, as an example, would rather go without sewers than encourage further New Deal involvement in town, and her opinion was important.

The success of the Democrats in Washington, where Roosevelt presided, and in

Hartford, where Wilbur L. Cross served as governor, encouraged a rebirth of that party in Fairfield. Led by John J. Fitzpatrick, the Democrats began to arise from their lethargy in 1933. On October 22, 1936, at just a little after five in the afternoon, Franklin Roosevelt came to town. The New Deal detractors must have stayed at home that day, because "staid, old Republican Fairfield yelled itself hoarse" when the president arrived.[3] FDR carried the town by 144 votes in the November election, the first time Fairfield had voted for a Democratic candidate since 1892, when it chose Grover Cleveland over Benjamin Harrison. The Democrats also sent a representative, W. Eben Burr, and a state senator, Winthrop B. Palmer—a woman—to the General Assembly from Fairfield in 1936.

But town government remained a Republican monopoly. In 1933, John Ferguson, the man who had dislodged Fred Burr, replaced Edward L. Barlow as the Republican candidate for first selectman. Barlow was the last member of a colonial Fairfield family to serve as first selectman, and Ferguson, born in Scotland, was the first foreign-born person to assume that office.

In 1938 Fairfield must have shocked political observers when it voted for a Socialist candidate over either the Republican or Democratic nominees for governor. Of course the Socialist was from right next door, a well-established Bridgeport roofing contractor and the Mayor of that city, Jasper McLevy. Whether town voters selected him because he was a neighbor or because they genuinely preferred him over Republican Raymond Baldwin and Democrat Wilbur Cross would be difficult to ascertain. But for most Fairfielders, a vote for McLevy was hardly a vote for the type of socialism that worried the folks on Sasco Hill. Fairfield was not given to radical causes. The Reverend Charles E. Coughlin, the leader of the National Union for Social Justice, attracted enough attention through his radio attacks on Roosevelt, labor unions, and the international banking community to allow his local followers to establish a Fairfield unit of the National Union, but its presence in town was largely a secret to everyone but its own members.

Fairfield residents had more interesting things to do than listen to Father Coughlin's ravings. In 1933, they were busy finally establishing a firehouse in Greenfield Hill and in 1936 celebrating the opening of the Fairfield Country Day School, originally located on Unquowa Road. An era ended in town at 1:45 A.M. on May 2, 1937, when motorman Anthony B. Ghiotto stepped down from trolley #1837, the last ever to travel through Fairfield. Henceforth riding public transportation meant taking a Connecticut Railway and Lighting Company bus.

The coming of the Merritt Parkway was the subject of years of speculation in Fairfield. Preliminary authorization for the parkway became law in 1927, but construction did not begin until April 1, 1932. From the very beginning, the people of Greenfield Hill were adamant that the parkway was going to intrude upon their neighborhood as little as possible. They were sure that its presence would mean "the complete change of the territory in this region from peaceful, beautiful countryside, to a gasoline alley for New York motorists, with suburban sub-divisions and building lots along the sides."[4]

State officials increased anxieties over the highway by refusing to announce its location. Even when the state began purchasing property for the road, confusion was still rampant. Once the route was revealed, Greenfield Hill residents set out to prevent the establishment of an entrance between Sturges Highway, on the Westport line, and

*Fairfield Beach in the wake of the 1938 hurricane.*

Black Rock Turnpike. The entrance's opponents, organized by the Greenfield Hill
Improvement Association, included several powerful persons among their ranks: Henry
B. Stoddard was chairman of the Town Plan Commission; Roger Wilkinson had both
time and energy to commit to the struggle; and Winthrop B. Palmer was an influential
Democrat, a member of the Merritt Parkway Commission, and the wife of Carleton
H. Palmer, the chairman of the board of Squibb and Company. The fact that the Palmers
lived only a few hundred yards from the proposed Redding Road entrance undoubtedly
encouraged Mrs. Palmer's determination to maintain the serenity of Greenfield Hill.

But on the other side of the question were arrayed the Fairfield Lions Club, a large
group of downtown businessmen who feared the parkway would mean a loss of trade,
and ultimately the town of Fairfield itself, which, in August 1939, voted in favor of
an entrance at Redding Road. By the beginning of November 1939, the parkway was
open through town and, although many who still wanted an entry in western Fairfield
remained committed to the fight, Greenfield Hill had, for the present, carried the day;
no interchange existed along that strip of the parkway that would come to be known
as "no man's land."

Construction crews were working on the parkway when the worst storm in history
struck the town. In September 1938, a hurricane ravaged New England. Fairfield residents
lost all telephone and electrical service. Trees were down from the shore to the Easton
and Weston lines, and roads were washed out by the flooding that accompanied the
storm. Rescue workers evacuated fifty families from coastal sections by boat. Recent
advances in weather forecasting and the abundance of radios in town saved untold lives;
only one Fairfield resident died. Probably the only good the storm accomplished was

*Fairfield: the biography of a community*

to clear the beach of dozens of ramshackle cottages, a major step in the drive to improve Fairfield's shore.

Several years before the hurricane of 1938, the town had acquired two large sections of beach. At the beginning of the 1933 summer season, A. M. Comley, the town attorney, announced, after a careful examination of the Town Land Records, that Fairfield owned the section of shoreline between Ash Creek and the Annie B. Jennings property. Apparently Andrew S. Wakeman had been mistakenly paying taxes on this land for many years. Comley's opinion proved valid, and the Park Department took control of that area the following month. A year later, town officials announced that Miss Jennings had given sixteen acres on the shore to be used as a public park. Acquisition of these two parcels allowed town residents more access to the beach than they had enjoyed since it had become popular for recreation. The timing was ideal, for few activities fit the constrained budgets of Depression Fairfield better than a trip to the beach. The Beach Club still existed for those who could become members; Jennings and Sasco beaches were reserved for Fairfield residents; and the Penfield Pavilion, the Restmore Pavilion, and the Idle Hour Pavilion provided for the needs of out-of-towners.

Fairfield had outgrown its Town Hall back in the middle 1920s. The building was entirely adequate for a government the size of the one that had existed in 1870, when it was last remodeled, but was too small to meet the town's needs by 1925. In 1929, Frederick Burr appointed a committee, chaired by Bradford G. Warner, to investigate what Fairfield might do about its town offices. Some residents wanted to enlarge the existing structure, while others supported either an entirely new building on the same location or elsewhere. After several weeks of study, Warner's committee recommended the construction of a new facility on the Town Hall Green. A minority report advocated a new building on a more centrally located site. Committee members, except for Annie B. Jennings, were unenthusiastic about keeping the old building and adding onto it.

The problems of the Depression overshadowed concerns over the Town Hall, and the question was abandoned for a time. But on March 24, 1935, Governor Wilbur L. Cross came to Fairfield to inaugurate the local celebration of Connecticut's tercentenary. Miss Jennings, town chairman of the event, arranged for an impressive program. The Bridgeport Symphony Orchestra performed, and dignitaries, both political and business leaders, lined the platform of the Roger Ludlowe High School. The big news of the evening came not from the governor but from Miss Jennings's sister, Emma Jennings Auchincloss. She announced that she would provide the materials needed to restore and update the Town Hall. Federal funds would pay the workers involved in the restoration. The project, directed by Fairfield resident and nationally prominent architect Cameron Clark, took more than a year to complete and cost Mrs. Auchincloss about $40,000.

The wisdom of restoring the old structure and retaining the town offices at their traditional location was obvious almost immediately. Situated within the Fairfield's center but still removed from the business district, the old site provided an ideal setting for the modern town's headquarters. The building, now liberated from its Second French Empire embellishments and restored to its Federal graciousness, stood as a monument to the town's heritage.

When Fairfield observed its own tercentenary in 1939, William O. Burr, chairman of the celebration, organized events throughout the entire town, but the culmination

*Miss Annie B. Jennings and her dogs circa 1910.*

*At far right is a view of the Sunnie-Holme gardens which were destroyed following her death in 1939.*

of the week-long festivities took place on the Town Hall Green. Observers could imagine no better setting for either the historic pageants that commemorated the arrival of Ludlow three hundred years before or the ethnic dancers who proclaimed their more recent but equally special contribution to the town's diverse culture.

Annie B. Jennings died in July 1939, two months before Fairfield celebrated its tercentenary. Her funeral marked not only her passing but also the demise of a certain style of life that was disappearing from town. There were still wealthy people in Fairfield, perhaps few as wealthy as Miss Jennings had been, yet still individuals with great financial resources. But the style of life that Oliver G. Jennings or Annie B. Jennings or the younger Frederic Bronson pursued had become an anachronism by the end of the 1930s. The Depression had proven that the wealthy had better attend to their fortunes or risk losing them. The paternalism that had characterized the Jenningses, the Bronsons, the Sturgeses, and other town benefactors no longer seemed appropriate; their generosity was no longer necessary, for Fairfield, even in the face of the Depression and the problems it created, was able, with the help of the federal government, to take care of itself and its residents. The middle class might complain about burgeoning government, but it heartily endorsed the concept of democracy—which it understood to mean rule by middle management—and this notion of democracy was impossible so long as towns like Fairfield were dependent upon the largess of rich people. Furthermore, the cost of maintaining armies of servants became prohibitively expensive once the Depression ended and prosperity returned; even Miss Jennings might have been unable to maintain thirty gardeners in 1945 or 1950. And estates like Sunnie-Holme would be impossible without the staffs to operate them. So Miss Jenning's death was probably timely. Much as she

*Fairfield: the biography of a community*

loved the town, she might have felt out of place in the new Fairfield.

F. Donald Coster's demise, on the other hand, was inopportune, for he died just as Fairfield was coming to know him for the man that he was. Coster sought the same status that the Jenningses and the Sturgeses had enjoyed for generations, but despite his immense talents—and he was a gifted individual—he ultimately failed in his quest. Coster was the man who transformed McKesson & Robbins of New York, a company with a celebrated past but a dubious future, into McKesson & Robbins of Connecticut, a diversified corporation that became a leader in the pharmaceutical industry. To a degree, he did this by accident. He was originally drawn into the pharmaceutical business during Prohibition in order to sell alcohol (illegally, of course) to some of the country's most notorious bootleggers. As president of the Adelphi Pharmaceutical Company and later as president of Girard & Company and eventually as president of McKesson & Robbins, he provided thousands of gallons of illicit alcohol to gangsters. Because he was such an able businessman, he also, almost inadvertantly, turned McKesson & Robbins into a huge, legitimate success.

Eventually the world learned not only that he was a crook but that he was in fact not even F. Donald Coster, M. D., Ph. D., University of Heidelberg. He was Philip Musica, a twice-convicted felon from New York's Lower East Side. The idea of returning both to prison and to a life and an identity that he had fought so hard to escape was more than Musica could bear. He refused to live without his eighteen-room mansion on Mill Plain Road, his yacht at the Black Rock Yacht Club, and his membership in the Greenfield Hill Country Club. As federal marshals armed with arrest warrants stood at his front door, on December 14, 1938, Musica took his own life.

*The Great Depression*

*Polish Catholic students of St. Anthony's School march in traditional costume in the 1939 tercentenary parade.*

By the beginning of 1939, Fairfield had survived both Philip Musica and the Great Depression. The grand list grew during 1938 despite both the construction of the Merritt Parkway and the havoc wrought by the hurricane that fall. Fairfield residents bought more than three hundred new vehicles in 1939, and that year saw a resumption of the building boom that had died in 1930. September 1939 was the busiest month the Fairfield Building Department had experienced since its creation fifteen years before.

The Depression had brought change to Fairfield, especially in terms of the town's relationship with the federal government. Although its population grew more slowly during the 1930s than it had during either of the two previous decades, the town included 21,135 residents by 1940. But still Fairfield retained a quality that had existed in town longer than even the oldest resident could remember. Thomas R. Gleason, the president of the Young Democrats Club, tried to describe this quality when he said: "Fairfield, unlike many towns of its size and attainments, is intensely local in its thoughts and its philosophy. Each individual seems to feel a keen sense of civic pride and duty, something innate and difficult to analyze, but nevertheless present." It was a trait of which Fairfield could be proud.[5]

NOTES

1. Livingston George Smith, Autobiography, 485. Peter Joseph Lombardo, Jr., "Connecticut in the Great Depression, 1929-1933," Ph.D. dissertation, University of Notre Dame, 1979, depicts state politics during these first years of economic dislocation.

2. *Fairfield News*, Sept. 12, 1931.
3. Ibid., Oct. 23, 1936.
4. Ibid., April 20, 1929.
5. Ibid., June 26, 1936.

# World War II
# and Its Aftermath

U NTIL THE SPRING of 1940, Fairfield
generally ignored World War II. Eager
to persuade themselves that the conflict
had little to do with their lives, Fairfielders tried to go about their business as usual.
But after France fell on June 22, the war suddenly had the town's full attention. In July
young men began enrolling in a military training course offered at the Wakeman
Memorial Boys' Club; Francis Blossom of Greenfield Hill, an engineer, accepted Secretary
of War Henry L. Stimson's invitation to come to Washington to oversee the transition
of the peacetime economy to one prepared for war. And Bullard's was recruiting
employees as energetically as it had in 1916.

During the autumn of 1940, with American participation in the war still more
than a year away, Fairfield men registered for another draft. Registration began on
October 16. James Hogath, who was then working at the Center Restaurant, was the
first of 3236 men to enroll that day. During November, the first Fairfield men began
taking preinduction physicals, and before the winter of 1940-41 was over, nearly one
hundred men from town had been drafted.

Simultaneously town leaders, acknowledging that it would be difficult for the
United States to avoid war, established a Fairfield Defense Board and set it to work
developing a comprehensive disaster plan. The Defense Board also studied air raid
procedures and recruited air raid wardens. The American Legion examined textbooks
used at Roger Ludlowe High School to make sure they were free of subversive or
anti-American materials.

When Howard A. Smith of Greenfield Hill created Connecticut's inaugural chapter
of the America First Committee, his efforts met with indifference from his neighbors.
The America Firsters hoped to keep the United States out of the war by encouraging
a defensive position in the Western Hemisphere that would be strong enough to preclude

*Armed forces recruitment photo taken in 1942 by Fairfield's George Weising on Fairfield Beach.*

the possibility of attack. Most Fairfield people, while not eager for another war, believed the United States would be better advised to defend itself by providing material aid to those nations then at war with Germany and Japan than by retreating into itself. James Truslow Adams's endorsement of Roosevelt's plan to send Lend-Lease supplies to Great Britain met with more local favor than did Smith's work on behalf of America First.

Meanwhile the war and the talk of possible American involvement caused area factories to flourish, and the economy to grow. Bullard's and Handy & Harmon added to their facilities, and Bridgeport Molded Plastics and J. L. Lucas and Son, manufacturers of machine tools, moved into town. The Building Department inspected 350 new houses built in 1940 and 302 constructed in 1941. The Depression was not forgotten, but obviously it was now a thing of the past.

Despite the draft and Lend-Lease and the disaster plan, Fairfield, like the rest of the country, was taken totally by surprise when Japan attacked Pearl Harbor. The town worried about the safety of the thirteen local servicemen who were stationed at the base or at other vulnerable locations in the Pacific on December 7, 1941. It was also anxious about local security. The Police Department doubled its patrols at Fairfield factories, and the town meeting authorized $12,683 for the establishment of a town guard; $9000 was designated for the purchase of rifles, and the remainder for uniforms. The guards would protect factories and other vital locations, such as the Hemlock Reservoir. The Auto Ordnance Company of Bridgeport, a machine gun manufacturer, donated one of its products to the guards.

Opportunities for civilians to demonstrate their patriotism existed in abundance. Richard M. Brett became the chief air raid warden for Fairfield. Aline Kate Fox served on the national Victory Garden Advisory Committee, and Sidney Maruse, urging his neighbors to "Get in the Scrap," took charge of salvage collections in town. Grover Benton directed the airplane observation post on Mill Hill. And although he rarely heard anything but criticisms and complaints, Robert C. Flack deserved the town's praise and thanks for his impartial direction of the local rationing board. Zealous area horsemen even organized a cavalry unit "designed to wage guerilla warfare in case of emergencies."

But much more than the previous world conflict, World War II, was directed from Washington. The New Deal had encouraged federal agencies to begin to reproduce; World War II caused them to proliferate so rapidly that they completely engulfed the earlier growth. The government was everywhere. It established gasoline rationing as of March 12, 1942. It required landlords to list their properties with the Bridgeport Defense Rental Unit Collector. It made fuel oil customers register with the rationing board; users who consumed more than five thousand gallons of oil a year were compelled to switch to coal, no exceptions. The government demanded that automobile owners have their tires inspected to determine when new ones would be required. In February 1943 11,955 Fairfielders lined up to obtain the blue ration stamps needed to purchase canned goods and processed foods and the red stamps required for rationed meat. Although meat, like gasoline and fuel oil and housing, was in short supply, merchants were not free to charge all the traffic would bear; the Office of Price Administration began setting price ceilings on meat in April 1943. Landlords likewise had to contend with rent control. Despite all their complaining to Robert Flack, Fairfield residents generally tolerated these restrictions because they believed them necessary to defeat the Axis powers.

They also accepted the idea, although not very graciously, of allowing the federal government to build two hundred houses on seventy-two acres near Knapp's Highway. Residents thought the housing, which was originally to be occupied by Bridgeport defense workers, would foster social problems in town. The influx of workers from other areas of the country into southwestern Connecticut had already led to increases in juvenile delinquency, venereal disease, and divorce. Fairfield was reluctant to encourage more of the same.

Eventually the town accepted not only the houses near Knapp's Highway but another two hundred on Melville Avenue. But final acceptance came only after the Federal Housing Administration had agreed to pay Fairfield 14 percent of the rents collected in lieu of taxes and promised also that Fairfield people would receive priority in the assignment of the dwellings. By February 1942, the first thirty-eight families, eighteen of whom had been living in Fairfield, had moved into the project.

If housing was scarce during the war, employment opportunities were abundant. Jobs were going begging as government contracts poured into local defense producers. In an attempt to gain an edge on the competition, Chance-Vought of Stratford established a mobile employment office in Fairfield. Many Fairfield women had already taken jobs outside the home; it hoped to convince even more. The Chance-Vought representatives came to town prepared to demonstrate that "war work is not only easy but interesting as well."

The abundance of jobs meant, of course, good pay and general prosperity. Until the end of 1942, some consumer goods were still freely available. Fairfield people bought more than three hundred new cars in 1942 before American industry converted completely to defense production. Some house construction went on throughout the war, but the few houses that were built were small; materials were difficult to obtain. As consumer goods became unavailable, especially during the last three years of the war, a larger and larger share of the wages of Fairfield men and women went into savings.

Unfortunately war was more than defense jobs and government housing projects. War also meant death and destruction. This was brought home to Fairfield in May 1942, when the town learned that Lieutenant Owen Russell Fish, a pilot in the United States Army Air Corps, had been killed in the Far Eastern Theater on April 27. Fish was the first town resident to die in the war.

The bad news kept coming. By Memorial Day 1944, twenty-nine Fairfielders were known to have died in the war, fifteen were missing in action, and nine were either German or Japanese prisoners of war. More flags flew in Fairfield on June 6, 1944, than even on Memorial Day. June 6 was D-Day, the day the Allied forces opened a second front in Europe. Superficially the day was like any other, but just below the surface lingered a funereal presence as the town waited and worried about the men storming the beaches at Normandy. By the next Memorial Day, May 31, 1945, eighty-nine Fairfielders had given their lives.

Despite the increased loss of life, Memorial Day 1945 was easier to face than the commemoration of 1944 had been; at 9 A.M. on May 8, 1945, twenty-three days before Memorial Day, residents had gathered around their radios to listen to President Harry S. Truman announce that Germany had surrendered unconditionally. At Roger Ludlowe High School students and teachers packed the auditorium to hear the broadcast. The war in Europe was over.

Just a matter of days before the collapse of Germany, on April 18, 1945, a young Fairfield soldier—he was only twenty at the time—performed acts of heroism that so awed his commanders and their superiors and eventually the United States Congress that he was awarded the Congressional Medal of Honor. He was Michael J. Daly, who had left the United States Military Academy at West Point to enlist in the army as a private. The recipient of a battlefield commission and already the holder of a Silver Star, Daly was a captain on April 18 and was serving in the vicinity of Nuremberg. Under continuous fire for forty-eight hours and seeing no other way to allow his men to advance safely, Captain Daly left the safety of his company's position, and, alone and in the face of intense enemy fire, attacked and destroyed an antitank patrol and three enemy machine-gun positions. In August, while both he and his father, Colonel Paul Daly, a highly decorated soldier in both World War I and World War II, were recovering from wounds, Fairfielders learned what the boy from Hulls Farm Road had done. The information could not make them forget the horror of the war, but it did remind them that man could also be a noble creature.

The news of Daly's heroism made the celebrations of Japan's surrender even more jubilant. Fairfield's first outburst of joy and relief came on August 15 and was a wild and spontaneous affair during which residents burned an effigy of the Japanese premier, Tojo. The official ceremony occurred on September 1, and included a parade, a town party at Legion Field, and a giant snake dance down Reef Road. Behind all the festivities, however, lurked the town's grief over the 110 residents who had died in World War II.

Between Pearl Harbor and V-J Day, the war overshadowed events that might otherwise have been the focus of town attention. In the autumn of 1944, Fairfield was once again struck by a devastating hurricane, not as calamitous as that of 1938, but one of the worst of the century. The storm failed to fluster the Roger Ludlowe High School football team. Going into the final game of the season, against Bassick of Bridgeport, the Ludlowe players had not lost in nineteen games, a streak that began in 1942. Opponents had scored only thirteen points against them during the entire 1944 season. Roger Ludlowe maintained its string of victories, defeating Bassick 20-0 on Thanksgiving Day.

Probably the biggest local news of the war years involved John Ferguson, the first selectman since 1933. Until late in 1942, Ferguson's control of both the local Republican party and the town government seemed secure. He kept spending to a minimum and no detail was too small for his attention. But in 1942, he angered a significant element in both the party and the town by selling Hearthstone Hall, the old Walter B. Lashar estate, to the New England Province of the Jesuit Order. The Depression had destroyed Lashar, leading to the town's seizure of his home for nonpayment of taxes. At the time the Superior Court ordered the tax lien foreclosure in December 1941, Lashar owed $51,599 in back taxes and interest. The following year, Ferguson, eager to encourage the Jesuits' plan to establish a university in Fairfield, sold them the forty-four-room mansion and 104 acres for $62,500. Many residents complained that the price was too low, that Ferguson had given away the estate, and that he should have retained the property on the tax rolls. The idea of having mischievous college students in town dismayed some Fairfielders. And doubtless another source of the protest was the lingering anti-Catholicism that still existed in town. Little was said openly on the subject, but the idea of creating a bastion of Catholicism right next door to Oliver G. Jenning's former residence was more than some old and powerful Fairfield families could tolerate. The fact that Jennings's heirs sold part of their father's estate to the Jesuits a few months later failed to ease the resentment.

The sale of Hearthstone Hall made Ferguson vulnerable. Among those eager to see the first selectman destroyed was his former friend and political ally, Arthur J. Bennett, once again chief of police. Bennett would have been well advised to have expended less energy on town politics and paid more attention to the affairs of his department. Morale among the police was so low that one disgruntled officer, Thomas Shaughnessey, apparently attempted to coerce Melvin Cole, who was then under a felony indictment, to testify that Bennett had stolen a diamond ring from him. During a crucial meeting in Bridgeport where Cole was to sign a statement accusing Bennett of taking the ring, a fight broke out between Shaughnessey and Cole. The Bridgeport police were summoned, and Cole brought assault charges against the Fairfield policeman. For reasons that Ferguson found difficult to explain, he had accompanied Shaughnessey and Cole to Bridgeport on the night of the clandestine meeting.

Because of this incident and because of the residue of ill-will that had lasted from the sale of the Lashar estate to the future Fairfield University, the Republican Town Committee refused to nominate Ferguson again in 1943. He took his fight to the Republican caucus, which endorsed him; he then went on to win reelection despite his uncertain role in the Melvin Cole affair.

The Bridgeport City Court subsequently found Shaughnessey not guilty of the assault charges, and he resumed his position on the police force. But because of the vituperative squabbling among the police, the town meeting, on September 20, 1943, appointed a committee to investigate the department. The committee, chaired by Johnson Stoddard, eventually recommended the dismissal of Shaughnessey but was mild in its criticisms of Bennett. On the basis of the report, the Police Commission—which consisted of the three selectmen—heard specific charges against Shaughnessey, including charges that he had traded favors for money and that he had conspired with Cole to discredit Bennett. In December 1943, the three commissioners voted to dismiss Shaughnessey.

Next the Police Commission heard charges against Bennett, brought by First Selectman Ferguson. From throughout the town came demands that Ferguson, who was known to despise Bennett, disqualify himself from these proceedings. He refused and at the conclusion of a closed hearing, voted, along with his Republican colleague, in favor of Bennett's dismissal. In January 1944, Bennett left the department.

Jeanne R. Brennan, editor of the *Fairfield News*, denounced Ferguson's role in the Bennett case. Even the Republican Town Committee, noting that Ferguson had initiated the case that he later decided, deplored and condemned Ferguson's role. Objective observers concluded that Bennett had been indiscreet in his political involvements and less than effective in maintaining morale within the Police Department but did not deserve the treatment he received at the hands of Ferguson. For Ferguson's part, his days as first selectman clearly were numbered. In September 1945, he announced that he would not be a candidate for reelection.

Clifford L. Johnson, who replaced Ferguson, oversaw Fairfield's initial adjustment to the postwar world. The task was not easy. As had been the case after World War I, layoffs and strikes followed the cessation of hostilities. The strikes at General Electric and at Bryant Electric in Bridgeport forced many unemployed Fairfield workers to seek the assistance of the town's Public Welfare Department. The strikes and the cutbacks were of shorter duration after the Second World War than they had been after the first. Accumulated savings and pent-up consumer demand—demand that frequently went all the way back to the Depression, when householders first began deferring major purchases—created a market for consumer goods that eased the transition to a peacetime economy. Once the initial period of readjustment had passed, the real problem was one of supplying the goods that people sought. Residents wanted new cars, for instance, but could only look on with envy when Bridgeport automobile dealers began receiving shipments in Fairfield in July 1946; the first cars to arrive had been reserved months before. Demand would exceed supply for two or three years.

The biggest postwar shortage in Fairfield was the shortage of homes. Building resumed right after the war. In early September, Carl Anderson announced plans to erect two hundred homes on Beach and Fern streets. Similar announcements quickly followed, but still many veterans returned home to find housing unavailable. The town began looking for property on which to construct veterans' housing in June 1946 and in October announced that it was establishing a Housing Authority to solve the veterans' housing

*The original members of the Fairfield Police Department organized
in 1930, in front of their Reef Road headquarters.*

crisis. In March 1947, Elwood Randolph, chairman of the authority, asked for bids to construct fifty four-room houses for veterans on lower Reef Road. The Connecticut Housing Authority gave its approval to the project in June, and in November the first families began moving in.

In all, 522 houses were built in Fairfield in 1947, most of them on Jennings Road and in the South Pine Creek, Mill Plain, and Fairfield beach areas. But these new homes failed to ease the problem. Rental housing was impossible to find. Social workers reported in October 1948 that sixty-eight town families had to be separated because they had been evicted and were unable to find quarters that would allow them to live together. Another 479 new houses in 1948 left the problem unresolved.

During the postwar years, Fairfield was inundated with newcomers. Between 1945 and 1960, the population jumped from 25,812 to 46,183, a 79 percent increase. What was happening was hardly peculiar to Fairfield. The country was in the midst of a mass migration to the suburbs. In retrospect, the reasons for the migration are clear. Between 1945 and 1960, almost 60,000,000 babies were born in the United States, most of them to veterans and their brides. Many of these newly formed families were unenthusiastic about living in Bridgeport or some other city. World War II had caused an influx of workers from various parts of the United States and the Caribbean into the nation's industrial cities, making them less attractive to many young families. Large numbers

*Aerial view of the triangle of Kuhn's Corner at the intersection of Tunxis Hill Road and Black Rock Turnpike shows the effects of the post World War II housing boom.*

of these new workers were black, some were Hispanic, and they had, many whites contended, a deleterious effect on public safety and public education. Places like Fairfield, whose black population was only .7 percent, seemed an ideal refuge.[1]

People were not only fleeing what they perceived to be increasingly undesirable cities but were also following a dream, the American dream of owning a single-family house complete with lawn, garage, and shrubs. The fecund postwar generation could afford to pursue this dream because the United States government made home ownership vastly more possible by creating FHA and VA mortgages, small down-payment mortgages written by private lenders but insured by the federal government. These programs opened suburban communities, like Fairfield, to people who otherwise might have had to resign themselves to an apartment in some city. The rapidly expanding national economy, which grew more between 1945 and 1970 than it had between the time Roger Ludlow arrived in Boston and 1945, also fostered the migration, as did technological and educational changes that created more white-collar than blue-collar jobs by 1956.

New people, houses, and automobiles arrived in town at a furious rate. On an average, the school system had to absorb six hundred more students each year during this period. In a typical year, almost as many new houses as additional students appeared; 3619 more homes existed in town in 1955 than in 1948. Cars materialized even more rapidly than did either students or houses; between 1948 and 1955, the number of cars grew from 7206 to 16,565, an increase of almost 130 percent.

Most of the population growth resulted from the movement to Fairfield of people who lived in Bridgeport or who had recently taken jobs there. Natural increase accounted

*Fairfield: the biography of a community*

for only about one-third of the growth. Twentieth-century Fairfield had exchanged places with nineteenth-century Bridgeport, now drawing away many of that city's most talented citizens just as Bridgeport had once taken many of its best and brightest. A variety of ethnic groups came to Fairfield, in particular Hungarians, their migration encouraged by the Hungarian Revolution of 1956 and urban renewal in west Bridgeport, an area that had once been derisively called "Hunky Town." One Bridgeport group that barely participated in this movement was the city's black population. Discouraged by the high cost of Fairfield real estate and by "gentlemen's agreements" among real estate agents who were afraid of offending their white clientele by encouraging minority buyers, blacks stayed away.

With the influx of population came new institutions. In 1954 Jacob Mellitz, Emmanuel Zimmer, and Hyman Berson formed the Fairfield Jewish Community Group. In 1957, the group purchased 3.5 acres on Fairfield Woods Road, and after 318 years, Fairfield finally became the home of a synagogue, Congregation Beth-El. Five years later, a second synagogue, Congregation Ahavath Achim, was dedicated by its Orthodox members; like many of its congregation, it had moved from Bridgeport. The recent establishment of these two synagogues indicates how small the town's Jewish population was until after World War II. The founding of St. Pius X Roman Catholic Church by the Bridgeport Diocese in 1955 acknowledged Fairfield's growing Catholic population. Located at the base of exclusive Greenfield Hill, the church served a well-educated, affluent congregation. Aware of the cravings of many suburban persons, especially corporate transients, for some substantial and consistent element within their often-rootless lives, the New York Conference of the Methodist Church created Faith Grace United Methodist Church in 1956. Unlike Congregation Beth-El or Congregation Ahavath Achim or St. Pius X, with their heavy emphasis upon tradition, Grace United Methodist found a majority of its members coming from other denominations, attracted to the church by a clergy that catered to the particular needs of suburban people.

The arrival in town of first Fairfield College Preparatory School and then Fairfield University was another indication that institutions as well as people preferred to be in the suburbs. The success of these schools undoubtedly encouraged Bishop Walter W. Curtis of the Bridgeport Diocese to locate both Notre Dame High School and Sacred Heart University in Fairfield rather than in Bridgeport itself.

Commercial and industrial establishments also sought out Fairfield. The late 1940s and the 1950s witnessed the renovation of Southport center, the construction of large shopping centers at the corner of Post Road and South Benson Road and on Black Rock Turnpike near Stillson Road, and the opening of new retail establishments all up and down the Post Road. Even the old McGarry blacksmith shop at the corner of Post Road and Sanford Street had to give way for a modern retail building. In 1960, 421 commercial establishments existed in town. Forty-seven factories were also operating then, although, relative to the total number of persons employed in town, a greater percentage worked in factories in 1953 than at any other point before or since. By 1960 the Alcoa plant had closed, but its facilities had become the property of Exide, the Electric Storage Battery Company of Philadelphia. By then also, Sturm, Ruger & Company was producing firearms in Southport.

All of this growth would have created chaos had not the town begun planning for expansion. The Town Plan Commission had existed since 1919 and the Zoning

*Congregation Ahavath Achim on Stratfield Road, a modern orthodox temple
built in 1958 to serve the growing family population in the area.*

Commission since 1924. During World War II, Walter Binger of Greenfield Hill, an engineer, strongly advocated the establishment of a postwar plan for Fairfield. To his voice was added that of the Post-War Planning Council; it listed a master plan and a sewer system as the town's greatest priorities. Herbert P. Elton, chairman of the council, pushed the idea of a plan, but C. Cameron Clark had taken his place before it became a reality. On December 7, 1948, at the Pequot Library, the council presented a master plan prepared by Technical Planning Associates, Incorporated, of New York to the public. Although never officially adopted by the town, the plan of 1948, together with the decisions of the Zoning Commission, provided enough guidance to permit vast growth without creating chaos. Neighborhoods, recreational facilities, and open spaces were sufficiently well preserved to allow future leaders to guarantee their permanence.

Town government also had to expand and become more modern. First Selectman Clifford L. Johnson, who had strongly supported the master plan of 1948, recognized the need for revision of the town charter. In August 1946, he and the other selectmen appointed a seven-member Charter Revision Commission, and just three months later, Norman King Parsells, chairman of the commission, presented that body's report. It advocated the establishment of a Representative Town Meeting (RTM) where delegates, each representing 250 voters, would make decisions that had all the authority of those previously made by the town meeting. The revised charter would also establish the position of first selectman as full time and would empower that officer to sit as an ex officio member on all town boards. In addition the commission urged that the Zoning Commission and the Town Plan Commission be combined into a single entity. Encouraged by the League of Women Voters to approve the revised charter, Fairfield voters confirmed the new document. The General Assembly and Governor James

McConaughy then gave their endorsement, and on June 13, 1947 the town again affirmed the changes, this time in a referendum. The new charter was a reality.

The biggest problem facing the town under its new charter was the growing school population. The town's educational establishment in 1945 consisted of a high school and three elementary schools. As its population soared, it added nine new elementary schools, a new junior high school, and a new high school. The school-age population was increasing much more rapidly than the population generally. Between 1950 and 1960, the total population increased by 51 percent while the school-age group grew by 91 percent. The school system enrolled 3669 students in 1945 and 9220 in 1960. The cost of education was growing at an annual rate of about 18 percent. With the notable exception of Vincent L. Busetti of the Fairfield Taxpayers League and Susan Deri of the Fairfield Property Owners League, town residents generally supported the recommendations of the Board of Education and the Board of Finance about expanding the school system during these years. Quality of education was one of the factors that continued to make Fairfield attractive to prospective residents.

In addition to building schools, the town was busy constructing roads. Subdividing more land created the need for more roads. Most of this construction caused no controversy, but one road construction proposal continued to divide the town. This was the question of an additional parkway entrance. First Selectman Dimill Kinnie, who replaced Johnson in 1949, called for an entrance at Redding Road. Once again the Greenfield Hill Improvement Association marshaled its forces, and once again the association demonstrated exactly how much muscle it had: no new entrance was added.

More alarming than even the original parkway plan was the state's 1951 proposal to build a truckway through Fairfield. G. Albert Hill, State Highway Commissioner, was determined to see a six-lane highway located along the shoreline of Connecticut; he believed the plan was essential to relieve the congested traffic along United States Route 1. The proposal threw Fairfield County into a frenzy of protest, but Hill refused to retreat. Instead, he pushed even more relentlessly. By August 1952, state representatives had already begun buying land. Their first purchase in Fairfield was the estate of Anna C. Buckingham on Mill Hill Road. Instead of convincing the opposition of the inevitability of the road, the purchase of the Buckingham property generated even more antagonism. When the General Assembly's Bridges and Roads Committee met in February 1953, it encountered a raft of bills designed to strip Hill of the power to continue the project. But before the month was out, Hill and his supporters had carried the day; the legislature left his power intact. In March Governor John Davis Lodge ordered Hill to begin engineering work on the truckway route.

Fairfield, with other shoreline towns, continued to fight throughout the spring. The RTM called upon Governor Lodge in May 1952 to halt work until a special commission could study several alternative routes. Mrs. D. Verner Smythe and Norman K. Parsells led a delegation of Fairfield people to Hartford to question Hill and Harry W. Lochner, the engineer who had established the route that Hill ultimately selected. The governor rejected the RTM suggestion outright, and Hill and Lochner politely listened to Smythe, Parsells, and the others before sending them on their way. The truckway was a reality, a fait accompli.

Actual construction began in September 1955. Now part of the largest public works project in the history of the United States, the Eisenhower Administration's interstate highway system, and now called the Connecticut Turnpike rather than the Shoreline Truckway, the route cost the town of Fairfield 153 houses, 570 building lots, 3 commercial buildings, 115 other buildings, and more or less 30 acres of undeveloped land. Built at a cost of $464 million dollars, the highway opened on January 1, 1958.

In the years after World War II, Fairfield needed sewers even more urgently than it did highways. First Selectman Johnson revived the Sewer Commission in April 1946. Originally created in 1929, it had been defunct since the early thirties. But Fairfield could no longer procrastinate. At the time the commission again became active, 80 percent of Fairfield's population of almost thirty thousand lived on only 10 percent on the total area of the town. In January 1947, the town received an initial grant of $128,850 from the Federal Bureau of Community Facilities, and in August the firm of Bowe, Albertson and Associates began designing a sanitary system. The project was vastly more expensive than it would have been twenty years earlier. In July 1949, Governor Chester Bowles signed legislation allowing the town to borrow beyond its legal limit in order to install sewers. The RTM then authorized the selectmen to borrow $1.6 million dollars. This was enough money to start construction, which incidentally did not actually begin until August 1950. Years would pass and millions of dollars would be spent before even most of the congested part of Fairfield would have both storm water and sanitary sewers.

Other changes came more rapidly. The town government again outgrew the Town Hall; in 1954, a two-story addition on the rear of the building provided space for the town clerk, the vault, and other town offices. Through these years, the work of the Town Plan and Zoning Commission never ceased, and the operation of the town government became more expensive and more complex. In 1947, the grand list amounted to about $61 million; by 1960 it had reached $252 million. Taxes collected in 1947 were about $1.8 million as compared to the nearly $7 million collected in 1960. The per capita costs of government expanded almost 150 percent during this period, largely because of the increased costs of education and debt service.

But the years between the end of the war and 1960 were not all years of work. There was fun as well. The composer Richard Rodgers lived in town at the time, and the shows that he organized to support the Fairfield Community Chest would have made much larger communities glow with pride. Sports continued to attract the town's attention. In the mid-fifties, Roger Ludlowe was a basketball power in the state. The student athletes from Ludlowe went to the New England Basketball Championship Tournament in March 1955 and, after a series of heart-stopping victories over some of the perennial basketball powers in the region, returned to Fairfield the champions, much to the delight of more than six thousand fans who welcomed them home. In 1960 Fairfield Prep won the state football title; and the following year, an undefeated and untied Roger Ludlowe team repeated the accomplishment. Andrew Warde High School, which opened in September 1956, had a difficult tradition to follow.

For those who found sports boring, there were other things to do. One could rant against the wild music the young people were enjoying, or complain about plans for the fluoridation of the water. Ira Follette Warner, director of the League of Connecticut Citizens Opposed to Fluoridation, tried to unseat Governor John Dempsey because of his support for the idea. More constructive was a program involving many Fairfield children to test a new antipolio vaccine devised by a then obscure physician named Jonas Salk.

*Fairfield: the biography of a community*

*Aerial view of Connecticut Turnpike construction in 1955. Mill River
is in the center and U. S. 1 in the extreme lower right corner.*

The Cold War was a source of concern and a subject of debate. United States
Senator William B. Benton of Sasco Hill tried to convince his neighbors that the so-called
"fall of China" had been encouraged more by the ineptitude of Generalissimo Chiang
Kai-shek than by Secretary of State Dean Acheson's lack of skill. Herbert A. Philbrick,
the author of *I Led Three Lives*, came to Roger Ludlowe High School to make sure that
Fairfielders realized the extent of Communist infiltration in the United States.

When war broke out in Korea in June 1950, residents hoped that it would end
quickly; after all, it was only a police action and not a genuine war. They came to understand how real it was when news arrived that William Bok, Jr., had become the town's
first casualty of the fighting. Grover Benton, who had watched for enemy aircraft during
World War II, became Fairfield's Civil Defense director. In the event that the limited
war in Korea became a general holocaust, he wanted Fairfield to be prepared.

The town's Republicans had problems choosing between Dwight D. Eisenhower
and Robert A. Taft in 1952, but once Ike became the nominee, he had little difficulty
swamping Adlai Stevenson in Fairfield. Eisenhower ended the war in Korea, and then
he and his Secretary of State, John Foster Dulles, set about protecting the United States
by threatening massive retaliation. Fairfield became the location of a NIKE missile site,
a bit of the Cold War right in everyone's back yard. Also to be found in some residents'
backyards were fallout shelters. A prefabricated refuge that would accommodate six
persons could be purchased locally for only $495. A shelter and a couple of $6.98

*World War II and Its Aftermath*

fourteen-day survival kits might make any family feel safer during those trying times of "brinkmanship."

Fairfield by 1960 differed vastly from what it had been twenty years before. More of everything, except undeveloped land, existed by then. Cars had insinuated themselves into every aspect of life. Fairfield men and women were more likely to work either in Bridgeport, where about 55 percent were employed, or in Fairfield, where another 24 percent made their livelihoods, than anyplace else. But thanks to the automobile, some residents drove great distances to their work places; growing numbers were heading in the direction of Stamford. They could also drive far afield to shop. Per capita retail sales in Fairfield were far below the state average while per capita income was well above the Connecticut figure, proving that Fairfielders were trading elsewhere.

Municipal boundaries grew meaningless as Fairfield became part of a "drive-in culture." The greatest physical change that came to town during the postwar years was the construction of the Connecticut Turnpike. The arrival of shopping centers and of drive-in restaurants was further evidence of what was happening. Before many more years would pass, Fairfield would even contain a drive-in church, Trinity Baptist Church, which stood as close to a turnpike entrance as any fast food establishment and which intentionally drew its congregation from a large area. The automobile, operating in tandem with both life in suburbia and the components of the communications revolution—the radio, motion pictures, and television—was forcing Fairfielders to become less aware of their town, more inclined toward privatism—that is, the tendency to center life inside the house rather than in the community—and more attuned to the standards of an increasingly monolithic civilization.

## NOTES

1. Anyone interested in Fairfield's development since 1945 will want to consult Arthur L. Anderson, *Divided We Stand: Institutional Religion as a Reflection of Pluralism and Integration in America* (Dubuque, Iowa, 1978). Carefully conceived and executed, Anderson's book, which is about Fairfield, has been of great value to me. Kenneth L. Jackson, *Crabgrass Frontier: The Suburbanization of the United States* (New York, 1985), is the best historical study of that important topic.

# The Sullivan Years

---

THE YEAR WAS 1936, and John J. Sullivan, a newcomer to Fairfield, was overseeing the installation of a sign above the flower shop that he was about to open on Post Road. As he watched to see that the sign was placed where he wanted, an automobile drew up to the curb and a woman emerged. She spoke precisely, but her meaning was initially unclear to Sullivan. "That is a hard name," she said, indicating the sign, which read "Sullivan's Flower Shop." Realizing she was not making herself understood, she repeated: "That is a hard name. A business with that name has little chance of success in Fairfield." Sullivan now realized that her reference was to his Irish name. "Wouldn't some other name do better?" she asked.

"I have no other name," he replied, "and that one has served both me and my family well. In fact," he continued, "I'd rather boil in hot oil than change it." Neither participant in that conversation could have guessed that for nearly a quarter of the twentieth century the name Sullivan would be better known than any other in town, would, in fact, become almost synonymous with the town.[1]

Sullivan came to Fairfield via Salem, Massachusetts, the University of Massachusetts, and North Kingston, Rhode Island. His first trip to town occurred in 1935, to see his brother, David, an engineer at the DuPont plant. John Sullivan liked Fairfield so much that he decided to make it his home. Eventually the town decided it liked him well enough to make him its first selectman, a position he held for twenty-four years.

The son of parents unable to agree about politics—his mother was an Al Smith Democrat and his father a Hoover Republican—Sullivan was a Democrat. And the process of getting a Democrat elected in Fairfield was, to say the least, a complicated one. John J. Fitzpatrick had begun to revive the Democratic party in the 1930s, before he became involved in state and national politics; he eventually served as Governor Robert Hurley's campaign manager, chairman of the Connecticut State Liquor Commission, and collector of the United States Department of Internal Revenue. After Fitzpatrick's departure, the party languished under the direction of Nicholas J. Phelan. Phelan was more interested

*The late Mary A. Katona, town clerk for twenty-one years during the Sullivan era and State Representative to the General Assembly.*

in distributing patronage than in winning control of the town government; whenever a Democrat won the governor's office in Hartford, Phelan enjoyed the privilege of dispensing positions on the Fairfield Town Court. All during the late 1940s and most of the 1950s, the Democrats put forward one weak ticket after another. But Phelan's control of the Democratic party was complete; he ran it with an iron hand.

After the establishment of the Representative Town Meeting, several bright young Democrats, some of them lawyers, decided to run for places on that body. Their experience on the RTM convinced them that if they were to develop any substantive legislative program, they had to have the support of their local party. Unfortunately Phelan had little interest in what they were doing; he saw them only as a challenge to his domination of the party. Once they realized this, these young Democrats—already called the Young Turks—decided to challenge Phelan's rule. In April 1958, in the wake of a town-wide primary, they unseated him and took over the Democratic committee. The not-so-young but politically astute Ralph Garofalo became the party chairman. In the fall of 1958, the Young Turks again demonstrated how effective their organization was when Democratic gubernatorial candidate Abraham Ribicoff carried the town, when John T. Fitzpatrick, one of the original Turks, was elected Judge of Probate, and when Mary Katona and James E. Murray III, both Democrats, went to the General Assembly from Fairfield.

In 1959 the new Democrats had to select candidates for the town elections. Having listened to the arguments of Fitzpatrick, Garofalo, John Darcy, and others, the town committee nominated John J. Sullivan and Robert G. Lee as first and second selectmen. Phelan and his cronies refused to accept their candidacy, however, and, after deciding

*Fairfield: the biography of a community*

to endorse Town Judge John H. Norton and Richard F. Root, announced that they would insist upon a primary election. Sullivan, Lee, and the other Young Turks were ready. They initiated "Operation Doorbell," during which Sullivan and Lee personally met almost half the six thousand Democrats in town. In the September primary, the two handily defeated Norton, Root, and the old guard.

The next step was to overcome Dimill Kinnie, the incumbent first selectman, who had held that office for almost a decade. Kinnie, a bright, articulate, and aggressive politician, had made himself vulnerable by attacking increases in the school budget, an unpopular position in education-conscious Fairfield, and by seeming to have neglected his office while buying and moving houses that were in the path of the Connecticut Turnpike. On the other hand, Sullivan and Lee appeared to be the perfect combination. Although possessed of little government experience, Sullivan was politically curious, had spent hundreds of hours attending various board and commission meetings, and enjoyed a memory that allowed him to recall specific details when others could remember only generalities. Lee was an ideal partner, an intellectual, a man who was compatible with Sullivan on the issues, and a representative of the town's Protestant establishment. Some voters would take Sullivan in order to bring Lee to office, and others were willing to accept Lee so long as Sullivan was first selectman.

Taking advantage of the momentum that they had developed during the primary, Sullivan and Lee won the general election. Not since 1910 had a Democrat been first selectman in Fairfield. As events would prove, the Young Turks had managed a political revolution, probably the most significant one in the town's entire history. The revolution resulted not merely from the election of a Democrat. Much more important, it came because the squabble in the Democratic party and the elections of 1958 and 1959 brought to important town offices persons who had strong ethnic ties, such as Hungarian-American Mary Katona, and Catholics. John J. Sullivan was the first Catholic to hold Fairfield's highest elective office. The revolution represented not only the return of a viable two-party system; it represented a widening of political participation in town.

The two Democratic selectmen brought a carefully conceived political philosophy to Town Hall. Sullivan understood that the main purpose of town government was to furnish services. But in addition he was aware that "in a fast growing community like Fairfield, it's not enough to provide for the present; we must also plan ahead to meet future needs."[2] He would emphasize planning more than any first selectman before him, even the farsighted Clifford Anderson. Sullivan and Lee were the first to prepare financial blueprints for the town—fiscal five-year plans. The first selectman wanted to see the community grow in balance; he refused to neglect one part of town for another or one segment of its economic or political structure for another. He viewed the town as a whole, a single entity.

He wanted to modernize town government by emphasizing the role of experts, the experts often being the heads of the various town departments. He also took advantage of the talents of his running mates, Lee initially and later James Eldridge, a successful executive at Sikorsky Aircraft. Sullivan insisted that all requests for funds come to him directly so that the administration could present a single budget to the Board of Finance. He made adjustments in the department petitions but always allowed the various directors to keep their original requests in the public record, so that if he mistakenly cut an item he, and not the department head, would be held responsible.

Sullivan believed that there should be one place in town government where the buck stopped, and he wanted it to be in the office of the first selectman. This aspect of his political philosophy was probably best demonstrated in 1961 when he challenged the volunteer firemen, a formidable force in town, over the issue of whether the fire commissioners should represent the individual fire companies or whether they should, as he believed, be responsible to and appointed by the selectmen. If he was ultimately responsible for the well-being of the town, he felt, he should have a fire commission that was answerable to him. Before he brought the matter to the town's attention, the various companies had chosen the commissioners, and the commissioners could use their budget as they saw fit. The issue went to a referendum, and Sullivan won.

On April 19, 1961, the Town Plan and Zoning Commission adopted a comprehensive plan to serve as a guide for future planning and zoning actions. The plan urged changes in the development of certain residential areas; the wetlands between Reef Road and South Pine Creek Road, for example, should be converted from residential lands to public lands that could be used for refuse disposal and as recreational and open lands. The plan recommended the establishment of three historic areas, on Old Post Road, in Greenfield Hill, and in Southport. It advocated the redevelopment of the State Street Extension area, an area where industry and housing met, and the Pine Creek Avenue section, a neighborhood crowded with summer cottages and inadequate waste disposal systems.

The 1961 plan also recommended ways to inject vitality into Fairfield's business center and into industrial development, industry then paying about 9 percent of all town taxes and occupying only 1 percent of the town's lands. New office and research areas should be encouraged, especially on a site near Hull's Highway and Mill Hill Road.

One aspect of the plan that especially appealed to Sullivan was the section that urged the town to buy additional land for open spaces. This was an idea first suggested by Andrew Huntington in the 1930s and kept alive in the 1940s and 1950s by Cameron Clark. As a trained horticulturalist, Sullivan understood that, if the town procrastinated about acquiring these lands, Fairfield could become, as the plan stated, "just another denatured blob of aging tract houses similar to large areas of Long Island and New Jersey." He also appreciated the recommendation to buy ten or twelve additional acres in the area of the Town Hall, including the Sun Tavern, the Warner estate, and the Rice estate; this would provide room for badly needed additional town office space and, by enhancing the town's identity, would "stave off the relative oblivion of becoming just another bedroom for Bridgeport."[3]

Except for the last four or five pages of the document, which suggested how Fairfield could pay for these recommended changes, Sullivan liked the Comprehensive Plan. He and Lee, he believed, could handle the finances better than the planners could. He set to work to make the plan a reality.

He had to make concessions from time to time. The 240-acre research and development park off Hull's Highway, for example, was abandoned. Neighboring residents, fearing that the park might degenerate into an industrial area, fought the concept so vigorously that in September 1963 Sullivan suggested the idea be eliminated from the plan.

On a few issues, Sullivan's opponents beat him. The King's Highway Urban Renewal Project was an example. The area had a history of mixed residential com-

*First Selectman John J. Sullivan in front of the historic Fairfield town hall.*

mercial, and industrial development. In 1958 the Connecticut Turnpike had cut through the heart of the section. The 67 acres of the project area included 54 industrial and commercial structures and 73 residential buildings. Of the slightly more than 100 dwelling units in the area, 92 were in "substandard buildings." Renewal would require relocating 45 businesses and almost 100 families, but the area was a prime prospect for redevelopment. In May 1962, the RTM appropriated $190,000 to survey the section and to develop renewal plans. The Sullivan administration hoped to obtain most of the money for the project from the federal government.

At first the project proceeded according to plan. In February 1964, the Fairfield Redevelopment Agency's Housing Authority set to work trying to relocate the families from the area. Then, in September, the federal government approved the agency's loan and grant application for $5.9 million. It seemed as if finally Fairfield's most blighted neighborhood was in for an overdue refurbishing.

But in early 1965, Fairfielders for Property Rights—Kenneth Adolphson, chairman—began to voice its opposition to the project. Adolphson's group represented businessmen in the area who preferred a plan of self-improvement over the scheme that Sullivan had put forth. In February the RTM approved the renewal plan and authorized $614,000 to get it started. Fairfielders for Property Rights responded by circulating a petition to force a referendum. Emotions were high in town by the middle of February

*The Sullivan Years*

as the referendum neared. "Sullivan and the radical left Democrats intend to bring crime, public housing, and urban renewal to Fairfield," declared the leaders of the well-organized and well-financed campaign against redevelopment.[4] They hoped to take advantage of local concerns about Washington's apparent increasing involvement in Fairfield, concerns that in 1963 caused Selectman Homer Cudmore to contend that "the current administration is merely the suckers on the tenacles of the octopus that is Washington." The Republican Town Committee, agreeing with Cudmore and hoping to cripple Sullivan, joined with Adolphson and his supporters. When the ballots were counted, renewal and Sullivan were the losers. More than 8000 voters opposed the plan, and fewer than 4000 endorsed it. Republican Town Chairman Peter Ball, reluctant to underestimate the importance of the vote, stated that "this may make a turning point throughout the country against federal interference in private rights and stimulate people toward self-help programs."[5]

Several efforts to revive the scheme fizzled. The self-help program about which the Fairfielders for Property Rights and Peter Ball spoke so positively proved to be only rhetoric. The area remained "an industrial mess." In 1985 Fairfield Economic Development Director Stephen Chipman targeted it once again for redevelopment.

In 1975 Sullivan had to abandon a $3 million recreational center that his administration planned for Tunxis Hill. As had been the case with the King's Highway renewal project, the RTM approved the Tunxis Hill center, but then a move developed to submit the whole question to a town-wide referendum. Many Fairfield residents feared that such a center located that close to Bridgeport would attract large numbers of unsavory urban characters. Although opponents of the center failed to defeat the idea in a referendum, Sullivan decided that they had enough votes to convince him that the plan really alarmed many residents. He asked the RTM to rescind its earlier approval.

Sullivan-endorsed attempts at charter revision also failed during his years. In 1967 T. F. Gilroy Daly chaired a Charter Revision Commission that urged Fairfield's voters to replace the Board of Selectmen with a mayor. Although those Fairfielders who bothered to come to the polls embraced the revision by more than 4 to 1, the proposal failed because it did not win the approval of 15 percent of the voters, as required by law. The following year another Charter Revision Commission, this one chaired by Robert G. Lee, made a similar recommendation; it also came to nought, and the same fate terminated the efforts of a 1970 revision commission, again headed by Daly.

But during his years in office, Sullivan won more battles than he lost, including a dozen elections. The election of 1961 was a major victory. Not only did he win the largest plurality in the history of Fairfield, but he also watched his fellow Democrats win control of the Board of Finance for the first time, and he celebrated Mary Katona's first election as town clerk. Because of her political wisdom and her influence within Fairfield's Hungarian community, she was as great an asset to him as were Robert G. Lee and James Eldridge.

The 1965 election was also an important one. Stewart McKinney, who later served in the United States Congress, contested Sullivan's hold as first selectman. A strong campaigner, McKinney was popular in Fairfield and had abundant financial resources behind him. Sullivan had been under fire for allowing the construction of apartments in town—another aspect of the 1961 Comprehensive Plan. Republicans denounced this "deliberate attempt to change Fairfield into a different and less desirable place to live." Despite these allegations, Sullivan beat McKinney by nine hundred votes.

The first selectman prevailed in policy battles as well. He managed to implement proposal after proposal from the 1961 Comprehensive Plan. Beginning in March 1965, the Town Plan and Zoning Commission examined in greater detail certain recommendations from the plan through a grant from the Housing and Home Finance Agency, and Sullivan, with considerable support in the now partisan RTM, accelerated his efforts. He appointed George O. Pratt and the other members of the Fairfield Historic District Commission. They began their duties in May 1964, by which time one historic district already existed in town, the Old Post Road Historic District, established in 1963. The commission added two others in 1966, one in Greenfield Hill and one in Southport. In September 1965, the RTM approved $370,000 to begin construction on the South Pine Creek Recreational Park, another step in the town's program to acquire and convert to public use the undeveloped land in that area. During the 1970s, Fairfield restored a large part of the Pine Creek salt marsh.

The idea of the Historic Civic Center was born before Sullivan's tenure began. In January 1957, the Town Plan and Zoning Commission recommended the idea to the selectmen. The concept found its way into the 1961 Comprehensive Plan. But it was Sullivan who made the plan a program. He oversaw the acquisition of the Burr Mansion from the Warner estate in 1962; the mansion served as a town office building until 1979, when it became a meetingplace for cultural and civic organizations. He also bought the Sun Tavern, obtained in 1978, and moved the Old Academy from its site next to St. Paul's Church, thus permitting the church's expansion and at the same time enhancing a civic complex of public and quasi-public buildings. Independence Hall, a town office building constructed in 1979, relieved much of the pressure on existing town facilities and became the fourth building in the center, a 21.5-acre tract that preserved a sense of the town's past despite its recent growth.

The acquisition of open spaces began in 1961 and continued through Sullivan's tenure. In 1965 the Town Plan and Zoning Commission issued the town's first Open Space Plan, and the Fairfield Conservation Commission began its search for six hundred acres of open spaces. The following year the RTM authorized the purchase of 264 acres in the Hoyden's Hill section. The price was $750,000, but Fairfield convinced the United States Department of Housing and Urban Development to contribute half that amount. The Sullivan administration bought 119 acres at Lake Mohegan in 1967 for $1.3 million. HUD's reluctance to direct more of its limited funds to Fairfield just a year after the Hoyden's Hill grant prompted Sullivan to begin looking for other sources of funding. The Interior Department's Bureau of Outdoor Recreation proved to be helpful. The first selectman's success with federal agencies was so dramatic that *Open Space Action*, a publication of the Open Space Action Institute, featured an article about Sullivan entitled "Grantsmanship: the Game and How to Play It." The article concluded that his success came because he was not simply after available money: "He is after it because it will help to buy what he believes in."

Sullivan, the horiculturist, understood the wisdom of dealing in tandem with flood control and open spaces. For this reason, he sought open spaces along the town's rivers. In the Mill River Valley, he eventually acquired lands at Lake Mohegan, at the Cascades, on the flood plain at Perry's Mill, and opposite Riverside Park. The result was both a green belt that extended from Southport far into the interior of town and, once the Mill River Valley Sewer Program was in place, a system to prevent the flooding of the river. During his administration, approximately twelve-hundred acres of land were acquired for open spaces.

The federal government helped with sewers as well as with open spaces. By being prepared to apply for funds as soon as they were available, Fairfield again obtained a disproportionately large share of the money. During the 1960s, it committed more than $16 million to its sanitary sewer system; almost $4 million was recovered from state and federal grants and about $11 million through assessments on benefited properties. The Mill River Valley Sewer Extension Program cost more than $19 million, less than $5 million of which had to be financed by the town. Almost 98 percent of the heavily populated areas of Fairfield had sanitary sewers by the end of Sullivan's administration.

Because Sullivan wanted to leave Fairfield's physical plant in good order when he returned to private life, he committed the same type of energy to road repair and school construction and maintenance. Between 1959 and 1983, every school in town was either extensively rehabilitated or replaced.

Even with federal help, these programs cost Fairfield taxpayers millions of dollars. Part of the cost was covered by the growth of the grand list. In 1959 it amounted to less than $250 million; by 1983 it had grown to about $1 billion. The single biggest increase came as a result of the General Electric Company's decision to locate its corporate headquarters in Fairfield. In 1971 GE bought slightly more than one hundred acres on Easton Turnpike near the Merritt Parkway. The company was able to obtain necessary zoning changes by paying careful attention to the concerns of its neighbors. Its plan was to create a corporate campus; all parking was underground or hidden. It also announced that it intended to donate twenty-nine acres to the open spaces program. The twenty-nine acres included the Cascades, one of the most beautiful locations in southwestern Connecticut. On August 12, 1974, the headquarters opened, and was formally dedicated two months later. GE, one of the ten largest corporations in the country, became Fairfield's most important taxpayer.

Like GE, the Exxon Corporation, decided in the 1970s to move from New York to a suburban location. Fairfield attracted Exxon's attention. In 1977, the company announced that it would move its corporate headquarters to a site near Black Rock Turnpike and the Merritt Parkway. In this instance, neighborhood opposition, led by the Zoning Preservation Committee, a group with strong ties to town Republicans, fought the Exxon move so vigorously that the company decided to abandon its plans and eventually found a home in Darien.

The Sullivan programs that were too large to be supported through the annual budget necessitated borrowing. During his first year in office, Fairfield had a bonded debt of approximately $15.5 million, which equalled 7.4 percent of the net grand list. By the time he left, the town's bonded indebtedness amounted to about $30.5 million, which was 3.3 percent of the net grand list. Eager to obtain credit as inexpensively as possible, Sullivan fought to improve the town's bond rating, which had slipped during the Kinnie years. Well before Sullivan left office, the town won an AAA rating from both Standard and Poor's and Moody's, the highest category possible and one that saved the town thousands of dollars in debt service costs.

*General Electric Company's corporate headquarters in Fairfield was dedicated in 1974.*

The Sullivan years could hardly be described as placid ones. Most of what he accomplished he achieved despite the opposition of one or another element in town. Even the most innocuous proposal might start a fight. When the Town Plan and Zoning Commission took the major step of endorsing "designed district" zoning, which allowed the TPZ to identify specific sites for condominium development, some residents were convinced that every neighborhood in town was in jeopardy. Sullivan eventually had to announce a moratorium on such projects. He also had to contend with furious growth in the 1960s. The town's population jumped from about 46,000 in 1960 to about 56,000 a decade later.

There were other problems. In 1966 Sullivan learned that John Pinchin, the tax collector, had been stealing from the town. Eventually auditors discovered that almost $500,000 had been taken over a period of many years. Because Dimill Kinnie had originally appointed Pinchin and because Kinnie had been in power during the years that Pinchin began his embezzling, the Republicans were unable to make as much of the scandal as they would have liked. Sullivan defused the situation further by taking legal action against the auditing firm that had failed for so many years to uncover Pinchin's thievery.

Sullivan also had to contend with James Kellis. Kellis became the Democratic Town Committee chairman after Garofalo retired. Kellis was an able man but insisted that Sullivan should make appointments only after consulting him. He tried a similar tactic with Judge of Probate John T. Fitzpatrick, who had the power to designate estate appraisers. Neither Sullivan nor Fitzpatrick believed that they should share their power with Kellis, a man answerable only to the Democratic party. Angered by their refusals,

Kellis set out to ruin Sullivan. He claimed that the first selectman, his family, and some associates were benefiting from corruption, were accepting favors from developers who wanted special considerations in town. Although Kellis was unable to provide any evidence to support his accusations, FBI and grand jury investigations followed. The inquiries resulted in exonerations for all those he accused.

The 1960s and 1970s were decades of social upheaval. Tensions existed between old-timers and newcomers, not surprising considering that so many of the people living in Fairfield in 1975 had arrived since the end of World War II. Some of the older members of Trinity Episcopal Church resented what one of their number described as the "status striving unreal people." Corporate transients frequently encountered a cool reception in the Greenfield Hill Congregational Church.

National issues kept invading the town. Edward J. McCallum, the chairman of the Prayers in Public Schools Committee, laid siege to the Board of Education in an attempt to convince it that the United States Supreme Court's decisions had no bearing in town. The Fairfield School Prayer Committee denounced Sullivan because he refused to hold a referendum on the question of school prayer; brushing aside the town's lack of authority to hold such a referendum. When the Board of Education suspended Blake Wade in 1968 for wearing a Beatles style haircut, anyone might have guessed that part of the problem between Wade and the board was a generational one, but the term "generation gap" was only then becoming popular. During the years it was in vogue, the town paid more attention than it ever had to its adolescents and their problems.

On the afternoon of April 7, 1968, Fairfielders gathered at the First Church to mourn the death of Dr. Martin Luther King, the black civil rights leader killed by an assassin. Exactly three weeks later, the first Wallace for President headquarters opened in Connecticut; the existence in Fairfield of that office, whose workers endorsed an avowedly racist candidate in George Wallace, stood in sharp contrast to the attitudes of those who had attended the King memorial service. Fairfield, although without any significant black population of its own, was obviously aware of the racial issues then facing the United States. Thomas J. Keegan, chairman of the Fairfield Board of Realtors, might declare that "there are no problems with discrimination in Fairfield County,"[6] but most residents knew otherwise, knew that Bridgeport, with its substantial minority population, shared a common boundary with Fairfield. "Just because it may be pleasant not to think about it doesn't mean we can avoid the problems of our neighbors," asserted Robert G. Lee.[7] Others who shared Lee's concerns spent much of the 1968-69 winter debating how Fairfield might work with Bridgeport to alleviate some of that city's difficulties.

Worry about segregation and about the problems of decay in Bridgeport gave way to anxieties over the Vietnam War. Modeling their tactics on those of civil rights demonstrators, local students organized marches and protests against the war. Discussion about the conflict often seemed to have more to do with how older Americans perceived their younger countrymen than it did with the wisdom or folly of American foreign policy. Charles Peden was Fairfield's Memorial Day speaker in 1966. He "spoke out against obstructionist youthful dissent and anti-Viet Nam war demonstrators and urged Americans to close ranks and present a united front for freedom." Even as he spoke young Americans were dying in Vietnam, Americans like Stephen Melnick, who had been a guard on Roger Ludlowe's 1961 state championship football team. He was the town's first casualty in the war.

The conflict prompted some residents to organize a Fairfield for McCarthy group; it gathered signatures to guarantee that antiwar activist Eugene McCarthy's name would appear on the presidential ballot in 1968. The war also encouraged Rabbi Dr. Victor Solomon of Congregation Ahavath Achim to trade the security of his position at the synagogue for the life of an Air Force chaplain. He explained that he was making the sacrifice out of respect for his parents. They had come to the United States from Russian Poland, and because of what they had endured in Europe, they loved the United States with a passion that perhaps few native Americans could understand. "They taught me," he stated, "to live a life of service in the most valuable area and the most appropriate time."[8] These were times that forced Fairfield men and women to make choices.

## NOTES

1. Author's interview of John J. Sullivan, Dec. 7, 1987. Henry Fountain's articles on Sullivan in the Fairfield *Citizen News*, Nov. 16, 18, 1983, are a rich source of information about the former first selectman.

2. Fairfield *Town Crier*, Aug. 15, 1965.

3. Fairfield Town Plan & Zoning Commission, *The Comprehensive Plan*, 1961.

4. Quoted in Fairfield *Citizen News*, Nov. 16, 1983.

5. Fairfield *Town Crier*, Feb. 14, 1965.

6. Ibid., July 31, 1966.

7. Quoted in George O. Pratt, *Fairfield in Connecticut, 1776-1976* (Fairfield, 1976), 92.

8. Fairfield *Town Crier*, March 30, 1968.

# Epilogue

THE VIETNAM WAR had been over almost a decade when Sullivan announced that he would not seek another term. The legacy that he left amounted to more than the aggregate of the sewers installed or the recreational facilities developed or the open spaces acquired. He had established a tradition of planned, orderly growth that his successors would have to continue. A new master plan, adopted in 1979, would help with this. He had brought to public affairs a quality of management that went beyond what the town had known earlier and that would provide a standard for the future; the era of the amateur was over. When the *Ladies Home Journal* in 1975 selected Fairfield as one of "America's best suburbs," it cited government efficiency among the town's principal assets. And finally, at a time when it could have been so easily lost, Sullivan had worked to preserve Fairfield's unique identity.

The preservation of that identity had perhaps been his greatest challenge; it would also try the skill of his successors. Located in one of the most affluent sections of the United States, southwestern coastal Connecticut, Fairfield has resisted more successfully than any of its neighbors of comparable size the pressure to become a bedroom community. Fairfield is a suburb, but its variety of ethnic and religious groups, its representatives of various social and economic strata, its diverse neighborhoods, and its persistent industrial sector set it apart from its more affluent and more homogeneous neighbors.

In the 1980s, Fairfield still included a Hungarian Catholic Church, a Slovenian Catholic Church, a Polish Catholic Church, two synagogues, and a variety of Protestant churches. It still included at least two areas—Greenfield Hill and Southport—where the mean family income far exceeded that of Fairfield County generally, and one or two where it fell significantly below the county figure. Many of its largest taxpayers were still industrial establishments; 23 percent of the 19,500 men and women employed in town worked in manufacturing.

But by the 1980s, Fairfield was under pressure to be something it had never been before: a community of older, affluent residents; a homogeneous suburban cocoon. With real estate prices increasing, more individuals, including persons born in Fairfield, found the town too expensive. The problem was compounded by Fairfield's opposition to moderate-income housing. "People don't want to do anything that will encourage a moderate-income element to move in," said Elizabeth S. Gray of the Fairfield League of Women Voters in 1978. "What the opponents don't stop to appreciate is that they themselves couldn't possibly afford to buy a single-family house in Fairfield today if they had to."[1] Sullivan understood. "The time is coming, and it is coming now when we have to face up to our responsibilities to all people, to the children who are born here and who will be looking for their own young families," he said in 1971. "We can't put our heads in the sand as far as a mix of population is concerned."[2]

Throughout its history, Fairfield has always included a generous blend of income and age groups. Other ingredients in its amalgam of residents have changed from time to time. Native Americans vanished, and English Protestants came to dominate. Before the American Revolution, Fairfield had a substantial black population; they had largely disappeared from town before the twentieth century. The coming of Irish and small numbers of Germans before the Civil War demolished the Anglo-Saxon monopoly and introduced Catholicism to Fairfield. This century has seen various groups arrive, Catholics, Protestants, and Jews. The recipe has been good. Fairfield children could grow up with a better understanding of America's heterogeneity than young people in some of the town's neighbors, many of them thoroughly homogenized suburbs.

After 1958 much of the town's diversity was finally reflected in its political life. The days when Fairfield's Protestant establishment had a hammer hold on the government were over. The election of a woman, Jacquelyn Durrell, as first selectman in 1983 expanded the town's political horizons even more. It took Fairfield almost three hundred years to elect its first female official and almost sixty more to choose a woman for its highest office. Durrell's election, many residents believed, indicated that the pool from which the voters could select officials now included all the town's able adults regardless of ethnic background, religious preference, economic and social status, or sex.

But to describe Fairfield as a "Camelot," as Congressman Stewart McKinney once did, would be hyperbole. Fairfield faces a real danger of becoming a single-class community. Given its ethnic, religious, and economic diversity, one familiar with the town must wonder how much genuine integration exists among its various groups.[3]

But Fairfield, of all its neighbors, remains unique. It has managed to retain both the atmosphere of a small town, something not easily found in modern America, and that variety which, in fact, is modern America. When Roger Ludlow created his settlement on the Sound in 1639, a sense of community was easily encouraged among his followers, all of whom came from the same religious, political, cultural, and ethnic background and all of whom were partners in a common experiment. During the years since Ludlow, Fairfield's history has been one of growing diversity. For such a mixture of people as live in Fairfield today to abide together amicably is noteworthy; for them to live together in sufficient peace to be truly a community is cause for celebration. Fairfield should celebrate. It has a heritage worth protecting.

NOTES

1. *New York Times*, July 2, 1978.
2. Fairfield *Citizen News*, Nov. 18, 1983.

3. Those who would ponder this question further should see Anderson, *Divided We Stand*.

*Epilogue*

# Illustrations and Credits

The great majority of illustrations which appear in this volume were drawn from the collections and photographic archives of the Fairfield Historical Society and only other sources are noted after the abbreviated captions in the following list. In all cases where known, the artist's, delineator's, or photographer's name is also included before the page number on which the illustration appears. The uncaptioned illustrations which embellish section and chapter lead pages have not been included. All of these are in the archives of the Society.

# Index

# Fairfield

*Designed by A. L. Morris,*
*the text of this volume was composed in Bem*
*and printed by Sherwin/Dodge, Printers,*
*in Littleton, New Hampshire*
*on Mohawk Vellum Text.*
*The jacket was printed on Monadnock Caress,*
*the endleaves on Strathmore Grandee Text,*
*and the binding in Holliston Mills Roxite*
*was executed by New Hampshire Bindery*
*in Concord, New Hampshire.*

# In Appreciation

*The Council and membership of the Fairfield Historical Society would like to take this opportunity to thank the following corporations, foundations, and individuals who have generously contributed to the financial underwriting of this endeavor. Without their support, this project would not have been possible.*

Anonymous

The Bank Mart

Bannow-Larson Foundation

Bridgeport Hydraulic Company

Camp-Younts Foundation

Citytrust

Collins Development Corporation

Connecticut National Bank

The E & F Construction Company

Fairfield Lumber & Supply Company

The Fairfield Store

Gateway Bank

General Electric Foundation

Mr. & Mrs. David S. Huntington

Lafayette Bank & Trust Company

Larsen Fund, Inc.

The Mandeville Foundation, Inc.

Marealty

Mechanics & Farmers Savings Bank

People's Bank

Mrs. John W. Ritter, Jr.

Southern New England Telephone

Mr. & Mrs. H. Noyes Spelman

Sturm Ruger & Co., Inc.

Town of Fairfield

Wilmot Wheeler Foundation